Exploring Innovation

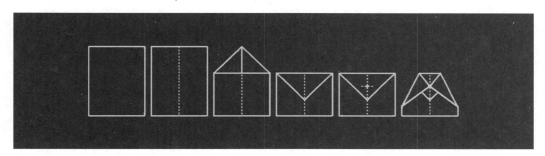

Second Edition

Praise for *Exploring Innovation, Second Edition*:

"This new edition of David Smith's *Exploring Innovation* provides the students with a solid vocabulary of innovation. Based on a firm foundation, the students are then provided with valuable exercises and cases to enhance their understanding of innovation practices and innovation management. Especially, the updated cases, the new topics like open innovation and a broader perspective on innovation management makes this book a strong handbook for undergraduate students with no prior knowledge on innovation. The book has also successfully been applied in our classes for engineering students enabling them to draw links between technological development and the market side to create and capture value from innovation. I can therefore only compliment David Smith on this new edition."

Mette Praest Knudsen
Professor of integrative innovation management
University of Southern Denmark

"I adopted Exploring Innovation in its first edition. I have found it to be pitched at just the right level for stage 2 undergraduates and it seems to have been well received by the students.

The case studies have also proven very useful as pedagogic aids and flexible enough to introduce my own questions and issues for discussion, whilst having the author's questions and answers available means that additional feedback can be provided to the students to reinforce their learning from the case. The revisions bring the text up to date with current research, whilst retaining its conciseness and clarity, and accessible style. I think it will prove even more useable than the first edition."

Neil Alderman
Senior Lecturer
Newcastle University Business School, Newcastle University

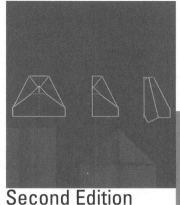

Second Edition

Exploring
Innovation

David Smith

McGraw-Hill
Higher Education

London Boston Burr Ridge, IL Dubuque, IA Madison, WI New York San Francisco
St. Louis Bangkok Bogotá Caracas Kuala Lumpur Lisbon Madrid Mexico City
Milan Montreal New Delhi Santiago Seoul Singapore Sydney Taipei Toronto

Exploring Innovation, Second Edition
David Smith
ISBN-13 978-0-07-712123-5
ISBN-10 0-07-712123-6

 **McGraw-Hill
Higher Education**

Published by McGraw-Hill Education
Shoppenhangers Road
Maidenhead
Berkshire
SL6 2QL
Telephone: 44 (0) 1628 502 500
Fax: 44 (0) 1628 770 224
Website: www.mcgraw-hill.co.uk

British Library Cataloguing in Publication Data
A catalogue record for this book is available from the British Library

Library of Congress Cataloguing in Publication Data
The Library of Congress data for this book has been applied for from the Library of Congress

First edition published in 2006

Commissioning Editor: Rachel Gear
Head of Development: Caroline Prodger
Freelance Editor: Emma Gain
Marketing Director: Alice Duijser
Production Editor: Alison Holt

Text Design by Hardlines
Cover design by Ego Creative
Printed and bound in the UK by Bell and Bain Ltd, Glasgow

ISBN-13 978-0-07-712123-5
ISBN-10 0-07-712123-6

The McGraw·Hill Companies

Dedication

For
John Keetley Smith
1917–2005

"My theory is that you do what your father wanted to do rather than what he did"
Alec Broers (2005)

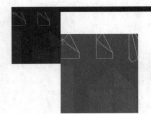

Brief Table of Contents

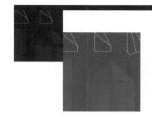

Detailed Table of Contents

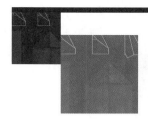

Preface

The response to the first edition of *Exploring Innovation* was very pleasing and surprising. Written primarily with UK students studying business administration in mind, the text has not only been well received and used in the UK, but found a market in other parts of Europe and even as far afield as South Africa and Malaysia. Consequently this revised edition retains the original format of fourteen chapters divided into four parts, though updated to include recent developments in innovation and major additions to the literature. As well, the opportunity has been taken to replace some of the more Anglocentric and dated case studies with more up-to-date material that hopefully has a wider appeal.

The chapter topics remain broadly unchanged, but some of the individual chapters have been extensively revised. Thus Chapter 1 now includes a more detailed treatment of the commercial aspects of innovation, stressing the importance of selecting an appropriate business model, while Chapter 5 includes more emphasis on user innovation and Chapter 6 introduces and explains the concept of open innovation. Chapter 8 has seen the biggest changes, with a shift in emphasis (and title) away from technology strategy to focus instead on innovation strategy. Another chapter to be re-titled is Chapter 11 which now specifically concentrates on the management of innovation, linking a number of managerial techniques to a specific model of the management process.

However, probably the biggest change is the replacement of several of the major case studies at the end of each chapter and many of the mini cases, with new cases that are more topical and up-to-date, reflecting recent innovations not just in products but services as well. Overall there are more than 20 new mini cases and six new full-length case studies. Among the new cases are ones on the *BBC iPlayer, Nintendo Wii, Linux, Blu-Ray, Mountain Bike, Predator boot, Videogames, Mark Shuttleworth, Dragon's Den* and *Ideo*, all topics that I hope will appeal to a generation of undergraduate students born in the 1990s.

At the same time the opportunity has been taken to reorganise the text. A new Further Reading section has been introduced at the end of each chapter to introduce students both to some important and valuable texts and provide them with guidance on where they can obtain additional information. Similarly the references that were located at the end of each chapter have now been concentrated into a single bibliography at the end of the book, which provides a central reference for the literature on innovation. Finally there is a new resources section near the end of the book. This is designed to help students access a wide range of additional materials, ranging from books and articles to websites, videos and even films!

Those who liked the case studies from the first edition that are not included in this revised edition, can be reassured that they are not lost for ever. They will be made available in the Online Learning Centre (OLC) that accompanies the book, together with additional materials in terms of lecture notes, questions for discussion, etc. Finally, since one of the aspects of innovation that is stressed throughout the book is the value of networking in facilitating knowledge transfer, let me say that I very much welcome feedback, suggestions and contributions which can reach me at: david.smith02@ntu.ac.uk.

David Smith, Nottingham, UK

Guided Tour

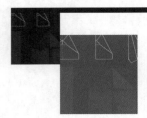

Learning Objectives

Each chapter opens with a set of learning objectives, summarising what readers should learn from each chapter.

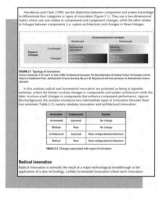

Figures and Tables

Each chapter provides a number of figures and tables to help you to visualise the various economic models, and to illustrate and summarise important concepts.

Mini Case Studies

Throughout the book these real life examples help you to understand the concepts of innovation more easily and enables you to relate abstract ideas to actual products.

CASE STUDY: HOWEVER THE INTERNET DEVELOPS,
WILL BENEFIT

YES, the Internet is helping to crunch down prices, but
is it doing to the whole production process?

This week the UK debate about interest rates has been
Wadhwani, a member of the Bank of England monetary co
paper that looks at the lessons from recent US experience
effects should become apparent here.

Crucially, productivity growth may be faster than expe
reason that much of an increase in productivity has not be
be partly because the costs of adjusting to the new technol
made. In any case he believes that business-to-business e-
savings in costs.

This being Britain, the argument leads into a debate abo
do not need higher interest rates to hold down inflation, be
competition and rising productivity will do it for us.

That spin is understandable. People care about their mo
borrowing costs, and both care about the level of sterling –
like the strong pound because it makes foreign holidays so
it because it makes exporting tougher.

But seeing the impact of the Internet through the prism
focus on one tiny effect of a great global phenomenon. Wh
industry, to the nature of competitiveness, to the ability of
delivering productivity gains – all this is vastly more impo

And we are still guessing wildly. At most we have thre
impact of the Internet, in practice more like 18 months. In
nothing, for you cannot really assess the implications of an
new economic event, until you have tracked it through a fu

Case Study

Each chapter contains a full-length case study with
questions. These comprehensive studies demonstrate the
material from each chapter and test your understanding of
the theories and principles covered.

6 Towards which of the innovation policy objectives of th
   Multimedia Super Corridor targeted?
7 To what extent is the Multimedia Super Corridor an exa
   pursuing the lead user objective?
8 What is the Smart card contributing to innovation in Ma

? **Questions for discussion**

1 Why should governments provide assistance to innovate
2 Why is market failure sometimes associated with innova
3 What are the UK government's objectives in promoting
4 What does Afuah (2003: p312) mean when he says that
   "shepherding" innovations by being a lead user?
5 When has the UK government acted as a lead user?
6 How do knowledge-transfer partnerships transfer knowl
7 How can science parks help to facilitate innovation?
8 Which university invented the science park and why?
9 What is the function of the SMART award scheme?
10 How do SMART awards help innovators?
11 How do R&D tax credits help innovators?
12 Why are regional development agencies increasingly in

Questions for Discussion

These questions encourage you to review and apply the
knowledge you have acquired from each chapter.
They are pitched at different levels.

✎ **Exercises**

1 Prepare a briefing document for the Nintendo Wii. This
   length and should provide the reader with a clear under
   well as the factors that account for its success as an inn
   you feel it holds for would-be innovators. As part of the
   enable you to make a presentation in class.
   To carry out this task you will need to classify the pro
   consumers, distinguish product features, identify compet
   to show what it is about the Nintendo Wii that makes it a
   You will need to carry out some basic fact-finding r
   and catalogues that stock the Nintendo Wii. If you know
   look at it, and more importantly ask them who uses it as
   newspapers such as *The Independent* and *The Guardia*
   about the Wii.
2 Prepare a profile of a company that you feel has a stron
   As well as providing background details on the com
   examples of successful innovations they have produced
   have been successful and try to identify the expertise ar
   the company to innovate.
   You will probably find that biographies, industry stu
   useful. You will find details of some these books in the
   well enable you to find short profiles of the innovations
   warned that such profiles often lack detail and tend to t
   unsophisticated and uncritical manner.

Exercises

A selection of more detailed questions is included,
designed to cover the material in more depth.

Further reading

1 **Freeman, C. and F. Louçã** (2001) *As Time Goes By: From Indus
   Information Revolution*, Oxford University Press, Oxford.
   This is one of very few books that focuses specifically on long v
   explanation of the origins and nature of long waves with extens
   contributions of Kondratiev and Schumpeter. It also examines i
   waves that has occurred since the industrial revolution.
2 **Dosi, G.** (1982) "Technological paradigms and technological tr
   11, pp 147–162.
   A brief introduction to the concept of the technological paradig
   paradigms is defined and then explained in detail.
3 **Florida, R.** (2002) *The Rise of the Creative Class: And How It's
   Community and Everyday Life*, Basic Books, NY.
   This is not a book about technological change. However, it is a
   readable account of the impact of technological change. The fo
   the nature of the knowledge economy but in the process it pro
   the wider impact of technological change in particular how dev
   have changed the way we work.
4 **Tylecote, A.** (1992) *The Long Wave in the World Economy: The
   Perspective*, Routledge and Kegan Paul, London.
   Since books on the long wave are very few in number, here is a
   helps to show that the long wave isn't an abstract concept but s
   analytical tool for analysing economic development.

Further Reading

A selection of further reading is discussed at the end of
each chapter, including web links, books and articles.

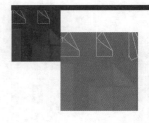

For Lecturers: Technology to enhance learning and teaching

Visit www.mcgraw-hill.co.uk/textbooks/innovation today

Online Learning Centre (OLC)

There is a supporting Online Learning Centre website to accompany this textbook.

For lecturers:
- PowerPoint slides for use in presentations or as class handouts
- Case Notes for the case studies in the textbook
- Tutor notes with seminar ideas and extra resources for teaching
- Additional cases, including favourite cases from the previous edition

For students
- Learning Objectives provide a chapter overview
- Resources appendix including web links
- Short self-test quizzes per chapter as an extra revision resource

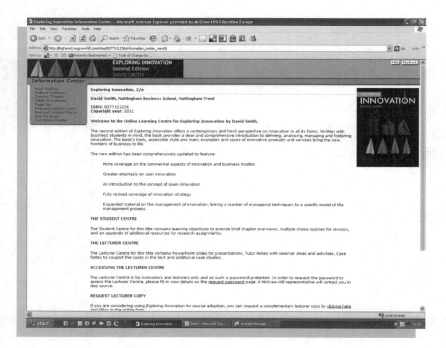

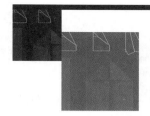

Custom Publishing Solutions: Let us help make our content your solution

At McGraw-Hill Education our aim is to help lecturers to find the most suitable content for their needs delivered to their students in the most appropriate way. Our **custom publishing solutions** offer the ideal combination of content delivered in the way which best suits lecturer and students.

Our custom publishing programme offers lecturers the opportunity to select just the chapters or sections of material they wish to deliver to their students from a database called Primis at www.primisonline.com

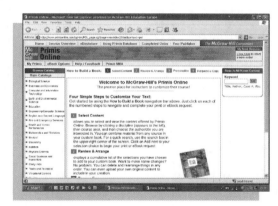

Primis contains over 2 million pages of content from:

- textbooks
- professional books
- case books – Harvard Articles, Insead, Ivey, Darden, Thunderbird and BusinessWeek
- Taking Sides – debate materials

across the following imprints:

- McGraw-Hill Education
- Open University Press
- Harvard Business School Press
- US and European material.

There is also the option to include additional material authored by lecturers in the custom product – this does not necessarily have to be in English.

We will take care of everything from start to finish in the process of developing and delivering a custom product to ensure that lecturers and students receive exactly the material needed in the most suitable way.

With a Custom Publishing Solution, students enjoy the best selection of material deemed to be the most suitable for learning everything they need for their courses – something of real value to support their learning. Lecturers are able to use exactly the material they want, in the way they want, to support their teaching on the course.

Please contact your local McGraw-Hill representative with any questions or alternatively contact Warren Eels **e:** warren_eels@mcgraw-hill.com.

Make the grade!

30% off any Study Skills book!

Our Study Skills books are packed with practical advice and tips that are easy to put into practice and will really improve the way you study. Topics include:

- Techniques to help you pass exams
- Advice to improve your essay writing
- Help in putting together the perfect seminar presentation
- Tips on how to balance studying and your personal life

www.openup.co.uk/studyskills

Visit our website to read helpful hints about essays, exams, dissertations and much more.

Special offer! As a valued customer, buy online and receive 30% off any of our Study Skills books by entering the promo code **getahead**

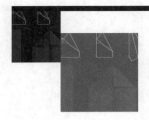

Acknowledgements

As always the reviewers who read and commented on earlier drafts, helped me enormously not just in spotting errors and inconsistencies, but in helping me to sharpening the focus of the text:

Mette Praest Knudsen, University of Southern Denmark
Dr Fiona Lettice, University of East Anglia
Peter Foong, Singapore Management University
James Bostock, Loughborough College
Dr Myfanwy Trueman, University of Bradford
Dr Neil Alderman, University of Newcastle
Dr Dolores Anon Higon, University of Aston
Terence Fan, Singapore Management University
Bryton Masiye, University of South Africa
Rene Pellissier, University of South Africa
Nina Hellman, Helsinki Metropolia University
Sunil Maharaj, University of Pretoria
Dr Hiro Izushi, University of Aston

In addition to the reviewers, lots of people have helped me, both directly and indirectly, with this edition of *Exploring Innovation*. Renu Agarwal of Macquarie University in Sydney, Australia, not only co-authored the final major case study about Australia's national innovation system, she also helped me to understand the recent contextual changes that have been taking place surrounding innovation in that country. Bob Crompton provided a most valuable input on innovations in automotive power steering systems, which do not feature as a separate case study but are covered in the text. Similarly Peter Robertson updated me on the OneClick Technologies case study.

The text has also benefited from many discussions and informal inputs from members of the team that helps with the teaching of *Competitive Strategy and Innovation* at Nottingham Trent University: James Bostock, Gamal Ibrahim, Paul Garratt, Karen Slater, Weili Teng, Michael Zhang and Arvind Yadav. My students over the last three years have also made a significant input, particularly helping me to understand the need for teaching materials to have currency and appeal for the Internet generation. They include undergraduate and postgraduate students at Nottingham Trent University as well as students I have taught at the University of Southern Denmark in Odense and Universiti Teknologi Malaysia in Jahor Bahru.

I have also benefited from insights into innovation and the innovation process provided by Phil Davis and Simon Gardner of the innovation consultancy, Impact Innovation in Leamington Spa in the UK. Finally Emma Gain and Rachel Gear at McGraw-Hill did a great job of simultaneously encouraging and motivating me while at the same time keeping me on target. Thank you all.

Every effort has been made to trace and acknowledge ownership of copyright and to clear permission for material reproduced in this book. The publishers will be pleased to make suitable arrangements to clear permission with any copyright holders whom it has not been possible to contact.

PART 01
What Is Innovation?

CHAPTER

01

Introduction

❖ **OBJECTIVES**

When you have completed this chapter you should be able to:

❖ appreciate the importance of innovation for business and the national economy

❖ understand the nature of innovation and be able to distinguish between invention and innovation

❖ describe the activities associated with innovation

❖ appreciate the part business models play in innovation

❖ understand the link between innovation and diffusion

Mini Case

Silicon Valley – the home of innovation?

Silicon Valley in California is synonymous with innovation. It is the quintessential example of a place that is all about innovation. Nowhere is so readily identified with new products and new services. Indeed in the last 50 years no other place on earth has been the location of so many innovations. Among the better known ones are:

- integrated circuit (Intel)
- personal computer (Apple)
- 3D graphics (Silicon Graphics)
- database software (Oracle)
- Web browser (Netscape)
- online auction (eBay)

It is not merely the number of innovations, it is the fact that Silicon Valley has gone on producing innovations over time.

There are other places in the world that have stronger records in scientific discoveries and scientific breakthroughs. Cambridge, in the UK, has an outstanding record in terms of scientific breakthroughs. These include: discovery of the electron, splitting the atom, and the identification of the structure of DNA. Though these achievements are the stuff of Nobel Prizes and as such highly significant, they are scientific breakthroughs, they are not innovations. Only Silicon Valley has an outstanding record in terms of innovation.

It wasn't always so. In the 1940s what is now Silicon Valley was a peaceful agricultural valley (Saxenian, 1983). Located at the southern tip of San Francisco Bay, Silicon Valley (or rather Santa Clara county) stretches from Palo Alto in the north to Gilray in the south. Covering 1,500 square miles and currently home to 2.5 million, today it is the densest concentration of high technology business on earth.

It is innovation that makes Silicon Valley unique. As one recent study (Lee *et al.*, 2000: p3) noted:

> 66 What sets Silicon Valley apart is not the technologies discovered there, but its record in developing, marketing and exploiting new technologies. 99

Silicon Valley's unique feature is its capability for developing new technologies and exploiting them commercially: in short, its capability for innovation. It is this capability that this book aims to explore.

Sources: Lee, Miller, Hancock and Rowen (2000); Saxenian, (1983).

What is innovation?

In 2002, listeners to the *Today* programme on BBC Radio 4, in a poll to mark 150 years of the UK Patent Office, voted for their top ten inventions (in descending order):

1 bicycle (Pierre Lallemente, 1886)
2 radio (Guglielmo Marconi, 1897)
3 computer (Alan Turing, 1945)
4 penicillin (Florey and Heatley, 1940)
5 internal combustion engine (Nicolaus Otto, 1876)
6 World Wide Web (Tim Berners-Lee, 1989)
7 light bulb (Thomas Edison and Joseph Swann, 1829?)
8 cat's eyes (Percy Shaw, 1936)
9 telephone (Alexander Graham Bell, 1876)
10 television (John Logie Baird, 1923)

The bicycle, invented by Pierre Lallemente in Paris in the 1860s, won by a landslide. Since the poll was organised to mark the opening of the Patent Office, it is not surprising that it was designed to elicit a top ten of inventions. The Patent Office is in the business of inventions. It issues patents to inventors whose ingenuity and perseverance has resulted in an "inventive step" that gives rise to an invention. Interestingly, all the inventions listed here are also innovations. Why? Because in each case the process did not end with invention. All the inventions became products that found markets and are still in use today. This is one of the key differences between invention and innovation. Not all inventions – even those that are registered for patents – get as far as being successful products in the marketplace. As Figure 1.1 shows, innovations represent a subset of a much bigger set of inventions. Why? Arduous though the task of invention is, the commercialisation process required to get an invention ready for the market is also lengthy and demanding, requiring a different range of capabilities so that many inventions do not make it to market and become successful innovations.

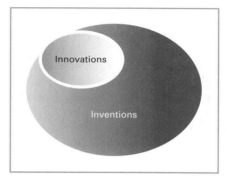

FIGURE 1.1 Inventions and innovations

Innovation defined

An innovation is something that is new. The word innovation is derived from the Latin word "nova" meaning new. However, merely being new does not quite catch the essence of innovation. An innovation is also normally something that is novel and different. Just how different, as we shall see later in this chapter, varies enormously, but typically most innovations have a degree of novelty about them. This newness and novelty is captured in most definitions of innovation:

> 66 An innovation is an idea, practice or object that is perceived as new by an individual or other unit of adoption.
>
> *Rogers (1995: p11)* 99

> 66 Innovations are new things applied in the business of producing, distributing and consuming products or services.
>
> *Betje (1998: p1)* 99

Although both of these definitions highlight the novelty of innovation, there are other aspects that they miss. In particular they do not help to distinguish innovation from invention. Hence more effective definitions are:

> 66 Innovation is the successful exploitation of ideas.
>
> *DTI (2004: p5)* 99

> 66 The first commercial application or production of a new process or product.
> *Freeman and Soete (1997: p1)* 99

These latter definitions are more effective because they refer to business and commerce, an important aspect of all innovations. They highlight the fact that innovation is about the commercial exploitation and application of ideas and inventions, so that they can be traded in the marketplace. The second definition is particularly helpful because it notes that innovation, as well as involving something new, also requires commercialisation in order to make an invention ready for market. However, Freeman and Soete's (1997) definition of innovation does have one particular weakness – it implies that innovation relates to physical objects or "things," i.e. products and processes. It fails to make clear that innovation also embraces services. New and novel services form an important class of innovation. Indeed the Internet has led to a growth in the proportion of innovations that are services. Facebook, eBay, YouTube and Flickr are examples of the many highly popular, new and novel services made possible through the application of Internet technology to meeting consumer needs.

Hence innovation embraces both a technological and a creative dimension, that we normally refer to as invention, together with a commercial dimension that involves the exploitation of the invention to turn it from a model or prototype into something that is available in the market for consumers to purchase. This latter aspect is much less heroic and less glamorous then invention, but it is crucial. Without it an invention is little more than a great idea, and all too often this is an element of innovation that is neglected, with disappointed consumers the result. Only when both aspects have been effectively handled does one have an innovation.

Mini Case

BBC iPlayer

The BBC has a world renowned reputation as a broadcasting organisation providing a wide range of TV and radio services and in December 2007 it launched an entirely new kind of service, an online video-on-demand service called BBC iPlayer. The new service allowed audiences in the UK to watch and listen to BBC programmes online for up to seven days after their initial broadcast.

Initiated in 2004 by the then Director-General of the BBC, Greg Dyke, the iPlayer project began at a time of intense technological change when it was not at all clear which method would be the most appropriate way to deliver this kind of video-on-demand service. By mid-2007, with the service due to be operational by the end of the year, iPlayer, despite having cost double-digit millions, wasn't ready. At this point the BBC's Head of Future Media and Technology, Ashley Highfield, brought in a South African, Anthony Rose, to head up the beleaguered iPlayer team. Rose's philosophy was simple: "It had to appeal to Mrs Smith, aged 65, who wants to watch EastEnders, as well as the Twitterati". To this end he was careful to make sure the development team paid particular attention to making the service easy to use.

By December 2008, a year after iPlayer was launched on schedule, it was clear that Rose and his team had succeeded. The new service was so easy to use that it attracted almost 10 per cent of the UK online traffic (it rose to 20 per cent during the Beijing Olympics), putting it in third place behind Google and Microsoft. With a million users everyday accessing 1.5 million TV and radio shows, it was clear that the British public found the new service extremely easy to use, leading one commentator to suggest that iPlayer had redefined TV and how we use it.

Source: Chibber (2009).

The scope of innovation: just how new is it?

Just how new and different does something have to be to make it an innovation? The answer is that the degree of novelty can be modest. Innovation covers a vast range of products and services, and in some cases the degree of novelty is barely discernible in technical terms and more a matter of marketing and presentation. Two particularly significant aspects of "newness" are new to market and new to a company. New to market implies that this is a product or service not previously offered in the market. The product or service is entirely new, though clearly something similar could have been offered in other markets and then adapted to the market in question. With products or services that are new to a company, there is probably less scope for novelty because other companies might already be offering the product or service.

Combining the two aspects of market and company gives the two-dimensional matrix shown in Figure 1.2. This identifies a number of common forms of innovation and serves to highlight how the degree of novelty can vary.

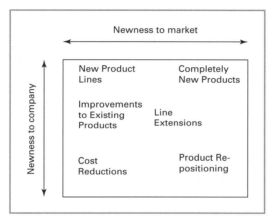

FIGURE 1.2 Degrees of innovation
Source: Adapted from Cooper (2001)

In the top right-hand corner of the matrix, we have products or services that are both new to the market and new to a company. Labelled "Completely New Products," these are products/services with the highest degree of innovation. A good example would be the Apple iPod or the Sony Walkman. They were, when first launched, both completely new products. The Sony Walkman was the world's first portable audio player. Prior to its introduction there simply was no practical way of listening to music while walking around. The iPod too was "completely new" because it was the first audio player to combine MP3 technology for listening to music with the capability to store a large quantity of music. There had been earlier attempts to produce this kind of product, most notably the PJB100 (Levy, 2006: p58), but they had been bulky and impractical and had not been a commercial success. The iPod possessed other novel features as well. It was extremely compact, it combined ease-of-use with a high degree of functionality. Consequently, one would have little difficulty in assigning the iPod to the position of a completely new product with a high degree of novelty.

Products or services that can be identified as "line extensions" score moderately on both the market and company axes. Line extensions are based on existing products. However, the product is altered in some way to give it new attributes. It is the addition of these new attributes that makes the product an innovation. However, the principle purpose behind the addition of new attributes is to enable the product to appeal to a new group of consumers. By so doing the product line is being extended, hence the term "line extension". One field where line extensions are common is pharmaceuticals. For example, the painkiller paracetemol has been in widespread use for many years. In recent years, line extensions have proliferated. Good examples include low-dose liquid forms of paracetemol for the market for children, slow-release versions of paracetemol in liquid form for those consumers wanting a treatment they can take overnight, and paracetemol powders that come packaged with a de-congestant for the "cold remedy" market. Each of these product offerings was in its time an innovation but the degree of novelty is limited. There is little in the way of new technology, rather it is a case of adapting the product by adding further formulations to give the product new attributes.

There will generally be less novelty with "re-positionings" and new product lines. New product lines are where companies introduce what for them are new products, but which are already available on the market. Thus Unilever's decision to introduce the "Clearblue" range of pregnancy testing kits (Jones, G., 2005: p293) was an example of a new product line. At the time, Unilever's product portfolio covered mainly cleaning and food products and the decision to produce medical diagnostic products was a case of introducing a new product line.

A classic case of re-positioning was Häagen-Dazs ice cream. Until this brand of ice cream was introduced in the early 1990s, children comprised the main customer base for ice cream, the product often being regarded as a reward or treat for special occasions. This was reflected in the marketing of ice cream. However this changed with the arrival of Häagen-Dazs. With its high-quality natural ingredients Häagen-Dazs was an example of re-positioning with the product aimed at adults rather than children. This re-positioning was graphically reflected in the early advertising for Häagen-Dazs, which featured a campaign that aimed to "eroticise" the brand through words and images emphasising sensuality and love-making, in order to enhance the appeal of the product to the adult market (Rutherford, 2007).

This analysis and the examples given serve to show that innovation is by no means a uniform concept. The degree of innovation in terms of just how novel the product is can vary enormously. In some cases the novelty associated with what some would term an innovation is at best superficial, some might say trivial. In other instances the degree of innovation is huge, as entirely new products that bear little relation to anything currently available appear on the market. This difference is taken up and analysed in more detail in Chapter 2.

Mini Case

Lucozade

Lucozade was first manufactured in Newcastle in 1927. Its inventor, a local chemist, had experimented for several years to produce a drink that would be a source of energy to aid sick children and invalids who were convalescing from illness. It went on sale in 1929 in a distinctive large glass bottle with an orange cellophane wrapper. It was promoted through an advertising campaign with the strap line, "Lucozade aids recovery". It was widely used for many years in hospitals and in the home to aid children recovering from a period of illness.

In 1983 the product underwent a re-branding designed to re-position it as an energy drink aimed at the growing fitness market. The advertising agency Ogilvy and Mather came up with a new strap line, "Lucozade replaces lost energy," and launched an advertising campaign featuring the Olympic champion Daley Thompson. The packaging was also changed to a smaller and more convenient plastic PET bottle. The effect of the re-positioning was dramatic. Between 1984 and 1989 the value of UK sales more than trebled to £75million.

Innovation: invention – commercialisation – diffusion

From the definitions of innovation it becomes clear that innovation is closely linked to invention. In fact invention forms part of (or even a stage in) the process of innovation.

Invention involves new ideas, new discoveries and new breakthroughs. These are developed via a process of experimentation to arrive at a workable invention. This typically forms part of the research element of research and development (R&D). Chapter 9 of James Dyson's autobiography (Dyson, 1997) provides a very realistic and detailed account of this process. A key feature of inventions is their "newness," which means that they incorporate some "inventive step". However, inventions are not normally ready for market at this stage. It is one thing to produce a single item, quite another to be able to produce it in large volumes at a cost and a level of reliability that meets the demands of everyday use.

Innovation therefore includes not only invention, but also activities that facilitate the introduction of new or improved products or services onto the market. These activities form part of the exploitation/commercialisation phase which is such an essential part of innovation. Figure 1.3 makes clear that innovation embraces both invention and commercialisation. The reason for the set of inventions shown in Figure 1.1 being much bigger than the subset of innovations is that commercialisation is often a lengthy and expensive process and many inventions, though they incorporate good ideas, never make it as far as the marketplace.

Commercialisation typically includes the development part of research and development (R&D) which involves ensuring that an invention is able to work reliably and safely, not only in the laboratory or workshop, but in the hands of actual users, and is capable of being produced in quantity in a manufacturing context. In addition commercialisation involves a range of business activities such as marketing, organisation and finance. These are required to prepare the invention for market, in particular to ensure that potential users are aware of it and can gain access to it.

While invention and commercialisation taken together make up innovation, there is a third phase, diffusion, which while it is not part of innovation is closely associated with it (Figure 1.3). Diffusion describes the rate at which consumers adopt the innovation. In some cases diffusion can be relatively slow, in other cases, as with many Internet related services such as eBay and Facebook, it can be very rapid.

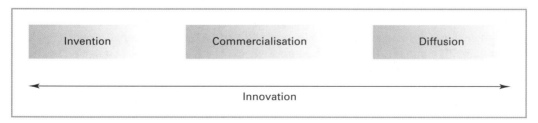

FIGURE 1.3 Invention, commercialisation and diffusion

Invention

The invention phase of innovation is the one that is most commonly associated with innovation. It is the phase where ideas are turned into workable inventions. It is the phase where the idea is made to work. As noted earlier, if the product or service in question is technological, this is a phase that is typically characterised by much experimentation. The function of the experimentation phase is to prove the concept and arrive at something that is workable. If the innovation is a modest one, with comparatively little novelty, as with line extensions and re-positionings, there may be little or no experimentation, nonetheless there may be a considerable amount of technical work to undertake in order to arrive at a product with the desired attributes.

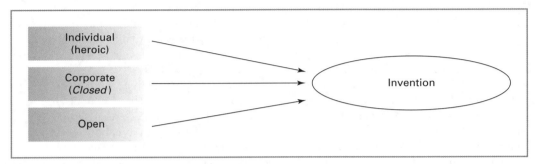

FIGURE 1.4 Three routes to invention

There are three models that describe how the invention phase of innovation can be undertaken. The first is what one might describe as the classic model of invention, where a lone inventor toils away on his or her own. In this instance the inventor is portrayed as a "heroic" figure, battling against the odds, isolated, lacking support and short of resources. Although examples regularly appear on the BBC TV programme *Dragon's Den*, this model is actually comparatively rare. However, there continue to be a small number that have a big impact and attract a high public profile. The Internet search engine Google, for instance, was established on the basis of data mining software developed by its founders, Larry Page and Sergey Brin (Vise, 2005), while they were postgraduate students at Stanford University in California. Similarly, the bagless vacuum cleaner was developed by James Dyson (Dyson, 1997) working on his own in the garage of his home near Bath. In both cases the invention was the product of individual effort.

Despite these high-profile examples of individual invention, this model has generally given way to a corporate model of invention, where corporate research and development (R&D) facilities in the form of R&D laboratories are the main engine of invention. From the mid-twentieth century large corporations like Dupont, IBM and AT&T were the basis of this model (Chesbrough, 2003b: p35). They possessed massive R&D facilities and they competed by the simple expedient of doing more R&D than anybody else in their industry.

Because most of the activities associated with invention take place within a single organisation, as do the associated commercialisation activities, the corporate model has in recent years come to be termed the "closed model" of innovation (Chesbrough, 2003a).

Latterly, however, we have come to see a new model emerge, which stands in marked contrast to the closed model of innovation. The open model of innovation (Chesbrough, 2003a) recognises that invention isn't only the product of corporate research labs. While this source is important there are other *external* sources which can be important today. These external or outside sources include other large corporations which, having developed new technologies, decide not to commercialise them. Having no immediate and obvious use for the technology themselves, they license the technology to others who are willing to innovate and turn the technology into new products. Another external source is small, entrepreneurial, high-tech companies. Perhaps formed as spin-offs of universities or other companies, these highly specialised companies possess knowledge and expertise in very narrowly defined fields. These enterprises may not have the facilities to achieve outstanding technical break-throughs, but they do have what much innovation demands, namely the capability to adapt the technology to a particular, highly specialised application. This specialisation, combined with a high degree of flexibility, enables these companies to produce potential commercial applications that can then be commercialised in collaboration with large corporations.

It is important to note that with the open model of innovation, while inventions can come from outside the organisation, nonetheless much innovation activity (i.e. commercialisation) is normally carried out internally. Such is the flexibility of open innovation, in contrast to closed innovation, that the invention may come about via the internal route, only for the external route to be used for the commercialisation phase as a third party commercialises the invention.

Mini Case

Antibiotics – Invention v. Innovation

Antibiotics are today a standard prescription/treatment for a vast range of infections, and yet it was only in the 1950s that they first came into widespread use. As an innovation antibiotics are today attributed to three individuals: Alexander Fleming, Howard Florey and Ernst Chain.

Fleming worked at St Mary's Hospital in Paddington in London. In 1928 he was studying a particular type of bacteria: staphlococci. To replicate an earlier study he prepared a number of cultures of staphlococcal bacteria and then left them to grow while he went on holiday. When he returned he noticed that on one of these cultures there was a growth of mould and that around this growth the colonies of bacteria had failed to develop. He called in a colleague, Charles La Touche, to investigate the mould and he identified it as a strain of penicillin. Fleming then proceeded to study a whole range of moulds but found that none had the anti-bacterial power of the one that had contaminated his experiment. He and his assistants then attempted to purify and stabilise the penicillin that they had been using, but were only able to produce a small amount in a very weak form. However, Fleming had found that penicillin provided a method of diagnosing influenza and this required only a small amount of penicillin. Fleming wrote up his work in a scientific paper outlining his test for influenza. Having identified penicillin as a potential diagnostic tool, Fleming took the development of penicillin as an antibiotic that could cure infections no further.

It was more than ten years later that a team at Oxford University under Professor Howard Florey began to look at the potential of penicillin as an anti-bacterial drug for treating infections. In 1939 Florey and his colleague, Ernst Chain, gained a grant from the Rockefeller Foundation to look further into the potential value of penicillin as an antibiotic. In May 1940 Chain began experimenting with mice, which had been given a lethal dose of streptococci. These quickly showed the therapeutic power of penicillin as an antibiotic. With great difficulty enough penicillin was produced to enable clinical trials on a small number of human cases suffering with life-threatening infections. The power of penicillin to combat infection was immediately evident and Florey and Chain reported their results in *The Lancet*. The problem remained how to produce penicillin in anything like the quantities where it could be used to treat humans. Florey tried to interest the British drug industry, but with war-time demands none was able to help. Undaunted, Florey and his team turned to the US. They approached the US government's Committee on Medical Research (CMR) who were quick to see the potential of the new antibiotic. As a stop-gap measure, the CMR enlisted the support of a US department of agriculture research laboratory in Peoria, Illinois, that was able to develop a laboratory-based method of producing penicillin. This was important in increasing the availability of penicillin for experimentation, but came nowhere near commercial production. To get this, Florey, with the support of the CMR, enlisted the help of a number of US drug companies including Merck, Squibb and Pfizer. It was the smallest of the three, Pfizer, that made the vital contribution. Pfizer developed a technique known as "submerged fermentation". From a situation where there was only enough penicillin to treat one human case in March 1942, by early 1943 there was enough for 500 and, with 21 firms producing it, there was sufficient to treat the needs of all the Allied casualties resulting from the D-day invasion of Normandy in June 1944. By this time limited distribution to civilians had also begun. As the new antibiotic came into general use in the late 1940s, so the price fell dramatically from $200 per million units in 1943 to only 50 cents in 1950.

Source: Kingston (2000).

Commercialisation: business models

Invention, discoveries and breakthroughs, though they may be of great interest to the technological community and on occasion attract much public interest, are actually of only limited value. This is because they may be dramatic, they may be exciting, they may be the product of a great deal of hard work, but they only release value when consumers start buying them. A way has to be found to transform the "technological potential" of an invention into economic value. The essence of the commercialisation element of innovation is to find an appropriate way to unlock what Chesbrough (2003a: p64) describes as the "latent value" of a technology in order to generate real value.

There are potentially many ways to commercialise an idea or a technology, though in reality only a very small number of them are likely to succeed. Commercialisation mechanisms are increasingly described as "business models". The rise of the Internet and the so-called "dot-com bubble" has fuelled interest in business models, partly because a number of new models have emerged and partly because the business model is perceived to be the key to unlocking the new opportunities created by the Internet.

What do we mean by a business model? Essentially a business model is an enabling device, that is, a tool that allows inventors to profit from their ideas and inventions. How does a business model enable innovation? According to Chesbrough (2006: p108) a business model performs two important functions as far as the commercialisation of an invention is concerned. These functions are: value creation and value capture. Value creation refers to a series of activities that enable the user to recognise the benefit and thence the value that he or she can gain from the invention. With new technologies in particular, this is a vitally important function, because the technology may be the product of a scientific breakthrough rather than a specific quest to meet a user need or solve a user problem. What the business model has to do is firstly, identify the users to whom the innovation is going to be of use and then articulate the "value proposition" so that users are aware of its purpose and the benefit they can expect to derive. Only when the user recognises the benefit to be gained from a new offering is he or she likely to be willing to consider purchasing it. No matter how enthusiastic the inventor, unless the articulation of value is effective potential users will not be interested.

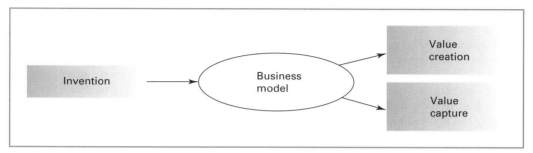

FIGURE 1.5 The functions of a business model

Flash of genius

Marc Abraham's recent film *Flash of Genius* tells the story of Bob Kearns, the inventor of the intermittent windscreen wiper and his battle to capture the value of his invention. The film begins in 1962 when Kearns was driving his Ford Galaxie in Detroit. Light rain caused the wipers to screech back and forth across the windscreen. Hearing the noise Kearns had his flash of genius – why can't wipers work like eyelids with a blinking action? Working at home in his basement Kearns devised an electronic timer for the wiper comprising a transistor, a capacitor and a variable resistor. When the voltage in the capacitor reached a certain level, the transistor turned on and the wiper wiped the windscreen. Running the wiper motor drained voltage out of the capacitor turning the transistor off and breaking the circuit thereby switching the wiper motor off after a single wipe. The wiper remained static until the capacitor recharged and the cycle began again.

Having patented his innovation with the help of a friend, Kearns showed it to engineers at Ford. They had been working on a similar device but based on vacuum technology rather than electronics. Ford's engineers were enthusiastic. Kearns was told that the new wiper would be incorporated into next year's model and he began to plan to put it into production. Then quite suddenly Ford said it wasn't interested in the technology after all. Kearns was devastated. Over time shock turned to anger when Ford models began to appear with an intermittent wiper. Other manufacturers followed suit. As the film shows it was to take Kearns 20 years of legal battles but eventually in 1990 a jury ruled that Ford had infringed Kearns' patent, and the car giant agreed to pay him $10.2million.

Source: Seabrook (2008).

An example of an innovation that suffered from poor value creation was the Sinclair C5. Launched in a blaze of publicity, its creator, Clive Sinclair, heralded it as an electric car that would transform urban transportation. When it appeared on the streets however it was clearly not a car. It was in fact a single seat electric tricycle, powered by a modified washing machine motor and car battery. With an effective range of 6.5 miles and a top speed of 12 miles per hour it bore little resemblance to a conventional car (Anderson and Kennedy, 1986). It was not clear at whom the C5 was aimed. It lacked the range required for all but the shortest of journeys, while as a leisure vehicle it lacked the capacity to take passengers. It was clear neither whom the C5 was intended for or what purpose it was designed to fulfil. In short, its business model suffered from poorly articulated value creation and, not unsurprisingly, it proved a commercial flop.

The second function of a business model is value capture. This involves appropriating value from the activities undertaken by the innovator. In this context the term "appropriating" means extracting or obtaining. The value that the innovator typically hopes to gain is revenue (i.e. money), though there could be other gains as well. The most obvious way of generating revenue is through outright sale where the consumer exchanges money in return for ownership of the product or service, but there are a variety of other methods of generating revenue including: renting, charging by transaction, advertising, subscription and charging for after-sales support (Chesbrough and Rosenbloom, 2002). However, it is rarely straightforward. If the innovation is very different from existing product offerings, consumers may be reluctant to pay using conventional revenue generation mechanisms used in the industry. Furthermore those working in the industry may be reluctant to break from the revenue generation mechanisms with which they are familiar. In Chesbrough and Rosenbloom's (2002) terminology they have a cognitive bias to existing mechanisms. Yet in order to capture value effectively it may be essential to break with the familiar and provide a different revenue generation mechanism. There is also the danger that some other party will appropriate the value by copying the innovation. Taking appropriate steps to protect the inventor's intellectual property (i.e. through patents) is essential to avoid this. It is precisely these sorts of issues that commercialisation has to tackle and that the selection of an appropriate business model aims to solve. For this reason revenue generation mechanisms are a key feature of business models.

Apple's iPhone mobile phone provides an example that illustrates some of the issues surrounding the choice of revenue generation mechanism. When Apple brought out its iPhone mobile phone in January 2007, it was applauded as a highly innovative product and much praised for the originality of the design. However, the iPhone is not just another mobile phone. According to Naughton (2008b) the iPhone is essentially a handheld computer which supports the powerful and widely used Unix operating system. This transforms the phone from a specialised gadget into something much more versatile. An important factor in boosting iPhone sales, and therefore Apple's revenues, is the wealth of software applications written and developed by third parties. Anyone can write programs for the iPhone and once approved by Apple they are available from the "Apps" branch of the iTunes store. The result has been what Naughton describes as an "explosion of iPhone applications" (Naughton, 2008b). The Apps store supplied more than 60 million downloads in its first month. Not only did this earn the developers of these applications $70million, it also provided Apple with a useful $30million (Apple splits revenues 30:70 with developers). More importantly, however, the presence of this wealth of additional, complementary material greatly boosted the "value proposition" that the iPhone represents. Hence as a revenue generation mechanism, the iPhone has become a "platform" that other firms are prepared to invest in. This costs Apple nothing, but from a user's perspective it boosts the value proposition that the product represents. And it would be wrong to see this as just a happy accident. Apple's revenue generation mechanism is predicated on taking deliberate steps to help and assist external organisations in developing new software applications and therefore new uses for the iPhone.

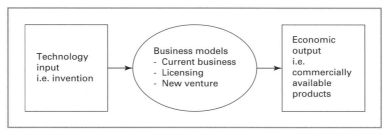

FIGURE 1.6 Three types of business model

Value creation and value capture are key aspects of business models. Just as there are a number of revenue generation mechanisms to facilitate value capture, so there are a number of generic business models. The three business models identified by Chesbrough (2003a: p63) to enable firms to convert technological potential (i.e. inventions) into economic value are:

1 incorporate the technology into the current business
2 license the technology to a third party (i.e. another firm)
3 launch a new venture to exploit the technology in new business arenas

These models determine who undertakes the commercialisation phase of innovation and how it is conducted. They are each in their own way mechanisms for bringing an invention to market. Examples of the application of the first model are very numerous, because it is the normal and logical step for a company that has taken time and effort to develop something new, to take. When Apple Computer developed the iPod in 2001 for instance, the company was very clear that, although audio players were not part of the company's existing product portfolio, nonetheless this innovation would be incorporated into the existing business and sold as an Apple product. Examples of the second business model are probably much more numerous than most people imagine, simply because many large companies receive a significant income from royalties resulting from the licensing of technology. An example of an innovator who initially went down this route is James Dyson, who when he had developed his dual cyclone technology for vacuum cleaners, decided that the best way for him to commercialise his invention was for him to use a business model that entailed him licensing it to an existing vacuum-cleaner manufacturer. Unfortunately this proved extremely difficult. While some vacuum-cleaner manufacturers appeared at least to see the technological potential in Dyson's dual cyclone technology, they were too firmly committed to a business model based, in part at least, on a revenue generating mechanism where revenue from replacement vacuum cleaner bags was important in capturing value, to switch to a new business model based on incorporating Dyson's new dual cyclone technology into their business (Dyson, 1997: p134). As a result Dyson, having generated some income from a small-scale licensing agreement with a Japanese firm, eventually opted for a business model in which he created a new venture. Called Dyson Appliances Ltd, the new venture eventually became a multi-million pound business. Another example of a firm that went down this route was the British automotive component manufacturer Lucas Varity. Having developed a revolutionary new electric system of power steering for cars, it chose to form a new venture, in the form of a joint venture with the US-based automotive component supplier TRW, in order to market the new technology to the world's leading car manufacturers.

The significance of business models for the innovation process can be gauged by the fact that the same technology taken to market through different business models will yield different amounts of value, a fact that many would-be innovators have failed to appreciate.

Mini Case

Xerox 914 Copier

Chester Carlson invented the modern plain paper copier and he teamed up with a little known company called Haloid Corporation in order to commercialise it. Believing there was great commercial potential in its new product, Haloid sought a strong marketing partner. However, approaches to IBM, General Electric and Kodak were all rebuffed. None could see any commercial potential in the new device. The reaction of IBM was typical. After much detailed analysis, they were unable to identify a significant value proposition. When IBM's consultants looked at the existing office copying market, they found two main types of product in use: "wet" photographic methods and low-quality dry thermal processes. The business model in use was to sell the copier at or near cost (typically about $300) generating revenue from sales of supplies and consumables, which were sold at relatively high prices. This was the "razor and razor blades business model". Since the average machine produced only 15–20 copies per day, consumers were happy.

The 914 on the other hand produced much better quality copies on plain paper using electrostatic technology. Though the variable cost of copies was at least on a par with the existing copiers, the 914 with its electrostatic technology, was much more expensive to manufacture. IBM reasoned that the typical consumer would not buy an expensive machine to produce a few hundred copies per month. Boldly Haloid chose to go it alone but with a different business model. Instead of selling the copier they offered to lease it for $95 per month with customers paying an additional 4 cents per copy beyond 2,000 copies per month. Haloid (soon to be re-named Xerox), provided all the required servicing as part of the lease. This was an attractive proposition to consumers. The cost was comparable to existing copiers. Only if the quality and convenience of the plain paper 914 led them to make much more use of the machine than they had done in the past would they pay more. Haloid was effectively betting that there was a great potential latent value in its electrostatic technology, and so it proved. The much improved quality and the convenience of using plain paper rather than special copier paper, led customers to use the new machines far more than they had ever done in the past. Such was the appeal of the 914 that consumers were soon using it to produce far more than 2,000 copies per month and in the first six months the machine generated as much revenue as Haloid had predicted for the whole life of the machine.

Sources: Chesbrough and Rosenbloom (2002); Owen (2004).

Diffusion

Diffusion is the process by which innovations are adopted and used by consumers, or in the case of process innovations, by other organisations. Diffusion describes the way in which innovations catch on and become popular. An innovation that becomes very popular and widely used very quickly can be said to exhibit a rapid rate of diffusion, while one that catches on more slowly will exhibit a slower rate of diffusion. Hence diffusion is the rate at which innovations are adopted.

Diffusion very rarely takes place at a steady linear rate. Instead the normal pattern is for the path of diffusion to exhibit an S curve (Geroski, 2000: p604). Consumers, initially unfamiliar with the new product or service and the potential benefits it has to offer, may be reluctant to purchase it. Consequently, during this initial period sales are modest, resulting in a low rate of diffusion. This will tend to be a period of awareness building, as consumers gradually become familiar with the innovation. According to Rogers (1995) "early adopters," highly esteemed individuals able to influence the views of others, may be particularly important in raising awareness at this stage. Over time as more consumers learn of the innovation and its benefits, the rate of diffusion starts to accelerate, sales pick up rapidly and the innovation starts to become popular. The diffusion path is now at the point where the curve is rising sharply. This is a phase of rapid diffusion. Eventually as the top of the curve is approached and the market starts to become saturated, sales begin to slow, a levelling out occurs and the rate of diffusion moderates. By now those adopting are the "laggards" (Rogers, 1995), isolated individuals who only adopt when forced to do so perhaps because of lack of alternatives. By this point the innovation may be said to have diffused as the end of the diffusion phase is reached (Figure 1.3).

Why does the diffusion path typically follow an S curve? Rogers (1995), suggests that social factors can be particularly influential in terms of the willingness of people to adopt an innovation. These social factors include things like peer pressure, fashion, word-of-mouth communication and social networks. They impact on innovation adoption by influencing would-be adopters. The so called "bandwagon" effect, where potential adopters are keen to jump aboard and adopt an innovation for fear of being left behind, illustrates how this can occur. In such cases adoption tends to be a function of the sheer number who have already adopted. Typically what happens is that once a certain threshold level of adoption has been reached, peer pressure, rather than rational assessment of potential benefits, causes many to adopt the innovation. The effect is to exaggerate the diffusion path making the S curve more pronounced. The power of social factors, particularly things like word-of-mouth communication and peer pressure, is well illustrated by the diffusion of recent Internet-based service innovations such as Facebook and YouTube. In both cases social factors have led to diffusion being much more rapid than it would otherwise be, with a steeply rising S curve.

What next?

This chapter has provided a brief overview of innovation. It is clear that innovation is a complex topic that draws not only on several academic disciplines, including economics, marketing and engineering, but also different fields of professional expertise (e.g. scientists, managers and lawyers). Each of the facets of innovation that this chapter has touched on is now considered in more depth in the chapters that follow.

Chapter 2 seeks to categorise innovations. It builds on the part of the current chapter that explored the scope of innovation. However, while this focused on the newness and novelty of innovations, the categorisation in Chapter 2 is more broadly based. Two well-known categorisations are presented. One is based primarily on novelty and complexity while the other is based on functionality. By presenting different, one might almost say alternative, categorisations of innovation, the reader hopefully comes both to understand the nature of innovation rather better and appreciate the range of things covered by innovation. Whereas Chapter 2 aims to enhance understanding of the nature of innovation, Chapter 4 presents frameworks that provide scope for analysing the course of innovation. These frameworks take the form of a number of theories of innovation. These it is argued, can be used, if not to predict the course of innovation, then at least to aid explaining it, in other words why some innovations occur when they do and why some have a much more profound impact than others.

The current chapter has shown that innovation generally is a two-phase process that involves an inventive/creative phase followed by a commercialisation phase, and the first of these is addressed in Chapters 3 and 5. Chapter 5 focuses on what one might term the creative dimension – that is how ideas that form the basis of an innovation originate. Chapter 3 on the other hand is devoted to the consideration of technology. In as much as new technologies are a source of innovation, it seeks to show how developments in technology impact upon innovation. Rather than look at specific technologies it focuses on the broader impact of technology.

Chapter 6 provides an overview of the process of innovation. As well as identifying the wide range of activities associated with innovation (i.e. what you have to do in order to innovate), it also explores different models of the process. This latter aspect shows that while there are a various activities that have to be undertaken, how they are undertaken, by whom, and when, can vary enormously.

One of the key messages coming out of the current chapter is that the second phase of innovation, commercialisation, is crucial if an invention is to stand any chance of commercial success. Commercialisation, it was noted, normally requires the use of a business model that performs two key functions: value creation and value capture. Value capture is the focus of Chapter 7 which provides detailed coverage of intellectual property rights. These rights are crucial if an innovator is to appropriate and therefore profit from his/her creativity. The other function of a business model is value creation, which is the function of Chapter 8 which looks at innovation strategy. By looking at how organisations and individuals position an innovation in relation to the market, innovation strategy is closely bound up with understanding the nature of the value that an innovation creates and for whom.

While value creation and value capture are clearly a vital part of commercialisation, there are other aspects to this phase of innovation. Earlier in the current chapter it was noted that commercialisation covers a range of business activities including marketing, organisation and finance. With aspects of marketing covered in Chapter 8 as part of innovation strategy, Chapter 11 explores the managerial aspects of innovation, while Chapter 10 highlights the difficulty of funding innovation and presents a range of funding mechanisms that can help to bridge the temporal gap that all too often exists between investment outlay on the development of a new product or service and the income stream that a successful innovation eventually brings in. Chapter 10 particularly focuses on the funding of innovation by new start-up businesses and to complement this, Chapter 9 examines the role of technical entrepreneurs, those individuals who found technology-based businesses.

Finally the remaining three chapters provide a public policy perspective. Chapters 12 and 13 examine some of the policy instruments available at national and regional levels to promote innovation, while the concluding chapter rounds off by considering national innovation systems, which comprise a country's infrastructure, in the broadest sense, for supporting innovation.

CASE STUDY: NINTENDO WII

Christmas 2006 was a strange time on the high street. If you'd looked through the window of almost any computer games shop in Britain, you would have seen lots of enthusiastic punters waving around a white object slightly larger than a mobile phone. Look a little further, and you would have seen that they were playing tennis or golf, but not as we know it. They were playing virtual tennis or golf using a Wii. The must-have present of Christmas 2006, the Wii, was Nintendo's new and highly innovative videogame console.

The Wii was unlike any other videogame console. A rival to Sony's highly successful PlayStation and Microsoft's Xbox, both of which relied on awesome processing power, state-of-the-art graphics and voluminous storage to make their "big beasts" market leaders (Fry, 2008), the Wii relied on a very different approach. Instead of using buttons and joysticks to enable the user to interact with the machine, as on conventional videogame consoles, Nintendo's new offering employed a wireless controller, the Wii Remote, a handheld device (the white object mentioned earlier), similar to a TV remote controller, that utilised wireless technology with built-in sensors to translate movement directly onto a TV screen, transforming the Wii into the most exciting mass market device in years.

And what does all this mean for the user? Strapped to the wrist, the Wii Remote is used as a pointing device that enables users to play sports-like tennis or golf, by swinging the wand in the air to hit virtual tennis or golf balls, using similar actions to real-life tennis players and golfers. This is altogether more realistic than using a conventional joystick physically connected to the console. So realistic is the Wii that not long after it was launched newspapers reported cases of enthusiastic users suffering bruised heads, black eyes and even damaged TV sets as they lost control of their wands, one of the penalties of playing tennis in the living room rather than out on the tennis court. Some players were even been reported to be suffering from a form of "tennis elbow". Recently Nintendo has supplemented the sporting element by launching the Wii Fit, an "add-on" which features a "balanceboard," which resembles a pair of bathroom scales, on which you can do yoga, step aerobics and ski slaloms. The Wii Fit will even calculate your Body Mass Index (BMI) enabling users to undertake a daily workout regime.

In terms of innovation, the Wii is about very much more than providing videogame players with a simulated game that is much more realistic, because one is no longer directly hooked up to the console and control of the ball is via motions that are much more like the real game. The Wii changed the nature of conventional videogaming.

What is different about the Wii is that, unlike Sony's PlayStation and Microsoft's Xbox, it appeals to consumers outside the "hard-core" gaming market, particularly female gamers and families. While titles such as the ultra-violent *Grand Theft Auto* sold well to traditional fans who want eye-boggling graphics and more complex adventures, Nintendo recognised that there was a vast untapped market of people who wanted simpler games that were fun to play (Fildes, 2007). The console's handset, the Wii Remote, revolutionised the market by allowing consumers "physically" to play simple games such as tennis and ten-pin bowling on the screen, in a manner very much akin to the real game, rather than with a joystick wired up to the computer. While these games are far more basic than the highly sophisticated modern games like *Halo 3* that boast the best graphics, this has not deterred consumers from outside the traditional videogames audience, attracted by the realistic human-computer interaction

▶

offered by the Wii. It is this human–computer interaction that has attracted millions of adults, for whom anything approaching running or lifting for fitness was out of the question on account of the ravages of time and ageing, and who wouldn't normally give videogames a second thought, because the Wii offers games that are fun and user friendly and facilitate participation with ease. It has also brought a whole new dimension to personal fitness.

Nintendo's decision to target non-traditional videogame users was part of a deliberate strategy. Having been the market leader in the late 1980s and early 1990s (Campbell-Kelly, 2004: p286), by the late 1990s Nintendo had lost its position as first Sony and then Microsoft entered the market. Introduced in 1995, the Sony PlayStation utilised 32-bit technology, thereby providing a "step-function improvement" (Campbell-Kelly, 2004: p287) over the 16-bit consoles that then dominated the videogame market. Not only was its software more advanced and capable of offering much improved graphics, the PlayStation, by using CDs instead of cartridges, was able to provide far more video, sound and game content within a videogame. These innovations quickly enabled the PlayStation to establish a dominant position in the videogame market and by 1998 it was the source of almost half of Sony's corporate profits (Chaplin and Ruby, 2006: p229). Microsoft's Xbox appeared in 2002 and it too provided serious competition, while Nintendo's attempt at going head to head with Sony and Microsoft with its GameCube videogame console triggered headlines proclaiming that Mario – the animated plumber that symbolised Nintendo's dominance of the computer games market in the 1980s – had finally run out of tricks (Fildes, 2007).

The launch of the Wii in late 2006 represented a very different approach. According to Nintendo's game designer Shigeru Miyamoto, the videogame consoles then dominating the market were a bit like dinosaurs – very powerful but inflexible – and as such were in danger of rendering each other extinct (Hall, 2006). Nintendo had identified that the computer gaming market had started to stagnate and despite increasing sales, the household penetration of consoles had for several years remained flat at around 30 per cent. Although more games were being sold they were actually being bought by the same narrow audience of committed game players.

Faced with this situation Nintendo went back to the drawing board and instead of starting with technical aspects such as blistering chip speeds or cutting edge graphics, focused on what might convince parents to buy the new console for their kids. When that happened, the discussion focused on basic concepts and goals, not the technical specifications of the console. The goal became how to come up with a machine that parents would want—easy to use, quick to start up, not a huge energy drain, and quiet while it was running. Rather than just picking new technology, Nintendo's engineers thought seriously about what a game console should be. The consensus was that the games should be fun. By offering fun it was hoped the new console would appeal to a mass market of first-time game players, women and older consumers not typically drawn to this form of interactive entertainment. Nintendo staked all on a cheaper, simpler device, that used a different kind of technology to enhance the personal relationship between player and machine, rather than the technical sophistication of its games. The project which was codenamed, Revolution, aimed to use a comparatively unsophisticated console, with Nintendo devoting its research and development (R&D) effort instead into developing a new type of controller that would dramatically improve the human–computer interface.

To create a new human–computer relationship Nintendo's engineers aimed to replace the conventional joystick controller and the associated messy wires with a wireless controller that could sense motion in three dimensions. To do this Nintendo's engineers planned to combine a number of different technologies to mimic three dimensional (3D) space recognition. The wireless controller they came up with incorporated an accelerometer, an instrument that accurately records how fast it is travelling, in three axes: backwards and forwards; up and down; left and right and rotating in any direction (Chu, 2008). In addition it also incorporated an infrared camera, which worked out where the controller was in space, relative to the screen on which the games were being played. Finally, there was wireless communication that fed all this data to the console. This enabled the console to detect the controller's position in 3D space and track its relative motion on a screen. However, the wireless controller took Nintendo's engineers two years to develop. Getting the pointer to work reliably proved particularly difficult. It worked fine in a workshop environment, but bright lights and sunshine interfered with its accuracy. So too did the size of room in which the machine was being used. Eventually, after two years of development, including exhaustive testing in a range of different environments, the wireless controller, or Wii Remote as it was known, was ready for market.

The development effort proved worthwhile for the Wii changed the rules of the videogame market completely. The result was a remarkable rebirth of Nintendo's fortunes. In its first full year the lower powered Wii sold as many consoles in the UK as the PlayStation 3 and Xbox combined, thanks to the appeal of its innovative motion-sensitive controller and family-friendly multi-player games. During the same year the Kyoto-based company overtook Sony in market capitalisation, at one point becoming Japan's third largest company behind Toyota and Mitsubishi. By April 2008 more than 25 million consoles had been sold worldwide.

References

Campbell-Kelly (2004); Chaplin and Ruby (2006); Chu (2008); Fildes (2007); Fry (2008); Hall (2006).

Questions

1 What was new and novel about the Wii?

2 Where would you locate the Wii in terms of the degrees of innovation matrix (Figure 1.2) and why?

3 How did Nintendo's approach to the inventive/creative phase of the Wii's innovation differ from its rivals Sony and Microsoft?

4 If the Wii was not as technologically advanced (in terms of graphics, chip speed etc.) as its rivals from Sony and Microsoft, how can it be an innovation?

5 What was the value proposition being put forward by the Wii and how did this differ from the PlayStation and the Xbox?

6 Who was the value proposition aimed at and why?

7 What was the business model and the associated revenue generation mechanism used for the Wii?

8 How does the Wii Fit contribute to Nintendo's business model?

9 Which of the three routes to invention did Nintendo use with the Wii (see Figure 1.4)?

10 What does the Wii tell us about the relative importance of technology and customer needs?

? **Questions for discussion**

1 Why do so many biographies of people associated with successful innovations appear more preoccupied with inventions?

2 Explain the difference between invention and innovation. Which do you consider the most important and why?

3 Outline the main phases in the process of innovation.

4 Explain what is meant by the term business model in the context of innovation.

5 Why is value creation likely to be a problem with innovations that involve a high degree of novelty?

6 Why is value capture an important issue for innovators, particularly individual innovators?

7 What personal qualities do you consider are essential for successful innovators?

8 Why is it that innovation is often now a collective activity?

9 Internet-related innovations have been associated with much discussion about business models – why?

Exercises

1 Prepare a briefing document for the Nintendo Wii. This should be no more than six pages in length and should provide the reader with a clear understanding of the nature of the Wii, as well as the factors that account for its success as an innovation and the important lessons you feel it holds for would-be innovators. As part of the briefing prepare some slides that will enable you to make a presentation in class.

   To carry out this task you will need to classify the product, identify prospective purchasers/ consumers, distinguish product features, identify competitor products, etc. Your aim should be to show what it is about the Nintendo Wii that makes it a good example of an innovation.

   You will need to carry out some basic fact-finding research. Possible sources are stores and catalogues that stock the Nintendo Wii. If you know someone who owns a Wii, have a look at it, and more importantly ask them who uses it and for what. The websites of newspapers such as *The Independent* and *The Guardian* can also be used to locate articles about the Wii.

2 Prepare a profile of a company that you feel has a strong record of innovation.

   As well as providing background details on the company, you will need to identify examples of successful innovations they have produced. Indicate why these innovations have been successful and try to identify the expertise and experience that you feel enabled the company to innovate.

   You will probably find that biographies, industry studies and similar sources will be useful. You will find details of some of these books in the bibliography. Internet searches may well enable you to find short profiles of the innovations you are interested in. However, be warned that such profiles often lack detail and tend to treat the subject matter in an unsophisticated and uncritical manner.

Further reading

1 **Dyson, J.** (1997) *Against the Odds*, Orion Business, London.
   If you only ever read one book that is in any way about innovation, this is the one. It describes in much detail how James Dyson developed the dual cyclone vacuum cleaner. It covers both the invention and commercialisation phases of innovation. The invention phase of innovation is described at length with plenty of coverage of prototype building and testing. But most important of all there is also plenty about the commercialisation stage of innovation. Business models may not be discussed specifically, but their importance clearly comes through in the text. Above all though it gives a valauble insight into just what innovation entails.

2 **Howells, J.** (2002) *The Management of Innovation and Technology*, Sage Publications, London.
   An unusual textbook about innovation. It isn't the usual highly structured account of innovation. But it is very readable and provides a fascinating perspective on innovation. It includes some excellent examples of innovation. These are not clearly signposted as case studies, but they are detailed and they provide valuable insights into the nature of innovation.

3 **Chesbrough, H.W.** (2003) *Open Innovation: The New Imperatives for Creating and Profiting from Technology*, Harvard Business School Press, Boston, MA.
   A highly influential text. It extols the virtues of a more open approach to innovation where inventions and breakthroughs come not just from internal sources but external sources as well. In the process it shows how the context of innovation has changed dramatically in recent years. It also highlights some of the key issues in innovation, most notably through giving very explicit consideration to business models.

4 **Van Dulken, S.** (2002) *Inventing the 20th Century: 100 Inventions that Shaped the World*, British Library, London.
   Titles can be deceptive. All of the inventions covered in this book are also innovations. It provides useful background information on many well-known innovations. It doesn't provide a great deal of data on each one, but it is a good starting point. Certainly this is a reference work that is worth consulting to build up quickly a picture of when and how a particular innovation occurred.

5 Textbooks on innovation
   These are increasing in number. Some of the more comprehensive ones are: Dodgson, M., D. Gann and A. Salter (2008) *The Management of Technological Innovation*, Oxford University Press, Oxford; Tidd, J., J. Bessant and K. Pavitt (2005) *Managing Innovation: Integrating Technological, Market and Organizational Change*, 3rd edn, John Wiley and Sons, Chichester; Trott, P. (2005) *Innovation Management and New Product Development*, 3rd edn, FT Prentice Hall, London; Von Stamm, B. (2008) *Managing Innovation, Design and Creativity*, 2nd edn, John Wiley and Sons, Chichester.

6 Journals on innovation
   Among the leading academic journals that specifically focus on innovation are: *Research Policy; R&D Management; Industry and Innovation; Technovation; International Journal of Innovation Management; Technology Analysis and Strategic Management; Journal of Product Innovation Management; Creativity and Innovation Management; European Journal of Innovation Management; International Journal of Innovation and Learning.*

CHAPTER 02

Types of innovation

❖ OBJECTIVES

When you have completed this chapter you will be able to:

❖ distinguish the different forms that innovation can take, such as product, process and service innovation

❖ differentiate and distinguish between the different types of innovation,

such as radical and incremental innovation

❖ describe each type of innovation

❖ analyse different types of innovation in terms of their impact on human behaviour, business activity and society as a whole

Introduction

The notion that innovation is essentially about the commercialisation of ideas and inventions suggests that it is relatively straightforward and simple. Far from it, not only is the step from invention to commercially successful innovation often a large one that takes much effort and time, but as Figure 1.2 previously indicated, innovations can and do vary enormously. Some involve a high degree of novelty, some a very modest degree of novelty. In addition the term "innovation" is widely used, and is often applied to things that really have little to do with innovation, certainly in the sense of technological innovation. This chapter builds on the discussion of the scope of innovation in the previous chapter, and tries to produce some order from the apparent chaos and confusion surrounding the term "innovation". Hopefully better informed, the reader can then proceed to more detailed analysis of innovation.

Making sense of innovation

If innovation comes in a variety of shapes and sizes and is used by different people to mean different things then making coherent sense of the subject is not an easy task. Grouping innovations into categories can help. Essentially, categorising innovations should make it easier to make sense of innovation as a whole, simply because one can then take each category in turn and subject it to detailed scrutiny. If it is easier to make sense of a small group than a large one then we should be on the way to making sense of innovation.

Innovations can be categorised in a number of different ways. In this chapter two of several potential methods of categorisation are used. One focuses on the form or application of the innovation (i.e. what it is used for), the other focuses on the degree of novelty associated with the innovation. Neither categorisation is exhaustive, but the difference between the two is illuminating and helps to shed further light on the nature of innovation.

Forms of innovation

The first categorisation, based on the form of innovation, distinguishes three principal applications for innovation: products, services and processes. Consumers use products and services. Products are tangible physical objects like mobile phones, audio players or cars, which consumers acquire and then use as part of the act of consumption. Product innovations take the form of new tangible objects. Services on the other hand are typically intangible things like healthcare or education, where the consumer benefits from the service but does not actually acquire an object. Service innovations are therefore intangible. Both product and service innovations are typically aimed at consumers. In contrast, producers produce products and deliver service and in order to do so they utilise processes. Typically these processes require equipment such as machinery which we refer to as "capital goods". An innovation in the form of new equipment or new methods and systems would be a process innovation.

This distinction is actually a simplification of what one finds in the real world, because clearly companies buy products and services as well as individuals as consumers. Similarly we could perfectly well argue that a washing machine, while being a consumer product bought on the high street, is also used for a process, namely washing clothes. In general when consumers acquire things it is part of consumption and when companies acquire things it is part of production or service delivery. However, while there is undoubtedly some overlap, the distinction between product, service and process innovations is a useful one. This is because of the distinction in terms of the benefit that results from innovation. Product and service innovations will typically benefit consumers giving them more functional products or faster and more effective services. Process innovations on the other hand typically benefit the corporate sector by improving the efficiency of their production or service delivery processes, thereby lowering their costs. Such innovations should also benefit consumers indirectly as lower costs eventually (but not inevitably) feed through into lower prices.

Product innovation

Product innovations loom large in the public imagination. Products, especially consumer products, are probably the most obvious innovation application. The Dyson bagless vacuum cleaner is an example of a product innovation. James Dyson developed what he terms "dual-cyclone" technology (Dyson, 1997) and used it to create a new, more efficient, vacuum cleaner. As a vacuum cleaner it is a consumer product and what makes it an innovation, i.e. what is "innovative" about it, is that it functions in a quite different way from a conventional vacuum cleaner. It is still a vacuum cleaner and it does what vacuum cleaners have always done – it extracts dust and other items of household debris from carpets and upholstery – but the innovation lies in the way in which it functions. Instead of employing a fan to suck dust into a bag, it dispenses with the bag and uses Dyson's patented dual-cyclone technology to extract dust and place it in a clear plastic container, resulting in a more effective cleaner. It is a good example of a product innovation because it is an everyday household product where you can actually see the innovation at work, a fact that James Dyson, an experienced industrial designer and entrepreneur, no doubt had in mind when he designed his first bagless vacuum cleaner, the Dyson 001.

From a commercial perspective the attraction of product innovations is that the novelty of a new product will often persuade consumers to make a purchase. Nor is it purely a matter of novelty. The introduction of a new technology into an existing product may similarly attract much consumer interest. It is no coincidence that "product development" is one of the four business strategies put forward by Ansoff (1988) for the future development of a business.

Service innovation

Often overlooked, but equally important, are service innovations which take the form of new service applications. One reason why service innovations fail to attract as much attention as product innovations is that they are often less spectacular and less eye-catching. This probably has something to do with the fact that, where innovation is concerned, the public imagination has always tended to identify with inventions, rather than innovation as such. Because of their high novelty value, inventions are usually products. Though often harder to identify, service innovations can have a huge impact on consumers. A service innovation involves the provision of a new or significantly improved service to the consumer. A new service may be the result of new technology which makes it possible to offer the consumer a service that has not previously been available. Service improvements in contrast typically result from delivery system (i.e. process) improvements which enable an existing service to be delivered more efficiently.

Facebook is an example of an entirely new service. Prior to the launch of Facebook in 2004, there were few if any social networking services available. Utilising the Internet, Facebook's founder, Harvard University student Mark Zuckerberg, made it possible for individuals to provide details of themselves, which others could access, thereby facilitating social networking. Other examples of new services resulting from the application of Internet technology are eBay and PayPal.

The creation of the "Direct Line" telephone insurance business is a good example of the second type of service innovation. For years the insurance business had been transacted via high street outlets, door-to-door, by post or through intermediaries known as insurance brokers. Peter Wood, the creator of the Direct Line telephone insurance business, realised that with appropriate online computer services, it would be possible to cut out these expensive and unproductive ways of dealing with the public and deal direct with the customer via the telephone, thereby making it much easier for consumers to access insurance services.

The growth of the Internet has led to a sharp rise in the number of service innovations. Some of these innovations have simply made existing services more extensive and more efficient. Amazon.com is a prime example. Bookshops have been around a long time, but online bookshops can offer a much greater range of books often at lower prices because they don't pay the cost of retail premises. Another field in which service innovations have brought significant benefits to consumers is air transport. The arrival of "no frills" airlines such as easyJet and Ryanair (borrowing a model first introduced by South West Airlines in the US), have dramatically increased the range of destinations served as well as lowering the cost.

Mini Case

South West Airlines

Founded in the late 1960s by Herb Kellner, it was South West Airlines that started the "no frills" revolution in air travel.

In Europe in the last ten years air travel has been transformed by the introduction of low-cost services offered by "no frills" carriers. The innovation which these carriers introduced has been the provision of easily accessible scheduled short-haul services at fares very much lower than those offered by conventional scheduled airlines. The result has been an enormous increase in both numbers travelling by air and the range of destinations served.

Yet this was not a European innovation. The pioneer of low-cost "no frills" air transport was South West Airlines based in Texas. Under its charismatic founder, Herb Kellner, South West Airlines had to fight legal battles with local competitors for the first four years of existence just to be allowed to fly. Competitors argued there simply was not enough business to warrant another airline in the region. When it did finally get airborne it was faced with a price war with Braniff and other airlines as they tried to drive it out of business.

Based at Love Field in downtown Dallas, South West Airlines was able to survive by offering customers a very different package from conventional airlines. The package included low fares (usually 60 per cent below conventional airlines), high frequencies, excellent on-time departure rates and direct sales (i.e. no travel agents). What was not being offered was meals, pre-assigned seats, different classes of seating and connecting flights. This was achieved by means of: a single aircraft type (then and now the Boeing 737), smaller low-cost airports, rapid turnarounds (typically 15–20 minutes), high load factors, and point-to-point services.

The "no frills" service package diverted some traffic away from existing carriers but, more significantly, it generated a lot of new business, especially leisure and business passengers who could be persuaded to fly rather than drive. As Herb Kellner (Dogannis, 2001: p128) put it: "we are not competing with airlines, we're competing with ground transportation".

De-regulation of airline services in the US in 1978 meant that South West Airlines was well placed to expand in Texas with this innovation in airline service. Traffic growth proved well above average. South West was able to expand by adding more capacity to its fleet, but instead of adding routes as airlines normally did, Kellner's strategy was to increase flight frequency on existing routes.

It worked. Today South West Airlines is the fifth biggest carrier in the US, and is the most consistently profitable airline in the country, yet it has stuck to its innovative business model. Not only that, the model has been copied with great success in Europe, first by Ryanair (Dogannis, 2001) and then by a host of other airlines including easyJet and BMI Baby to create a low-cost revolution in air travel across the continent.

Source: Procter (1994).

Process innovation

If service innovation comes second behind product innovations, then process innovation almost certainly comes a poor third. Yet process innovation often has an even bigger impact on society than product/service innovation. The early nineteenth-century Luddite movement in and around Nottingham (Chapman, 2002), where stocking knitters who worked on machines in the home took to rioting and breaking the new, more efficient, machines located in factories, because they feared that the new machines would destroy their livelihoods, is testimony to the power of process innovation.

By process innovation we typically mean innovations in manufacturing processes, although as we have already seen it also includes innovations in service delivery processes (though this might well simply be included under service innovation). However, process innovation in fact extends beyond both spheres to include innovations in administrative and office systems.

A classic example of a process innovation that dramatically improved the efficiency of a production process is the "float glass" process developed by Alistair Pilkington, in which plate glass is manufactured by drawing glass out across a bed of molten tin (Quinn, 1991). Prior to the introduction of this process innovation, plate glass used for shop windows and office windows was expensive and of poor quality, largely because the only way of getting a flat surface was to grind it and polish it. The float glass process at a stroke eliminated the need for time-consuming grinding and polishing, leading to a dramatic fall in costs. Architects and property developers could now afford to specify large sheets of plate glass when constructing new buildings, where in the past they would have been prevented because of the cost. The result can be seen in building construction in the past 30 years, where everything from office blocks and hotels to airports and shopping malls now employs large expanses of glass.

Assembly Time	Craft production, 1913 (minutes)	Mass production, 1914 (minutes)	Reduction in effort (%)
Engine	594	226	62
Magneto	20	5	75
Axle	150	26.5	83
Components into vehicle	750	93	88

TABLE 2.1 Craft v. mass production at Ford 1913–1914
Source: Womack, J. P., D. T. Jones, and D. Roos (1990) *The Machine That Changed the World*, Rawson Associates/Scribner, an imprint of Simon and Schuster Adult Publishing Group, New York © 1990 by James P. Womack, Daniel T. Jones, Daniel Roos and Donna Sammons Carpenter

Nor are process innovations confined to technology in the form of improved equipment (i.e. capital goods): they can also include improved methods of working and improved systems. F.W.Taylor's "scientific management" (sometimes refered to as work study or organisation and methods) formed a new method of organising work. It led to big increases in productivity as work activities were re-organised using Taylor's principles of scientific management. Another new production method was Henry Ford's introduction of the moving assembly line at his Detroit factory in 1913. Table 2.1 shows the dramatic reduction in manufacturing effort this produced. Improved productivity on this scale led Ford to reduce the price of his Model T car which in 1908 sold for $850, to $600 in 1913 and $360 by 1916 (Freeman and Louçã, 2001: p275). As Ford reduced his prices, demand took off and the car, which had hitherto been an ostentatious toy only available to a small wealthy elite, was opened to a broad cross-section of society.

Since process innovations are not confined to manufacturing, it is not surprising that, as we have already seen, process innovations frequently occur in service industries. An example of a service transformed by the introduction of improved methods to give a process innovation is the parcel service Federal Express (Table 2.2). This was the brainchild of Frederick W. Smith, who pioneered the idea of overnight delivery using a "hub-and-spoke" system (Nayak and Ketteringham, 1993). During the day trucks collect parcels and bring them to an airport hub where they are sorted and then flown overnight to another hub near their destination ready for delivery the next day. The result is a much faster and more efficient parcel delivery system.

Table 2.2 includes SABRE, the computerised airline reservation system introduced by American Airlines (Campbell-Kelly, 2003), which provides an example of a service innovation brought about by improved equipment, namely the computer. When first introduced in the late 1960s SABRE transformed the experience of air travel, because for the first time it became possible for travel agents booking passengers on to flights to ascertain accurately whether an airline actually had vacant seats on a particular flight. Prior to SABRE, airlines could only estimate how many people had booked to fly. Passengers were required to "confirm" their booking by telephone before the flight and airlines left a certain proportion of seats empty to cover bookings still being processed by the unwieldy paper-based systems then being used. Not only did the uncertainty mean a poor quality of service for passengers, it often led to low load factors on many flights, inevitably making flying more expensive. SABRE paved the way for the massive growth in air travel that has occured over the last three decades.

Today we are in the midst of a process revolution. All sorts of organisations from banks and insurance companies to supermarkets and cinemas are providing facilities for consumers to carry out transactions online. Even government is getting in on the act as activities, such as taxing a car and applying for a driving licence, are increasingly carried out online. Transacting business online means greater efficiency because there are no people to serve the customer and no papers to process. Instead the customer inputs the data and everything else (well, just about everything else) is done electronically. This is dramatically reducing the need for paperwork and those who process paper, namely administrators, resulting in faster and cheaper processes and greater efficiency. It is no surprise that all sorts of businesses from airlines to insurance

Form	Innovation	Innovator	Country
Product	iPod	Steve Jobs/Apple	US
	Ballpoint pen	Laszlo Biro	Hungary
	Velcro	Georges de Mestral	Switzerland
	Computer mouse	Douglas Engelbart	US
Service	Telephone insurance	Peter Wood/RBS	UK
	Social networking website	Mark Zuckerberg	US
	World Wide Web	Tim Berners-Lee	UK
	"No frills" airline	Herb Kellner/R King	US
Process	Moving assembly line	Henry Ford	US
	Float glass	Alistair Pilkington	UK
	Hub + spoke delivery system	Fred Smith	US
	Computerised airline reservations (SABRE)	IBM/American Airlines	US

TABLE 2.2 Forms of innovation

companies offer a discount for carrying out transactions online. One has only to look at the size of the discounts offered to get an idea of the efficiency gains that firms can make.

One final point to bear in mind about categorising innovations in this way is that it helps to highlight the nature of process innovation. Process innovation is one of the unsung heroes of innovation in the sense that it attracts much less attention than product or even service innovation, and yet its impact is typically much greater. The rising standard of living that the world has enjoyed since the industrial revolution, is largely the product of successive process innovations. By making production and service delivery processes more efficient these process innovations have improved productivity, thereby making us all better off.

Types of innovation

As well as focusing on applications to differentiate innovations, there are other approaches to analysing the extent of innovation through some form of categorisation (Dodgson, Gann and Salter, 2008). One widely used approach is to focus on the degree of novelty. This was broadly the approach taken in Chapter 1 on the scope of innovation. However, here a more systematic approach is used. The advantage of using this sort of categorisation is that it brings the extent of the change involved in an innovation into sharp relief. One focuses on just how new an innovation is, which in turn highlights the technological effort associated with an innovation. Quite literally one is examining the "innovativeness" of an innovation. In an era when lots of things are described as innovative, this kind of analysis can help to qualify such terms and enable judgments to be made about the degree of change embodied in an innovation.

It has long been noted that innovations vary greatly, from those which are completely new and different from anything that has gone before, to those that involve little more than "cosmetic" changes to an existing design. In the first instance the degree of novelty would be high while in the latter it would be very low. This distinction between big-change and small-change innovations has led some to a categorisation of innovation that differentiates between radical and incremental (Freeman, 1974) innovations. In this categorisation, innovations involving major breakthroughs, new technologies and major scientific advances would be in the radical category. More modest innovations involving product improvements that result in changes to product attributes, such as small improvements in performance or greater functionality, rather than new products, would be in the incremental category.

However, differentiating innovations using just two classes in this way is rather limited and does not bring out the subtle but important differences between innovations. In particular it often fails to show where the novelty really lies. To cater for this Henderson and Clark (1990) have developed a more complex and more sophisticated analysis. This incorporates the concepts of radical and incremental innovation within a broader framework. Henderson and Clark's (1990) analytical framework provides a typology that allows us to analyse a range of innovations in more detail than simply classifying them as radical or incremental, and at the same time predict their impact in terms of both competition and the marketplace. The analysis does have its limitations, most notably that it is very product oriented, though it can be used for service and process innovations. But it does at least help to show the sheer range of things that can be covered by the term innovation, and importantly it helps to focus on where the novelty in an innovation really lies.

At the heart of Henderson and Clark's analytical framework is the recognition that products, services and processes are actually systems. As systems they are made up of components that fit together in a particular way in order to carry out a given function.

Henderson and Clark (1990) point out that to make a product, service or process normally requires two distinct types of knowledge:

■ Component knowledge

i.e. knowledge of each of the components that perform a well-defined function within a broader system that makes up the product. This knowledge forms part of the "core design concepts" (Henderson and Clark, 1990) embedded in the components.

■ System knowledge

i.e. knowledge about the way the components are integrated and linked together. This is knowledge about how the system works and how the various components are configured and work together. Henderson and Clark (1990) refer to this as "architectural" knowledge.

Mini Case

Automatic washing machine

The modern automatic washing machine is the product of a variety of innovations. The washing machine is a system for washing clothes. The components comprise: motor, pump, drum, programmer, chassis, door and body. These components are linked together into an overall system. Component knowledge is the knowledge that relates to each of the components. System knowledge, on the other hand, is about the way in which the components interact. The interaction is determined by the way in which the system is configured. Responsible for the design and development of the system, washing machine manufacturers frequently buy in component knowledge by buying components and then assembling them into a finished product.

Washing machines have been affected by both incremental and architectural innovation. Changes in the spin speed are an example of incremental innovation. The spin speed determines how dry the clothes will be when they come out of the machine. In the mid-1970s automatic washing machines typically had a maximum spin speed of 700 rpm. In 1976 Hoover launched its A3058 model which boasted a maximum spin speed of 800 rpm. Two years later and Hoover's A3060 introduced a further innovation in the form of a maximum spin speed of 1,100 rpm. Since then a steady stream of innovations has seen the speed rise to 1,200, 1,400, 1,600 and now 1,800 rpm. Although these advances have resulted in improved performance (i.e. drier clothes), the system has remained unchanged. However, there have also been architectural innovations in the washing machine field. The Dyson Contrarotator™ washing machine launched in November 2000 was an architectural innovation. This had not just one drum, as on a conventional machine, but two that rotate in opposite directions. This change in the configuration of the system produced an entirely different washing system.

Henderson and Clark (1990) use the distinction between component and system knowledge to differentiate four categories or types of innovation (Figure 2.1). They use a two-dimensional matrix where one axis relates to components and component changes, while the other relates to linkages between components (i.e. system architecture) and changes in those linkages.

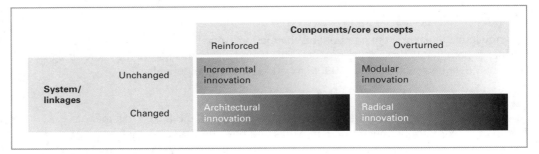

FIGURE 2.1 Typology of innovations
Source: Henderson, R. M. and K. B. Clark, (1990) 'Architectural Innovation: The Reconfiguration of Existing Product Technologies and the Failure of Established Firms', *Administrative Science Quarterly*, **35**, pp 9–30. Reproduced with kind permission of *Administrative Science Quarterly*

In this analysis radical and incremental innovation are polarised as being at opposite extremes, where the former involves changes in components and system architecture while the latter involves small changes in components that enhance component performance. Against this background, the analysis introduces two intermediate types of innovation between these two extremes (Table 2.3), namely modular innovation and architectural innovation:

Innovation	Components	System
Incremental	Improved	No change
Modular	New	No change
Architectural	Improved	New configuration/architecture
Radical	New	New configuration/architecture

TABLE 2.3 Changes associated with types of innovation

Radical innovation

Radical innovation is normally the result of a major technological breakthrough or the application of a new technology. Unlike incremental innovation where each innovation typically draws heavily on what has preceded it, radical innovation is non-linear and discontinuous involving a step change from what has gone before. Hence radical innovation is about much more than improving an existing design. A radical innovation calls for a whole new design. In Henderson and Clark's (1990) terminology: "Radical innovation establishes a new dominant design, and hence a new set of core design concepts embodied in components that are linked together in a new architecture". This new architecture, with new components linked together in a different way, often results from the introduction of a new technology (see Table 2.4). In some cases this will be a transforming technology, which brings a different set of priorities in to play both in the market and the industry. Thus in terms of the degree of novelty, radical innovations involve a high level of novelty because they employ a new design with new components integrated into a new system architecture. A radical innovation may well involve the use of a new business model, as when Haloid (later Xerox) introduced the electrostatic copier. In short with radical innovation just about everything changes.

The flat-screen TV is an example of a radical innovation. What makes the flat-screen TV a radical innovation? Prior to its introduction, TVs and computer monitors utilised a cathode ray tube (CRT) to display an image. Compared to a TV utilising a CRT display, a flat-screen TV incorporates a completely different technology, namely a liquid crystal display (LCD). LCD technology, which has its origins back in the 1970s, operates on entirely different principles. The LCD uses liquid chemicals whose molecules can be aligned precisely when subjected to an electrical current. First used for pocket calculator and wrist watch displays, LCD technology owes nothing to CRT technology. Compared to a CRT-based TV, the system architecture is different as are the components. Thus the flat-screen TV represents a discontinuous change rather than a linear one. CRT displays benefited from a string of linear innovations over many years, that improved their display characteristics, but the introduction of the flat-screen TV represented a break with CRT technology. The net result is a product that has to be manufactured in a completely different way, rendering CRT manufacturing facilities and the knowledge surrounding them redundant.

Radical innovation	Technology	Impact on society
Jet engine	Gas turbine	Permits mass travel for first time
Carbon fibre F1 racing car	Carbon fibre	Much better handling and safer
Transistor radio	Transistor	First portable radio (+ lower cost)
Personal computer	Integrated circuit	Computing for everyone
Digital camera	Digital imaging	Photography becomes more flexible and accessible
MP3 player	MP3 files	Greater access to recorded music

TABLE 2.4 Radical innovations

Table 2.4 provides some more examples of radical innovation. What is noticeable about them all is that they employed a new technology. There was no mere tinkering to provide a small improvement in performance, give the product a new look, or provide appeal to a new group of consumers. Each innovation represented a radical break from the past, with a new technology working on new principles to give new product characteristics. To bring the new technology to market was a big task. There was a high degree of uncertainty. Would the technology work? Would it provide products or services with characteristics that consumers wanted? Thus radical innovation is both difficult and risky.

Radical innovations are, however, comparatively rare. Rothwell and Gardner (1989a) estimated that at the most about 10 per cent of innovations are radical. Radical innovation is often associated with the introduction of a new technology (Table 2.4).

Radical innovations tend to have more dramatic consequences than other types of innovation for the organisations that develop them. Typically a radical innovation will require them to ask a new set of questions, to draw on new technical and commercial skills and to employ new problem-solving approaches (Henderson and Clarke, 1990). The jet engine provides a good example of a radical innovation that had far-reaching consequences in terms of organisational capabilities. Compared to its predecessor, the piston engine, the jet operates on quite different principles. Among the problems it presented were the need for new materials that could withstand very high temperatures. In terms of technical skills it required a knowledge of aerodynamics. Nor did it stop there, for the jet had very different things to offer potential customers (i.e. commercial airlines), namely speed and smoothness.

Because different organisational capabilities are often required with radical innovations, it is not unusual for them to be launched, not by existing players in an industry, but by new entrants. The iPod is an example. Working on different principles from earlier audio players, it provided an opportunity for a new entrant, Apple Computer, to enter the market. Apple was not at a disadvantage because the technology of MP3 was new and the existing firms didn't have many years of accumulated experience to draw on. Nor is this a one-off example: we saw in the previous chapter how a radical innovation, electrostatic copying, provided an opportunity for Haloid (later re-named Xerox) to enter the market very successfully.

The concept of radical innovation is closely linked to Christensen's (1997) notion of "disruptive technologies". By "disruptive" he means inducing significant changes in markets and industries, often leading to high levels of uncertainty. In terms of markets these changes might mean completely new markets or new customers or new products/services. In industry terms the changes often mean the arrival of new entrant firms better able to marshall the necessary organisational capabilities now required, and the departure of existing firms.

Thus radical innovation typically has much more far-reaching consequences than any other type of innovation. The changes that accompany radical innovation often lead to periods of considerable uncertainty, perhaps with competing designs and increased competition. Eventually, however, as we shall see in the next chapter this state of uncertainty subsides and radical innovation is followed by successive incremental innovations.

Incremental innovation

Incremental innovation involves modest changes to existing products/services (or processes) to exploit the potential of an existing design. The changes are typically improvements to components, possibly the introduction of new components, but always within the confines of an existing design. However, it is important to stress that these are improvements not major changes. In other words the level of novelty is low. Christensen (1997) defines incremental innovation as: "a change that builds on a firm's expertise in component technology within an established architecture," and this highlights an important feature of incremental innovation, namely that it is typically the product of existing practice and expertise associated with an existing technology rather than the introduction of a new technology.

Incremental innovations are the commonest type of innovation. Gradual improvements in knowledge and materials associated with a particular technology lead to most products and services being enhanced over time. These enhancements typically take the form of refinements in components rather than changes in the system. The technology is improved rather than replaced. Thus incremental innovation is something that occurs quite frequently to create an essentially linear process of continuous change. The changes exploit the potential of an existing design using an existing technology. Thus, a new model of an existing and established product (perhaps described as a 'mark 2' or new and improved version) is likely to leave the architecture of the system unchanged and instead involve refinements to particular components. In the case of the automatic washing machine (see mini case), incremental innovation describes the way in which manufacturers have improved the efficiency of the machine by fitting more powerful motors to give faster spin speeds. With the system and the linkages between components unchanged and the design of the components reinforced (through refinements and performance improvements) this places such innovations in the top-left-hand quadrant of Figure 2.1, where they are designated "incremental innovations".

New models of the iPod provide another example of incremental innovation. Originally introduced in October 2001, there was nothing incremental about the iPod when it first appeared. It was a radical innovation. However, since then Apple has produced a steady stream of new versions of the iPod – different sizes (e.g. Mini and Nano), different storage capacities and different colours. Throughout though the technology and how it is configured has remained the same.

The impact of incremental innovation in terms of markets and industries is likely to be quite different from radical innovation. Incremental innovation, by using existing technology and the knowledge and expertise associated with it, tends to reinforce the position of incumbent firms. Similarly in terms of markets one is typically talking about increasing market penetration or entering new market segments rather than the creation of new markets. Thus incremental innovation favours existing players. They are likely to be the ones with an established stock of knowledge and expertise in a given technology. In that sense they will probably be the ones best placed to generate a steady (i.e. linear) stream of incremental innovations.

Mini Case

Never ask permission to innovate

In 1956, a small American company invented a device called the "Hush-a-Phone". It was a plastic cup designed to be attached to the microphone end of a telephone handset in order to facilitate telephone conversations in noisy environments – rather like cupping your hand over the phone.

When Hush-a-Phone appeared on the market, AT&T – then the monopolistic supplier of telephone services to the US public – objected, on the grounds that it was a crime to attach to the phone system any device not expressly approved by AT&T. Hush-a-Phone had not been thus approved. The Federal Communications Commission agreed with AT&T. The fact that the device in no way 'connected' with the network was neither here nor there. Hush-a-Phone was history.

A few years later, when Paul Baran proposed the packet-switching technology which eventually underpinned the Internet, AT&T first derided and then blocked its development. One of AT&T's executives eventually said to Baran: "First, it can't possibly work, and if it did, damned if we are going to allow the creation of a competitor to ourselves".

Note the verb "allow". In a single word it explains why we should never permit the established order to be gatekeepers of innovation.

This is not widely understood by legislatures or governments, and it is particularly not understood by our own dear DTI (aka the Department of Torpor and Indolence), which thinks that the way to encourage innovation is to get all the established players in an industry together and exhort them to do it.

Innovation comes in two forms. The first is incremental – the process of making regular improvements to existing products and services. This is a cosy, familiar business which is easily accommodated by the established industrial order and by its regulatory bodies. It is what governments and corporations have in mind when they declare they are in favour of innovation.

The second kind of innovation is the disruptive variety – defined as developments that upset, supersede or transform established business models, user expectations and government frameworks and create hitherto unimagined possibilities. In other words, change that upsets powerful apple-carts.

This is the kind of innovation that the established order really fears – and often tries hard to squash. Yet, if our societies and economies are to remain vibrant, it is the only kind of innovation that matters. We are thus faced with a dilemma: on the one hand, we need disruptive innovation; on the other, the established order will never make it happen. So what do we do?

This is the central policy issue confronting every modern government. Yet the answer – as a striking new pamphlet by Demos argues – is staring us in the face. It involves learning from the history of the Internet. The reason it spurred such an explosion of disruptive change is that it was an innovation commons – an uncontrolled space equally available to all. A whole raft of powerful technologies – for example, the World Wide Web, streaming audio, video-conferencing, Internet telephony, instant messaging, peer-to-peer networking, interactive gaming, online auctions, chat – came into being because their inventors had unfettered access to the network. They did not have to ask the permission of AT&T or BT or the DTI to implement their ideas. If the invention was good enough, then it could, and did, conquer the world.

The lesson for the UK – and particularly Ofcom, the new omnipotent communications regulator – is that the preservation of a commons is vital if real innovation is to be nurtured here. This means, for example, that when analogue TV is switched off, some of the liberated spectrum should be retained as an unlicensed commons so that people can experiment and innovate with it.

Like all great ideas, it is simple. The only question is whether it is simple enough for the DTI to get it.

Source: Naughton (2002).

Modular innovation

Modular innovation uses the architecture and configuration associated with the existing system of an established product, but employs new components with different design concepts. In terms of Henderson and Clark's framework, modular innovation is in the top-right quadrant.

Mini Case

Clockwork radio

An example of modular innovation would be the clockwork radio, developed by Trevor Baylis. Radios have been around for a very long time. They operate on the basis of electrical energy, normally provided via either an external power supply or batteries. The clockwork radio is an innovation that employs a different form of power supply, one that utilises a spring-based clockwork mechanism. The other components of the radio, such as the speakers, tuner, amplifier, receiver, etc. remain unchanged. As a radio, the clockwork radio operates in the same way as other radios. It employs the same kind of architecture in which the various components that make up the system are configured and linked together in the normal way. However, being clockwork it does not require an external power sources and this is a very valuable feature in those parts of the world which do not benefit from regular uninterrupted power supplies.

Source: Baylis (1999).

As with incremental innovation, modular innovation does not involve a whole new design. Modular innovation does, however, involve new or at least significantly different components. In the case of the clockwork radio it is the power source that is new. The radio operates in much the same way as any other radio.

The use of new or different components is the key feature of modular innovation, especially if the new components embrace a new technology. New technology can transform the way in which one or more components within the overall system can operate, but the system and its configuration/architecture remains unchanged.

Clearly the impact of modular innovation is usually less dramatic than is the case with radical innovation. The clockwork radio illustrates this well. People still listen to the radio in the way they always have; but the fact that it does not need an external power source means that new groups often living in relatively poor countries without access to a stable and reliable supply of electricity can get the benefit of radio. Clockwork radio has also opened up new markets in affluent countries – for example, hikers who want a radio to keep in touch with the outside world. It has also provided an important "demonstration" effect as it has led to other products, such as torches, being fitted with this ingenious and environmentally friendly source of power.

Architectural innovation

With architectural innovation, the components and associated design concepts remain unchanged but the configuration of the system changes as new linkages are instituted. As Henderson and Clark (1990: p12) point out: "the essence of an architectural innovation is the reconfiguration of an established system to link together existing components in a new way". This is not to say that there will not be some changes to components. Manufacturers may well take the opportunity to refine and improve some components, but essentially the changes will be minor, leaving the components to function as they have in the past but within a new re-designed and re-configured system.

Sony Walkman

The Sony Walkman provides a good example of architectural innovation. The Walkman, when it first came out, was a highly innovative new product, but it involved little or no new technology. All the main components that went into the Walkman were tried and tested having been used on a variety of other products. Portable audio tape recorders that could both play and record music had been on the market for many years. Designers at Sony started with an existing, small, audio cassette tape recorder, the Pressman (Henry and Walker, 1991), a small lightweight tape recorder designed for press reporters. They proceeded to remove the recording circuitry and the speakers, and added a small stereo amplifier. A set of lightweight headphones completed the package. Because there were no speakers the new machine needed much less power. The absence of speakers meant it could be made much smaller, while the fact that it needed much less power meant it could use only small batteries making it very much lighter. A very different kind of system with a very different kind of architecture began to emerge. So the Walkman was born. It was a new type of audio product. It was a personal stereo, that enabled its young, mobile users to listen to music whenever and wherever they wanted, and without being harassed by older generations concerned about noise.

Source: Sanderson and Uzumeri (1995).

The Walkman was a huge commercial success, selling 1.5 million units in just two years (Sanderson and Uzumeri, 1995). However, the significance of the Walkman is not just that it sold well. It illustrates the power that is sometimes associated with architectural innovations. As well as securing Sony's future as a consumer electronics manufacturer, it had a much wider impact on society. It was soon copied by other manufacturers, but more significantly it changed the behaviour of consumers. Young people found they could combine a healthy lifestyle while continuing to listen to music so that the Walkman may be said to have helped promote a whole range of activities like jogging, walking and use of the gym.

The value of an innovation typology

As was the case with the forms of innovation, none of the types of innovation outlined using this framework is entirely watertight. Inevitably there is overlap and there will be many occasions when it is a matter of judgment as to in which category an innovation should be placed. However, this is not really the issue. What matters is the general value that comes from attempting a categorisation of innovations. Categorisation helps to show that innovations are not homogeneous. Innovations vary. Consequently, any analysis of innovation needs a degree of sophistication that can isolate exactly where the nature of the innovation lies. In the process this should enable the more discerning analysts to cast a more critical eye upon some of the wilder claims surrounding objects that are described using that much over-used adjective: "innovative".

Categorising innovations into types ranging from radical to incremental can also help to show that the influence of technology and technological change can vary considerably.

Technology works in a variety of ways. However, its impact will differ enormously when applied to whole systems or when, for comparison, it is applied to individual components. Hence, this form of categorisation has a predictive power, such that those who use it can much more effectively evaluate the potential impact of a particular innovation.

Distinguishing four different types of innovation can also help to explain why the responses of firms to the introduction of new technologies will often vary. The analysis means that perhaps we should not be surprised that some firms do not respond positively to some new technologies. If the technology affects components we can expect a rapid take-up of a new technology, because it is likely to reinforce the competitive position of incumbent manufacturers. On the other hand, if the technology leads to system changes and the introduction of new architectures, the incumbents are less likely to be happy about the changes, as their position may be eroded. In Schumpeter's words, we are likely to see "creative destruction" at work.

This typology can also help in understanding the evolutionary process associated with technological change. When a new technology appears, it frequently leads to a proliferation of competing system designs each with a different architecture. One could see exactly this happening when the first cars were developed – there was a multiplicity of competing architectures, and again when the first video recorders appeared. Eventually through a process of "shake-out" a common system architecture or "dominant design" evolved and was adopted by all manufacturers. This kind of evolutionary process is in fact very common and carries major implications for would-be innovators and entrepreneurs. They will need to recognise that, if they enter the industry during its early years, they can expect there to be a period of shake-out eventually. It is even more important that they recognise that a dominant design is likely to emerge and that it is not always technically superior to its rivals. The QWERTY keyboard is evidence that sometimes technically inferior designs emerge as the dominant design.

However, this typology does have its limitations. Firstly it is very product oriented. While most products are assembled from components configured through a product architecture that describes the way they fit together, this is often much less apparent with services. Services therefore don't lend themselves to this sort of analysis nearly as easily. Secondly there are some products that aren't assembled from components and therefore don't possess an architecture. Products like chemicals and pharmaceuticals provide appropriate examples of such products. Hence the typology is not universally applicable even to products. Thirdly the typology is technologically oriented and while it may be good at differentiating the degree of innovation in technological terms it doesn't necessarily differentiate in terms of the wider impact of an innovation on society. There are examples of architectural and even modular innovations that have had what one might describe as a radical impact in terms of their impact on society. The personal computer provides a good example. One has only to consider that 30 years ago virtually no one had a personal computer on their desk at work – whereas today virtually everyone does (certainly of those who work in offices). And yet in technological terms the personal computer is an example of architectural innovation. The mobile phone and the Sony Walkman provide further examples.

(This is an abridged version of an article from the *New York Times*, 30 November 2003.)

Two years ago this month, Apple Computer released a small, sleek-looking device it called the iPod. A digital music player, it weighed just 6.5 ounces and held about 1,000 songs. There were small MP3 players around at the time, and there were players that could hold a lot of music. But if the crucial equation is "largest number of songs" divided by "smallest physical space," the iPod seemed untouchable. Yet the initial reaction was mixed: the thing cost $400, so much more than existing digital players that it prompted one online skeptic to suggest that the name might be an acronym for "Idiots Price Our Devices".

Since then, however, about 1.4 million iPods have been sold. For the months of July and August, the iPod claimed the No. 1 spot in the MP3 player market both in terms of unit share (31 per cent) and revenue share (56 per cent), by Apple's reckoning. It is now Apple's highest-volume product. Whether the iPod achieves truly mass scale – like, say, the cassette-tape Walkman, which sold an astonishing 186 million units in its first 20 years of existence – it certainly qualifies as a hit and as a genuine breakthrough.

So you can say that the iPod is innovative, but it's harder to nail down whether the key is what's inside it, the external appearance or even the way these work together. One approach is to peel your way through the thing, layer by layer.

The aura

Before you even get to the surface of the iPod, you encounter what could be called its aura. The commercial version of an aura is a brand, and while Apple may be a niche player in the computer market, the fanatical brand loyalty of its customers is legendary. Leander Kahney has even written a book about it, *The Cult of Mac.* As he points out, that base has supported the company with a faith in its will to innovate – even during stretches when it hasn't. Apple is also a giant in the world of industrial design. The candy-colored look of the iMac has been so widely copied that it's now a visual cliché.

But the iPod is making an even bigger impression. Bruce Claxton, who is the current president of the Industrial Designers Society of America and a senior designer at Motorola, calls the device emblematic of a shift toward products that are "an antidote to the hyper lifestyle," which might be symbolized by hand-held devices that bristle with buttons and controls that seem to promise a million functions if you only had time to figure them all out. "People are seeking out products that are not just simple to use but a joy to use". Moby, the recording artist, has been a high-profile iPod booster since the product's debut. 'The kind of insidious revolutionary quality of the iPod," he says, "is that it's so elegant and logical, it becomes part of your life so quickly that you can't remember what it was like beforehand".

The idea of innovation, particularly technological innovation, has a kind of aura around it, too. Imagine the lone genius, sheltered from the storm of short-term commercial demands in a research lab somewhere, whose tinkering produces a sudden and momentous breakthrough. Or maybe we think innovation begins with an epiphany, a sudden vision of the future. Either way, we think of that one thing, the lightning bolt that jolted all the other pieces into place. The Walkman came about because a Sony executive wanted a high-quality but small stereo tape player to listen to on long flights. A small recorder was modified, with the recording pieces removed and stereo circuitry added. That was February 1979, and within six months the product was on the market.

The iPod's history is comparatively free of lightning-bolt moments. Apple was not ahead of the curve in recognizing the power of music in digital form. Various portable digital music players were already on the market before the iPod was even an idea. The company had, back in the 1990's, invented a technology called FireWire, which is basically a tool for moving data between digital devices – in large quantities, very quickly. Apple licensed this technology to various Japanese consumer electronics companies (which used it in digital camcorders and players) and eventually started adding FireWire ports to iMacs and creating video editing software. This led to programs called iMovie, then iPhoto and then a conceptual view of the home computer as a "digital hub" that would complement a range of devices. Finally, in January 2001, iTunes was added to the mix.

And although the next step sounds prosaic – we make software that lets you organize the music on your computer, so maybe we should make one of those things that lets you take it with you – it was also something new. There were companies that made jukebox software, and companies that made portable players, but nobody made both. What this meant is not that the iPod could do more, but that it would do less. This is what led to what Jonathan Ive, Apple's vice president of industrial design, calls the iPod's "overt simplicity". And this, perversely, is the most exciting thing about it.

The surface

The surface of the iPod, white on front and stainless steel behind, is perfectly seamless. It's close to impenetrable. You hook it up to a computer with iTunes, and whatever music you have collected there flows (incredibly fast, thanks to that FireWire cable) into the iPod – again, seamless. Once it's in there, the surface of the iPod is not likely to cause problems for the user, because there's almost nothing on it. Just that wheel, one button in the center, and four beneath the device's LCD screen.

"Steve (Jobs) made some very interesting observations very early on about how this was about navigating content", Ive says. "It was about being very focused and not trying to do too much with the device – which would have been its complication and, therefore, its demise. The enabling features aren't obvious and evident, because the key was getting rid of stuff".

Later he said: "What's interesting is that out of that simplicity, and almost that unashamed sense of simplicity, and expressing it, came a very different product. But difference wasn't the goal. It's actually very easy to create a different thing. What was exciting is starting to realize that its difference was really a consequence of this quest to make it a very simple thing".

Only Apple could have developed the iPod. Like the device itself, Apple appears seamless: it has the hardware engineers, the software engineers, the industrial designers, all under one roof and working together. "As technology becomes more complex, Apple's core strength of knowing how to make very sophisticated technology comprehensible to mere mortals is in even greater demand." This is why, (Jobs) said, the barrage of devices made by everyone from Philips to Samsung to Dell that are imitating and will imitate the iPod do not make him nervous. "The Dells of the world don't spend money" on design innovation, he said. "They don't think about these things."

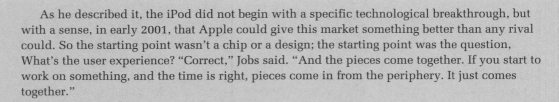

As he described it, the iPod did not begin with a specific technological breakthrough, but with a sense, in early 2001, that Apple could give this market something better than any rival could. So the starting point wasn't a chip or a design; the starting point was the question, What's the user experience? "Correct," Jobs said. "And the pieces come together. If you start to work on something, and the time is right, pieces come in from the periphery. It just comes together."

The guts

What, then, are the pieces? What are the technical innards of the seamless iPod? What's underneath the surface? A lot of people were interested in knowing what was inside the iPod when it made its debut. One of them was David Carey, who for the past three years has run a business in Austin, Tex., called Portelligent, which tears apart electronic devices and does what might be called guts checks. He tore up his first iPod in early 2002.

Inside was a neat stack of core components. First, the power source: a slim, squarish rechargeable battery made by Sony. Atop that was the hard disk – the thing that holds all the music files. At the time, small hard disks were mostly used in laptops, or as removable data-storage cards for laptops. So-called 2.5-in hard disks, which are protected by a casing that actually measures about 2 3/4-in by 4-in, were fairly commonplace, but Toshiba had come up with an even smaller one. With a protective cover measuring just over 2-in by 3-in, 0.2-in thick and weighing less than two ounces, its 1.8-in disk could hold five gigabytes of data – or, in practical terms, about a thousand songs. This is what Apple used.

On top of this hard disk was the circuit board. This included components to turn a digitally encoded music file into a conventional audio file, the chip that enables the device to use FireWire both as a pipe for digital data and battery charging and the central processing unit that acts as the sort of taskmaster for the various components. Also here was the ball-bearing construction underlying the scroll wheel.

Exactly how all the pieces came together – there were parts from at least a half-dozen companies in the original iPod – is not something Apple talks about. But one clue can be found in the device itself. Under the Settings menu is a selection called Legal, and there you find not just Apple's copyright but also a note that "portions" of the device are copyrighted by something called PortalPlayer Inc. That taskmaster central processing unit is a PortalPlayer chip.

Most early MP3 players did not use hard disks because they were physically too large. Rather, they used another type of storage technology (referred to as a "flash" chip) that took up little space but held less data – that is, fewer songs. PortalPlayer's setup includes both a hard disk and a smaller memory chip, which is actually the thing that's active when you're listening to music; songs are cleverly parceled into this from the hard disk in small groups, a scheme that keeps the energy-hog hard disk from wearing down the battery.

Apple won't comment on any of this, and the nondisclosure agreements it has in place with its suppliers and collaborators are described as unusually restrictive. Presumably this is because the company prefers the image of a product that sprang forth whole from the corporate godhead – which was certainly the impression the iPod created when it seemed to appear out of nowhere two years ago. But the point here is not to undercut Apple's role: the iPod came together in somewhere between six and nine months, from concept to market, and its coherence as a product given the time frame and the number of variables is astonishing. Jobs and company are still correct when they point to that coherence as key to the iPod's appeal; and the reality of technical innovation today is that assembling the right specialists is critical to speed, and speed is critical to success.

Still, in the world of technology products, guts have traditionally mattered quite a bit; the PC boom viewed from one angle was nothing but an endless series of announcements about bits and megahertz and RAM. That 1.8-in hard disk, and the amount of data storage it offered in such a small space, isn't the only key to the iPod, but it's a big deal. Apple apparently cornered the market for the Toshiba disks for a while. But now there is, inevitably, an alternative. Hitachi now makes a disk that size, and it has at least one major buyer: Dell.

The system

My visit to Cupertino happened to coincide with the publication of a pessimistic installment of *The Wall Street Journal's* Heard on the Street column pointing out that Apple's famous online music store generates little profit. About a week later Jobs played host to one of the "launch" events for which the company is notorious, announcing the availability of iTunes and access to the company's music store for Windows users. The announcement included a deal with AOL and a huge promotion with Pepsi. The message was obvious: Apple is aiming squarely at the mainstream.

This sounded like a sea change. But while you can run iTunes on Windows and hook it up to an iPod, that iPod does not play songs in the formats used by any other seller of digital music, like Napster or Rhapsody. Nor will music bought through Apple's store play on any rival device. This means Apple is, again, competing against a huge number of players across multiple business segments, who by and large will support one another's products and services. In light of this, says one of those competitors, Rob Glaser, founder and C.E.O. of RealNetworks, "It's absolutely clear now why five years from now, Apple will have 3 to 5 percent of the player market".

Jobs, of course, has heard the predictions and has no patience for any of it. Various contenders have come at the iPod for two years, and none have measured up. Nothing has come close to Apple's interface. Even the look-alike products are frauds. "They're all putting their dumb controls in the shape of a circle, to fool the consumer into thinking it's a wheel like ours," he says. "We've sort of set the vernacular. They're trying to copy the vernacular without understanding it". (The one company that did plan a wheel-driven product, Samsung, changed course after Apple reportedly threatened to sue.) "We don't underestimate people," Jobs said later in the interview. "We really did believe that people would want something this good, that they'd see the value in it".

The core

What I had been hoping to do was catch a glimpse of what's there when you pull back all those layers – when you penetrate the aura, strip off the surface, clear away the guts. What's under there is innovation, but where does it come from? I had given up on getting an answer to this question when I made a jokey observation that before long somebody would probably start making white headphones so that people carrying knockoffs and tape players could fool the world into thinking they had trendy iPods.

Jobs shook his head. "But then you meet the girl, and she says, 'Let me see what's on your iPod'. You pull out a tape player, and she walks away".

Source: © 2003 – The New York Times Magazine, *30 November.*

Since this article was written in 2003, Apple has continued its inexorable rise and expanded its range of products. In addition to the Classic iPod discussed in this article, Apple has launched variants for different sectors of the market, including the "nano", "shuffle" and the "touch", each with different features. In April 2007, Apple announced via its website (http://www.apple.com/pr/library/2007/04/09ipod.html) that 100 million iPods had been sold worldwide. In January 2007 it combined its latest iPod technology, including touch screen facility, within a mobile and internet communication device, in the shape of the iPhone. They have also created an "Apps" store which allows content in the form of small applications to be uploaded onto the device for free or purchased for a small fee. In June 2009 they had sold over a million iPhones (http://www.apple.com/pr/library/2009/06/22iphone.html). It remains to be seen where Apple will direct its energies in 2010 and beyond, but it shows no sign of resting on its laurels.

Questions

1 What is novel about the iPod?

2 What type of innovation would you class the Sony Walkman as and why?

3 What type of innovation would you class the iPod as and why?

4 What does the author mean by "lightening-bolt" moments?

5 If "the iPod did not begin with a specific technological breakthrough" as Steve Jobs maintains, how can it still be classed as an innovation?

6 What is licensing and why did Apple choose to license its Firewire technology?

7 Why, according to the author, does innovation especially technological innovation, have an "aura" around it? Give an example of another product with an aura.

8 What do you think Steve Jobs means when he says that the iPod is about "navigating content"?

9 Why does Steve Jobs believe that imitators of the iPod like Dell do not pose a threat?

10 By April 2007, 100 million iPods had been sold worldwide. What does this imply about the prediction of Rob Glaser of RealNetworks for the iPod's market share?

11 From what you know about how the iPod has evolved since 2003, do you think that Apple has continued to innovate? Why?

? Questions for discussion

1 What is the value of being able to categorise innovations?

2 Why may large established firms be wary of radical (disruptive) innovations?

3 Why do product innovations tend to attract more public attention than service or process innovations?

4 Why do process innovations sometimes have wide-ranging consequences for society?

5 Identify two process innovations which have had a big impact on society.

6 Differentiate between component knowledge and system knowledge.

7 Choose an example of an everyday household object (e.g. an electric kettle) and identify some of the incremental innovations that have taken place.

8 Why are only a small proportion of innovations typically radical?

9 Why is the Sony Walkman an example of architectural innovation?

10 What type of innovation is Apple's iPod?

Exercises

1 Using any household object of your choice (e.g. vacuum cleaner, hairdryer, etc.) identify and analyse the following:

- System function

- Components

- System linkages

- Incremental innovation

Outline what you consider to be the rationale behind ONE recent incremental innovation.

2 Identify a product that has been the subject of modular innovation. Analyse where the innovation has occurred and the impact this has had on the product. Explain why you think this is a case of modular innovation, noting how the system architecture has remained unchanged.

3 What is a system? Take an example of a system and analyse it using a diagram to show the components and the linkages between them. Indicate where there have been examples of a) incremental innovation and b) architectural innovation.

4 What is meant by radical innovation? Take an example of radical innovation and analyse the impact it has had on society. Take care to differentiate between the different groups within society that have been affected.

5 What is meant by the term "creative destruction". Explain, using appropriate examples, the link between creative destruction and radical innovation.

Further reading

1 Henderson, R.M. and K.B. Clark (1990) "Architectural Innovation: The Reconfiguration of Existing Product Technologies and the Failure of Established Firms", *Administrative Science Quarterly*, 35, pp9–30.
This paper is an excellent starting point. It gives a clear overview of the different types of innovation. Not only is there a rationale for the typology but each type is explained in detail.

2 Christensen, C.M. (1997) *The Innovator's Dilemma: When New Technologies Cause Great Firms to Fail*, Harvard Business School Press, Boston, MA.
This provides a detailed examination of radical innovation, although the term that Christensen uses is "disruptive technology". Several extensive and highly detailed case studies of radical innovations are provided.

3 Dahlin, K. and D. Behrens (2005) "When is an Invention Really Radical? Defining and Measuring Technological Radicalness", *Research Policy*, 34(5), pp717–734.
Another useful paper that discusses the nature of radical innovation at length.

4 Tushman, M.L. and P. Anderson (1986) "Technological Discontinuities and Organisational Environments", *Administrative Science Quarterly*, 31, pp439–465.
Although this paper does not set out to provide a typology, it does provide some valuable insights into different types of innovation.

CHAPTER 03

Technological change

❖ **OBJECTIVES**

When you have completed this chapter you will be able to:

❖ distinguish between science and technology

❖ describe the nature of technology

❖ analyse the link between technological change and the long wave cycle

❖ describe the phases of the long wave cycle

❖ explain and analyse the nature of a technological paradigm

Introduction

Innovation and technology are closely linked. Although it is possible to have innovations that don't involve technology, it is comparatively rare and innovation typically involves a new application of a new technology, a modified technology or a technology from another field.

For its part technology is often seen as something that is constantly moving forward through a series of spectacular advances or breakthroughs, to give us a stream of ever more ingenious products and services. These technological advances are often referred to collectively as technological change. Technological change describes a whole range of advances and breakthroughs in technology. In turn the advances in technology that form part of technological change lead to technological innovations. Hence technological change is one of the main drivers of innovation. The more advances in technology the more the scale of innovation increases, resulting in more capable and more sophisticated products and services for consumers.

In the popular imagination, technological change is typically portrayed as something that is speeding up and accelerating. Each year there are more breakthroughs, each more dramatic than the last (or so we are often led to believe), resulting in more innovations and more sophisticated products. However, as Richard Florida (2002) recently indicated (see Time Traveller mini case), this view is actually misleading and presents an inaccurate perspective on technological change. Certainly technological change is constantly advancing, but not necessarily at an accelerating rate. Florida's point is that the rate of technological change *varies*; not only that, but on occasions some existing technologies are much more affected by technological change than others.

In the period from 1900 to 1950 there were technological breakthroughs in fields such as aerospace (the Wright brothers' pioneering aircraft first flew in 1903), in cars (particularly Ford's system of mass production introduced in 1913–14) and electronics (e.g. the invention of radio and television). These new technologies led to new forms of transport and new consumer products that dramatically altered the lives of ordinary people. In the period from 1950 to 2000, there have continued to be technological advances, but the more dramatic ones, and certainly the ones to have had the greatest impact, have occurred in different fields, particularly fields surrounding computing and telecommunications, leading to changes in the way in which we handle and process information. Hence technological change has been variable, in the sense that it has affected some areas much more than others. Not only that, the actual rate at which breakthroughs have occurred, has varied.

Portraying technological change as something that varies, affecting some fields more than others, gives a much more realistic perspective on technology, which in turn gives a more realistic perspective on innovation. This chapter focuses on technological change. The aim is not only to provide a clearer perspective on what we mean by technological change, but also to analyse any identifiable patterns in the course of technological change, so that we can have a better appreciation of just how technology affects innovation and in turn how there may be patterns to innovation. To facilitate the analysis, theories and models are introduced as potential analytical tools, most notably Kondratiev's long wave cycle.

Mini Case

The time traveller

Here's a thought experiment. Take a typical man on the street from the year 1900 and drop him into the 1950s. Then take someone from the 1950s and drop him Austin Powers-style into the present day. Who would experience the greater change?

Thrust forward into the 1950s, a person from the turn of the twentieth century would be awestruck by a world filled with baffling technological wonders. In place of horse-drawn carriages, he would see streets and highways jammed with cars, trucks and buses. In the cities, immense skyscrapers would line the horizon, and mammoth bridges would span rivers where once only ferries could cross. Flying machines would soar overhead, carrying people across the continent or the oceans in a matter of hours rather than days. At home, our 1900-to-1950s time-traveller would grope his way through a strange new environment filled with appliances powered by electricity: radios and televisions emanating musical sounds and even human images, refrigerators to keep things cold, washing machines to clean his clothes automatically and much more. The newness of this time-traveller's physical surroundings – the speed and power of everyday machines – would be profoundly disorienting. A massive new supermarket would replace daily trips to the market with an array of technologically enhanced foods, such as instant coffee or frozen vegetables to put into the refrigerator. Life itself would be dramatically extended. Many once-fatal ailments could be prevented with an injection or with a pill. The newness of this time-traveller's physical surroundings – the speed and power of everyday machines – would be profoundly disorienting.

On the other hand, someone from the 1950s would have little trouble navigating the physical landscape of today. Although we like to think ours is the age of boundless technological wonders, our second time-traveller would find himself in a world not all that different from the one he left. He would still drive a car to work. If he took the train, it would likely be on the same line leaving from the same station. He would probably board an airplane at the same airport. He might still live in a suburban house, though a bigger one. Television would have more channels, but it would basically be the same, and he could still catch some of his favourite 1950s shows on the reruns. He would know how, or quickly learn how, to operate most household appliances – even the personal computer, with its familiar QWERTY keyboard. In fact with just a few exceptions, such as the PC, the Internet, CD and DVD players, the cash machine and a wireless phone he could carry with him, he would be familiar with almost all current-day technology.

On the basis of big, obvious technological changes alone, surely the 1900-to-1950s traveller would experience the greater shift, while the other might easily conclude that we'd spent the second half of the twentieth century doing little more than tweaking the great waves of the first half.

Source: Florida (2002).

The nature of technology

The term "technology" is defined by Simon (1972) as:

> knowledge that is stored in millions of books, in hundreds of millions or billions of human heads, and, to an important extent in the artifacts themselves.

This definition probably strikes a chord with most of us, since we generally associate technology with things, especially machines and equipment whether for the direct use of consumers or for use as part of manufacturing processes.

Frequently technology is linked to science, with scientific discoveries and breakthroughs seen as focusing the development of technology. Although there are links between the two, in fact science and technology are distinct. As McGinn (1991: p18) notes:

> Technology is the human activity which is devoted to the production of technics [material products of human making or fabrication] – or technic-related intellectual products – and whose root function is to expand the realm of practical human possibility

while:

> Science is that form of human activity which is devoted to the production of theory-related knowledge of material phenomena whose root function is to attain an enhanced understanding of nature.

Thus, technology is concerned with practical knowledge of how to do things and how to make things. To develop technology it is not necessary to understand fully the principles behind phenomena. Science on the other hand is all about understanding. Science involves the application of systematic rigorous methods of enquiry in order to develop logical, self-consistent explanations of phenomena (Littler, 1988). A critical aspect is the application of the scientific method involving observation, the development of hypotheses and the systematic collection of data in order to arrive at explanations. The rigorous application of scientific method results in knowledge being recorded and codified as a formal body of knowledge that can be transferred through books and papers.

Technology on the other hand is embedded in "artefacts" – that is equipment and machines – which form the most obvious examples and readily identifiable forms of technology. However, as Forbes and Wield (2002) note, technology is not only embedded in artefacts, but also in people and organisations. This form of knowledge is proprietary, i.e. firm-specific. Some is explicit: that is to say, it is codified in documents as patents, drawings, manuals, standard operating procedures and databases. On the other hand much of this proprietary knowledge is tacit. That is to say, it is knowledge that resides within the individual, known but extremely difficult or in some cases impossible, to articulate or communicate adequately (Newell *et al.*, 2002).

While science and technology are different, they are nonetheless connected. An understanding of phenomena can assist the development of technology. Sometimes scientific breakthroughs lead to advances in technology. Sometimes it is the other way round. However, in recent times not only has the relationship between science and technology become closer, but developments and advances in science have increasingly led to developments in technology.

It is developments in technology that give rise to technological change. Informed, if not led, by advances in science, the development of technology gives rise to innovations in the form both of new products/services and new processes. These innovations form part of technological change. New products/services lead to new patterns of consumption and new behaviours. New processes lead to new ways of working. The outcome is significant changes in the economic and social facets of human existence – precisely the things that typically go hand-in-hand with technological change.

Long wave cycle and technological change

One has only to reflect on the course of technological change to appreciate that it is not constant, being sometimes rapid, as in the early years of the Internet, and sometimes relatively sluggish. Nor are the Internet boom years of the late 1990s different from other periods. The 1870s and 1880s saw a flurry of innovations surrounding electricity. This same period also saw innovations surrounding the internal combustion engine. Further evidence of the cyclical nature of innovation and the technological change that accompanies it can be found in the cyclical nature of academic work. It is no coincidence that the rise of the Internet in the early 1990s was accompanied by a renewed interest on the part of academics in technological change, manifested in an increase in academic output of journals and books.

The cyclical pattern of innovation is not a short cycle of five to ten years like the business cycle, but is much longer. The idea of a long cycle or long wave was analysed by Nicholai Kondratiev (1892–1938), a Russian economist who founded and directed the Institute of Conjuncture in Moscow in the 1920s (Freeman and Louçã, 2001).

Kondratiev was not the first to put forward the idea of a long cycle. Economists had pointed to long-term cyclical changes in prices, interest rates and trade before the First World War. However, Kondratiev's analysis in the 1920s did much to bring the idea to a wider audience. As a result, he is particularly associated with the notion of a 50-year cycle of economic activity stretching from a phase of depression through recovery and boom back to depression again. Such was his contribution that this long cycle, or "long wave" as it is sometimes termed, is often referred to as the "Kondratiev cycle".

Starting with the industrial revolution of the late eighteenth century, some four long waves have been completed since then, and we are today well into the fifth cycle or fifth Kondratiev (Table 3.1) (Hall, 1981).

Date	Cycle/wave	Technology
1780–1830	First	Cotton, iron, water power
1830–1880	Second	Railways, steam power, steamship
1880–1930	Third	Electricity, chemicals, steel
1930–1980	Fourth	Cars, electronics, oil, aerospace
1980–	Fifth	Computers, telecommunications and the Internet

TABLE 3.1 Long wave cycles

The idea of a long wave cycle was taken up by Joseph Schumpeter, who came across Kondratiev's work in Germany before he moved to Harvard University in the US. Schumpeter used the long wave cycle as a feature of his work on business cycles. Schumpeter (1939) put forward the idea that each long wave represented the application of a new group of technologies, each of which had a very powerful transforming effect on the economy, effectively bringing about another industrial revolution. In Schumpeter's analysis each revolution was based on a major technological change that, just like the first industrial revolution, brought major shifts in productivity, consumption and the organisation of productive activity. The technological change of the first long wave centred on the development of iron smelting using coal, pioneered by Abraham Darby, the application of water power and above all the mechanisation of the textile industry especially cotton manufacture in Lancashire. Associated with these new technologies was an organisational innovation – the development of the factory system, initiated by Richard Arkwright with his mill at Cromford in Derbyshire.

The second long wave ran from the 1830s to the 1880s and involved technological change again based on a group of new transforming technologies, principally in the form of steam power and the introduction of the railways (Freeman and Louçã, 2001). The tendency of major innovations to group together or "swarm" in this way is a feature of the long wave cycle.

The introduction of the new technology of the railway led to a speculative boom. The "railway mania" of the 1840s saw the flotation of a large number of railway companies aiming to profit from the application of the new technology of railways and the anticipated growth in traffic (Figure 3.1). Like most financial booms it led eventually to a financial crash.

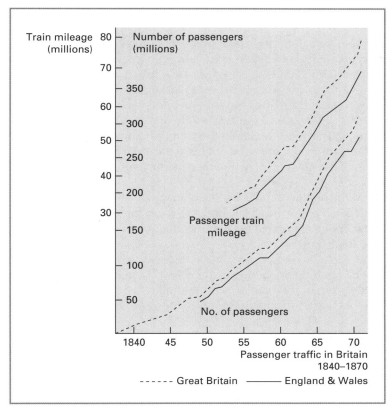

FIGURE 3.1 Passenger traffic in Britain 1840–1870
Source: Freeman and Louçã (2001: p189)

The dot-com bubble (1995–2001)

The '**dot-com bubble**' was a speculative mania that began in the mid-1990s and was based on the new technology of the Internet. The height of the bubble was in March 2000 when the US stock market peaked. The period was marked by the founding of a large number of new Internet-based companies known as "dot.coms". Most of the companies floated as part of the bubble were ones that offered new services derived from the Internet or traditional services delivered via the Internet. Many were unproven and highly speculative. A combination of factors helped to fuel the bubble. These included availability of venture capital keen to invest in the sector, widespread optimism about the prospects for Internet-based companies and the appearance of new, unusual and in many cases highly optimistic business models. The latter were often predicated on the so-called network effect which demanded a rapid build up of market share rather than profitability. The bursting of the dot-com bubble in 2001 marked the beginning of a mild downturn in economic activity.

Mini Case

The bubble really began with the dramatic uptake of the Internet in the early 1990s. This encouraged venture capitalists to support the flotation of so-called dot-com companies like Amazon.com that utilised the Internet to deliver services. Many of these flotations were heavily oversubscribed and the prices of newly listed companies rose sharply, despite the fact that many of these companies had yet to make a profit. Encouraged by sharply rising stock prices, venture capitalists moved faster and with less caution than usual. Low interest rates in 1998–99 increased the availability of capital. Although some new entrepreneurs had realistic plans and both the technical knowledge and managerial capability to make them work, many did not but were able to convince investors of their potential by virtue of the novelty of the Internet and the corresponding difficulty of valuing these ventures.

At the height of the bubble the share price of many newly floated companies reached dizzy heights, driven up by investors keen to cash in on the new technology. In the process many very young entrepreneurs became wildly rich on paper in a very short space of time. As so often in previous booms many new companies committed themselves and their executives to a lavish corporate lifestyle. However, many of the stocks were wildly over-valued with little or nothing in the way of a track record of profitability. Historically, the dot-com bubble can be seen as similar to a number of other technology-inspired booms of the past, including railways in the 1840s, and cars and radio in the 1920s.

In the aftermath of the bubble many dot-com companies went bankrupt and many others ceased trading, including many in the communications sector who had invested heavily in new infrastructure to support the anticipated dramatic growth of the so called "new economy". By October 2002 $5trillion had been wiped off the market value of technology companies in the US, but despite this the ensuing recession was mild and short-lived. Some of the larger dot-com companies not only survived but went on to prosper, including Amazon.com and eBay. Recent research suggests that as many as 50 per cent of the dot-com companies survived, an indication that in fact most were small players who were able to weather the aftermath of the financial bubble. A number of factors have been attributed to triggering the bursting of the bubble, including rising interest rates (the most likely cause), a court action by the federal authorities aimed at curbing Microsoft's monopoly and poor Christmas sales in 1999 on the part of many Internet retailers.

The third long wave, based on the new technologies of electricity, chemicals and steel (Freeman and Louçã, 2001) was from the 1880s to the 1930s and was largely complete by the time Schumpeter was writing. It was accompanied by managerial innovations such as scientific management and the rise of the first large corporations (Freeman and Louçã, 2001). The new transforming technologies themselves found widespread applications in products and services. With a new and much more flexible source of power new industries arose to manufacture the equipment to distribute the power, as well as new industries to make new machines, appliances, instruments and tools. Similarly, the availability of cheap, high-quality steel helped transform existing industries (Figure 3.2). The railways switched from iron rails to steel as did shipbuilding. Along with the new technologies themselves came improvements in productivity derived from the use of scientific management.

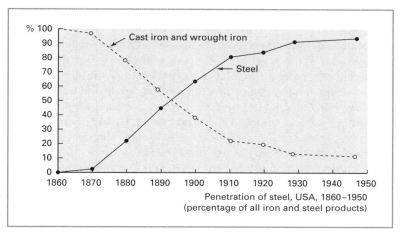

FIGURE 3.2 Penetration of steel, US, 1860–1950 (percentage of all iron and steel products)
Source: Freeman and Louçã (2001: p233)

The fourth long wave from the 1930s to the 1980s brought new technologies associated with electronics, cars, oil and aerospace. The car industry not only grew dramatically, but also had a wide-ranging impact on the economy. Increased use of cars led to major investments in infrastructure, while the introduction of Fordist mass production led to dramatic changes in working practices. Changes in electronics led to the manufacture of consumer electrical products, most notably radio and television. The fourth Kondratiev was truly the period of the mass market.

The fifth long wave, as we shall see in the next section, was based on yet another raft of transforming technologies, this time in the form of computers, telecommunications and biotechnology.

Among the most significant features of the long wave is that it follows a regular course. A long climb up from depression involving recovery and prosperity phases leads to a maturity phase where a shallow decline leads to a steep fall in the depression phase (Figure 3.3). Each of these phases has implications for the pattern of innovation.

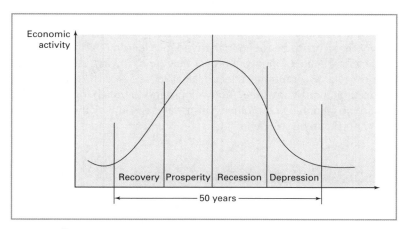

FIGURE 3.3 The long wave cycle

In the recovery phase the discoveries of scientists and investors are developed into new innovations that create entirely new opportunities for investment, growth and employment. Often these new opportunities will be created by newcomers (i.e. new firms) who view technology in a new way. At this point in the cycle there is often a high degree of uncertainty that produces a variety of competing product configurations. Offering significant improvements in performance and a high novelty value, these innovations command a price premium. Under these conditions there will often not be particularly strong pressures for production efficiency. As yet these innovations are finding only a specialist market. Higher prices mean higher profits from these innovations, these act as a decisive impulse for new surges of growth which in turn act as a signal for imitators (Freeman, 1986) to enter the fray.

In the prosperity phase the innovations begin to diffuse to a wider range of applications through finding a broader market. As the innovations and their associated new technologies reach a wider market they become better known and imitations frequently appear. They may well catch the mood of the popular imagination. Often there will be a "bandwagon" effect as others try to cash in on the new technology. The combination of appropriate financial conditions and a large number of would-be imitators can easily lead to a speculative boom (e.g. the "railway mania" of the 1840s and the "dot-com" boom of the 1990s) as investors try to cash in on the technological advances. Over-ambitious and unrealistic plans combined with the ever-increasing cost of capital lead to the inevitable financial crash. Such a crash typically heralds the onset of the third phase.

In the third phase, with surplus capacity and diminishing returns as the limits of technological advance become evident, price competition becomes intense. It is at this point that the focus of innovation shifts. The new technology which has hitherto been applied to create new products now begins to spill over into process applications. This may well be where the transformative capacity of the new technology is at its greatest. New production processes can sweep away old working practices, leading to dramatic improvements in productivity.

Finally market saturation leads to ever-greater price competition and declining profitability which are the features of the depression phase of the long wave cycle. So too are decreasing returns that begin to set in as the technological advance reaches its limits. The result is mergers and acquisitions in pursuit of greater efficiency. This is the "shake-out" phase. Despite the depressed and difficult trading conditions, this phase is also the point at which the discoveries, breakthroughs and inventions that will form the basis of the next long wave begin to take place. In Schumpeter's analysis the innovations that occur in the recovery phase will tend to cluster. Hence, the early stages of each long wave are associated with a "swarm" of new innovations.

The same phenomena are to be found in the work of Mensch (1979). He showed that, as Schumpeter predicted, the rate of innovation over time tends to vary. According to Mensch, innovation is subject to a "wagon-train" effect (Hall, 1981: p534). Thus, while inventions and discoveries can occur at almost any time, innovations tend to bunch together at the end of one long wave and the beginning of another. This is one reason why the transforming effect of technological change can be so dramatic.

The Internet: Our very own long wave

Freeman and Louçã (2001) argue that we are currently witnessing a fifth Kondratiev long wave. Beginning in the 1980s, this long wave is associated with new transforming technologies, comprising computers, telecommunications and the Internet together with developments in biotechnology. These technologies have between them begun to transform a variety of aspects of our daily lives. According to Freeman and Louçã (2001) the "dot-com bubble" of the late 1990s shares many of the characteristics of similar bubbles seen in earlier long waves, such as the railway mania of the 1840s and the Wall Street crash of 1929.

As with previous long waves the origins of the many transforming technologies lie in the breakthroughs and inventions that occurred in the downward phase of the fourth Kondratiev. Nonetheless, each technology has itself been transformed by more recent breakthroughs which have gained additional momentum as a result of technological convergence.

Developments in electronics underpin developments in all three of the transforming technologies. Jack Kilby's idea that, instead of transistors being linked together and mounted on a circuit board, they could simply be manufactured from a single piece of silicon, led to the production of the first integrated circuit (IC) as far back as 1958 (Campbell-Kelly, 2004). ICs were initially very expensive and used for specialist defence applications such as the guidance system of the Minuteman missile. However, Moore's Law, that the capacity of ICs would double every year, led in time to a dramatic reduction in the price of a core technological input. The development of the first microprocessor by Intel in 1971 was another decisive event. Though it still required successive incremental improvements to deliver appropriate performance, these advances in electronics paved the way for big changes in other technologies.

One of these technologies was computing, where the availability of ICs led to the development of the first personal computers. Though they were at first lacking in power and flexibility, within a decade the PC had begun to challenge computing orthodoxy based on large mainframe applications. As the PC grew more capable through advances in electronics, so it multiplied.

Developments in electronics also fed through to telecommunications. Transistors were first used for switching in the 1960s. With the introduction of digital technology in the form of pulse code modulation (PCM), the scope for extending the application of electronics grew still further. Developments in fibre optics and the introduction of packet switching transformed the capacity and versatility of the system.

In the 1990s the three technologies converged to give rise to the Internet. Computers and telecommunications are important transforming technologies in their own right, but it is the Internet that exhibits the greatest transforming potential. Initially giving rise to business-to-consumer (B2C) applications (e.g. Amazon.com, the online bookstore) in the upward phase of the long wave, as the cycle appears to be reaching its apex we are now seeing the technology of the Internet diffuse into process applications through business-to-business (B2B) applications (e.g. e-commerce).

As with previous long waves, the transformation does not stop at the technology itself. The transformation is changing working lives, business models, leisure patterns and the structure and shape of business organisations themselves.

The implications of the long wave cycle

The notion of the long cycle has a number of important implications for technological change. First, the idea of technological change being cyclical helps to break away from the popular notion that the rate of technological change is simply accelerating over time (see time traveller mini case). If technological change is cyclical, one can expect different effects at different points in time. The cycle predicts that the distinct phases will be: a hesitant start, fast growth, subsequent saturation followed by decline and stagnation as the limits of technology are reduced.

This point has been taken up by Abernathy and Utterback (1978) in their analysis of the life cycle of technologies and industries. This helps to explain a second point: why innovation can vary over time. Product innovations that occur early in the long wave cycle give way eventually to process innovations as a technology diffuses through the economy. This was emphasised by Schumpeter (1939) who argued that the diffusion of innovations was inherently uneven. In the early stages of the recovery phase only a few firms and individuals will be far-sighted enough to bring forward innovations. In the prosperity phase many firms will follow in the wake of successful pioneers. In the maturity phase, diffusion shifts from products to processes.

Third, the long wave cycle reinforces the notion of different types of innovation. In the early phases of the long wave, radical innovations are more likely, while in later phases one can expect to find incremental innovations.

Fourth, the long wave cycle shows how some technologies can have a much bigger impact than others. In particular one can differentiate transforming technologies. These innovations are so wide-ranging in their impact that they cause major perturbations in the economic and social system (Freeman, 1986). Steam power, electricity, oil and latterly the Internet all come within this category. These technologies are not merely important in themselves, they are also important because of the impact they have on a wide range of industries. As a result their transforming power is much greater than other technologies.

Fifth, the long wave cycle shows how technologies often go hand-in-hand with institutional changes (Freeman, 1986). These institutional changes include:

- education and training
- industrial relations
- corporate structures
- systems of management
- capital markets
- the legal framework

Each of the five long waves identified in Table 3.1 was associated with significant institutional changes. In the first long wave it was the introduction of factory production. This not only facilitated the application of new technologies and innovations in textile production, it also brought with it big increases in productivity. These in turn led to lower prices, thereby stimulating demand and major shifts in consumption. In the second wave the institutional change was the joint stock company that facilitated access to greater supplies of capital and permitted larger enterprises. In the third wave it was scientific management and the rise of the large corporation, while in the fourth it was mass production and the large, vertically integrated corporation. Finally, the fifth long wave has been accompanied by further institutional changes, most notably network structures for organisations, alliances and joint ventures and outsourcing.

The significance of these institutional changes lies not just in the impact that they have had on the economic and social life of nations but also in the way in which the long wave cycle shows that they are linked to technological change. This in turn shows that technology is not merely important for its own sake, but for the things that it brings with it. This is where the power of the long wave cycle lies, in its ability to link technology to economic and social aspects of life. The new technology of the internal combustion engine combined with the introduction of mass production did not merely create a new class of product in the form of the car. It changed the nature of work for millions of industrial workers, it brought massive improvements in productivity and, as Freeman and Louçã (2001: p263) show, it permitted an unprecedented degree of personal mobility that in turn induced massive growth in infrastructure and supply industries. Dramatic as these changes were at the time, the long wave cycle helps to show that this was neither the first time that technological change had occurred on this scale nor – as we are currently experiencing – was it the last.

Finally, as Perez (1983) describes it, the long wave cycle highlights the impact of transforming technologies and costs. The railways, for instance, were not only the leading industrial sector in terms of investment and employment generation in the Victorian boom of the 1850s and 1860s, they also had a big impact on the costs of many industrial sectors. The ability to transport coal cheaply reduced dramatically the cost of energy for the whole economy. Similarly, in the Internet age developments in information technology have dramatically reduced the cost of storing, processing and transferring information. This in turn has facilitated knowledge acquisition and knowledge transfer, significantly altering the cost base of a wide range of industries.

Technological paradigms

Another attempt to distinguish differences in the pattern of technological change is embodied in Dosi's (1982) notion of the technological paradigm.

Mini Case

Thanks, Gutenberg – but we're all too pressed for time

The FIRST Law of Technology says we invariably overestimate the short-term impact of new technologies while underestimating their longer-term effects. The invention of printing in the fifteenth century had an extraordinary short-term impact: though scholars argue about the precise number, within 40 years of the first Gutenberg Bible between 8 and 40 million books, representing 30,000 titles, had been printed and published. To those around at the time, it seemed like a pretty big deal.

"In our time," wrote the German humanist Sebastian Brandt in 1500, "… books have emerged in lavish numbers. A book that once would've belonged only to the rich – nay, to a king – can now be seen under a modest roof … . There is nothing nowadays that our children … fail to know". They didn't know the half of it.

They didn't know, for example, that Gutenberg's technology, which enables lay people to read and interpret the Bible for themselves, would undermine the authority of the Catholic church and fuel the Reformation. Or that it would enable the rise of modern science by facilitating the rapid and accurate dissemination of ideas. Or create new social classes of clerks, teachers and intellectuals. Or alter our conception of "childhood" as a protected early stage in the lives of young people. In an oral culture, childhood effectively ended at the age when an individual could be regarded as a competent communicator, i.e. about seven – which is why the Vatican defined that as "the age of reason" after which individuals could be held accountable for their sins.

In a print-based culture, communication competence took longer to achieve and required schooling, so "childhood" was extended to 12 or 14. All these long-term repercussions were not – indeed, could not have been – foreseen. Yet they represent the profound ways in which Gutenberg's technology transformed society.

Today's Gutenberg is Sir Tim Berners-Lee, inventor of the Web. In the 17 years since he launched his technology on an unsuspecting world, he has transformed it. Nobody knows how big the Web is now, but estimates of the indexed part hover around 40 billion pages, and the "deep Web" hidden from the search engines is between 400 and 750 times bigger than that. These numbers seem as remarkable to us as the avalanche of printed books seemed to Brandt. But the First Law holds we don't know the half of it, and it will be decades before we have any real understanding of what Berners-Lee has wrought.

Occasionally, we get a fleeting glimpse of what's happening. One was provided last week by the report of a study by the British Library and researchers at University College London. The study (available from tinyurl.com/2eslnr) combined a review of published literature on the information-seeking behaviour of young people more than thirty years ago with a five-year analysis of the logs of the British Library website and another popular research site that documents people's behaviour in finding and reading information online.

The findings describe "a new form of information-seeking behaviour" characterised as being "horizontal, bouncing, checking and viewing in nature. Users are promiscuous, diverse and volatile." "Horizontal" information-seeking means "a form of skimming activity, where people view just one or two pages from an academic site then 'bounce' out, perhaps never to return". The average times users spend on e-book and e-journal sites are very short: typically four and eight minutes respectively.

"It is clear", says the study, "that users are not reading online in the traditional sense, indeed there are signs that new forms of 'reading' are emerging as users 'power-browse' horizontally through titles, contents pages and abstracts, going for quick wins. It almost seems that they go online to avoid reading in the traditional sense." These findings apply to online information seekers of all ages.

The study confirms what many are beginning to suspect: that the Web is having a profound impact on how we conceptualise, seek, evaluate and use information. What Marshall McLuhan called "the Gutenberg galaxy" – that universe of linear exposition , quiet contemplation, disciplined reading and study – is imploding, and we don't know if what will replace it will be better or worse. But at least you can find the Wikipedia entry for "the Gutenberg galaxy" in 0.34 seconds.

Source: Naughton (2008a).

The term "technological paradigm" borrows heavily from science, in particular the notion of scientific paradigms (Kuhn, 1970) used to identify particular scientific schools of thought. According to Dosi (1982) technological paradigms represent a general area or field of technology in which the search for innovation is conducted by a significant group of innovators, within a particular historical context. As examples of technological paradigms Dosi (1982: p152) cites nuclear technologies, semiconductor technologies and organic chemistry technologies. As such, a technological paradigm sets what Von Tunzelmann (1995) describes as "the technological domain within which technologies evolve".

A particular technological paradigm therefore effectively delimits the field of enquiry within which innovation is pursued. By setting the boundaries of knowledge in this way, as far as innovation is concerned it confines the search process in terms of the direction of enquiry and the prescriptions sought. A technological paradigm is likely to be based on a selected set of principles. These principles in turn are likely to confine the innovation process in terms of:

- the field of enquiry
- the problems to be solved
- the procedures used
- the generic tasks to which it is applied
- the properties it exploits
- the materials technology it uses

Hence a technological paradigm plays a big part in setting limits to the field of enquiry by defining "the rules of the game," even though this may be quite unintentional. Indeed Dosi (1982: p153) notes that technological paradigms tend to have a powerful "exclusion effect" that confines the efforts and technological imagination of engineers and whole organisations, making them "blind" to other technological possibilities.

When a new technological paradigm emerges, it represents a major discontinuity, or shift in thinking. A paradigm shift is likely to be associated with some form of radical innovation that ushers in a new technology. As an example of a paradigm shift Dosi (1982) refers to the switch in electronics from thermionic valves to semiconductors. This involved new principles of operation, new materials and a whole new set of tasks. Similarly, in the field of aerospace the switch from piston to jet engines was another example of a change of technological paradigm. The jet engine demanded new materials in the form of high temperature alloys, new scientific principles and new control systems, and meant confronting an entirely different set of problems.

When a paradigm shift occurs, it can be very difficult for existing or incumbent firms who have made big investments in irreversible capabilities in production, skills, marketing and product support, as well as production capacity and reputation, to make the transition to the new technology. When the new technology of electronics impacted on the cash register industry, it brought major problems for incumbent manufacturers such as NCR who were firmly wedded to the older mechanical technology. NCR's investment in plant capacity, R&D, patents and intellectual property and service networks were rendered obsolete. Even more problematic was the need to rethink the nature of the product. NCR, for instance, saw the new technology of electronics as a way of building cash registers that could add numbers more quickly. Unlike the new entrants into the industry they were unable to re-conceptualise the product as a means by which their customers could manage inventories and supplier relations more effectively (Afuah, 2003).

Similarly, Christensen (1997), who uses the term "disruptive technology" rather than technological paradigm, shows how new technologies can transform an industry, as new firms embrace the new technology while established firms who do not or are slow to do so, are wiped out. Using the mechanical excavator industry as a case study he shows how existing firms found it hard to re-conceptualise their product when cable technology began to be challenged by the new technology of hydraulics in the 1960s. Failure to rethink the product led to new entrants, such as Joseph Bamford with his "JCB" hydraulic excavator, taking over the market.

CASE STUDY: HOWEVER THE INTERNET DEVELOPS, IT IS THE CONSUMER WHO WILL BENEFIT

YES, the Internet is helping to crunch down prices, but by how much – and what else is it doing to the whole production process?

This week the UK debate about interest rates has been given a new twist by Sushil Wadhwani, a member of the Bank of England monetary committee. He has just written a paper that looks at the lessons from recent US experience and argues that after a lag, similar effects should become apparent here.

Crucially, productivity growth may be faster than expected as a result of the Net. The reason that much of an increase in productivity has not been evident outside America may be partly because the costs of adjusting to the new technology have obscured the gains being made. In any case he believes that business-to-business e-commerce will result in significant savings in costs.

This being Britain, the argument leads into a debate about interest rates. Put crudely, we do not need higher interest rates to hold down inflation, because the combination of greater competition and rising productivity will do it for us.

That spin is understandable. People care about their mortgages, companies care about their borrowing costs, and both care about the level of sterling – though private individuals rather like the strong pound because it makes foreign holidays so affordable, while companies dislike it because it makes exporting tougher.

But seeing the impact of the Internet through the prism of British interest rate policy is to focus on one tiny effect of a great global phenomenon. What it does to the structure of industry, to the nature of competitiveness, to the ability of developed economies to continue delivering productivity gains – all this is vastly more important.

And we are still guessing wildly. At most we have three or four years' experience of the impact of the Internet, in practice more like 18 months. In normal economic terms this is nothing, for you cannot really assess the implications of any new technology, or indeed any new economic event, until you have tracked it through a full economic cycle. Once we have come through the next downswing and seen how the Internet has altered the response of the economy to a fall-off in demand then we can start to make some better guesses. But even then they will still be guesses.

But we can, thanks to the couple of years of US experience, see some of the issues that matter, and it might be helpful here to identify two: the impact of business-to-business e-commerce and the fragility, or otherwise, of current ratings of technology stocks.

The first matters because it will determine the outcome of the key micro-economic issue facing the world: whether the business community really can deliver a sharply improved economic performance. The second matters because it will determine the key macro-economic issue: might a crash of share values be the thing that plunges the world into the next downswing?

The starting point with e-commerce is to realise that the bit we all write about, what businesses are doing to use the Net to sell services to the consumer, is much less important than the bit we do not write about, what businesses are doing to use the Net to streamline their production chain. Growth in business-to-consumer e-commerce is tiny compared with business-to-business and the gap is likely to widen. Quite suddenly, companies are figuring out ways of using the Net to cut out human beings and paper from the complex business of ordering components, managing stocks, maintaining equipment, and so on.

Humans make mistakes and paperwork costs money and time. You know the story about an automated factory that was run by a man and a dog? Why a man and a dog? The man was there to feed the dog and the dog was there to bite the man if he tried to touch any of the machinery. The Internet makes it possible to apply this principle to the entire production process. But it takes time to learn how to do it, and many factories are in the transition process, spending money on new kit and making it work, without yet obtaining the savings in labour and the improvement in quality and time that the technology promises.

The first assessment of the impact of business-to-business investment from people like Goldman Sachs suggests that it will boost long-term productivity growth and reduce the sustainable rate of unemployment and thereby boost economic growth of developed countries by one percentage point a year for five years.

There is an offset to this over the next five years from a decline in the growth of the labour force, but the very long-term effect will still be to boost economic activity by about the 5 per cent figure.

My own guess, for what it is worth, is that this estimate is both too high and too low. In the short-term it is too high. One percentage point a year across the entire economies of the developed countries requires an enormous shift in the way every business operates. It is a tall order. On the other hand, the effect of this new technology will not just last five or ten years. This will affect the way we live for a generation or more. It will take a full generation refining the technology and figuring out how to use it before we can be sure that we have exploited its full potential. In the long term the 5 per cent figure is therefore too low.

The markets, of course, have bought the hi-tech story, up-rating these stocks again and again. As my colleague Jeremy Warner has pointed out on several occasions, were it not for a couple of hi-tech sectors we would, in Britain at least, be in a bear market. Have the markets pushed too far, demanding with these ratings improvements in growth that cannot be achieved?

Goldman here argues that it is "a tough call, but not necessarily fatal". Interestingly, it also believes that the trigger for a downgrading of equities will not be the aggressive valuations put on technology stocks. If there is a trigger, it will most probably be a reassessment of the cost of capital (higher interest rates) or a reassessment of the earnings outlook. They do not see either happening soon and remain reasonably confident of the hi-tech sector.

We will see. The big point here surely is that we are seeing something akin to the railways, the steamship, the telegraph, the radio, the car, maybe even the moving production line of Henry Ford. New technologies fuel economic growth. They also inspire booms. Some of the protagonists get immensely rich. Others fail. The only thing we can be really sure of is that ultimately the certain beneficiaries are the consumers.

Source: McRae, H. (2000).

Questions

1 What is productivity and how can improvements (gains) in productivity enable developed nations to continue to grow?
2 Why does McRae think we are still guessing about the likely impact of the Internet?

3 What is the difference between business-to-consumer (B2C) and business-to-business (B2B) e-commerce?

4 Why, according to McRae, is business-to-consumer less important than business-to-business e-commerce?

5 Where would you expect to find (i) business-to-consumer e-commerce and (ii) business-to-business e-commerce in the phases of the long wave?

6 What does the long wave cycle predict in terms of the sorts of organisations likely to be important in the development of the Internet?

7 Why does McRae regard the Internet as comparable to the railways, the steamship, radio and the car?

8 Why is business-to-business e-commerce likely to lead to big productivity gains over the long term?

? Questions for discussion

1 What is a technological paradigm? Use examples to illustrate your answer.

2 Why do process innovations tend to occur during the later phases of the long wave cycle?

3 Where does the "credit crunch" fit within the long wave cycle? To what extent do you consider it to have been predictable?

4 What is technology? Use examples to illustrate your answer.

5 Distinguish between science and technology.

6 What is tacit knowledge and why is it an important aspect of technology?

7 What is the Kondratiev long wave cycle?

8 How can the Kondratiev long wave cycle contribute to our understanding of innovation?

9 What is meant by the term "diffusion" and why is it an important aspect of innovation (you may want to refer to Chapter 1)?

10 How did Joseph Schumpeter link together innovation and the long wave cycle?

Exercises

1 What is technology and what is the link between technology and economic development?

2 Using a period of your choice, show how the long wave cycle is associated with the introduction of one or more new technologies.

3 What is a speculative boom? How would you account for the dot-com boom of the late 1990s?

4 What is the link between innovation and the long wave cycle?

5 Why does the emergence of a new technological paradigm often seem to create problems for existing manufacturers? Use examples to illustrate your answer.

Further reading

1 **Freeman, C. and F. Louçã** (2001) *As Time Goes By: From Industrial Revolutions to Information Revolution*, Oxford University Press, Oxford.
This is one of very few books that focuses specifically on long waves. It provides an explanation of the origins and nature of long waves with extensive consideration of the contributions of Kondratiev and Schumpeter. It also examines in detail each of the long waves that has occurred since the industrial revolution.

2 **Dosi, G.** (1982) "Technological paradigms and technological trajectories," *Research Policy*, 11, pp147–162.
A brief introduction to the concept of the technological paradigm. The nature of such paradigms is defined and then explained in detail.

3 **Florida, R.** (2002) *The Rise of the Creative Class: And How It's Transforming Work, Leisure, Community and Everyday Life,* Basic Books, NY.
This is not a book about technological change. However, it is a provocative and highly readable account of the impact of technological change. The focus of the book is really on the nature of the knowledge economy but in the process it provides a fascinating insight into the wider impact of technological change in particular how developments in computing have changed the way we work.

4 **Tylecote, A.** (1992) *The Long Wave in the World Economy: The Present Crisis in Historical Perspective,* Routledge and Kegan Paul, London.
Since books on the long wave are very few in number, here is another one. Useful because it helps to show that the long wave isn't an abstract concept but something that can be used as analytical tool for analysing economic development.

PART 02
What Does
Innovation Involve?

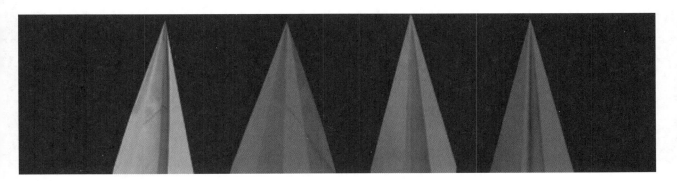

Part Contents

CHAPTER

04

Theories of innovation

Introduction

Innovation is not inevitable. We have already seen that there are different types of innovation. It can occur in different ways and take place at different rates. Similarly, the impact of innovation varies according to the type. This is where theory comes in. Theories help us to make sense of innovation. In particular theories enable us to identify patterns of innovation. These patterns will be linked to different types of innovation. At the same time innovation theories possess a predictive capability that allows us to indicate the likely course of innovation and the impact that it will have. Given that innovation theories allow us to make sense of innovation, they provide powerful tools of analysis. These tools mean that the analysis of innovation is not just a matter of describing what happened. Using theories one can identify patterns of innovation, make comparisons between innovations and predict possible outcomes from the process of innovation.

This chapter aims to introduce a number of theories of innovation. They come from a variety of sources, though most are closely linked to technological aspects of innovation. In addition the chapter shows how these theories can be used as tools for analysing innovations and provides scope for gaining practical experience of doing this. This should enable the reader to come to a clearer appreciation of the nature of innovation.

Who needs theory?

Innovation is a practical business. We have already seen that it is concerned with the "commercialization" of discoveries and inventions. Inevitably this has a lot do with practicalities, e.g. finding a market for the product or working out how the product can be manufactured relatively cheaply and easily. Despite this, it is actually very important to be able to relate innovations to a body of theory. Why should this be?

Innovation has a number of features, but three in particular stand out as being ones where theory in one form or another can contribute to our understanding. These features are:

- complexity
- populism
- interest in success/failure

Innovation is a complex phenomenon and one that embraces a number of academic disciplines. Essentially scientific and technological by nature, as a phenomenon it has important economic and social consequences. This overlap makes it all the more necessary to have a body of theory that can aid and assist in analysing the phenomenon. Otherwise, we are in danger of trivialising innovation because there is no single easily identifiable body of knowledge upon which we can readily and easily draw.

Probably because it is new and exciting, innovation attracts a lot of column centimetres in the press. As a result much that is written about innovation tends to be journalistic. While this helps to popularise innovation and bring it to the attention of a large number of people, it can sometimes make analysing and accounting for innovation difficult. In particular it tends to mean that a good deal of what is written about innovation tends to highlight personalities, particular events and success stories, rather than the range of activities, collective effort and organisational support that are a vital part of innovation. It also means that accounts of innovation often include a lot of extraneous material and lack hard data.

Finally, much that is written about innovation tends to focus on success or failure. The fact that an innovation is successful is what makes it interesting. Accounts of innovation therefore tend to be written for a variety of purposes including entertainment, personal aggrandisement, money and the like. All too often the reasons for the success (or for that matter the failure) are ignored, with attention instead focusing on the extent of the success. Yet, if we are to understand innovation, what matters is to understand the reasons for success, and theory can help in making sense of events to enable identification and evaluation of these reasons.

Theories of innovation

There are many theories associated with innovation, of which four are presented here. The selection of four theories is fairly arbitrary. One could very easily have included many more. However, the four selected here offer scope for applying a number of different theories in different contexts without unduly complicating the picture. There are other texts that can provide the reader with further theories should these be required (Ettlie, 2006).

The four theories are:

- technology S-curve
- punctuated equilibrium

- dominant design
- absorptive capacity

These theories are associated primarily with technological innovation. Despite the emphasis on technology within the process of innovation, they all provide adequate scope for analysing innovations in general.

Technology S-curve

One of the central ideas behind the theory of the technology S-curve is the notion of a technology life cycle. This implies that over time the capability of a technology to deliver improved performance will vary. Early in the life cycle the potential for a given investment of engineering effort to deliver improved performance will be high. Successive amounts of additional engineering effort produce ever greater improvements in performance. This is the well-known "learning curve" effect, which results from a new technology becoming better understood, better controlled and more widely diffused. Eventually this will begin to lessen in terms of the relationship between inputs and performance until a point is reached where increasing engineering effort produces diminishing returns in terms of performance improvement. This implies that a given technology eventually reaches some kind of "natural limit" as it matures (Figure 4.1).

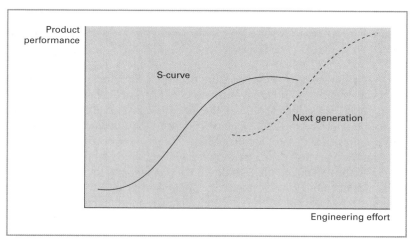

FIGURE 4.1 Technology S-curve
Source: Foster (1986)

Why does a technology mature?

Foster (1986) argues that technologies simply have physical limits. He cites the technology of sailing ships whose speed was limited by the physics of wind and water. The tea clippers that traded between China and Europe in the last years of the nineteenth century were amongst the most efficient sailing ships ever built, representing the high point of sailing-ship technology. They were eclipsed by steamships which substituted the new technology of steam power for wind. As a technology matures so performance improvements get less and less and it requires a radical innovation associated with a new technology. The piston-engined aircraft of the Second World War represented the physical limit of propeller technology in terms of speed. To go any faster required a new technology. That technology took the form of the jet engine pioneered by Whittle in the UK (Golley, 1996) and Von Ohain in Germany (Conner, 2001). The jet engine worked in a completely different way from the piston engine, requiring new skills, new knowledge and new materials. Yet it had the potential to power aircraft at much higher speeds.

Sahal (1981) suggests that technological maturity is also a matter of scale and complexity. Scale is a matter of the product getting impossibly large in the pursuit of improved performance, while complexity is a matter of there being more and more components. In order to avoid the problems caused by scale and complexity a radical innovation is required to break free of the limits of the technology.

Christensen (1997: p34) suggests that the technology S-curve can be useful not only in terms of its descriptive value (i.e. the extent to which it represents what happens in real life) but also in terms of its predictive value. By this is meant the ability of the technology S-curve to predict the course or developmental path of innovation. The predictive power of the technology S-curve is that the point of inflection shows the point at which the existing technology has reached maturity and is going into relative decline. The technology may still be making an effective contribution, but the point has been reached where one might expect to find a successor technology (i.e. another technology S-curve) to arise. The challenge is to identify and develop the successor technology. The inability to anticipate new technologies has been cited as the reason why incumbent firms often fail and as the source of advantage for new entrants.

Mini Case

Disk drives

A hard disk drive is a storage device used to store data on a computer. The first ones were developed by IBM in the 1950s and today most modern PCs have a hard disk drive. Indeed adverts for PCs typically stress the capacity of the hard disk drive (e.g. 200 gigabyte hard disk) as a feature. The hard disk drive consists of a read-write head mounted on an arm that swings over the surface of a rotating solid disk (much like the operation of a record-player deck for playing vinyl records). The first hard disk drives used on large mainframe computer installations were 14-in in diameter. In the 1970s smaller 8-in drives were developed for a new generation of microcomputers produced by firms such as Data General and Hewlett-Packard. These smaller drives were produced by new entrant firms such as Shugart and Quantum. Gradually the capacity of the smaller 8-in hard disk drives rose and they began to invade the mainframe computer market where their lower cost and greater reliability began to tell. Then in the 1980s Seagate Technology introduced a 5.25-in hard disk drive. These were of no interest to microcomputer manufacturers, so Seagate pioneered new applications. They turned to the makers of the new personal computers such as Apple and IBM. At this point it was by no means certain that PC users wanted a hard disk drive – data storage was by so-called "floppy disks".

By the early 1990s the first 3.5-in hard disk drive had appeared developed by a small Scottish company – Rodine. Again there was little interest from existing PC manufacturers. But the idea was taken up by a new company, Connor Peripherals, a spin-off from 5.25-in, hard drive manufacturer, Seagate Technology. The 3.5-in, drive differed significantly from its 5.25-in counterpart. Many of the mechanical parts were replaced with electronics, making the drive significantly lighter and more rugged. These attributes were of no particular concern for existing PC manufacturers, so again firms like Connor Peripherals sought new applications such as the growing market for portable and laptop PCs where weight, ruggedness and power consumption were critical issues. In time the 3.5-in hard disk drive became the industry standard.

Source: Christensen (1997).

Punctuated equilibrium

Abernathy and Utterback (1978) used the distinction between incremental and radical innovation to show how established industries go through periods of stability with changes confined to incremental innovations. They recognised that eventually the stability is broken by a radical innovation that is highly disruptive, bringing the period of stability and equilibrium to an end. According to Loch and Huberman (1999) this is caused by initial uncertainty surrounding the new technology, leading to experimentation and instability. As the technology becomes better understood the changes become incremental and stability and equilibrium return.

Punctuated equilibrium is an evolutionary theory. As a theory of innovation, technology is a central force shaping the pattern of innovation. Tushman and Anderson (1986) note that it is the evolution of technology that gives rise to the distinctive pattern of innovation associated with punctuated equilibrium. Technology evolves not on a smooth continuous basis, but via a succession of fits and starts. Major technological breakthroughs are relatively rare. Tushman and Anderson (1986) cite the cases of Chester Carlson and the development of xerography (photocopying) and Alistair Pilkington and the development of the float glass process for manufacturing plate glass, as examples of discontinuities. They observe (Tushman and Anderson, 1986: p41) that technological change is: "a bit-by-bit cumulative process until it is punctuated by a major advance".

Both xerography and float glass were major advances. Each in its own way was highly disruptive, but it was followed by a period of relative stability. This is what occurred in both instances. Innovations followed the major advances but they were incremental innovations that resulted in modest product improvements rather than significant changes.

The discontinuities that punctuate periods of equilibrium are linked to major technological innovations. These represent technical changes that are step changes. Tushman and Anderson (1986: p44) describe them as: "so significant that no increase in scale, efficiency or design can make older technologies competitive with the new technology". The new technology represents a step change which is why no amount of incremental change for the existing technology will render it competitive.

A key feature of technological discontinuities is that they require new skills, new abilities and new knowledge in both the development and the manufacture of the product. As a result such innovations can be "competence destroying". This means that existing firms are unable to use the knowledge and experience they have accumulated during the period of equilibrium. Given that the existing knowledge represents a big investment made over a long period of time, they are likely to want to make use of this knowledge. Hence they are more likely to opt for incremental innovations.

Nor is it just that "incumbent" firms possess knowledge and expertise linked to the old technology that gives rise to inertia; other factors include:

- traditions
- sunk costs
- internal political constraints
- commitment to outmoded technology

If working practices have changed very little in a long time, they may have become so widely accepted and so deeply ingrained in the organisation that they have become traditions. As traditions, the rationale and reasoning behind the working practices in question may have long since disappeared, but because this is the way things have been done for a long time, traditions are very hard to break. Nor are traditions confined to working practices: they can cover all aspects of a business.

Sunk costs are costs associated with prior investments. These could cover equipment, buildings, systems or even training. Firms make investments all the time, but where the investment is technology-specific the cost of the investment is a sunk cost. The key aspect is that the investment cannot be transferred to the new technology – it is sunk in the old technology. If the organisation has invested heavily, then it may be expecting to spread the cost over future output. As a result the organisation may be reluctant to break from the old technology.

Internal political constraints can arise for all sorts of reasons. If managers have a strong commitment to the old technology – perhaps by virtue of their training or their knowledge – they may well be reluctant to embrace a new technology they know little about. Not only will this lead to a reluctance to innovate on their part, it may even stop others pursuing innovation.

All of these factors serve to constrain or limit the responsiveness of existing firms. This helps to account for the existence of equilibrium. Under these conditions existing firms may confine themselves to incremental innovations, thereby prolonging the period of equilibrium. Eventually, however, radical innovations lead to discontinuities that punctuate the equilibrium. A period of "ferment" then ensues, when technological uncertainty leads to a number of competing product architectures or product designs. This can extend not only to technical aspects such as product configuration and product performance, but also to marketing aspects such as product pricing and market boundaries.

Mini Case

Carbon fibre in Formula One

Ever wondered how it is that drivers in Formula One are able to survive crashes at speeds up to 200 mph? The answer lies in the material used to build their cars. The chassis (the internal frame in which the driver sits and to which the wheels and engine are fitted) of a modern racing car is constructed not of metal (as with a conventional road car), but of a form of plastic called carbon fibre. Carbon fibre is both extremely strong and extremely light. It is also very rigid, which was the main attraction of the material when designers first came to us it.

Racing cars have used a variety of materials for chassis construction. In the 1950s racing cars used steel, with lengths of steel tubing welding together to create what was termed a "spaceframe" chassis. Although cheap and easy to build, a spaceframe chassis was relatively heavy because it required the bodywork to be built separately and then attached to the car. Spaceframe chassis also gave relatively poor handling, which made cars slow through the corners. Then in the 1960s Colin Chapman at Lotus came up with an entirely new design, the "monocoque" chassis. Built of aluminium sheets riveted together to form a strong tub, monocoque chassis were lighter and stronger than spaceframe ones. However, the key difference was that there was no longer separate bodywork which made the monocoque much more rigid giving better handling. Lotus cars were soon winning races and within three years the alumimium monocoque had become standard in Formula One.

In the 1980s cars got faster and faster as manufacturer produced ever more powerful engines and designers found other ways of improving performance. The emphasis turned to aerodynamics, particularly "ground effects" where the shape of the car is used to create an aerofoil shape that creates down force which improves both traction and handling. In the quest for better aerodynamics designers made the chassis narrower. Unfortunately a narrower chassis was less rigid, cancelling out the improvement in handling. It was to combat this that John Barnard at McLaren came up with an entirely new idea: a car with the chassis made entirely of carbon fibre. A form of plastic, carbon fibre is lighter than aluminium and stronger than steel. Widely used in the aerospace industry, Barnard subcontracted the construction of the new carbon fibre chassis to Hercules Aerospace a US company that made carbon fibre parts for the AV8B jump-jet and the F-18 fighter. The McLaren MP4 was soon winning races and in a very short time all the Formula One teams had followed suit and were building cars using carbon fibre.

Source: Cooper (1999).

These circumstances, with a high level of technological and market uncertainty, offer opportunities for new entrants. During a period of equilibrium, new entrants would normally find they were at a disadvantage to incumbents, but when technological discontinuities arise and a process of ferment occurs, the tables may be turned. While incumbents may be stuck with "legacy" problems such as sunk costs, unwanted skills and obsolete plant, new entrants can respond more effectively to the new conditions precisely because they are unencumbered by the baggage of an old technology, traditional ways of doing things and an outdated view of the world.

As a theory that helps to explain the pattern of innovation exhibited in real life, punctuated equilibrium has its limitations. It is a theory in which technology plays a central role. Some might argue that it is a theory of technological evolution. Similarly it is an external theory in the sense that it tells us little about how innovation is carried out inside the firm. However, despite this, punctuated equilibrium is of value as an innovation theory. It helps to explain inertia, in particular the reluctance of existing firms to adopt a new technology, which in turn explains why some innovators find it hard to interest existing firms in new ideas. The case of James Dyson (Dyson, 1997) and his attempts to get established vacuum cleaner manufacturers to embrace his new more efficient dual-cyclone technology which eliminated the need for a dust bag, is a good example. What was happening was that incumbent firms were comfortable with the equilibrium that existed in the vacuum cleaner industry. Dyson's ideas posed a technological discontinuity that threatened their investments in know-how and manufacturing capability. Consequently, they were not keen to embrace the new technology. Another merit of punctuated equilibrium is that it integrates the typology of innovation that distinguishes radical and incremental forms of innovation. Finally, punctuated equilibrium provides a good fit with reality where technological discontinuities can be very disruptive.

Dominant design

Mini Case

The spreadsheet

Microsoft's Excel is familiar to all, so much so that few of us use any other spreadsheet and many people would be hard pressed to name another. Today Excel represents a dominant design where spreadsheets are concerned, yet it was a comparatively late entrant. The first spreadsheet was VisiCalc which appeared about 1980. Despite an early lead, within two years VisiCalc had more than 20 competitors including Supercalc, Lotus 1-2-3, Multiplan (Microsoft's offering later re-named Excel) and Quattro. Each competitor was able, as a follower and imitator, to incorporate additional features into its spreadsheet software. Quattro introduced a WYSIWYG (What You See Is What You Get) facility, while Lotus 1-2-3 introduced integrated presentation graphics and a small database into the spreadsheet. Whereas VisiCalc had been designed to work on the Apple II computer, the newer spreadsheets were designed to operate on newer PCs as they became available. As the IBM PC replaced the Apple II as the most widely used personal computer and became the desktop computer used not only by small companies but large ones as well, spreadsheets designed from the outset for this machine, such as Lotus 1-2-3, began to get the upper hand in the marketplace. VisiCalc, though it had been the innovator as the first spreadsheet to go on the market, was soon eclipsed. Lotus 1-2-3, very rapidly took over the market. In time Microsoft revamped its own spreadsheet, Excel. With GUI facilities, Microsoft's Excel built up a strong position in the Apple Macintosh market but was completely overshadowed by Lotus 1-2-3 in the IBM PC market. However, in the late 1980s Microsoft released Excel for Windows. At this time the Windows operating system was something of a novelty, but as it came to dominate the IBM PC market in the early 1990s, Lotus was caught without a Windows version of its product. Users wanting to take advantage of the new operating system had to buy Microsoft Excel, because it was the only spreadsheet for Windows then available (Campbell-Kelly, 2003). Within a very short space of time Microsoft Excel completely dominated the market.

Source: Campbell-Kelly (2004; 2003).

A dominant design is a design or product configuration that comprises "the one that wins the allegiance of the marketplace, the one that competitors and innovators must adhere to if they hope to command a significant market following" (Nordström and Biström, 2002: p713). Quite literally it is a configuration that all or most firms eventually follow.

The theory of a "dominant design" is linked to ideas about the evolutionary development (Teece, 1986) of science. In science ideas are constantly evolving. The process of evolution comprises two stages: a pre-paradigmatic phase, when many ideas are circulating and no one explanation of a phenomenon holds sway, and a paradigmatic phase, when a single explanation or theory becomes widely accepted. The switch to the latter phase and the emergence of a dominant paradigm signals scientific maturity. This paradigm remains the accepted view until perhaps even it is eventually overturned by another paradigm, as in the seventeenth century when Copernicus's theories of astronomy overturned those of Ptolemy (Teece, 1986).

Dosi (1982) provides a perspective of technological innovation that evokes this evolutionary principle and parallels notions of scientific evolution. According to Dosi the early stages of technological innovation are characterised by a state of "flux" or "ferment" (Anderson and Tushman, 1990), where product designs and configurations are fluid. There will be large numbers of competitors, with rivalry based on competing designs, each of which is markedly different. In this pre-paradigmatic phase no one design or configuration stands out. The evolution of the bicycle (Rosen, 2002), which generated a proliferation of competing designs or forms in the late nineteenth century, including the famous "penny-farthing", illustrates this pre-paradigmatic period of flux.

Eventually an evolutionary process involving variation, selection and retention (Basalla, 1988) leads to the emergence of a single design that forms the dominant design (see Figure 4.2). Teece (1986) likens this to a process akin to a game of "musical chairs" where competing designs gradually fade away to leave a dominant design. Others have used the term "shake-out" to describe the way in which most of the early designs fall away. When a dominant design emerges, competition then shifts away from design and towards other variables such as branding, promotion and price. Under these new circumstances new factors, such as scale and learning, become more important and specialised capital assets begin to replace general-purpose capital assets as firms seek lower unit costs through economies of scale and learning. In the case of the bicycle, the dominant design was the "safety bicycle" that emerged at the end of the nineteenth century from the proliferation of different forms, to include a variety of features we would all recognise today, including a triangular all-metal frame, bearings, chain drive to the rear wheel and pneumatic tyres (Anderson and Tushman, 1990).

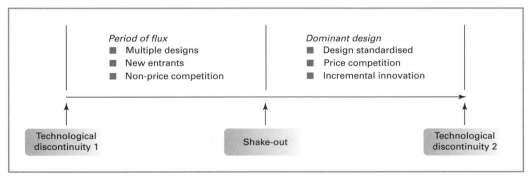

FIGURE 4.2 Dominant design and the technology cycle
Source: Adapted from Anderson and Tushman (1990)

Utterback (1993) has shown that dominant designs are more likely to appear in mass markets, such as typewriters, bicycles, sewing machines, televisions and cars (Freeman and Louçã, 2001), which can justify the investment in specialised capital assets. This is borne out by well-known examples of dominant designs that include the QWERTY typewriter keyboard, Ford's Model T car, Douglas's DC3 airliner, JVC's VHS video recorders and Microsoft's Windows operating system.

How do dominant designs arise? Abernathy and Utterback (1978) suggest three possible factors that can give rise to dominant designs. First, consumer preference, where a particular package of factors present in one design finds favour with consumers in meeting their requirements. These factors will not all be technical. In fact, dominant designs are rarely technically superior to rival designs, but the particular package of features appeals to consumers. Sometimes it is the market power of a dominant producer that is the key factor. Abernathy and Utterback (1978) cite the case of IBM and its 360 series mainframe computer which became the de facto industry standard. Finally regulation, either by government or some form of industry body, may be instrumental in a dominant design appearing.

The theory of dominant design contributes to our understanding of innovation in a number of ways. It highlights the importance of the user, who may be less interested in technical features and more interested in usability. It also highlights the importance of standards particularly where compatibility is an issue for the user. Finally it shows the importance of business strategy within innovation. In the spreadsheet case, for instance, Lotus, like many software companies, lost out to Microsoft because its business strategy anticipated OS/2 succeeding MS-DOS as the principal operating system for PCs (Campbell-Kelly, 2004: p253), and invested in software products to reflect this.

Mini Case

Blu-ray

The home entertainment industry is emerging from a period of flux brought on by the arrival of high definition (HD) television. Nowhere has this flux been more apparent than in the DVD market. The home DVD market is worth £12.3 billion a year, but has lately contracted in the face of uncertainty surrounding the format for the new generation of high definition DVDs. There has been intense competition between two competing new formats, Toshiba's HD DVD and Sony's Blu-ray.

Toshiba was first into the market and initially seemed to have the upper hand. Its HD DVD appeared to have a number of advantages. Its discs were cheaper to produce and sales were initially strong in Japan. In the movie field Toshiba was quick to sign up Dreamworks, while in the computer games field it signed up Microsoft, maker of the best selling X-box 360 videogames console.

However, Sony's Blu-ray now appears to have the upper hand. Its discs, though more expensive, have 25 gigabytes of storage compared to Toshiba's 15 gigabytes. Sony held back the launch of its own videogames console, PlayStation 3, and picked up much criticism from consumers at the time, precisely because it wanted to ensure that it came with Blu-ray installed. The Microsoft X-box 360 on the other hand, while it supports the HD DVD format, requires a separate plug-in HD DVD player. As sales of PlayStation 3 have now passed the 10 million mark this has helped to ensure a substantial base for Blu-ray among videogame users. By contrast only about 1 million HD DVD players have been sold and then mainly in Japan.

With the two formats competing neck and neck, Toshiba was dealt two severe blows in the early months of 2008. Firstly, Warner Bros, the world's largest DVD producer, opted to stop selling the new style DVDs in both formats opting instead for Blu-ray alone. Warner which accounts for about a fifth of the lucrative US DVD market was the last big Hollywood studio producing discs in both formats. MGM, Fox, Walt Disney and Sony Pictures had already signed up to the Blu-ray format. The second major blow was the decision by Wal-Mart, the world's largest retailer, to dump HD DVD across its 4,000 stores in the US. Wal-Mart's move followed a similar decision by consumer electronics retailer, Best Buy and online video rental firm Netflix.

These twin blows effectively sealed the fate of Toshiba's HD DVD and confirmed the place of Blu-ray as the dominant design for high definition DVDs. Sony's success was in sharp contrast to its experience with VCRs where its Betamax system lost out to the rival VHS system produced by arch rival JVC.

Source: Wray and McCurry (2008).

Absorptive capacity

The theory of absorptive capacity differs from previous theories by virtue of the fact that it integrates both the external dimension of innovation, which is concerned with the evolution of technology, and the internal dimension, which is concerned with learning and the knowledge transfer process within the innovating organisation. The emphasis within absorptive capacity upon learning marks it out as providing a very different analytical framework from the S-curve or punctuated equilibrium. This is reflected in the words of Cohen and Levinthal (1990: p128), in a seminal article that first expounded the notion of absorptive capacity, when they identified it as being concerned with: "the ability of a firm to recognise the value of new, external information, assimilate it and apply it to commercial ends".

Figure 4.3 provides a schema in which one can see recognition, assimilation and application at work. In this schema the external environment where technological evolution takes place is at the top and the internal environment of the firm is at the bottom. The process of recognising external trends and technological opportunities is represented by the arrow linked to the box on the left. This box represents the part of an organisation's absorptive capacity that focuses on assimilation. Hence the link from the external environment to this box represents a conduit or channel through which external ideas and opportunities are fed into the organisation. The capacity of the conduit is a crucial feature of organisations with a strong absorptive capacity. If it is effective, the organisation will be good at recognising external ideas.

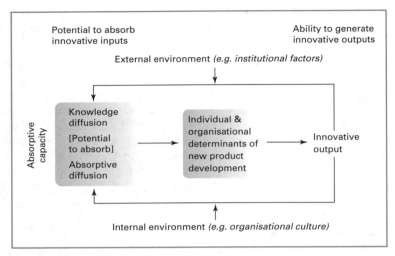

FIGURE 4.3 Absorptive capacity
Source: Ettlie (2006: p83)

While Cohen and Levinthal (1990) acknowledge that "external influences" are vital for innovation, recognition of such influences is only one feature of absorptive capacity. For effective innovation there has also to be a capability to assimilate ideas within the organisation. As Figure 4.3 shows, assimilation is dependent upon an ability to bring external ideas in and to absorb such ideas within an organisation. Termed "knowledge diffusion" this has to extend right across an organisation and to all levels within it. The "silo" mentality has no place within the theory of absorptive capacity. Accordingly, the theory of absorptive capacity sets considerable store by internal communication systems that effectively transfer knowledge across the different parts of the organisation. In this context Cohen and Levinthal note that shared knowledge and expertise is necessary for good communication.

Nor is this the end of the story since, for effective innovation, the ideas once absorbed within an organisation have to be applied. An organisation's capability to apply ideas it has absorbed is represented by the box in the centre of Figure 4.3. What determines an organisation's ability to recognise, absorb and apply new ideas so as to achieve effective innovation? Ettlie (2006) reminds us that there is a constant tension between inward-looking (the bottom channel in Figure 4.3) and outward-looking (the top channel in Figure 4.3) absorptive capacity. Effective absorptive capacity requires the organisation to maintain a balance between the two if it is to lead to effective innovation.

The theory of absorptive capacity places a great deal of emphasis on an organisation's ability to learn. Three factors are identified by Cohen and Levinthal (1990) as being critical in developing and extending an organisation's capacity to learn and thence its ability to assimilate and apply new ideas:

- exposure to relevant knowledge
- presence of prior related knowledge
- diversity of experience

Exposure to relevant knowledge means that the organisation and its staff need to utilise appropriate networks in order to ensure that they keep abreast of developments in the field.

The importance attached to prior related knowledge is linked to the assimilation process. Cohen and Levinthal (1990) argue that the ability to recognise the value of new knowledge and assimilate it into the organisation is a function of the accumulated prior knowledge within the organisation. This in turn emphasises the importance of knowledge within this theoretical model. Assimilation requires that knowledge be evaluated, which in turn requires prior knowledge. It is because of the learning process that Cohen and Levinthal also stress diversity of experience. The greater the range of experience within the organisation, the greater the scope for recognising external ideas and stimuli.

The mini case of the carbon fibre chassis in Formula One provides a powerful illustration of the theory of absorptive capacity (see also Chapter 5). Carbon fibre had been known about for some time (Henry, 1988). Designers had used small amounts of carbon fibre in non-structural applications such as wings, but it took a relative outsider to the Formula One community, like John Barnard, to attempt to build an entire chassis out of carbon fibre. Significantly it was his external contacts, particularly in the aerospace industry and the US, that gave the McLaren team access to the necessary knowledge and expertise.

In this context Bruce and Moger (1999) observe that there is a danger that organisations that place excessive emphasis on increasing efficiency and cost reductions through the pursuit of increased specialisation using mass-production-type activities risk impairing the organisation's absorptive capacity. This is because the division of labour aimed at producing repetitive, mass-production-type activities reduces the diversity of experience of those working within the organisation, and as a result the scope to build up absorptive capacity, which Cohen and Levinthal argue is a cumulative process, is limited.

Absorptive capacity is more sophisticated than some of the other theories of innovation. It highlights the importance of external knowledge as a critical component in innovation. It helps to explain why some organisations, even where they are exposed to external knowledge, may be poor innovators, because they cannot absorb and make use of the knowledge, and it serves to show why networks and networking can be so important to innovation. However, probably the greatest strength of absorptive capacity and the reason why it has been widely used by those researching the field is that it integrates and brings together a number of ideas. These include ideas about technological evolution, the learning process and networking. Absorptive capacity offers a synthesis that draws these different strands together. In the process it offers a powerful tool for analysing innovation.

How does theory help the innovator?

Theories of innovation, like any other form of theory, have three main contributions to offer when it comes to analysing innovation. These contributions are:

- descriptive
- analytical
- predictive

The descriptive contribution includes the identification of key events, the description of the course of events and how the events are linked so as to provide an accurate account of the process of innovation based on relevant evidence. Most people when asked about innovation will describe a process. This is not surprising, because innovation typically involves a linear process in which activities follow one from the other. While describing the course of innovation in this way often makes a good story – hence the large number of books about innovations (especially biographies which recount how the innovation came about) – unfortunately it does not provide a great deal in the way of explanation.

The analytical contribution is all about uncovering and explaining why the innovation occurred. In order to be able to offer an explanation of why one innovation occurred in the way that it did, or why another innovation was particularly successful, one needs to be able to identify patterns or points of commonality between innovations. This permits the identification of causal relationships so that the success or failure of an innovation is not seen as merely a succession of accidents. At the same time it helps to be able to draw comparisons between different innovations. Undertaking these sorts of activities requires some tools of analysis. Innovation theories can provide these analytical tools.

Finally, the predictive element allows us to understand why particular innovations succeeded or failed so that others can learn and in future take actions that will enhance the likelihood of success. Why should this be? Prediction can offer a number of benefits:

- the course of events associated with innovation can be anticipated
- problems and difficulties can be predicted in advance
- there is scope for planning so that resources can be used more effectively
- there is a greater likelihood of a successful outcome to the innovation

Consequently, while theories of innovation may appear to be abstract and unrelated to the practical problems associated with innovation, in fact they can offer some very practical benefits, all the more so when one considers that there is often a high level of uncertainty associated with innovation.

CASE STUDY: HIGH FIDELITY

In June 1948 Columbia Records, a division of the giant US media corporation CBS, transformed listening to music by launching the long playing (LP) record. Its 12-in vinyl disc utilised microgrooves and rotated at 33$\frac{1}{3}$ rpm. This was much slower than the 78 rpm records which had been the dominant form of music recording since the introduction of the gramophone in the early twentieth century. 78 rpm records lasted just 4 minutes, meaning that with classical music it was necessary to change the record before the piece had finished. Engineers at Columbia had in fact calculated that some 90 per cent of classical pieces lasted for 17 minutes or less. Columbia's new long-playing record provided a previously unheard of uninterrupted 25 minutes of playing time. For the first time it was possible to hear an "album" comprising several songs or a major classical piece without having to stop to change records.

Columbia Records was keen to see its new music recording system become the new standard format. So keen was it that it didn't even patent the technology which had been invented by Ed Wallerstein and his research team. Columbia Records hoped that by letting other record companies use the technology without paying a royalty, it would be quickly adopted and become the de facto standard. This did in fact happen but not before CBS's great rival, RCA Victor, refusing to admit that they'd been beaten by a competitor, had devoted enormous research effort and resources to developing their own "new and improved" system. Quite simply the senior management of NBC which owned RCA Victor, thought the company was a sufficiently powerful force in the marketplace to force its technology on the consumer. But they underestimated Columbia's first mover advantage. RCA, in fact, would be the last of the major labels to finally release its own 33$\frac{1}{3}$ rpm albums, three years later in 1951.

Although LPs appeared first in the classical market, with the rising disposable income of young people they quickly caught on in the market for pop music. Thus throughout the 1950s, 1960s and 1970s the vinyl "LP" was the dominant format for recording and playing music.

However, a breakthrough appeared in 1962 when the Dutch electronics firm, Philips, launched the first compact audio cassette tape. This utilised an entirely new medium: magnetic tape. This had been in use for some time but Philips perfected the packaging of magnetic tape into a cassette using a much narrower tape than used previously. The result was quite literally a standardised cassette that was much more compact and easy to use. Unfortunately while the cassette was easy to use it couldn't offer the quality of recording inherent in the high fidelity vinyl LPs then on the market. Consequently the first audio cassette applications were in dictating machines rather than as pre-recorded cassettes that could be used to listen to music.

This situation changed in the late 1960s when an American working in England, Ray Dolby, patented the Dolby A noise reduction system in 1966. This improved the sound quality of audio cassette tapes by reducing the "hiss" inherent in the use of a relative narrow magnetic tape. Dolby's innovation proved crucial in the popularising and commercial success of audio cassette tape, which became a key feature of the "hi-fi" market of the 1970s. The cassette was also helped by Sony's launch of the "Walkman" in the late 1970s, which popularised listening to music on the move. Even though a rival eight-track cartridge system appeared, offering superior sound quality, the small size and durability of the audio cassette won out and it was the dominant medium of the later 1970s and 1980s.

▶   The 1980s were to see the appearance of an entirely new recording medium: the digital compact disk (CD). The CD was the product of a huge research effort by Sony and Philips working together. They set up a joint taskforce in 1979 that brought together two research teams with different technologies and expertise. The CD worked on entirely different principles from magnetic tape. Music was stored digitally on an optical disc and a laser was then used to read the disc. Although the laser had been invented as far back as 1958, it was primarily used as a piece of expensive laboratory equipment. Making it sufficiently robust to operate in a domestic environment presented many challenges as did the problem of simplifying the technology so that it could be mass produced and sold at a price consumers could afford. By working together rather than in competition Sony and Philips hoped to avoid some of the pitfalls that had affected the earlier and relatively unsuccessful laser disc. The format finally agreed was a compromise in terms of overall performance. Compared to the compact audio cassette the CD offered greater capacity and greater durability, but at the expense of slightly reduced sound quality. These benefits were not lost on consumers who were quick to adopt the new technology. The first commercial music offered on a CD was Abba's "The Visitors" album released in 1982. By 1990 CD sales in the US amounted to 288 million annually. By 2007 more than 200 billion CDs had been sold worldwide.

While the CD was the dominant format for listening to music during the late 1980s and 1990s, by the end of the latter decade a new technology had appeared: MP3. MP3 stands for Motion Picture Experts Group Layer-3. The Motion Picture Experts Group, as its name implies had nothing to do with the music industry. Rather it was a committee of technical experts set up by the International Standards Organisation (ISO) an international body that tries to create common standards for products and technologies in the hope of improving compatibility and safety. The remit of the group mainly covered video and was intended to establish common standards for displaying video and audio using compression techniques to reduce the amount of storage space required without compromising sound quality. The use of compression techniques for digital audio provided a format that would allow music to be turned into computer files, that could then be relatively easily transferred from one device to another and which would require much less storage space. In the early 1990s the Motion Picture Experts Group (MPEG) agreed three standards, of which MP3 was the third. (hence 'MP3'). It didn't take long for the manufacturers of audio products to take advantage of the new standard.

In 1998 the first MP3 players appeared. Diamond Multimedia's Rio 100 MP3 player was launched in the US at much the same time as the Korean manufacturer Saehan introduced its MPman. Three years later the American computer giant Apple burst onto the scene with its iPod. It combined MP3 technology with very small high-capacity hard disk drive making it possible to store 1,000 songs on a portable audio player.

The popularity of MP3 players meant that consumers, instead of buying CDs, chose instead to download music files from the Internet. Thanks to Apple's iTunes and other legal download providers sales of downloaded music surged. By 2006 music downloads accounted for 78 per cent of all singles sales, up from 24 per cent in 2004 (Hickman, 2006). As downloading increased in popularity so inevitably CD sales declined and MP3 became increasingly the norm.

Source: Hickman (2006); Levy (2006).

Questions

1 Which theory do you think best explains innovations in the music industry?
2 How would you describe the periods between the technological breakthroughs?
3 If the technical breakthroughs described in the case study form radical innovations, what sorts of innovations would you expect to find in the periods between them?
4 Apply the theory of punctuated equilibrium by drawing a diagram showing innovations in music recording over the last 60 years.
5 How effectively does the theory of punctuated equilibrium explain innovations in the music industry?
6 What evidence is there that at times of technological breakthrough one has a number of new competing designs?
7 Why was Columbia Records keen to establish a standard for vinyl LP records?
8 What evidence is there that the technological breakthroughs required other factors to ensure they were successful?
9 Why was it beneficial for Sony and Philips to collaborate to develop the CD format?
10 What does the case study tell us about the importance of standards?

? Questions for discussion

1 Which of the four theories outlined makes the greatest contribution to our understanding of innovation and why?
2 How can a theory of innovation have a predictive capability (use appropriate examples to support your case)?
3 Many potential innovators who have developed and patented an innovation have found they could attract little interest when they sought to persuade established companies to take out a licence. To what extent do any of the theories of innovation provide an explanation for this behaviour?
4 Why do innovations often come from outside the industry?
5 Explain what is meant by a technological discontinuity and show how such discontinuities are linked to theories of innovation.
6 Use the theory of the technology S-curve to distinguish between radical and incremental types of innovation.
7 Draw the technology S-curve for the washing machine. How does this theory help to explain innovations in the field?
8 According to the theory of punctuated equilibrium, why is the rate of innovation not constant?
9 What is the significance of knowledge transfer within the theory of absorptive capacity?
10 How might outsourcing reduce a firm's absorptive capacity?

Exercises

1 Take an account of innovation (this could be from a biography of an innovator, or a television programme or a film) and use any *one* theory of innovation to explain why and how innovation occurred.

2 Provide a detailed critique of any one of the theories of innovation.

3 What is the connection between notions of evolution, particularly technological evolution, and theories of innovation?

4 What is the value of theories of innovation for (a) would-be innovators and (b) policy-makers?

Further reading

1 Tushman, M.L. and P. Anderson (2004) *Managing Strategic Innovation and Change*, 2nd edn, Oxford University Press, New York.
One of few readers on innovation. The collection of papers includes some useful ones on innovation theory. These include Anderson and Tushman on punctuated equilibrium and Christensen and Bower on the technology S-curve.

2 Ettlie, J.E. (2006) *Managing Innovation: New Technology, New Products, and New Services in a Global Economy*, 2nd edn, John Wiley & Sons, NY.
A textbook treatment of innovation theory. In fact there is only one chapter of this book that deals with theory, but don't be put off, it provides a comprehensive overview of a range of innovation theories and the references point the enthusiastic reader to the original sources.

3 Christensen, C.M. (1997) *The Innovator's Dilemma: Why New Technologies Cause Great Companies to Fail*, Harvard Business School Press, Boston, MA.
This book provides an excellent opportunity to see how the theories of innovation can be applied to analysing and understanding why and how innovation occurs. The theories of dominant design, technology-S curve and punctuated equilibrium are much in evidence in Christensen's analysis innovations in mechanical excavators and hard disk drives.

4 Foster, R.J. (1986) *Innovation: The Attacker's Advantage*, Summit Books, NY.
Although this book doesn't set out to examine theory, it is does focus at considerable length on the technology S-curve. What is of particular interest is that it shows how a theory can be used as analytical tool to analyse innovation.

Sources of innovation

05

❖ OBJECTIVES

When you have completed this chapter you will be able to:

❖ review the innovation process

❖ distinguish the different ways in which the innovation process can commence

❖ analyse the diverse sources of innovation

❖ identify recent changes in the relative importance of particular sources of innovation

❖ evaluate the relative importance of different sources of innovation

Introduction

This chapter focuses on the invention stage of the innovation process rather than the later points which are concerned with commercialisation and getting an invention ready for market. It is concerned with where new ideas for innovation come from. In a sense it is concerned with the "Eureka" moment, when an individual or team has an idea or makes a discovery that forms the basis of a new product or service or production process. In reality of course innovation is rarely so straightforward. Innovations can have a range of different starting points and that is the purpose of this chapter, which aims to identify the various different origins or sources of innovation. As well as examining the various sources of innovation, the chapter also aims to show how these sources vary in importance, both between different contexts (i.e. different industries or sectors) and over time. The chapter shows how research laboratories such as AT&T's Bell Labs and Xerox's PARC are now relatively less important than they were in the second half of the twentieth century. Instead it is noted that there has been a "democratisation" (Von Hippel, 2005) of innovation, where ideas and discoveries emanate from a wider range of sources and not just research labs. The range of sources is illustrated in Figure 5.1.

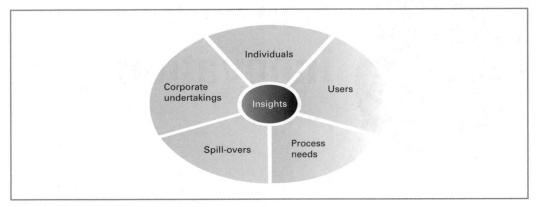

FIGURE 5.1 Insights and sources of innovation

Insight – a flash of genius

Models of the innovation process that portray the process as linear and sequential and formal models of new product development (NPD) both place idea generation as the starting point of the process. Within a very structured new product development process this might well involve the application of a variety of creative techniques (e.g. brainstorming), designed to throw up a number of possible ideas that can then be developed and evaluated. However, innovation is not always so structured; sometimes ideas come from some form of sudden "insight" that arises almost by accident or after months or even years of painstaking research. It is this insight that really lies at the heart of the invention phase of the innovation process. Insight is the starting point that leads to invention and thence to innovation.

Insight is the moment of inspiration when an idea occurs to an individual and forms the basis of an idea. According to Usher (1954) insight is the point where a mental act goes beyond the skill normally expected of someone trained in the field. How does the insight arise? Is it simply a sudden moment of inspiration or are there any patterns one can observe?

There appear to be at least some patterns that form the basis of insight:

- association
- adaptation
- analogy
- serendipity/chance

Association

Association involves the bringing together of two apparently unconnected ideas. With association, insights in one field provide solutions in another. There might be two different fields, but essentially the same activity can be used to solve a problem. The insight arises as a result of bringing work from two different fields together. Bette Nesmith Graham provides an example of insight arising through association. She was working as a secretary in a Texas bank when she devised a method of removing typing errors. She noticed that sign-writers working across the street painted over errors in order to remove them, and decided to take a small paintbrush and some white paint to see if they would enable her to correct her typing mistakes. The results were sufficiently encouraging for her to try and develop the idea further. Working on a trial and error basis in her kitchen, with occasional technical help from her son's chemistry teacher, after five years she had perfected the idea to the point where it was a practical product. When IBM, then the largest manufacturer of electric typewriters, showed no interest in her invention, she set up production on her own in her garage. The business prospered and in time her corrective fluid became a mass market product sold and used all over the world. Amazingly, it even survived the coming of the word processor which should have rendered it obsolete.

Adaptation

Adaptation on the other hand involves taking an existing solution to a problem and adapting it so that it can be used for a different purpose in another field. James Dyson's dual cyclone bagless vacuum cleaner provides an example of this form of insight (Dyson, 1997). Dust-extraction using a cyclone was well established for industrial applications, and it was while working on an industrial dust-extraction system designed to remove fine particles of paint from the atmosphere that the idea occurred to him that the cyclone principle could be applied to vacuum cleaners. The amount of adaptation required was considerable. Indeed, the originality of Dyson's system was that it employed not one but two cyclones.

Analogy

Analogy is exemplified where a principle used in one situation is used for a different purpose in another. Georges De Mestral's invention of the Velcro fastener provides an example of analogy leading to an insight. De Mestral was a Swiss engineer who began to think about alternatives to conventional zip fasteners (Van Dulken, 2002). While walking through the woods with his dog one night he noticed how burs stuck to his dog's fur and his own clothing. Curious, he examined the burs under a microscope and discovered that the surface of the bur contained large numbers of tiny hooks. It was these tiny hooks that caught in the strands of fur and the loops of wool on the clothing. After some eight years of effort De Mestral finally developed a method of reproducing the hooks and loops in woven nylon. He called the new product Velcro which was short for Velours Croché, meaning hooked velvet.

What is the difference between analogy and adaptation? Clearly they are very similar. However, with analogy a technique or principle in one context suggests a new way of doing something, rather than being transferred directly from one context to another. Thus in the case of Velcro, burs are seeds that stick to things in order that seeds may be widely distributed. It was the method by which burs attached themselves to a dog's fur that suggested a new way of attaching two surfaces together.

Serendipity/chance

Finally there is chance, or as it is sometimes termed "serendipity," where supposedly random occurrences giving rise to a new insight form the basis of an idea that ultimately leads to an innovation. Taylor (1996) gives the example of Alexander Graham Bell and the invention of the telephone. It was in June 1875 while working on improvements to the telegraph system, which enabled messages to be transmitted over telegraph wires using Morse code, that one of his assistants by chance over-tightened a clamping screw. When the telegraph was used Bell heard a sound and began to realise how sound waves in the air could be made to vary the strength of electrical current in a wire. It was almost a year later that Bell, having filed a patent, was able to transmit the first words. Nevertheless, the idea that formed the basis of the innovation was the result of the earlier chance event. And it would be quite wrong to think that this is an isolated example, for Meyers (2007) shows that a wide range of medical innovations, including penicillin, chemotherapy, X-rays, anti-depressants, the Pap smear and Viagra, resulted from serendipity.

Whatever the reason for the insight – whether it is association, adaptation, analogy or even serendipity – a common reaction of most people is to think how obvious the idea is. This highlights a very important feature of insights: no matter how they arise, the skill, indeed some might say the genius, is being able to recognise their potential value. In Bell's case it was his prior knowledge of the field that enabled him to interpret the event in such a way that he was able to gain an insight. Had others, lacking Bell's knowledge and experience, witnessed it, it is highly unlikely that they would have had an insight in the same way. Clearly Bell was fortunate that a chance event occurred in his presence, but one should not underestimate the requirement for a combination of chance, prior knowledge and experience; only then is there any likelihood of what Seabrook (2008), in his recent book on inventions, terms, "a flash of genius".

Sources of innovation

Notions of "insight" tend to assume that idea-generation is something carried out by individuals. Certainly all of the examples that have just been given in relation to insight focus on individuals and the insights that they have gained. However, too much emphasis on individuals is misleading. While lone individuals who quite independently have ideas and work them up into feasible products/services are a source of innovation, it is important to appreciate that there are multiple sources, not least because individuals can take a number of roles, e.g. users or employees, as well as being individual inventors. We have already seen that the research labs of large corporations are an important source of innovation. In reality innovation can be sourced not only from individuals and corporations but from a range of other sources as well. Hence the full range of innovation sources is more likely to be:

- individuals
- corporations
- users
- employees
- outsiders
- spill-overs
- process needs

Recognition of multiple sources of innovation, particularly sources other than "heroic" individuals and mighty business corporations with large research labs, reflect the changing nature of innovation and the changing context within which it takes place. The increasing use of "open" models of innovation (Chesbrough, 2003a) in which innovation is sourced from outside a business organisation (or if necessary commercialised outside) has led to the growth of other sources of innovation. This has been helped by new, more flexible institutional arrangements in the form of various types of inter-firm collaboration such as strategic alliances and joint ventures. No longer must innovation be the preserve of the large, vertically integrated business corporation because only it has the required resources. The new institutional arrangements have facilitated collaboration. In particular they provide a mechanism whereby small start-up companies can work with large corporations. Such arrangements can be complementary, with the small firm providing ideas and inventions and the large firm providing the resources for commercialisation. In this type of environment, with flexible arrangements for undertaking innovation, it is perhaps not surprising there are many sources of innovation.

Individuals

In the popular media, derived from biographies, television documentaries, films (e.g. Marc Abraham's recent film *Flash of Genius*), press reports and business magazines, the individual in the form of the lone inventor (Seabrook, 2008) reigns supreme. According to this model, individuals have ideas for potential new products and services typically quite independent of any third party or business corporation. Where do the ideas come from? Sometimes the ideas are derived from work (e.g. Bill Gore and the development of Gore-tex (Parsons and Rose, 2003)), sometimes from involvement in sports and hobbies (e.g. Trevor Baylis and the clockwork radio (Baylis, 1999)), sometimes from a sense of frustration at the poor quality and performance of existing product (e.g. James Dyson and the bagless vacuum cleaner (Dyson, 1997)), sometimes from spotting a gap in the market (e.g. Dan Bricklin and the development of VisiCalc, the world's first spreadsheet (Campbell-Kelly, 2003b)) and sometimes from chance events (serendipity) such as Bob Kearns driving through the rain in Detroit and suddenly thinking – why can't a windscreen wiper behave like an eye and blink (Seabrook, 2008)?

Individual	Product name	Product	Link to innovation	Reference
Bill Gore	Gore-Tex	Waterproof fabric	Work experience	Parsons & Rose (2003)
Trevor Baylis	n/a	Clockwork radio	Hobby	Baylis (1999)
James Dyson	Dyson Dual Cyclone	Bagless vacuum cleaner	User and work experience	Dyson (1997)
Dan Bricklin	VisiCalc	Spreadsheet	User who spotted gap in market	Campbell-Kelly (2003)

TABLE 5.1 Individuals and their innovations

The individual inventor/innovator is often described as the "garage" model of innovation (Audia and Rider, 2005). In this model an individual, perhaps working with a partner, develops an innovation at home in his or her garage or somewhere similar. Among the most famous innovators who have used this model and quite literally developed an invention in the garage are William Hewlett and David Packard who developed a prototype audio oscillator in the garage of Hewlett's home at 367 Addison Avenue in Palo Alto in California and James Dyson who developed his bagless vacuum cleaner in the garage/coach-house of his home near Bath (Dyson, 1997).

In fact it was the individual as innovator that was the model first used by Joseph Schumpeter (Pavitt, 2005). In his early writing (sometimes referred to as Schumpeter Mark 1 (Fagerberg, 2005)), Schumpeter stressed the role of individuals as the source of innovation. Schumpeter particularly highlighted the character and determination of outstanding individuals who had not only the ingenuity to develop technical inventions, but more importantly the perseverance to see them through the long and demanding commercialisation stage required to bring them to market successfully.

A study by Jewkes *et al.* (1969) showed that despite much speculation that only large firms now have the resources necessary to undertake technology-based innovation, the individual inventor/innovator was alive and well. In a study that covered some 70 important innovations that occurred during the twentieth century, Jewkes *et al.* (1969) found that in around half the cases the source of the innovation was a single person either working on his or her own or at least independently of a corporate undertaking. Only one-third of the innovations had as their source the research laboratory of a corporate undertaking, the remainder being simply difficult to classify. More recent studies (Amesse *et al.*, 1991) support the general pattern identified by Jewkes *et al.* (1969).

The resilience of the individual inventor is linked to a number of factors. First, there is the growth in the small-firm sector that has taken place during recent years. Second, a variety of organisational devices, such as strategic alliances, have enabled small firms to work with large firms. Third, innovation is associated with the applications of technology and, while large firms may be proficient where the development of technology is concerned, small firms will often have greater knowledge of applications. A further factor has been the increased popularity of spin-off companies. Not only do these provide a means for individual inventors to leave the corporate sector and set up on their own in order to develop an innovation, they also, as in the case of Silicon Valley, provide a powerful role model for would-be innovators. In this context the growth of the venture capital industry over the last three decades has provided a powerful force to support this kind of trend. Finally, as Christensen (1997) has pointed out, the emergence of disruptive new technologies is something to which the corporate sector often finds it difficult to adapt. Consequently, some of the new technologies of the last quarter of the twentieth century have helped promote the cause of the individual inventor/innovator. Not least of these have been some of the technologies associated with computing. The examples of Steve Jobs and Steve Wozniak and the personal computer and Dan Bricklin and the spreadsheet stand as testimony to the success of the individual inventor/innovator in this context.

Corporations

Although Schumpeter originally identified individuals as the primary source of innovation, in later life he underwent something of a conversion and his later work identified large business corporations as the chief source of innovation (the so-called Schumpeter Mark 2 (Fagerberg, 2005)). Schumpeter's reasoning was that as innovation became increasingly to be technology based it required extensive research and development (R&D). Only large firms had the resources to operate industrial research laboratories in which such R&D could be undertaken. The use of industrial R&D laboratories first emerged in the chemical industry in Germany and was rapidly taken up by the electrical industry as electrical technologies became an increasingly important source of innovation.

Pavitt (2005) notes that industrial R&D became increasingly integrated into large manufacturing firms during the course of the twentieth century. Large, vertically integrated business corporations invested in research laboratories whose R&D activities became a source of technical breakthroughs that led to innovations across the business world.

Outstanding examples of this approach were to be found in the US where, in the telecommunications field, AT&T's Bell Labs earned six Nobel Prizes for inventions such as the laser and the transistor (*The Economist*, 2007a), while in computing IBM picked up three. Nor was the model confined to high-technology industries like aerospace, automotive and electronics; in food processing, detergents, cosmetics and industrial materials one finds a similar pattern. Companies like Procter and Gamble, Unilever and 3M used their R&D capability to produce a steady stream of innovations across the full range of their product portfolios.

While there is no doubt that the corporate model of innovation is still the primary source of innovation, it has increasingly been recognised that the R&D undertaken in industrial research labs is not the only way in which corporations can innovate. According to Chesbrough (2006: p48) the proportion of R&D undertaken by large firms (i.e. with more than 25,000 employees) has fallen from 70.7 per cent in 1981 to 41.3 per cent in 1999. Increasingly R&D is being done by smaller firms (less than 1,000 employees) whose share of R&D has risen from 4.4 per cent in 1981 to 22.5 per cent in 1999. This change reflects the increasing use of "open innovation" (Chesbrough, 2003a) where large corporations increasingly buy in new technology by licensing it from other firms. The greater flexibility that open innovation provides has enabled large corporations to continue to play a very important part in innovation, only now they sometimes innovate with someone else's technology rather than their own.

Users

The idea that users are a source of innovation is unsurprising since one might reasonably assume that they are best placed to know what they need. However, it needs to be stressed that what we mean by users as innovators is not users telling manufacturers what to make, rather like some form of market research, but users being actively involved – indeed they may well initiate and oversee the innovation process.

Users as an important source of innovations is particularly associated with the pioneering work of Von Hippel (1976). He was among the first to show that in certain industry sectors users play a critical role not only in generating ideas for innovations, but also in their subsequent development. Von Hippel's work focused on the scientific equipment industry, particularly the sectors producing instruments used for gas chromatography, nuclear magnetic resonance spectrometry, ultra absorption spectrometry and transmission electronic microscopy. Von Hippel was able to show that in each case the idea that formed the basis of the instrument came from, and was initially developed by, a user who was a member of the scientific community; only when the idea had been developed into a working prototype was it transferred to a manufacturing company for commercial production, and the user still remained actively involved in the programme.

It is significant that Von Hippel focused on scientific equipment as an industry sector. This sort of equipment is widely used in scientific research and as Rothwell (1986) points out, in this field scientific researchers form the focal point of state-of-the-art expertise. In addition, the nature of their work – research – means that they often have to construct new kinds of equipment in order to allow them to move forward the frontiers of knowledge. Experimentation by its nature requires monitoring and measuring equipment, and new forms of experimentation may well require new forms of equipment. Similarly, in chemistry, chemists working in government laboratories and universities often need to devise new forms of analytical equipment in order to further their research. As Von Hippel points out, manufacturers of scientific instruments are simply not sufficiently closely involved in scientific research to perceive or predict the new requirements in the field which would enable them to make the initial invention. Similarly, users do not possess the capability to manufacture scientific instruments so that once they have developed a working prototype, they then turn to manufacturers to produce the equipment in quantity.

More recently, Von Hippel (2005) has described what he calls the "democratising" of innovation as the involvement of users as a source of innovation has extended to many more industries. Among the industries where users are now an important source of innovation are:

- software development
- library information systems
- mountain bikes
- outdoor clothing and equipment (e.g. jackets, sleeping bags, etc.)
- extreme sporting equipment (e.g. skateboards, windsurfers, etc.)

Over the last decade there has been a steady stream of research studies detailing user involvement in these industry sectors. In software development Hertel *et al.* (2003) looked at user involvement in the development of the Linux operating system. Morrison *et al.* (2000) did the same for library information systems. Parsons and Rose's (2003) recent history of the outdoor clothing industry shows how climbers and walkers played a crucial role in developing innovations in this sector in the 1980s and 1990s. Lüthje *et al.* (2005) describe how users in Marin County, California, developed the first mountain bikes, while Shah (2000) did the same thing for sports equipment, highlighting the importance of "learning by doing" in developing innovations in skateboarding, snowboarding and windsurfing.

Why are users in these industries increasingly becoming the source of innovation? A variety of factors have been put forward as facilitating the involvement of users in new product development. Firstly, improvements in communication such as the appearance of the Internet, cheaper and better telecommunications, the growth of the media (especially media catering for special interests, e.g. specialist magazines and web sites) have given users much improved access to each other and to manufacturers and suppliers, as well as much improved access to knowledge.

Secondly, improvements in computing, particularly things like CAD, spreadsheets and project-management software, have enabled users to develop their own new product development (NPD) capability. Thirdly, greater levels of education, particularly greatly increased rates of participation in higher education, have given users both an increased knowledge capability and greater access to knowledge. Finally the growth of open innovation has provided user innovators with another route to market (i.e. via large companies).

These factors, combined with much greater flexibility of technology and lower costs in many instances, have enabled users to play a much more active role in innovation in certain industry sectors. No longer forced to be passive recipients of what manufacturers conceive as appropriate products, users have been "democratised" and given access to an active role in innovation. In many sectors enthusiastic users have leapt at the opportunities presented by their democratisation and developed new products. This is particularly the case in areas like sport, outdoor pursuits and cycling where enthusiasts are able to acquire and build up specialist knowledge that enables them to produce better products and services.

Energising users to play a very active role in innovation in this way has also been helped by new institutional arrangements. New financial institutions such as the rising venture capital sector have provided a means for users to set up and grow their own start-up ventures, while increased use of forms of collaborations such as alliances and joint ventures has provided them with a means to work with manufacturers and distributors on equal terms.

Mini Case

Linux

Linux was developed originally by a Finnish student, Linus Torvalds, at the University of Helsinki in the early 1990s. It is an alternative to Microsoft's Windows operating system. Linux is similar to AT&T's UNIX operating system but with one big difference – it is available free of charge as a piece of open-source software. Torvalds developed Linux as a hobby in order to enable him to use a UNIX-like operating system on his PC. He didn't intend it to be a conventional piece of commercial software. Because Linux shared features with another UNIX-like operating system called MINIX, which had an established user group, Torvalds posted a message about his new operating system on the group's message board. The message prompted an offer of space on a server at the Helsinki University of Technology, so that people could download the source code of the new operating system for themselves.

From the outset Linux was "copy lifted" – meaning that potential users could use the software without charge and because they had access to the source code were encouraged to modify and improve the software, fixing any bugs they encountered. Within months there were 100 Linux users engaged in news group discussions and active in providing improvements (on a part-time basis). Within a year there was a fully functional Linux operating system available for the IBM PC family of machines. Today there are estimated to be around 10 million Linux users. Not only that, upwards of 10,000 of these users are programmers actively involved in Linux news groups and the provision of improvements and enhancements to the software. One might imagine that having a huge number of people contributing to innovation on a part-time basis would be a recipe for chaos. Far from it. Linux is a remarkably stable and robust product – precisely because so many people are involved in checking it out and improving it. Indeed Linux has emerged as a serious rival for the operating system that currently dominates the PC field, namely Microsoft's Windows.

Sources: Naughton (2003); Moody (2002).

The Predator

Craig Johnston is an Australian from Lake Macquarie in New South Wales. He was a keen soccer player as a child, encouraged by his father who had been a professional footballer. Craig too followed in his father's footsteps and in 1986 achieved a childhood ambition when he scored one of the winning goals for Liverpool in the 1986 FA Cup Final. However, two years later Johnston quit the game and returned to Australia.

In retirement Johnston coached the Lake Macquarie junior team. Coaching children, Johnston came to realise how difficult ball control was for youngsters. He began to think about the idea of a new type of football boot that would perform better than existing boots. A chance call from fellow Australian, Harold Hunter, who had been experimenting with high friction surfaces for football boots to give better grip, set Johnston on the path to innovation. Hunter's experimental boot incorporated a serrated plastic surface and while it did give better grip Johnston realised its sheer bulk made it too cumbersome. Johnston found the solution while windsurfing. Having borrowed a pair of windsurfing shoes, he quickly realised that they were light yet provided excellent grip in the wet. Lightness was achieved by using one-piece mouldings utilising thermoplastic rubber.

Johnston determined to find out more about windsurfing shoes and while in Europe for the 1990 World Cup he visited a French company, Okespor, one of the leading manufacturers of specialist sporting footwear for sports such as windsurfing, golf and ice-skating. Johnston met with an Okespor director, Roger Ours. Impressed by what Okespor was doing, Johnston commissioned the company to make a prototype soccer boot. The boot would utilise the same thermoplastic as the windsurfing shoe to provide grip in the wet, but with a flattened top to give a larger area of contact with the ball. The new design was actually based on a modified golf shoe and development of the prototype cost Johnston £15,000.

Testing the boot against a wall outside the Okespor factory in Paris, Johnston found it provided much improved control but with only a modest improvement in grip. To improve grip Johnston etched grooves into the boot to improve grip in the manner of a car tyre. The result was improved grip but at the expense of reduced control! Johnston experimented further, but even after three or four months' effort he had made little improvement. Then one day while visiting a children's toy store the idea came to him to use the same rubber as used for toy "superballs" which have a very high rebound capability. Johnston bought some superballs and tried attaching pieces from them to the boot. The result was a dramatic improvement in performance.

A specialist rubber consultancy advised Johnston on how to obtain the rebound capability he required and a low rate of wear by vulcanising the rubber. However, injection moulding a boot had proved prohibitively expensive to develop further, so Johnston devised a flat mould incorporating the same fins as before but which could easily be vulcanised.

One cold winter's day Johnston tried the new boot against the wall of a tennis club in Paris. He was delighted and got a young player from the Paris St Germain team to try the new boot. Johnston was convinced the new boot gave a player's shot greater power and greater accuracy.

However, by now he had spent £250,000 of his own money and having patented his final design, he decided to get someone else to make it. He approached the sports footwear manufacturer Adidas in Nuremberg. At first sceptical, their scientists agreed to test the boot and compare it with their conventional leather boots. A few weeks later he was summoned to hear the results of the tests. Tense at the prospect of having his design rejected, Johnston need not have worried as Adidas' scientists gave him a standing ovation when they announced the results. Adidas offered Johnston a deal whereby he would work with their designers to produce a marketable product. Adidas called the new boot The Predator. Launched in 1994, two years later more than a million pairs had been sold, and by 2004 it was the world's best selling football boot.

Source: Taylor (1996), www.press.adidas.com, Sept 2009.

Employees

Employees are a much under-estimated source of innovation, and yet Adam Smith (1776) in *The Wealth of Nations* noted that employees, by virtue of their close involvement in work, often find "easier and readier methods of performing it".

Today a small number of companies have actively recognised the value of Adam Smith's observation. Some companies operate "suggestion schemes" that encourage and reward employees who come up with ideas for new products and services or devise improvements in production processes. Other companies take the suggestion scheme a stage further and allow their employees to devote a modest proportion of their time at work to developing new ideas. WL Gore & Associates, the manufacturer of the waterproof fabric Gore-tex, for instance actively encourages its employees to spend around 10 per cent of their time working on speculative ideas (Deutschman, 2004). 3M operates a similar scheme, referring to this type of activity as "bootlegging".

As companies come increasingly to recognise the importance of innovation in providing them with competitive advantage, then we may well see more companies devising ways of encouraging employee innovation.

Outsiders

A consistent feature of innovation over many years, has been the substantial proportion derived, not from those working within a given technological paradigm (see Chapter 3), but from outsiders who have hitherto had little to do with it. There is a case for arguing that outsiders provide an important source of innovation. Table 5.2 provides some examples of innovations developed by outsiders.

Innovation	Company	Innovator	Date
Photocopier	Haloid Corporation	Chester Carlson	1938
Personal computer	Apple Computer	Steve Jobs & Steve Wozniak	1977
Carbon fibre Formula One racing car	McLaren-International	John Barnard	1981
Internet bookstore	Amazon.com	Jeff Bezos	1995

TABLE 5.2 Outsiders as innovators

To what extent were they outsiders? Chester Carlson, the inventor of the photocopier, worked for P.R. Mallory & Company a manufacturer of electrical and electronic components (later better known for its Duracell batteries), analysing patents (Owen, 2004). Steve Jobs and Steve Wozniak, the pioneering Apple computer innovators (Campbell-Kelly, 2003), were college drop-outs and although Wozniak worked for Hewlett-Packard, he was in calculators, not computers. John Barnard, the designer of the McLaren MP4, the world's first carbon fibre racing car, was new to Formula One, having previously worked in the US on Indycars (Cooper, 1999). Finally, Jeff Bezos, who pioneered Internet-based retailing through the creation of Amazon.com, was a fund manager in the financial services industry (Cassidy, 2002).

None of these individuals worked in the field in which they were to achieve success as innovators. They were not part of the community in which their innovation was based and in that sense they were outsiders.

What do outsiders have that industry insiders lack? In analysing why outsiders are important as a source of innovation it is worth exploring the role of industry insiders. Within any industry there will tend to be what Galbraith (1958: p35) describes as the "conventional wisdom," which comprises "the ideas which are esteemed for their acceptability". In more technologically based industries this may amount to what Dosi (1982) terms a "technological paradigm" (see Chapter 3) where the domain of what is technologically possible is informally prescribed by industry insiders. In short, assumptions may well be deeply embedded and as such go unquestioned. Where people work in a group of like-minded specialists or belong to such groups, the phenomenon may be even more pronounced. Similarly, groups can be insulated from the world around them, sharing a collective perspective that leads all too easily to assumptions and ideas going unquestioned. The insularity may be worse if firms have close relationships with their customers. It was noted by Christensen (1997) that, in some circumstances, paying close attention to customers and customer needs may actually be counter-productive for innovation, in so far as it leads to greater insularity as the firm's outlook becomes more specialised and ignores some of the wider trends in technology and potential customers.

Outsiders may be able to avoid at least some of these pitfalls. Since they are not part of an established community, they are likely to have fewer inhibitions when it comes to challenging accepted ideas. Similarly, outsiders may be more willing to try unorthodox ideas precisely because they are not familiar with the "conventional wisdom". The case of Chester Carlson illustrates this well. When trying to develop a means of copying he found that the conventional wisdom prescribed chemical methods for reproducing photographs, a field closely related to his experimental work on document copying. Lacking expertise in chemistry, Carlson was obliged to pursue a completely different direction involving the use of an electrical method which he later called "electrophotography" (Van Dulken, 2000). As well as being willing to try unorthodox ideas and approaches, outsiders may also be more willing to try simple ideas. However, one of the biggest advantages enjoyed by outsiders is that they often have external contacts in fields which may be unrelated but nonetheless prove useful. A feature of these contacts is likely to be their diversity, enabling the innovator to draw from a relatively wide knowledge base. This was true of John Barnard when he designed the McLaren MP4 racing car. The established practice was for the chassis of a racing car to be constructed from sheets of aluminium rivetted together to form a tub. This was light, strong and relatively easy to build. While carbon fibre had been used on racing cars, it had only been used for single components, such as the aerodynamic wing at the rear of the car. The idea of building the whole chassis (which was the main part of the car) from carbon fibre was revolutionary. However, Barnard had a friend who worked for British Aerospace in Weybridge where the Harrier jet was built. The friend explained how carbon fibre was being used in the aerospace industry. In this way Barnard was able to confirm that his idea was feasible. Unfortunately, it still proved impossible to get anyone in the UK to undertake the construction of anything as big as a car chassis from carbon fibre. At this point Barnard was again able to call on one of his contacts outside Formula One, in this case a former colleague from the US, who suggested that Hercules Aerospace of Salt Lake City, Utah, who built guided missile components using carbon fibre, might be able to help. (Henry, 1988). Hercules Aerospace not only had the expertise and the facilities, they also had an R&D section willing to undertake one-off jobs. Thus outsiders may possess a range of advantages over industry insiders – not only are they likely to be more open to new approaches and willing to challenge existing ideas, but the range of external contacts they can draw on means their absorptive capacity, as far as external linkages are concerned, is likely to be greater too.

Spill-overs

Spill-overs typically occur when one firm benefits from another firm's investment in R&D. Afuah (2003) gives the example of a firm conducting research on cholesterol drugs, where the knowledge that it gains about how the body makes cholesterol spills over to its competitors. The nature of spill-overs can vary, but they might for instance result from one firm making an investment in R&D that leads to a scientific discovery or development of a new product that other firms are able to imitate or copy. Alternatively, if the firm that has developed the new product chooses not to commercialise it, it might license it to others. Either way a firm, other than the one that made the initial investment, is able to bring an innovative new product to market. Two examples illustrate this source of innovation. Dan Bricklin and his company, Software Arts, developed VisiCalc, the world's first spreadsheet in the late 1970s. However, the spreadsheet idea was soon copied by other firms including Lotus with its spreadsheet 1-2-3, Borland with Quattro and Microsoft with Multiplan (later renamed Excel). Although Software Arts was the first mover (being the first to get a product to market), it was ultimately overtaken first by Lotus and latterly by Microsoft. Quite literally after Software Arts had developed the spreadsheet and proved the concept in the marketplace, the idea then spilled over and became public knowledge to be taken up by others. (At the time software could not be patented in the US, unlike the situation today.) Similarly, when Du Pont developed Teflon in the late 1950s, it chose not to become heavily involved in applications on the grounds that this was not its area of expertise. Instead it was left to Bill Gore, a researcher at Du Pont, to go it alone and develop fabrics using Teflon, in particular the high-performance, weatherproof fabric Gore-tex.

Spill-overs are likely to occur in situations where it is difficult to prevent others from appropriating the benefits from an invention. Intellectual property rights are the means by which inventors normally endeavour to prevent others appropriating benefits. Success is dependent on being able to engage a tight appropriability regime. Sometimes despite best endeavours this proves difficult. Software Arts was hampered by the fact that at the time it developed VisiCalc, software could not be patented and the Software Arts' founders had to rely on copyright. A similar thing happened with EMI's CAT scanner, where the principle was relatively easily understood and complementary assets such as training, product support and servicing proved key features of competitive advantage (Teece, 1986). Under these circumstances, even though patents were employed, it was not possible to prevent knowledge spilling over into the public domain for other firms to take up.

Spill-overs are also more likely in situations where staff move around a lot. This is referred to as staff "churn" and greater mobility of staff tends to mean that just as staff move around, so does knowledge. Similarly, if there is a lot of contact between staff in different companies one can expect the movement of knowledge and therefore spill-overs.

Process needs

Sometimes the demands of a manufacturing process will act as a stimulus to innovation. Abernathy and Utterback (1978) note that this is most likely to occur in industries which have reached a point of maturity in terms of industry evolution, particularly those producing established commodity products in large volumes, such light bulbs, paper, glass, steel and chemicals. Here pressures for cost reduction are like to be at their most intense, acting as a spur to process innovations that can make an already efficient production process even more efficient.

Alistair Pilkington's development of the "float glass" process in the 1960s and 1970s exemplifies just such conditions. At that time the manufacture of plate glass, which was increasingly being used in construction, was expensive and time consuming because it required sheets of glass to be subjected to grinding and polishing in order to obtain a flat surface. The float glass process developed by Pilkington did away with these stages in the production process. Instead glass was drawn directly from the furnace over a bed of molten tin. Although it took several years to perfect this innovation, it did eventually result in plate glass being produced much more quickly and at much lower cost. So great was the improvement that Pilkington's were able to license the process to other glass-makers and it is still widely used today. The significance of float glass as an innovation is that it is a clear case of a process need – in this case effectively a production bottleneck – being the source of the innovation. As is often the case it was the existence of a bottleneck that provided the stimulus to innovate.

CASE STUDY: THE MOUNTAIN BIKE

A sea change in sales of bicycles across North America and Europe has taken place over the last 20 years. This change has seen consumers switch from road bikes to mountain bikes. Introduced into the UK the late 1980s, mountain bikes quickly caught the imagination not only of the emerging "yuppie" culture, but commuters as well, attracted to this stylish but sturdy new type of bicycle (Rosen, 2002: p133). The introduction of this new type of bike led to a new boom in the cycle industry and the emergence of a new dominant design. This was the biggest change in bicycle design since the so-called "safety bicycle" challenged the "penny farthing" back in the 1890s (Berto, 1999: p11). Just how big an impact mountain bikes had on the bicycle can be gauged by sales figures for the UK market. In 1988 sales of mountain bikes made up just 15 per cent of the 2.2-million-unit UK market. Two years later sales of mountain bikes had not only risen dramatically to 50–60 per cent of the bikes sold in the UK, they had helped to push the overall market to 2.8 million units (Rosen, 2002: p133).

Among the changes brought in by the new mountain bikes were a switch to fat "balloon" tyres instead of thin ones, the adoption of an erect riding position instead of a crouched one, the substitution of flat handlebars for dropped ones, the use of front and rear derailleur gears to provide at least 15 speeds, cantilever brakes and thumb operated gear shifters (Berto, 1999: p20). Dramatic though the change was, its origins lie not with the big bicycle manufacturers but with riders themselves. The particular riders all came from Marin County, California on the pacific coast of the US.

Marin County is located to the north of the Golden Gate Bridge in San Francisco, California. It is quite literally on the opposite side of San Francisco bay to Silicon Valley. Marin County is a hilly area comprising dense woodland. These woodland areas cover the slopes of Mount Tamalpais, and in the early 1970s a group of young cyclists, mostly men in their teens and twenties, made up of high school and college students, firemen, bike-shop mechanics and members of the general public, began to use them for off-road racing. They particularly liked the rough fire roads that ran through the forests. These dirt tracks were steep and ideal for downhill racing. One run in particular was the infamous "repack run" a steep descent down Mount Tamalpais that dropped 1,300 feet in less than 2 miles. Riders would make the ascent in the back of a truck and then race each other down. The ride got its name from the effect it had on the bikes taking part. The bikes were single speed models with old fashioned coaster brakes which would overheat with the excessive use to which they were subjected, forcing the rider to repack the hub with grease before making another descent (Rosen, 2002: p135).

Existing commercial road bikes were not suited to the rough conditions (Lüthje *et al.*, 2005). Hence the young downhill racers turned instead to older more robust models. Among the bikes used for downhill racing were old Schwinn models with fat "balloon" tyres. Particularly prized was the Schwinn Excelsior, the classic "newsboy" bike of the 1930s and 1940s. Though the frames of these bikes were heavy, they were sturdy enough to withstand the rough treatment meted out in downhill racing and the extra strength more than compensated for the extra weight. The use of old-fashioned models like the Schwinn, bought second-hand from backyards for no more than a few dollars, led to the bikes being nicknamed "clunkers".

Though the early clunkers were comparatively unsophisticated, their riders gradually found ways of adding features to improve a "clunker" bike's performance for downhill racing.

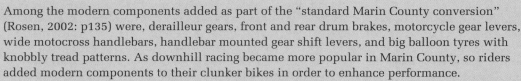

Among the modern components added as part of the "standard Marin County conversion" (Rosen, 2002: p135) were, derailleur gears, front and rear drum brakes, motorcycle gear levers, wide motocross handlebars, handlebar mounted gear shift levers, and big balloon tyres with knobbly tread patterns. As downhill racing became more popular in Marin County, so riders added modern components to their clunker bikes in order to enhance performance.

A cottage industry (Lüthje *et al.*, 2005: p954) developed in Marin County as clunker riders built bikes not only for themselves but for friends and even fellow riders. By the late 1970s half a dozen small assemblers existed in Marin County. However, the core of each bike was still an old Schwinn frame. Unfortunately the supply of old Schwinns was limited and newer Schwinn models were of no use because they were lighter and not as strong. Riders scoured the state of California for old Schwinn bikes that they could convert in to clunkers. Old fashioned cycle repair businesses proved to be a valuable source of supply. When they found a cycle repair business that had old Schwinn models, usually piled up as scrap, riders would buy them up and take them back to Marin County.

Such was the interest generated by clunker bikes that in time the supply of old Schwinn models began to dry up. Some riders then began to build their own frames. These frames improved on the Schwinn design and provided the additional components as standard. Among the first riders to build his own frame was a rider called Joe Breeze (Berto, 1999: p43). Not only was Breeze an experienced downhill racer he was also an experienced frame-builder. His frame was lighter and stronger than the original Schwinn design. Although Joe Breeze only built a handful of frames, the custom-built bikes that he built using his frame were widely seen and much admired. They came to be known as "Breezers" and they were the first modern mountain bikes (Berto, 1999: p45). They quickly acquired a reputation. The Breezers began to expand the market beyond Marin County.

Breeze only produced a very small number of custom-built mountain bikes and there were soon other riders building frames, though always in very small quantities for downhill racing in and around Marin County. However in 1979 it wasn't long before two riders, Gary Fisher and Charlie Kelly teamed to form a company that would produce and sell mountain bikes on a commercial basis. They called their company MountainBikes (Rosen, 2002: p136). Fisher and Kelly needed someone who could build frames, not on a custom basis 'but in quantity' and they teamed up with frame-builder Tom Richey who was based in Palo Alto in Silicon Valley on the other side of San Francisco Bay. Using frames produced by Richey (and occasionally other local frame-builders), MountainBikes built, equipped and marketed the first commercial mountain bikes. Within a couple of years there were more than a dozen firms making mountain bikes, but in each case the quantities produced were relatively small, and the market for mountain bikes was generally confined to the West Coast of the US.

At the same time as the first commercial mountain bikes were appearing on the market, cycle-component manufacturers such as Shimano and Sun Tour began producing and distributing components such as derailleurs, crank sets, tyres and handlebars that were specially designed for off-road use (Lüthje *et al.*, 2005: p954). Not only that, companies like Shimano continued to develop componentry that helped to make cycling, particularly using mountain bikes, more "user friendly". Shimano developed index shifting (for gear changing), integrated gearing and improved braking systems that not only enhanced performance but also improved functionality and reliability (Rosen, 2002: p138), making the use of mountain bikes more straightforward and less problematic for inexperienced users.

In 1982 another Californian cycle company, Specialized, a bike- and bike-parts importer that supplied Marin County bike assemblers, took the next step and brought out the first mass-produced mountain bike (Berto, 1999). They had a Fisher-Kelly-Ritchie design mass produced in Japan. Marketed as the "Stumpjumper" it represented the general public's introduction to the mountain bike. Major cycle manufacturers soon followed with similar designs which were retailed through conventional cycle outlets first across the US and then across Europe.

By the end of the 1980s the mountain bike was fully integrated into the mainstream cycle market. By 2000 total retail sales of cycles in the US amounted to $5.89 billion, of which some 65 per cent were sales of mountain bikes. However, the process of innovation didn't stop here. As mountain biking dramatically increased in popularity so mountain biking enthusiasts found new uses for their machines and the demand for improvements in performance continued. This demand was met by a steady flow of innovations derived from riders.

Sources: Berto (1999); Lüthje et al. (2005); Rosen (2002).

Questions

1 Who were the innovators in this case?

2 From which of the sources identified in this chapter, did the innovation of mountain bikes come?

3 Which model of the innovation process best describes the way in which mountain bikes were developed?

4 Draw a diagram to describe the innovation process and the various parties involved in this instance.

5 What do you understand by the term "cottage" industry, and why were the early producers of "clunkers" thus described?

6 What do you consider is the significance of mountain biking having originated in a narrowly defined geographical area, i.e. Marin County?

7 Which academic writer has been a leading proponent of the notion of user-innovators?

8 Why, according to Christensen, are incumbent firms often relatively slow to innovate?

9 Why were incumbent cycle manufacturers relatively slow to introduce mountain bikes?

10 Which of the four theories of innovation gives prominence to "outsiders" in initiating innovation?

?   Questions for discussion

1 What factors have led to a resurgence of innovation by individuals?

2 Why does innovation require a "flash of genius"?

3 Give examples of how "chance" can lead to innovation.

4 Account for the apparent decline of "corporate labs" as a source of innovation.

5 Why do large firms often have a poor record of innovation?

6 What advantages do users have as a source of innovation?

7 What does Von Hippel mean when he talks about the "democratisation of innovation"?

8 Why are outsiders often an important source of innovation? Give examples of innovations by outsiders.

9 What do we mean by spill-overs and how can spill-overs contribute to innovation? Use an example to illustrate your answer.

10 How can process needs lead to innovation?

Exercises

1 Take two examples of innovation where in each case the source of innovation is different. Compare and contrast the innovation process.

2 Research an example of user innovation. Draw a diagram to show the various parties involved in the process of innovation. Comment upon the different roles taken by these parties and the nature of the links between them.

3 Take an example of user innovation and show how user communities have facilitated user engagement in innovation.

4 Why has innovation become "democratised"?

5 Read *The Economist article* "Out of the Dusty Labs" (*The Economist*, 2007a) and discuss why in spite of advances in technology there has been a relative decline in big industrial R&D laboratories like Bell Labs.

Further reading

1 **Von Hippel, E.** (1976) "The Dominant Role of Users in the Scientific Instrument Innovation Process", *Research Policy,* 5(3), pp212–219.
A path-breaking piece of research that first highlighted the importance of users as a source of innovation. A sequel to this work is in Von Hippel (2005), a book entitled *Democratising Innovation,* which brings Von Hippel's work right up to date. It represents a powerful alternative perspective on the process of innovation that plots the spread of user-initiated innovations. It provides detailed accounts of several recent pieces of research into sectors where user innovators are prevalent. It cites several recent research studies into user innovation.

2 **Leadbeater, C.** (2006) *The User Innovation Revolution: How Business Can Unlock the Value of Customers' Ideas,* National Consumer Council, London.
This report provides an excellent overview of user innovation. It is well structured and written in a clear and readable style. User innovation is contrasted with more traditional forms of innovation. Examples are widely used. Although the emphasis is on the practicalities of user innovation, there are plenty of informative and up-to-date references.

3 **Parsons, M. and M.B. Rose** (2003) *Invisible On Everest: Innovation and the Gear Makers,* Northern Liberties Press, Philadelphia, PA.
A study of the development of the outdoor clothing and equipment industry written by a practitioner and a business historian. Chapter 8 in particular is an invaluable source that

provides accounts of innovations in outdoor clothing (e.g. Gore-tex jackets) initiated by users in the form of climbers and walkers, particularly in the UK in the 1970s, 1980s and 1990s.

4 Meyers, M.A. (2007) *Happy Accidents: Serendipity in Modern Medical Breakthroughs,* Arcade Publishing, New York.

Focusing on the world of medicine, this text shows how in the case of a number of major medical innovations, serendipity was a crucial factor. The text provides detailed case studies showing the role of serendipity in each of four major fields of medical advance – infectious disease, cancer, heart disease, and mental disorders.

CHAPTER

06

The process of innovation

❖ OBJECTIVES

When you have completed this chapter you will be able to:

❖ differentiate commercialisation from invention

❖ distinguish the steps in the innovation process

❖ differentiate and distinguish the different activities associated with the process of innovation

❖ evaluate the techniques available to facilitate the process of innovation

❖ differentiate and evaluate different models of the innovation process

❖ compare and contrast the open and closed forms of innovation

Introduction

The innovation process is concerned with the various activities necessary to turn an idea or discovery into a commercial product or service which consumers, be they individuals or firms, will purchase. This chapter explores the nature of this process. In particular the various activities involved with the exploitation of inventions to make them into commercially viable products and services are examined and explored. In this way the chapter explains what is involved in carrying out innovation. One might say it looks at how firms innovate.

As well as looking at the activities associated with innovation the chapter also looks at different ways of organising these activities to create a process. Several different models of the innovation process are examined. The existence of a number of models of the process reflects the fact that there are distinct and different ways in which firms approach or carry out innovation. It also reflects the changing nature of innovation, especially the increased importance of knowledge and the various different ways in which that knowledge can be channelled into innovation.

The steps in the innovation process

To progress from an idea to a product or service that is on the market and available for consumers to purchase involves a number of activities that are linked together to form a process. Figure 6.1 presents a generic model of the innovation process. It highlights the main steps that have to be undertaken, shown as a particular sequence starting with the generation of an idea or research leading to new discovery at one end, and the finished product going onto the market at the other. It is important to stress that this is an *idealised* model designed to highlight the activities that have to be undertaken. In real life innovation is rarely as neatly packaged as this. The steps or stages will often not be as clearly differentiated as shown in the model, some may even be absent, and some may not come in quite this sequence. However, for the purposes of explaining the nature of the various activities associated with innovation, it is helpful to use an idealised model and portray innovation as taking place as a generic process comprising well-defined steps or stages.

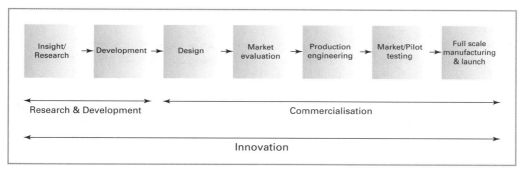

FIGURE 6.1 A generic-model of the innovation process

Figure 6.1 distinguishes a total of seven steps in the innovation process. All seven are associated with innovation and can be said to be part of the innovation process. However, as the diagram makes clear, the first two steps (insight/research and development) are particularly associated with the invention. The remaining five steps turn an invention into an innovation. Labelled "commercialisation" they were briefly touched on in Chapter 1 and are the activities involved in transforming an invention into a commercially viable product. Whereas an invention is usually produced as a one-off, it requires innovation to transform it into something that can be produced in quantity and with the standards of reliability that consumers have come to expect.

Insight/research

This generic model of the innovation process begins with an insight that gives rise to an idea, or a new discovery as the result of research. How is it possible to have dual sourcing in this way? Essentially some innovations, particularly technological ones, are the product of a big investment in research, while others are more the result of individual human ingenuity. The former are likely to be associated with scientific discoveries and technological breakthroughs, the latter with the application of new technologies in order to devise better products.

As we saw in the previous chapter, ideas for innovation arise in all sorts of ways. Sometimes the insight that provides the basis of the idea that leads to the innovation comes from association – quite literally something triggers an idea. Sometimes the idea is an adaptation of an existing product. Sometimes it is by analogy that a way of solving the problem is discovered. And sometimes it just happens, more or less by chance.

However, not all innovations arise from individuals having a fresh insight into something. Much innovation, especially in technological fields, arises as a result of extensive scientific research carried out over many years often by large teams of people. This sort of research is typically carried out in research laboratories. Sometimes the laboratories are located in universities, in some cases they are government laboratories and in others they are the laboratories of large business corporations.

Mini Case

Bell Labs

The Bell Laboratories (or Bell Labs as they are usually known) of the American telecommunications company AT&T have a quite outstanding record of innovation. Since they were founded in 1925, Bell Labs (which today is part of Alcatel-Lucent) has earned six Nobel Prizes and registered more than 25,000 patents. Nor is it just that they have come up with a large number of innovations; many of them have been highly successful and have had a huge impact on the way we live our lives. Amongst the most significant innovations developed at Bell Labs over the years have been: the transistor, electrical sound recording, the solar cell, digital switching and the laser. These innovations were not the product of individual human ingenuity but rather of sustained collective scientific endeavour, for at their height Bell Labs employed a staff of 25,000.

Source: The Economist *(2007a).*

In the mini case shown above, innovations were the result of an intense research effort on the part of the laboratories concerned. These were corporate laboratories run by a private company and their remit was to engage in research in pursuit of technological breakthroughs. Having made the breakthroughs, the technology was then passed on to other parts of the company in order to initiate the rest of the innovation process. This contrasts sharply with insights/ideas of individuals in the sense that the breakthroughs were not associated with specific products or specific customers. In the case of the laser, it was to be many years before the technology was incorporated into products.

Although the innovations emerging via these two different routes – insight of individuals and the research effort of corporate undertakings – can be very different, often there is a degree of overlap. Take the case of Mosaic (Cassidy, 2002; Naughton, 2002), the first web browser that could be used by non-computing people. Mosaic was produced by a team working in a large, publicly funded research laboratory based at the University of Illinois in Urbana-Champaign, yet it was an individual – undergraduate computer science student, Marc Andreessen – who had the insight to create an accessible web browser.

Development

Development is about turning ideas and technologies into products. The product that results from the development stage will not be ready to sell to consumers, but it will have many of the operational characteristics of the final product. In short, the product will work, and so will demonstrate the feasibility of placing it on the market, even if there is still more to do before it is produced in the volumes and to the standards of reliability demanded by consumers.

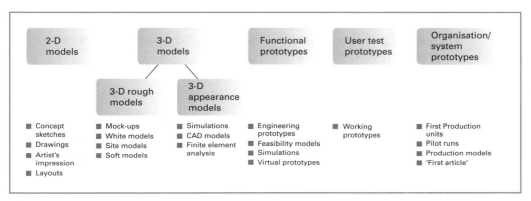

FIGURE 6.2 Models and prototypes
Source: Adapted from Leonard-Barton (1991)

Central to the development stage of the innovation process is the construction of models and prototypes (see Figure 6.2). The purpose of models is to convey the form, style and "feel" of an object (Leonard-Barton, 1991). Models serve to communicate the appearance of the proposed product. They are typically used to give an impression of what the product will actually look like. 3D examples, whether they are mock-ups, white models or computer-aided design (CAD) models, enable people to visualise the form of the product. Computer-generated 3D models can be particularly useful with complex products, where potential problems such as incompatibility, clashes or lack of space, can be highlighted by "walking through" the model long before the real thing is built.

Prototypes in contrast usually have little to do with form and instead are all about function. Hence the term "functional prototypes" in Figure 6.2. Unlike the final product, a prototype is a version of the product constructed as a one-off. Prototypes are typically constructed on a "jobbing" basis using general-purpose equipment rather than specialist purpose-built equipment. They are often made with different materials from those that will go into the final product. This is normally because the materials used for prototypes are easier to work with and more flexible. James Dyson explains how he made prototypes:

> 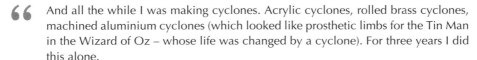 And all the while I was making cyclones. Acrylic cyclones, rolled brass cyclones, machined aluminium cyclones (which looked like prosthetic limbs for the Tin Man in the Wizard of Oz – whose life was changed by a cyclone). For three years I did this alone.
>
> *Dyson (1997: p122)*

Functional prototypes usually form the basis of the experimentation and testing that lies at the heart of development. Experimentation and testing has to take place to ensure that the product works in the way intended, in particular that it will work consistently and with the kind of performance that consumers are likely to demand. This means that development is usually a slow and laborious process. Accounts of new inventions frequently dwell on just how slow and painstaking the development stage can be. James Dyson's account of the development stage of his dual-cyclone vacuum cleaner is typical:

> 66   This is what development is all about. Empirical testing demands that you only ever make one change at a time. It is the Edison principle, and it is bloody slow. It is a thing that takes me ages to explain to my graduate employees at Dyson Appliances, but it is important. They tend to leap into tests, making dozens of radical changes and then stepping back to test their new masterpiece. How do they know which change has improved it and which hasn't?
>
> *Dyson (1997: p124)*   99

Prototypes do have other uses too. They are used to facilitate the integration of components and sub-systems. This is particularly the case with complex products which have a large number of components and sub-systems that have to interact and work together. Another function of prototypes is to facilitate learning. The process of testing enables those who have developed a new technology to learn about its properties, through the acquisition of formal technical knowledge. Where innovation is concerned, knowledge is cumulative and hours spent testing prototypes can help developers to learn about the properties of a new technology. However, learning in terms of the acquisition of tacit or informal knowledge can be just as important. User-test prototypes, in the form of working prototypes, are often used to enable firms to learn about users and user behaviour.

Finally, prototypes have a part to play in risk reduction. Tests carried out with prototypes can help to identify potential risks. It is technological rather than market risks that will be identified in this way. With products that generate significant safety issues if they do not function correctly, as with many mechanical products, this can be extremely important. Of course, having identified these sorts of risks, firms may occasionally choose, for whatever reason, to ignore them.

Mini Case

Hyfil carbon fibre fan blades

The large jet engines developed to power modern wide-bodied jets such as Boeing's 747 "jumbo jet," feature a very large fan at the front of the engine. Aero-engine-manufacturer, Rolls-Royce, developed a novel fan for its RB211 engine. It comprised fan blades made not of metal, but of carbon fibre. Known as Hyfil, the attraction of using what was then an entirely new technology, was that carbon fibre was much lighter than the titanium normally used. The resulting weight-saving made for an appreciably lighter engine, which in turn was much more fuel efficient. However, Rolls-Royce's expectations of carbon fibre were dashed when a prototype engine fitted with a carbon fibre fan was subjected to the "dead chicken" impact tests. This test was designed to simulate a "bird strike" where a bird is sucked into the engine. The test involved firing 2-lb chickens (purchased frozen from a local supermarket and duly defrosted) into the fan blades of a prototype engine operating under full power. The impact caused a blade to snap resulting in a failure to contain the broken blade within the engine casing. The prototype engine's carbon fibre blades, though immensely strong, were insufficiently strong at the edges, which meant there was a risk that in the event of a bird strike when the engine was in service, parts of the engine could have pierced the fuselage or the wings, causing the plane to crash. As a result, carbon fibre blades had to be abandoned and replaced with conventional titanium ones. Rolls-Royce continued to develop carbon fibre eventually using the material for engine nacelle doors.

Source: Spinardi (2002).

By the time the development process is complete, fully functioning prototypes should be in operation. They will not necessarily look like the final product but they will have the final product's operating characteristics. By this point there should be a reasonable degree of certainly that the product will work in the way intended.

Design

Design is required to determine the attributes and features of the final product that will go on sale in the marketplace. This is likely to involve specifying:

- the precise shape of the product
- the tolerances to which it will be manufactured
- the materials to be used in manufacture
- the process by which the product will be manufactured

Design is a process that will generate a design specification that not only includes drawings (normally computer-generated) specifying exactly the form of the product, but also gives details of the geometry, materials and tolerances of all the components that make up the final product. In more complex products there will also be system-level design taking place. This is required in order to show the systems architecture of the product, particularly the way in which the different sub-systems interact in order to achieve a fully functioning product.

In producing a design, the designer has to factor in a number of constraints and come up with a design that will both appeal to the customer and enable the firm to make money. These sorts of constraints are all likely to form part of the design brief. Most designers or design teams will have a design brief to work to that incorporates the requirements of the various stakeholders responsible for the product. Accordingly, the design brief will outline what is required of the design and note a number of constraints. These constraints will typically come from other functional areas of the business such as marketing, manufacturing and finance. The design brief will also include constraints derived from the work that has been done with the prototypes.

The designer's task is to take the design brief and translate it into a design that meets the requirements of the team responsible for the product. This means that it has to operate effectively, while appealing to consumers and being capable of being manufactured at a cost that will both enable the consumer to afford it, and generate a return for the firm.

In reality there may be no single designer. Instead there may well be a design team that brings together different types of designer including: technical designers able to design systems; industrial designers able to ensure functionality; and more traditional designers able to create a form that will have appeal for consumers. Often some or all of these design skills will not be available in-house and will need to be bought in, probably from a design house that has expertise and experience in the field.

Market evaluation

Inventions may be technically very sophisticated and result in what are technically great products but, as Chesbrough (2003a: p64) reminds us:

" There is no inherent value in a technology per se. **"**

Indeed he goes on to point out that:

" the economic value of a technology remains *latent* until it is commercialized in some way. **"**

By latent he means untapped and unrealised. Thus commercialisation has a critical role to play in the innovation process. For its part commercialisation requires the implementation of a "business model". A business model, as we learnt in Chapter 1, serves the dual function of enabling value capture and value creation (Chesbrough, 2006: p108) to take place and it is at the market evaluation stage that decisions about the business model are made.

Value creation as we saw in Chapter 1 involves articulating the "value proposition". This determines the actual value (i.e. benefit) that the new product/service provides for the customer, while at the same time specifying who the customer is. This in turn will mean specifying the particular markets and market segments in which the new product/service can be sold. The extent of the value proposition will not necessarily be related to the sophistication of the technology. Seemingly modest advances in technology can result in products that deliver very powerful value propositions as far as customers are concerned. In the case of photocopiers, the small desk-top copiers developed by Japanese manufacturers in the late 1970s were not technically very sophisticated, but they offered a much more flexible, personalised service (Chesbrough, 2003a), something that customers valued highly. By the same token technical staff often overvalue technical sophistication. Also some products require "complementary assets" such as product support, after sales service and training, and it is essential that this is recognised and arrangements made to ensure such assets will be available. Without these aspects of an innovation being clearly defined there is a real danger that the innovation will appeal to no one other than the inventor.

Value capture on the other hand involves figuring out how to make money from the innovation, in particular the type of revenue generation mechanism that will produce the highest possible return. A variety of revenue generation mechanisms are possible, including outright sale, leasing and the razor and razor blades model where the product is sold at or below cost while consumables are charged at a high margin. Selecting the most appropriate revenue generating mechanism can be critical. This was the case with Xerox and the introduction of the world's first plain paper copier, the Model 914 (Owen, 2004). Recognising it had limited marketing expertise, Xerox initially tried to license its novel plain paper copier technology to big firms like IBM, Kodak and General Electric, but given the sophisticated technology associated with plain paper copying, they figured that the new copiers would be too expensive and were not interested. In the end Xerox hit on the idea of leasing the copier and charging a royalty for any copies beyond normal monthly usage. It was an almost instant success because leasing offered a low-cost way of acquiring the machine, and once acquired companies found the new technology was so easy to use and gave such good results, that staff made far more use of the new copiers than had been expected.

Thus market evaluation has a vital role to play in presenting an accurate picture of the potential value of a new product/service. Without a clear perspective on the value proposition for instance, there is a risk that the value of a new product/service remains unquantified. This in turn raises the prospect that those developing the new technology may seriously overvalue it, resulting in poor sales and ultimately a failed innovation.

Production engineering

Essentially production engineering is concerned with how the product will be manufcatured. Whereas prototypes are usually made on a one-off basis, the final product is likely to be manufactured in substantial quantities and this calls for quite different processes and skills.

The initial decisions surrounding production engineering concern who is to undertake manufacture. Will the product be made in-house or will it be outsourced to subcontractors? Developments in IT combined with improvements in communication mean that it is now possible to design a product on one side of the world and produce it on the other. In a whole range of industries it is now commonplace for manufacturing to be contracted out.

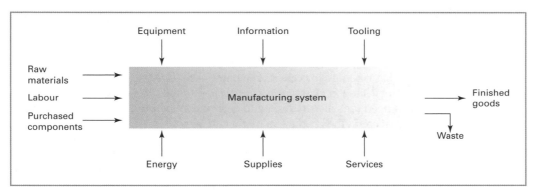

FIGURE 6.3 A manufacturing system
Source: Ulrich and Eppinger (2003)

Assuming manufacture is going to take place in-house, production engineering involves a raft of decisions surrounding the way in which the product is made. Many of these decisions will in turn be linked to the type of manufacturing system (see Figure 6.3) being used. There are very often big differences between a functional prototype used for development and the final product, and this reflects the fact that at the production engineering stage the product is often revised to make it easier and cheaper to manufacture. Such work typically centres on a close examination of assembly operations. With careful preparation and effective design it is usually possible to simplify the design, thereby eliminating a number of assembly operations. Ulrich and Eppinger (2003) provide a number of examples of design changes of this type:

- reducing the parts count
- using standardised components
- using self-aligning parts
- using assembly operations that require a single, linear motion

Changes such as these reflect the volume of production that is anticipated. With the prospect of volume production it is worthwhile redesigning and revising the product in order to make assembly quicker, easier and cheaper.

Trott (2002: p150) gives the example of a toolbox. Manufactured as a prototype, it is produced on a one-off jobbing basis initially in which the various components are held together with industrial fasteners. With a satisfactory prototype, the production-engineering function then proceeds, with the help of the designers, to simplify the design to make it suitable for manufacturing in large batches. This entails eliminating the need for fasteners and investing in specialist machinery that will shape the individual components. The result is a big drop in the number of parts required and an assembly process that involves all the parts being held in place via "push and snap" operations undertaken by assembly workers. Hence one gets a product that has the external characteristics and functionality of the original design and yet is capable of being assembled more quickly and more cheaply. Not only does this indicate the sort of activities carried out at the production-engineering stage, it also illustrates an important principle, highlighted by Trott (2002): namely that, as the volume of production increases so the most appropriate method of manufacture also changes.

Market/pilot testing

Having ensured that the product can be made in a way that will ensure it appeals to consumers, while at the same time making money for the company, further testing has to be carried out to ensure that it can go into the marketplace. The testing is likely to be of two types. There will be market testing to elicit customer reaction to the product, while at the same time there may well be a need for statutory testing to ensure that the product meets appropriate safety requirements or to accredit the product so that it can be sold.

Market testing involves launching the product on a trial basis, usually within a limited geographical area. This kind of testing typically has two objectives, described by Baker and Hart (1999) as mechanical and commercial. Mechanical testing is designed to ensure that the distribution systems that deliver the product to the customer are functioning effectively. With innovations this can be particularly important. By launching the product in a limited and controlled fashion it should be possible to identify potential problems and rectify them. Commercial testing on the other hand is designed to gather data from which to construct sales forecasts and budgets and to see the reaction of competitors.

As well as market testing there may well be a requirement for further physical testing, this time with the final product or something that is very close to the final product. Testing at this stage will have less to do with developing the product and more to do with ensuring it will be safe in the hands of consumers. Consequently, much of the testing at this stage will involve interaction with consumers. Testing may be a statutory requirement or necessary for the product to gain type approval or certification before it can be used to provide public services (e.g. crash tests for cars and blade-off and bird strike tests for aero-engines).

Full-scale manufacture and launch

Before full-scale manufacture can actually take place the equipment that forms part of the manufacturing system (see Figure 6.3) has to be commissioned. This is designed to ensure that not only are the individual items of equipment that comprise the manufacturing system functioning as they should, but that they are also interacting effectively. With a complex manufacturing system and a sophisticated control system this can be a demanding task. Pieces of equipment will often work perfectly in isolation, but put together they become quite ineffective. Consequently, the commissioning process is intended to prove the system and ensure it is functioning as planned.

Even with a fully effective manufacturing system, those who are going to operate it have to be recruited and trained. This is something that has changed over the past 20 years as companies in the West have learnt from Japanese companies the importance of careful planning and preparation as far as the labour force is concerned. Not only is it important to select people with appropriate aptitude and skills, they have to be trained to use the equipment.

Finally manufacturing can begin. Even this is not likely to be full-scale manufacture to begin with. Typically, firms will deliberately plan their production so that initially they are producing at perhaps 20 per cent or 30 per cent capacity. This allows those operating the system to move up the "learning curve" as they become more familiar with the system. The learning curve concerns the way in which, particularly in batch operations, it will often take less time to manufacture the hundredth item than the first. This can be an important feature of manufacturing in some industries. Aerospace is a good example. Firms like Airbus and Boeing find that, even with sophisticated production systems, it will typically take much less time to produce an airliner as output expands. This reflects the fact that this sort of learning relies heavily on tacit knowledge and is a cumulative process. Consequently, as output expands, learning increases and it can take less time to manufacture the product.

There are other reasons why firms will typically "ramp up" (Ulrich and Eppinger, 2003) production gradually from a relatively low base. Products produced during the ramp-up can be evaluated to spot potential flaws. They can also be supplied to preferential customers who will not only evaluate the product but also provide valuable marketing data in terms of their perception of the product. In addition ramping up gradually can also help with stock building. It can be disastrous to raise customer expectations by promoting a new product, only to deny customers access to it because the product has not yet reached retail outlets. Gradually building up production can allow time for distributors to build up stocks prior to the product being formally launched. Then, eventually full-scale production can get under way.

The market-launch phase brings another round of potential problems. The activities involved are likely to be quite different from those encountered earlier, however. Since the market-launch phase is mainly concerned with marketing it will not be covered in detail here.

The market-launch phase essentially requires the co-ordination of a whole range of different activities. Some of the activities include:

- ensuring that retail outlets have appropriate stocks
- booking advertising space
- designing and producing advertisements
- booking exhibition space
- ensuring that literature about the product has been designed, written and printed
- informing the press and ensuring that they have had time to familiarise themselves with the product

The list is at best indicative of the sorts of activities that have to be undertaken. They all form part of the process of introducing the product to the public. While it may require a different set of skills, getting this phase of the innovation process right is just as important as all the others.

This reinforces one of the central features of the innovation process and one that researchers have increasingly come to recognise. It is very easy to see innovation in heroic terms. The pursuit of new ways of doing things, the struggle to get something to work, these are usually the things that people think of when they think of innovation. Yet there is actually a lot more to innovation. It is a lengthy process, even when activities are carried out concurrently. It is also a process that includes many different activities, and all of these activities are important. The feature of the innovation process that is increasingly recognised is that it is important for all of them to be carried out effectively.

Models of the innovation process

While the generic model of the innovation process enables the various activities associated with innovation to be identified, it does not reflect the range of different approaches to innovation that are available. In particular, it fails to take account of some of the newer models of the innovation process that have been introduced in recent years.

Rothwell (1994) identifies no less than five models of the innovation process. Significantly, he suggests that these models form part of a continuum that has seen new models of innovation introduced over the last half-century. All five of these models are presented here.

Technology push

The technology push model (Figure 6.4) is very much the traditional perspective on the process of innovation. It is effectively the research-led version of the generic model presented earlier, since one of the features of this model is that it is driven by developments in science and technology. It assumes that more technology, brought about by additional expenditure on R&D, will lead inexorably to more innovation. The process is entirely linear and sequential, each stage following on from the completion of the previous one. The model virtually ignores the marketplace, which is portrayed as being passive and simply taking what technology has to offer. The model is naïve as far as the process itself is concerned. We are told very little about the nature of the process. Having said that, there are industries where the innovation process does take place in very much this way – for example, the pharmaceutical industry.

FIGURE 6.4 Technology push process
Source: Republished with permission, Emerald Group Publishing Limited

Demand pull

Recognising the passive role given to marketing, theorists in the late 1960s and early 1970s came up with a new perspective on the process of innovation. In the demand pull model, the role of the market is central. According to Rothwell (1994), the move to a more market-centred type of innovation process reflected the maturing of many technology-based industries and a growing realisation that consumer requirements were becoming more sophisticated.

In the demand pull model (Figure 6.5), the market forms the source of ideas for new innovations. Knowledge of consumer requirements is seen as driving research and development rather than the other way around. This is a variant on the generic model, if one sees consumer needs as the source of new ideas that lead to innovation.

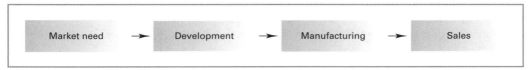

FIGURE 6.5 Demand pull process
Source: Republished with permission, Emerald Group Publishing Limited

This model of the innovation process is appropriate for mature technologies/industries where firms' innovation effort is devoted to minor improvements that are better at meeting consumers' requirements.

Mini Case

Barbed wire

Kevin Costner got it all wrong. In the Western *Open Range* Costner, like other Hollywood actors before him, pits himself and Robert Duvall as prairie cattlemen or "free rangers" fighting a powerful local ranch owner. Only this time the ranch owner has the local town, including the sheriff, in his pocket. In reality ranchers did not need to rely on intimidation, they had barbed wire, and it was barbed wire rather than the six-gun that helped win the West.

As cattle ranches spread across the treeless Great Plains in the 1870s, the ranchers found their activities constrained not by prairie cattlemen like Costner and Duvall, but by a severe shortage of timber for fencing. As Basalla (1988: p51) notes: "Between 1870 and 1880 newspapers in the region devoted more space to fencing matters than to political, military, or economics issues".

Such was the scale of the problem that westward expansion across the vast open spaces of the Great Plains was constrained by the high cost of fencing which was itself a function of the treeless landscape. As Howells (2005) points out, there was a pressing need for a "wooden fence substitute". One solution was the planting of hedges made of Osage orange (Basalla, 1988). Unlike many forms of hedging, the long thorns growing at right angles to the stem on the Osage bush meant it was sturdy enough to restrain cattle. Native to Texas and Arkansas, it was planted in the Great Plains region. Unfortunately it proved too slow-growing to be entirely effective. Smooth-wire fencing provided a cheap substitute, but it was ineffective in restraining roaming livestock, which loosened the fencing poles and broke the wire by constantly rubbing against it.

It was against this background of well-defined and articulated consumer need holding back economic development, that in the 1870s inventors in Illinois on the eastern edge of the Great Plains began to experiment with various forms of barb that mimicked the Osage bush, in order to create a new type of fencing. J.F. Gidden perfected and patented a form of wire that became the pattern followed by most other wire producers. Very quickly barbed wire solved the fencing problem and, with the bottleneck removed, economic development could continue westward, to the detriment of prairie cattlemen.

Sources: Basalla (1988); Howells (2005).

Coupling

For many industries both technology push and demand pull innovation processes are flawed. They both rely on innovation being a linear, sequential process. Unfortunately, processes like this are said by some to encourage what is often described as 'over the wall' behaviour (Trott, 2002: p215), where the departments responsible for each stage carry out their task in isolation, providing little in the way of guidance and help to the next department. It was to overcome precisely these kind of problems that the coupling model (Figure 6.6) evolved.

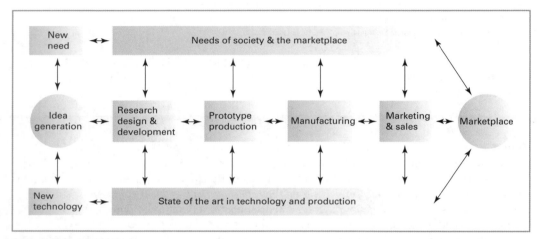

FIGURE 6.6 Coupling model process
Source: Republished with permission, Emerald Group Publishing Limited

A crucial difference between this model and the earlier ones is the presence of "feedback loops". The lines of communication between the various functions carry a two-way traffic. No longer can functions operate on an "over the wall" basis, forgetting about the process once their immediate tasks have been completed. In the coupling model one has a series of distinct functions or stages, but they are interacting and interdependent. Each phase is also linked or coupled (hence the name) to the marketplace (see top of diagram) and the state of technology (see bottom of diagram).

Integrated

The 1980s were characterised by powerful forces for change. In many fields the old order and the old certainties that had prevailed in the years since the Second World War gave way to new and much more intense competitive pressures. Developments in technology, both in the computing and the communications fields, led to the introduction of IT-based manufacturing systems that shortened product life cycles. In parallel with changes in manufacturing technology came new ideas about manufacturing management. Many of these new ideas, such as just-in-time production and set-up reduction, came from Japan. Among the most powerful ideas were notions of concurrent or parallel development. Applied to new product development, this implies an end to the strictly linear and sequential processes prevalent in the three models of the innovation process presented so far. Japanese companies rely on project teams that integrate the various functions. Under such arrangements the functions are brought into the new product development process from the start, and joint group meetings ensure that issues such as manufacturability are considered early in the process rather than near the end. Team-based new product development therefore represents a much more integrated process (Figure 6.7).

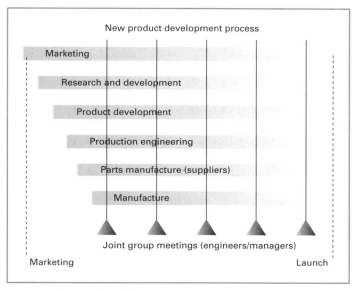

FIGURE 6.7 Integrated model process
Source: Republished with permission, Emerald Group Publishing Limited

Mini Case

Lessons from Apple

Not invented here, and very welcome.

Innovation can come from without as well as within. Apple is generally perceived to be an innovator in the tradition of Thomas Edison or Bell Laboratories, employing gifted scientists and engineers who come up with new ideas and new products that are the result of their moments of inspiration. In fact, its real skill lies in bringing together its own ideas with technologies from outside and then wrapping the results in elegant software and stylish design. The idea for the iPod, for example, was originally dreamt up by a consultant whom Apple hired to run the project. It was assembled by combining off-the-shelf parts with in-house ingredients such as its distinctive, easily used system of controls. And it was designed to work closely with Apple's iTunes jukebox software, which was also bought in and then overhauled and improved. Apple is, in short, an orchestrator and integrator of technologies, unafraid to bring in ideas from outside but always adding its own twists.

This approach, known as "network innovation," is not limited to electronics. It has also been embraced by companies such as Nike, Rolls-Royce, Marks and Spencer and several drugs giants, who now appreciate the value of admitting that not all good ideas start at home. Making network innovation work involves cultivating contacts with start-ups and academic researchers, constantly scouting for new ideas and ensuring that engineers do not fall prey to "not invented here" syndrome, which always values in-house ideas over those from outside.

Source: Adapted from The Economist *(2007b).*

Network

Finally, the 1990s saw the advent of what Rothwell (1994) describes as a "fifth-generation" innovation process. Termed the network model (Figure 6.8), this reflects the way in which some organisations increasingly rely not only on their own internal resources for innovation, but instead draw on external resources, either for the development of major sub-systems and components or to undertake specific phases of the innovation process (see Table 6.1). This is normally achieved through alliances, agreements and contracts with third-party organisations. The use of networks reflects continuing developments in computing and communications which have facilitated information transfer and outsourcing. The resulting vertical disintegration has led to organisations ceasing certain activities such as research and some forms of development, preferring instead to buy them in as and when needed. Companies that utilise the network model of innovation increasingly take on the role of systems integrator where they manage the innovation process and the integration of the development activities carried out by partners. An example would be Apple's role in developing the iPod (see mini case).

Company	Product	External partners
Apple	iPod	Sony (battery); Toshiba (hard disk); PortalPlayer (CPU); Wolfson (DAC); Texas Instruments (FireWire interface controller); Linear Technologies Inc (power management system)
Marks & Spencer	Chilled ready meals	Small food manufacturers (meals); Packaging firms (microwave tolerant packaging); Logistics firms (transport); Computer companies (EPOS)
Rolls-Royce	Trent 900 engine	Hamilton Sundstrand (FADEC); Fiat Avio (gearbox); Marubeni (engine components); Volvo (intermediate compressor); ITP (low pressure turbine); Goodrich (fan casings); Honeywell (pneumatic system)

TABLE 6.1 Examples of network innovation
Sources: Cox *et al.* (2003); Sherman (2002)

Network innovation is by no means universally practised. Only in certain industry sectors has it proved popular. Good examples are pharmaceuticals, aerospace and computing. In pharmaceuticals, developments in biotechnology have fostered the growth of small specialist biotechnology companies on which large pharmaceutical companies increasingly rely as a source of innovation. In computing, the growth of specialist companies making computer peripherals has helped to make Silicon Valley in California viable. Finally, in aerospace, the prohibitive cost of developing a new airliner or a new engine has led many aerospace giants to put together joint ventures and partnerships that bring together a number of suppliers to engage jointly in new product development.

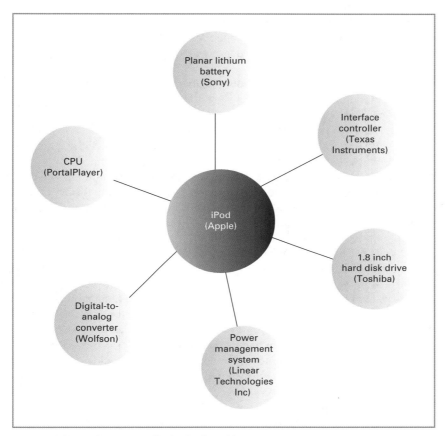

FIGURE 6.8 Network model: the iPod – Apple and its partners
Source: Sherman (2002)

While developments in IT and communications have helped to make the sort of "collaborative innovation" implied by the network model viable (i.e. through the electronic transfer of CAD-generated design data to the manufacturing function), the use of this approach is not entirely the result of facilitating factors. Rising consumer expectations and increasing emphasis on choice and variety have also helped to fuel an increasing emphasis on innovation and new-product development. Thus, companies anxious to provide consumers with ever greater choice have increasingly sought to look outside their own organisation for ideas and technologies. By looking outside they have access to a greater range of capabilities. Again the Apple iPod provides a very good example of this type of network innovation, for although Apple can undoubtedly claim the credit for this highly successful innovation, in reality, as Figure 6.8 shows, the company relied on a number of key partners for many aspects of the innovation.

Connect & Develop

Proctor and Gamble is a multinational company well known for its wide range of consumer products, covering everything from snacks to hygiene products and detergents. It has a massive research capability employing some 7,500 scientists whose task is to generate a steady stream of new products. A measure of this research capability is Proctor and Gamble's $5 million annual spend on R&D and the eight patents per day that its scientists notch up (Dodgson, Gann and Slater, 2006).

However, by 2000 there was concern about the ability of the company's conventional invent-it-ourselves model of innovation to deliver a sufficient number of new products. The company's senior management realised that changes in the business environment meant that increasingly innovation was being carried out by small and medium-sized companies. Recognising that simply spending more on R&D was unlikely to produce the number of new products required, Proctor and Gamble opted for a new strategy.

Called "Connect & Develop," the new strategy was based on research into the performance of a small number of innovations derived not from the company's own labs but from external sources (i.e. other companies, universities, etc.), which showed that many of these innovations had been very successful. The goal of the Connect & Develop strategy was that ultimately some 50 per cent of the company's innovations should come from external sources. Retaining its commitment to its existing lab's the company hoped that by using external sources as well it could significantly increase its overall level of innovation. As part of the strategy Proctor and Gamble systematically searches throughout the world for promising ideas and technologies, and then applies its own manufacturing, marketing and procurement capabilities to turn them into successful innovations. Examples of products that have come through this route are: Olay Regenerist, Swiffer Dusters and Crest SpinBrush.

How does it work? Every year Proctor and Gamble produces a top-ten needs list for each of its businesses, showing those consumer needs which, if addressed, would generate the highest sales growth. The needs lists are then developed into scientific problems to be solved. The company uses its own proprietary networks as well as a range of open networks, to seek out potential technologies that can address these needs. The proprietary networks include some 70 technology entrepreneurs working out of 6 regional connect-and-develop hubs focusing on technologies that are the speciality of the region, who seek out potential new technologies by meeting with university and industry researchers around the world. Proctor and Gamble also uses its top 15 suppliers as a network. The open networks used comprise a range of independent technology-seeking networks, including NineSigma and Innocentive, commercial enterprises who specialise in connecting companies seeking solutions to technology problems with companies, universities, government and private labs and consultants with the capability to solve the problems. Once a potential technology has been identified through one of the networks, then it is given an initial screening by one of the technology entrepreneurs before being sent to the business concerned for more detailed evaluation by its R&D staff and brand managers. If the technology is evaluated positively then the company's external business development (EBD) group will begin negotiations to acquire a licence or set up an appropriate form of collaboration. Proctor and Gamble hasn't yet reached its target for externally sourced innovations, but at 35 per cent it is well on the way. More significantly the Connect & Develop strategy has effected a cultural change within the company in terms of how it goes about innovation.

Source: Huston and Sakkab (2006).

Open innovation

The first four of Rothwell's five models are all effectively *closed* models of innovation, in which a single firm uses its own internal resources and capabilities to undertake all the activities that form part of the generic innovation process. Such companies are typically vertically integrated. In contrast much attention has in recent years come to focus on what Chesbrough (2003a) terms "open innovation," where innovating companies increasingly utilise external sources in order to carry out innovation.

The network model is effectively a form of open innovation, because it relies on a measure of externalisation in order to complete the activities required for innovation. The ideas/discoveries will come from inside the company, but when it comes to developing them into innovations, outside external organisations may be used for certain activities. In the development of chilled ready-meals for example, Marks & Spencer relied upon a number of external partner organisations to implement its ideas for innovation (Cox *et al.*, 2003). Other examples are shown in Table 6.1.

Open innovation carries the logic of the network model a stage further. With open innovation firms utilise external resources for innovation in one of two possible ways:

- either, taking internally generated ideas/discoveries and using an external route to market via a third party organisation (perhaps through a licensing agreement) so that the latter then develops the ideas/discoveries into marketable products/services which it then markets;

- or, actually sourcing ideas/discoveries themselves from external organisations, with subsequent development taking place internally using the firm's own resources/facilities.

Each of these possible paths to innovation is portrayed in Figure 6.9, which also shows the route followed for closed innovation.

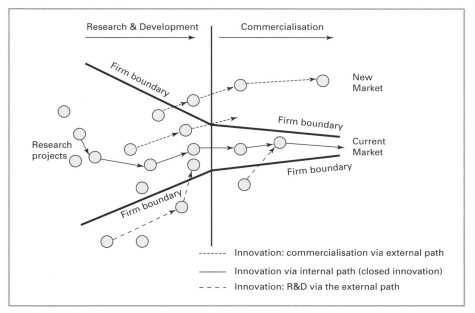

FIGURE 6.9 Open innovation
Source: Adapted from Chesbrough (2003a)

The rise of open innovation has been matched by the decline of the "corporate" form of innovation which Chesbrough (2003a) terms "closed innovation". Under this system innovation was a technology-led affair mainly undertaken by large, vertically integrated, companies with huge corporate R&D labs, like Xerox's PARC and AT&T's and Bell Labs (Vaitheeswaran, 2007), which were the source of new discoveries driving the innovation process, and where success relied on retaining tight control of intellectual property and being first to market. This was the model of innovation that was extolled by Schumpeter and became dominant during the second-half of the twentieth century. However, the rise of first network-based models of innovation and now open innovation has challenged (but by no means eliminated) the closed innovation model.

Why? What has led to this change? The reasons for this are changes in the external environment, or what Chesbrough (2003a: pxxv) refers to as the "landscape". Of these changes two have been of particular significance:

- greater mobility of knowledge, brought about by the growth of universities and their research capability, a massive increase in the proportion of graduates in the labour force and greatly increased mobility of staff who are no longer willing to stay with the same company for life
- greater mobility of capital which, through the rise of venture capital in all its forms, has led to a big growth in technology-based spin-off, spin-out and new start companies

Open innovation implies a clear move away from an approach to innovation based on vertical integration (the old corporate model) to one based on vertical disintegration, where innovation instead becomes much more flexible both in sourcing new ideas/discoveries and in realising the commercial potential of internally generated ideas/discoveries. Businesses that take the open innovation route become very much more fluid and flexible with ideas, discoveries and inventions increasingly flowing both in and out of the organisation (Dodgson *et al.*, 2008).

However, there is considerably more to open innovation than simply increased flexibility. Some of the key features of open innovation are:

- it explicitly recognises that no one firm can hire all the best brains, hence the importance of accessing external knowledge/expertise
- networking in various forms can provide the means of linking to external knowledge/ expertise
- it recognises that there are other innovation strategies than a first mover strategy
- the management of intellectual property is vitally important in order to ensure to maximise its value, but this can be achieved in a variety of ways

Under these circumstances it becomes vitally important to extract as much knowledge from the external environment as possible.

How is open innovation conducted? If we think of open innovation as having two forms:

- external sources
- external routes

then for each there are a range of options available. Among the external sources are large companies, start-up companies, universities and technology brokers. Large companies will tend to be ones with significant research facilities that may have intellectual property that falls outside their normal product portfolio; start-up companies are likely to be small, highly specialised enterprises with a research capability but without the resources to bring new products to market; universities are likely to have intellectual property derived from their research activities; and technology brokers are in the business of linking owners of intellectual property with users of intellectual property. External routes on the other hand will typically be some form of licensing agreement or new venture creation, perhaps through a joint venture or a spin-off company.

It would be wrong to imagine that open and closed innovation are mutually exclusive choices. They are not. Most companies that use open innovation are likely to use closed innovation as well. Proctor and Gamble, one of the best known users of open innovation, for example currently obtains about 35 per cent of its innovation (Huston and Sakkab, 2006) from external sources. Impressive though this figure is, it still means that Proctor and Gamble maintains a very substantial research capability, though one that is now complemented by externally sourced technologies.

CASE STUDY: THE CHILLED MEALS REVOLUTION

What did you have for dinner last night? We are increasingly eating a range of exotic meals eaten not in restaurants or collected from the takeaway but prepared in our own homes in a matter of minutes. Chicken tikka, chicken Madras, mango chicken curry, chicken chow mein, these are just a few from the wide range of ready-meals that are available in the chiller cabinets of our supermarkets these days. They offer high-quality, ready-prepared meals at reasonable prices. But it was not always so. Chilled ready-meals such as chicken tikka are a relatively recent innovation that only began to appear on our supermarket shelves in the early 1990s, pioneered initially by multiple retailer Marks & Spencer.

Prior to the introduction of chilled food, ready-made meals were available in our supermarkets, but they came as frozen foods. Unilever's frozen food subsidiary Birds Eye introduced the first "TV dinners" as they were known in 1969. Over the years, the freezer cabinets of Britain's supermarkets became home to a range of ready-meals. Social changes in the 1970s and 1980s, such as the increasing number of women working full-time and the increasing number of single-person households meant a steady increase in the popularity of these kinds of products. Though the range of meals became steadily more sophisticated, the products themselves did not. They might look attractive, but when it came to eating them, most were nothing like the ready-meals we have today. As frozen foods, they were hampered by the fact that freezing food and then thawing it to reconstitute it had an adverse effect on both the texture and the flavour of the food that inevitably made the meals less palatable. This was a major drawback that constrained the growth of the market for ready-prepared meals sold in supermarkets. The solution was not to freeze the food but simply to chill it. Chilling involves lowering the temperature of the food to about 5 degrees centigrade but not actually freezing it. Keeping food at a low temperature helps to preserve it (for a time at least), while not actually freezing it avoids the problem of damaging the texture and flavour of the food. However, as Cox *et al.* (1999) point out, chilling presents formidable logistical difficulties, since the meals are highly perishable and have a very limited shelf-life with the result that the maximum period of time that can elapse between production and final consumption of such products is a few days rather than weeks or months in the case of frozen foods. Without very careful and precise co-ordination of supply and demand, the premium price associated with delivering to the consumer a superior product would be more than absorbed by high wastage rates.

By the late 1980s Marks & Spencer felt recent developments in technology, combined with their proven and long-standing skills in relational contracting in the textile and clothing sector, offered scope for offering a range of chilled products in the form of ready-meals.

The technological developments that formed part of this innovation covered both consumption and production. On the consumption side, the introduction of microwave ovens in the early 1970s and their widespread use in domestic households meant that a means of quickly and easily preparing and heating chilled ready-meals was readily available. On the production side, developments in IT systems, especially in the field of communications technology and data management, helped to provide retailers with an unprecedented degree of control over their operations.

The IT developments centred on electronic point of sale (EPOS) systems based on laser-scanning technology introduced in the 1980s. These helped to transform retailers' ability to exercise detailed operational control over the goods going through their stores. EPOS systems, which scanned all the goods going through the check-outs, enabled retailers to link their inventory replenishment to consumer requirements. No longer did they have to estimate demand, since EPOS systems enabled them to link their purchases of replacement inventory directly to consumer purchases. A key feature of this was the use of electronic data interchange (EDI) systems. EDI in particular enabled retailers to manage inter-firm co-ordination, between themselves, manufacturers and distributors, in real time. Working in real time brought an unprecedented degree of precision, both to inventory management and purchasing. No longer was it necessary to estimate demand by laboriously checking the stock on the shelves to see which were empty or at least needed re-stocking. EPOS systems using bar codes on all items of stock did this automatically. The systems were also highly efficient as EDI replaced paper-based administrative systems with computer links. Effective inter-firm co-ordination required a high degree of systems compatibility in order to provide links that would facilitate data transfer between retailers, manufacturers and logistics/distribution companies. The achievement of the necessary compatibility can be directly attributed to the work of a trade association (Bamfield, 1994), the Institute of Grocery Distributors (IGD). The IGD brought together retailers, manufacturers and distributors to establish a set of common standards for bar-coding. Bar-coding was an essentially element in ensuring rapid and easy data transfer.

To add to the wealth of data that retailers now possessed in relation to the goods going through their stores came developments in data warehousing and data mining. Retailers introduced store loyalty cards in the 1990s so that they could link the data coming from their EPOS/EDI systems to individual consumers. This in turn permitted retailers to record the activities of consumers on a regular basis. Then, using data mining they could establish consumer buying patterns and trends. Armed with this sort of data, retailers were in a position to exercise a high level of co-ordination between all the parties involved in producing and selling goods to consumers. This was particularly significant for food items where the perishable nature of the goods was an important issue.

The introduction of these various technologies created an infrastructure that provided scope for innovation in ready-meals, driven not by manufacturers but by retailers. Marks & Spencer began with a range of meat pies and quiches marketed under its St Michael brand name. Their strategy for chilled ready-meals was that they should be promoted as a substitute for takeaway meals or even restaurant meals, which had been increasing both in popularity and the range of dishes available. The key elements in promoting these products were variety, novelty and quality (Cox *et al.*, 2003). As such chilled ready-meals were marketed as high-quality, premium-priced products.

Marks & Spencer's strategy was that as quality substitutes for restaurant meals, their range of chilled ready-meals should offer an extensive and constantly changing array of new products that mirrored customer eating trends. To provide them with the necessary variety and choice, as well as new offerings, they turned to small specialist food manufacturers. These ranged from micro-kitchens employing less than five people to larger concerns such as Hazlewood Foods, though most were relatively small concerns. For retailers like Marks & Spencer the advantage of using several small manufacturers was the flexibility offered by small suppliers (Cox *et al.*, 1999). These small firms manufacture in small batches, which is highly desirable given the relatively short shelf-life of the product. Being small, these firms are also highly specialised. Many specialise in particular product bases (e.g. poultry, fish, etc.) and "ethnic" recipes (e.g. Indian, Thai, Italian, etc.). Specialisation provides scope for retailers offering a very broad product range and also facilitates the rapid development of new products. Given the access to customer behaviour provided by customer loyalty schemes (like Tesco's clubcard), retailers were anxious to be able to identify new market niches and fill them with new products as quickly as possible. Of the small specialist food manufacturers used by the major retailers, S & A Foods of Derby is typical. The company was started in 1986 by Perween Warsi after she despaired of ever finding a decent samosa in her local supermarket in Derby. S & A Foods began as a micro-kitchen supplying a range of chilled Indian ready-meals sold as own label products for retailers like Marks & Spencer and has grown to the point where it has two factories manufacturing Indian meals. As a specialist food manufacturer S & A Foods does not engage in marketing, branding or distribution, focusing its efforts instead on developing new products.

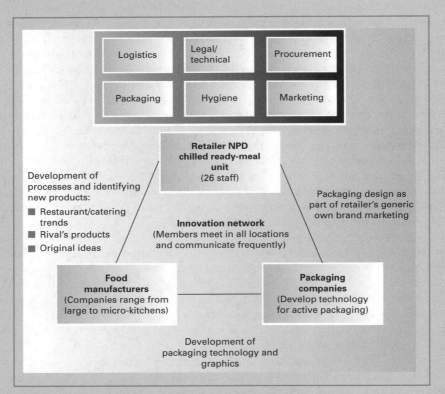

FIGURE 6.10 The innovation network for chilled ready-meals
Source: Cox *et al.* (2003)

In developing chilled ready-meals, firms like Marks & Spencer assembled new product-development teams that brought together employees from the specialist food manufacturers with employees from the packaging companies and their own staff drawn from their food technology and hygiene departments. The new product teams formed a network for pooling knowledge and drawing on data from a variety of sources in order to facilitate innovation. From the retailer came data on purchasing patterns and trends derived from its IT system. From the specialist food manufacturers came ideas for new dishes and guidance on which dishes would be more suitable for chilling and re-heating. From the packaging companies came guidance on packaging materials suitable for use in microwave ovens. This was particularly important as microwavable meals necessitated the development of "active" forms of packaging designed specially for use in microwave ovens. Working on a collaborative basis the new product development teams devised a range of ready-meals suitable for chilling.

While the innovation network based on new product development teams generated new products, retailers like Marks & Spencer were able to use their IT systems to co-ordinate product and distribution to ensure that the right amount of stock got to the right store at the right time at the right temperature so that it was available when consumers wanted it.

To gauge the success of chilled ready-meals as an innovation one has only to travel a few miles on a motorway and count the number of large trucks with the words "Chilled Distribution" painted on the side. Similarly, a visit to any supermarket will reveal rows of chiller cabinets offering a wide range of Indian, Chinese, Thai, Italian and traditional British ready-meals. A more conventional evaluation reveals that sales of chilled ready-meals almost doubled between 1993 and 1999.

Year	£m	Index
1993	340	100
1994	380	112
1995	435	130
1996	475	140
1997	497	146
1998	551	162
1999	596	175

TABLE 6.2 UK retail sales of chilled ready-meals 1993–1999
Source: Cox *et al.* (2003)

Questions

1 Why did retailers like Marks & Spencer choose to use small firms as their suppliers?
2 What aspect of Marks & Spencer's prior knowledge and experience proved particularly useful in terms of the innovation process used to develop chilled ready-meals?
3 Which model of the innovation process did Marks & Spencer adopt in order to bring about the innovation of chilled ready-meals?
4 What benefits did Marks & Spencer (and the other retailers) obtain from the particular innovation process they used?
5 What alternative models of the innovation process might Marks & Spencer have used?
6 What enabling factors permitted firms like Marks & Spencer to use their chosen model of the innovation process?
7 What do you think were the critical factors in achieving successful innovation in this case?
8 Why was co-ordination vitally important and how was it achieved?

9 Using an appropriate series of market research reports, such as Mintel or Key Note reports, show:

■ how the market for chilled ready-meals has grown in the last decade

■ how the shares of the chilled ready-meal market have changed over the last decade.

Questions for discussion

1 Why is innovation often a lengthy process?

2 Where do innovations come from?

3 What are the relative merits of technological change and the market as sources of innovation?

4 Why can it be problematic portraying innovation as a series of phases?

5 Distinguish between research and development.

6 Why is testing such an important part of the development process?

7 Which personal qualities do you think are required of those engaged in development work?

8 What do you consider to be the most important feature of the network model of the innovation process and why?

9 Which do you consider provides the better explanation of innovation – technology push or demand pull?

10 Why has the network model of innovation become popular in recent years?

11 What kinds of organisation are likely to be associated with closed innovation?

12 What factors have led to the decline in closed innovation in recent years?

13 What are the implications of open innovation as far as individual lone innovators are concerned?

14 What are the implications for policymakers of the increased popularity of open innovation?

Exercises

1 Using an account of an innovation of your choice, prepare a report that describes the process innovation. The report should:

a make clear the type of innovation

b use one of the models of the innovation process to make clear how the innovation was conducted

c identify and describe the various steps or stages in the innovation process.

2 What is open innovation? What factors have led to this way of undertaking innovation becoming much more popular in recent years?

3 Using one example of an innovation with which you are familiar, explain what is meant by the term network innovation.

Further reading

1 Dyson, J. (1997) *Against the Odds*, Orion Business, London.
James Dyson's autobiography is one of the best studies of the innovation process. Covering the 15-year period from conceiving the idea for a cyclone vacuum cleaner to his finally getting one into production and onto the market, it explains in detail the steps involved including: how the idea arose, the building of prototypes, testing them, design of product, the acquisition of manufacturing facilities and the problems he faced in getting his new cleaner into the shops.

2 Owen, D. (2004) *Copies in Seconds: How a Lone Inventor and an Unknown Company Created the Biggest Communications Breakthrough since Gutenberg – Chester Carlson and the Birth of the Xerox Machine*, Simon & Schuster, New York.
Another tale of how an invention found its way to market. The Xerox plain paper copier was an extraordinarily successful innovation. This book outlines just how hard it was to get the invention to market. It also provides very useful insights into business models and how important they can be.

3 Chesbrough, H.W. (2003) *Open Innovation: The New Imperatives for Creating and Profiting from Technologies*, Harvard Business School Press, Boston, MA.
Although many of the ideas of open innovation have been around for years, this is the book that put it all together in a logical and coherent way. Well worth spending time in detail. It not only provides a very coherent explanation of the nature of open innovation, it also provides some first class case studies. Perhaps it is a bit Silicon Valley-centric, but some very valuable insights and details none the less.

4 Bruce, M. and J. Bessant (2001) *Design in Business: Strategic Innovation Through Design*, FT Prentice Hall, Harlow.
A textbook that looks at the innovation process. As the title indicates this is a book that focuses primarily on design and the management of the design function. However, it nonetheless provides a valuable insight into how innovation comes about. It provides very specific inputs on key features on design aspects of the innovation process.

5 Ulrich, K.T. and S.D. Eppinger (2003) *Product Design and Development*, McGraw-Hill, New York.
Another textbook, this time that explains the technical aspects of the innovation process. For those without a technology background this book provides an excellent account of the various activities that make up the innovation process. One might almost say this is a "how to do it" book.

CHAPTER 07

Intellectual property

❖ OBJECTIVES

When you have completed this chapter you will be able to:

❖ appreciate the rationale behind the various rights associated with intellectual property

❖ identify the various types of intellectual property right (IPR)

❖ distinguish the benefits conferred by intellectual property rights

❖ differentiate the remedies available to those whose intellectual property rights have been infringed

❖ show how intellectual property rights can be used to create value for their creator

Introduction

This chapter is about intellectual property in general and intellectual property rights in particular. The nature of intellectual property and how it arises is considered. The different forms of intellectual property right are introduced and explained in detail. So too are the various mechanisms and procedures for registering these rights.

Having acquired an intellectual property right what do you do with it? The chapter goes on to explain the different forms of protection associated with each intellectual property right. Similarly the various institutions and individuals associated with the process of registration are analysed. There is then consideration of the forms of protection offered by intellectual property rights, and finally a short section showing how intellectual property can be used, in particular how it can be traded in order to create value for its creator.

Intellectual property and intellectual property rights

In so far as innovation involves a creative effort that gives rise to something new, it is concerned with intellectual property. However, creative effort takes many forms and is not just about new ideas for products or services, but includes designs and computer programs for instance, as well as literary and artistic works. Similarly, the concept of intellectual property extends beyond creative effort and encompasses aspects of commercial reputation. Whether one is talking about a new product, a new logo or a new publication, all involve creative effort and as such are the result of intellectual activity on the part of individuals which requires the application of knowledge and skills leading to the creation of something new. Intellectual property may therefore be seen as the product of the application of knowledge and skills.

One of the problems with any form of intellectual activity is that the greater its potential value, the stronger the incentive for others to copy it in order to reap some form of commercial gain. Copying has the potential to deny the creator any commercial benefit from his or her creative endeavour. This in turn acts as a major disincentive for potential creators. Why invest a lot of time, effort and resources in something, only for someone else to profit from it? With such a disincentive surrounding creative effort, society will be the poorer because those individuals with the creative intellectual powers to originate new ideas will be less inclined to bother with innovation.

To overcome this potential loss to society, the law provides legal recognition of the ownership of the products of creative effort. In turn the proprietor can use this legal recognition to stop other people exploiting his or her property. Hence intellectual property rights create for the innovator a system by which he or she can benefit from their ingenuity. As with other forms of property, the proprietor, as the owner, may choose to sell the intellectual property rights or license them to others. However, since many intellectual property rights are monopolistic in nature, the state in many cases requires that certain rigorous tests be met before such rights will be granted.

In the UK a government agency, the Patent Office, is responsible for granting intellectual property rights. The main forms of intellectual property right are shown in Figure 7.1.

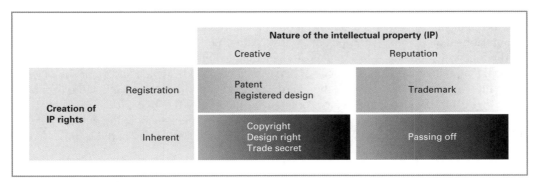

FIGURE 7.1 Forms of intellectual property and associated rights
Source: Bainbridge (2007: p4)

Each of these rights provides legal recognition of ownership for the creator of a new design, new product or written work. Ownership in turn gives the owner of the intellectual property right the right to stop others from exploiting his or her intellectual property, for a time at least. In this way intellectual property rights provide the creator with a system by which he or she can ensure that they benefit from their creative and intellectual endeavour.

Intellectual property rights through registration

Patents

A patent is a 20-year monopoly right (in the UK) granted by the state to an inventor. The object of a patent is to buy a breathing space for the inventor. It is a reward for invention, designed to provide the patent-holder with an exclusive right to benefit from it, but for a limited period of time. Exclusivity gives the patent-holder the right to prevent others from making or selling a patented product or using a patented process. It is a "social bargain" designed to promote innovation and the spread of new ideas, and in return for exclusivity the patent-holder is obliged to provide the Patent Office with full details of how the invention works (Figure 7.2).

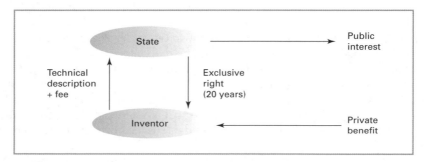

FIGURE 7.2 Patents and the state

The origin of the patent system in the UK goes back to medieval times when the monarch granted individuals monopolies for a variety of purposes. The actual term "patent" is derived from the Latin *litterae patentes* meaning an open letter intended for public display. Over time it became abbreviated from "letters patent" to just "patent".

The function of patents is to stimulate and encourage innovation. Any innovator faces the problem that, if the invention is a success, it may well be quickly copied and he or she may derive little in the way of reward for their hard work and effort in developing it. If the likelihood of copying can be reduced, the chances of financial success for the innovator are greater. This is actually a matter of public policy, as the state has to weigh the benefit to the public interest of encouraging innovation against the cost (to the public) of a slower rate of diffusion (i.e. take-up) of the innovation.

In practice it has been found that a 20-year monopoly gives the innovator a sufficient incentive to invent, while ensuring that the resulting innovation does not command a premium price for too long because of the lack of competition. The state has to weigh the benefits of diffusion leading to the rapid spread of a new technology against the benefits to creativity and innovation arising from granting inventors exclusivity.

In the UK the body that deals with patents on behalf of the state is the Patent Office. Before a patent is granted by the Patent Office, an inventor has to show that the invention is new. In practice this means meeting three conditions:

1 Novelty

An invention must be new. According to the Patents Act 1977 an invention may be considered new if it "does not form part of the state of the art". State of the art is all about whether the invention has been made public prior to the date at which the patent application is filed. Making something public is quite narrowly defined. Using an invention on a single occasion in one location would be sufficient for an invention to be part of the state of the art. In the "windsurfer" case it was held that a 12-year-old boy who had built a sailboard and used it in public at Hayling Island in Hampshire had effectively anticipated a later patent for a sailboard (Bainbridge, 1999: p351). This has important implications for innovators. Demonstrating an invention, perhaps to potential investors, prior to filing a patent could easily jeopardise the eventual granting of a patent. Hence as Bainbridge (1999) advises, anyone contemplating field trials of a prototype invention ought to file a patent application before conducting any such trials, if there is a possibility of members of the public seeing the invention.

2 Inventive step

An invention must involve an "inventive step". Essentially this means that it must not be obvious. This raises the question of obvious to whom? The answer is that it must not be obvious to someone skilled in the art, which is to say a notional skilled worker. The notional skilled worker does not have to be an expert: rather he or she is implied to have a general knowledge of the subject. Hence, the notion of an inventive step implies that the apparatus being patented would strike someone with a reasonable general knowledge of the subject as incorporating something that constitutes a genuine invention. In the case of *Dyson Appliances Ltd v. Hoover Ltd* (2000) for instance it was held that, because the vacuum cleaner industry was firmly committed to the use of bags in vacuum cleaners, a bagless cleaner was not obvious and therefore involved a genuine inventive step.

3 Industrial application

An invention has to be capable of being used in some kind of industry. This reflects both the history of patents, which were at one time referred to as "industrial" property rather than "intellectual" property and their practical nature. The requirement for an industrial application rules out scientific discoveries. The discovery has to be incorporated into some sort of apparatus, device or product if it is to be patentable. Alternatively, if it is produced by an industrial process it may be patentable. Thus, the discovery of the drug pencillin was not patentable as such but it could be patented when it was produced through an industrial process.

Providing it can meet these three tests then an invention is patentable. However, certain items are excluded (though this is effectively covered by the need for an industrial application). Scientific theories, mathematical models and aesthetic creations (e.g. literary or artistic works) are excluded. Computer software and business methods (at least outside the US) are among those excluded. It is possible to patent software-related products. If the software results in the introduction of a "technological innovation" then it may be patentable. The critical point, in Europe at least, is that as long as the software brings about a "technical effect" leading to an inventive step that goes beyond the normal physical interaction between the new program and the hardware leading to a technical improvement in the running of the computer or an attached device (such as making the computer memory usage more efficient), then it may be patentable. In the US around 15 per cent of the 170,000 patents granted each year are for software (Gapper, 2005).

BTG sues Amazon over tracking software

BTG, the British patent licensing company, is suing a group of American retailers including Amazon.com, the largest online retailer in the world, for allegedly infringing its rights over a technology to track customers' use of the Internet.

The company's lawsuit, filed in a Delaware court, claims the retailers are using a technique it has already patented, to monitor when customers move from one site to another. The technology is important because retailers will normally pay a fee to other sites that direct traffic their way.

BTG is claiming an undisclosed amount of damages from the group, which also includes BarnesandNoble.com, the electronic version of America's pervasive bookshop chain. BTG buys patent rights to new technologies and licenses them to manufacturers. It also sets up its own companies to develop technology and is best known for its subsidiary Provensis, which is testing a revolutionary varicose vein treatment. The treatment ran into trouble at the end of last year when US regulators suspended its tests.

The company, originally set up by the government to protect and patent the country's inventions, has a history of taking on opponents much larger than itself to protect its wide-ranging intellectual property rights.

Earlier this month BTG sued Microsoft and Apple for including patented technology in their operating systems that allows users to obtain software updates over the Internet.

In a statement about the latest lawsuit, BTG said: "The suit asks for unspecified damages for past infringing activity and an injunction against future use of the technology". It also said it had tried to reach an agreement but had failed. Fighting the case in court could take three years, making it possible that the parties will yet reach an agreement over the technology.

Ian Harvey, BTG's chief executive, said the patents are "fundamental to the tracking of users for online marketing programmes," adding that the technology's commercial potential is "significant". BTG's shares moved ahead 4p to 140p.

Source: Griffiths (2004: p48).

Obtaining a patent

To obtain a patent in the UK, an inventor has to follow a procedure with a number of clearly defined steps:

1 Making an application to the Patent Office: the application, on forms supplied by the Patent Office, has to contain:

- a request for a patent
- identification of the applicant
- a description of the invention

The description has to be sufficiently clear and complete; otherwise the level of protection will be limited. Once the application has been received by the Patent Office it is said to be "filed".

2 Search and publication: once a claim for a patent has been filed and a search fee paid (within a 12-month period) a preliminary search will be undertaken by a Patent Office examiner who will go through the records of previous patents to see if the invention meets the necessary conditions and is in fact new. At this point the application is published.

3 Full ("substantive") examination: this is the final stage in the process. The applicant pays a further fee within six months of publication and detailed examination of the description then takes place to see if it meets all the relevant legal requirements of the Patents Act 1977. Attention will focus on whether documents reported at the search stage and any others which have come to light since indicate that the invention is not in fact new or is obvious. The applicant gets a report and may make amendments at this stage. Once the examiner is satisfied that it meets all the requirements the patent is issued.

There is no such thing as a worldwide patent. In general, an application for a patent must be filed and a patent granted and enforced in each country where patent protection for the invention is sought, in accordance with the law of that country. It is possible to obtain a patent on a regional basis through regional bodies like the European Patent Office (EPO) or the African Regional International Patent Organization (ARIPO). It is also possible to file an international patent application under the terms of the Patent Cooperation Treaty (PCT) with the World International Patent Office (WIPO) in Geneva (Mostert, 2007). This has the effect of a national patent application in all filing countries (currently 125). However, the PCT application has to be followed by national applications in those countries where patent rights are desired. (The advantages of using this route are that the inventor is given more time and there are cost reductions.)

What protection does a patent provide?

A patent will not stop others from copying the invention. As with most forms of intellectual property, a patent is a legal right that is enforceable by legal action. If a direct infringement of the patent occurs, i.e. someone brings out a very similar product without the patent owner's consent, then the inventor has to take legal action through the courts in order to secure a remedy.

There are four main remedies (Bainbridge, 2007) that the courts provide:

- an *injunction* restraining the defendant from carrying out activities that infringe the patent
- *damages* to compensate for the loss suffered as a consequence of the infringement, or an *account of profit* where instead of damages the award is based on the profits actually made and attributable to the infringement
- an *order* that the infringing articles be destroyed or delivered up (i.e. handed over to the patent-holder)
- a *declaration* that the patent is valid and has indeed been infringed by the defendant

The last-named may seem a bit like stating the obvious, but is in fact very important. It is quite common where a case of patent infringement is alleged, for the accused to counter-petition alleging that the patent is not valid, should never have been granted to the patent-holder and should therefore be rescinded. When James Dyson for instance took action against Hoover, alleging that their Triple Vortex cleaner infringed the patent on his dual cyclone technology, Hoover promptly started a counter-action claiming that Dyson's patent wasn't valid in the first place. Under these circumstances the court is obliged to consider the validity of the patent and if it upholds it, then this is valuable reassurance for the patent-holder. An injunction in contrast is a restraining order that halts production of the offending article immediately, thereby preventing any further instances of infringement. Damages and an account of profit are both designed to provide a measure of financial compensation, while an order either removes the prospect of further infringement at some later point or calls upon whoever has perpetrated the infringement to hand over the counterfeit items so that the patent-holder can destroy them. Very occasionally the copies are so good and so like the real thing that the patent-holder may choose to sell them. In the case of the Workmate, the portable workbench developed by Ron Hickman and licensed to the American DIY manufacturer Black and Decker, the Japanese "Kinzo" was such a good copy that when the manufacturers were required to deliver up the offending counterfeit stock as part of an out-of-court settlement, Black and Decker was able to re-label the confiscated items and sell them (Landis, 1987).

Just which of the four remedies the court will apply varies according to the circumstances. Sometimes, as was the case with Hoover's infringement of James Dyson's patent, all four remedies are applied. It should be stressed that in the UK at any rate, the financial penalties imposed are typically modest. They may well not cover all the legal costs involved in prosecuting the infringement. For instance, Ron Hickman's legal costs for defending the patent on his Workmate workbench, came to significantly more than he or Black and Decker ever received in damages. However, despite this, the cumulative effect of more than 20 legal actions was to eventually produce the desired effect, namely discouraging counterfeit products (Landis, 1987). Of course for this to happen it is essential that great care is taken in drafting the patents in the first place. But if the patent has been properly drafted, then if the inventor does have to resort to the courts it should enable him or her to eliminate counterfeit copies, at least for the 20 years that a patent remains in force.

'Floor Wars'

James Dyson's bagless vacuum cleaner, was a breakthrough in vacuum cleaner technology when it first appeared on the UK market in 1993. Prior to then virtually all vacuum cleaners worked on the principle of extracting dust and dirt by passing the stream of dirty air through from a bag which acted as a filter in which the dirt collected. Vacuum cleaners employing a bag to filter the dirt formed a dominant design and had done so since Hoover pioneered the vacuum cleaner back in 1908.

The principle of cyclonic separation utilised in Dyson's new cleaner was not new and formed part of the "prior art". What was new was the use of more than one cyclonic separator in series to provide successively better filtering (Van Dulken, 2000). This was the technology which Dyson developed and patented. Unable to persuade any of the existing vacuum-cleaner manufacturers to adopt his patented dual cyclone technology, Dyson was forced to set up on his own company. His DC01 bagless vacuum-cleaner racked up £2.4 million of sales in its first year and within two years it had become the UK's best selling vacuum cleaner. Eventually some of the established vacuum-cleaner manufacturers produced their own "bagless" designs. One such company was Hoover (the European subsidiary owned by the Italian firm Candy), who brought out their own bagless vacuum cleaner, the Hoover Triple Vortex (HTV) in 1999. It was similar to Dyson's dual cyclone cleaner. So similar that Dyson brought an action against Hoover alleging infringement of his European Patent (UK) No. 0042723 entitled "Vacuum Cleaning Appliance". Dyson sought an injunction, delivery up and either damages or an account of profits. Dyson's claim for patent infringement rested on Hoover's use of three cyclones. The first is cylindrical and of lower efficiency. The second does not deposit particles but rather serves to create two air streams. The third is high efficiency. Unique to the HTV is that air is re-circulated through the second and third cyclones.

Hoover in turn challenged the validity of Dyson's patent, with a counter-claim requesting that the patent be revoked. The first part of Hoover's challenge to Dyson's patent was that "prior art" anticipated Dyson's patent. The court rejected that any of the prior art cited by Hoover, anticipated Dyson's patent. In particular the court looked at US Patent No. 2 768 707 for an industrial unit entitled "Separator for use with Vacuum Cleaning". The court also looked at the Johnston/Donaldson (US Patent No. 4 204 849) appliances and found that they could not be described as cleaning devices since in reality they were dust-control apparatus.

For the second part of Hoover's challenge, the court considered the "windsurfer test" (as set out in *Windsurfer International v. Tarbur Marine*), and in particular looked in some detail at the relevant skilled man and common general knowledge. The court held that it was not obvious to move to the invention from the prior art and that the technology of the prior art was a long way away from the patent.

With Dyson's patent upheld, Hoover had to defend its alleged infringement. Hoover's case for non-infringement was that the first and second cyclones were not connected in series as required by the patent. The court rejected this. Hoover also argued that Dyson's patent required the appliance to be unidirectional, whereas Hoover's appliance was not. The court said that re-circulation of the air, was not relevant to the issue of infringement. Hoover also tried to argue that its highest efficiency cyclone was not "frusto-conical" shaped as the patent required, but was in fact trumpet-shaped. The court rejected this very literal interpretation of frusto-conical. The High Court ruled that Hoover had indeed infringed Dyson's patent (Dyson, 2003). Although Hoover appealed, the company was required to stop production of its Triple Vortex cleaner, deliver up existing machines, and in due course pay Dyson £4 million in damages together with £2 million in costs.

Sources: Dyson (1997 and 2003); Tidd et al. (2001); Eaglesham (2001); Van Dulken (2000).

Registered designs

There are two forms of protection available for designs: registered designs and design rights. Registered designs require registration, design rights do not. While there is considerable overlap between the two forms of protection, registered designs cover designs where outward appearance is important, while design rights cover designs that are more functional. It is important to note in both cases the protection applies to the design and not the product or article.

The purpose of a registered design is to provide protection for the look or appearance of products. Registered design tends to apply particularly to aspects of products such as shapes or surface patterns. As a form of protection a registered design is likely to be particularly appropriate for products where appearance is a key attribute, such as jewellery, glassware and furniture. However, the Designs Registry, the part of the Patent Office that deals with this particular intellectual property right, receives applications from every branch of technology including: cars, laptop computers, washing machines, tennis racquets and even such mundane items as paperclips!

What is a registered design?

In essence it works in a similar way to a patent in that it too is a monopoly right that can be bought and sold and which is used to stop copying. However, it is a monopoly right that covers the outward appearance of an article. The main features of a registered design are:

- the design must be new and materially different
- it covers appearance resulting from the lines, contours, colours, shape, texture or materials of a product
- two exceptions are – must-fit and must-match
- two- and three-dimensional objects are covered
- duration – 5 years but it can be extended to 25 years.

As with patents, a design has to be new if it is to be registered. A design is regarded as new if it has not been made public in the UK. There is more flexibility than with patents, because a design can be shown for purposes such as marketing during the 12 months preceding registration. Just as patents involve disclosure of the details of the invention to the public, so too designs that have been accepted as registered designs are open to public inspection at the Patent Office.

The significance of appearance highlights the main distinction between this form of intellectual property right and patents. For registered designs, outward appearance is important – one cannot rely on function, operation, manufacture or material of construction of an article, as in the case of a patent. What constitutes an article has recently been extended by an EC Design Directive to include: "… any industrial or handicraft item intended to be assembled into a complex product, packaging, get-up, graphic symbols, and typographical typefaces, but excluding computer programs".

In terms of the two types of exception, the must-fit exception relates to function and means that it is not possible to gain a registered design for a design that is purely a matter of function. Therefore, one could not gain a registered design for the jaws of a spanner, because the jaws form part of the function of a spanner. Similarly the must-match exception relates to parts of a design. One cannot gain a registered design for part of a design where the part is determined by the shape of the whole. It is not possible to gain design rights for things like the front-wing panel of a car, because the shape is determined by the overall shape of the car.

What does one gain from a registered design?

As with patents the main benefit is the exclusive right in the UK to make any article to which the design has been applied. The significance of this right is that the owner can then take legal action against anyone who infringes upon this exclusivity, which in turn forms a deterrent to would-be copiers.

Trademarks: introduction

Intellectual property does not only apply to the products of creative effort but also covers commercial reputations. Specifically this refers to trademarks. A trademark is a sign used to distinguish the goods or services of one trader from those of another. The law defines a trademark as:

 … any sign capable of being represented graphically which is capable of distinguishing goods or services of one undertaking from those of other undertakings.

Typically the term covers words, logos and pictures, although these days it has been extended to include other forms used to identify particular goods or services.

Registration of a trademark

Trademarks have been an important feature of commercial life for a very long time. Since medieval times they have been used by traders to differentiate their goods from those of others. Trademarks have taken many different forms. In the eighteenth century, as shops became more widespread, signs were used by shopkeepers to denote the type of goods they were selling. In the nineteenth century the appearance of manufactured and standardised consumer products led to trademarks being used by manufacturers to differentiate their products. Among the first products to use trademarks in this way were everyday household items like soap, tea and chocolate.

As the means for communicating with customers have been extended and become vastly more sophisticated (i.e. through television, animation, computer graphics, simulation and special effects), so the scope for differentiating products has expanded and trademarks have become more widely used. Developments in marketing such as branding and relationship marketing have increasingly led companies to enhance the image and reputation of their products and services, and trademarks have normally formed an important part of this process. Similarly, the increased emphasis on merchandising has also led to trademarks assuming greater importance.

Although some protection is available for trademarks without registration through common law by means of an action for "passing off," registration of a trademark provides the most comprehensive protection for a name, brand name, logo or slogan. Registration via the Patent Office lasts for ten years and can be renewed indefinitely. It was first introduced in the UK in 1875 through the Trade Marks Registration Act of that year. The very first registered trademark was registered by the brewing concern Bass in the form of a red triangle symbol for one of its pale ales. The trademark is still in use today and Bass reckons that over the years it has had to deal with 1,900 cases of infringement (Bainbridge, 1999).

In the past only words or logos or combinations of the two were registrable, but the Trade Marks Act 1994 was a landmark piece of legislation that greatly expanded the range of things that could be registered as trademarks. Among the more recent and more unusual registrations have been:

- the Coca-Cola bottle
- a Chanel perfume bottle
- Bach's *Air on a G-string*
- the colour green
- the sound of a dog barking
- the colour yellow
- the slogan "exceedingly good cakes"

These registrations reflect the new classes of trademark that were eligible for registration under the 1994 Act. Specifically the items that can now be registered include:

■ domain names
■ logos
■ music
■ slogans
■ colours
■ shapes

Another change introduced by the Trade Marks Act 1994 is in relation to infringement of trademarks. The Act places a statutory duty upon trading standards officers to take action against those who trade in counterfeit goods using unauthorised trademarks. Trading standards officers have the power to seize counterfeit goods, thereby assisting in the enforcement of trademarks.

In order for a trademark to be registered, an application has to be made to the Patent Office. This needs to satisfy a number of criteria:

■ section 1(1) of the Trade Marks Act 1994 which specifies what can be registered and now includes colours, shapes and pieces of music
■ distinctiveness – in the sense that the trademark singles out the company and its product from its competitors
■ non-deceptiveness – in the sense that it should not in any way mislead the public or lead them to believe that the product has attributes that are not in fact present
■ no conflict with existing trademarks

Mini Case

Mr Men

More than 100 million of the Mr Men books have been sold since Roger Hargreaves published the first in 1971, making him the second-best selling author in the UK after JK Rowling, the creator of Harry Potter. The Mr Men phenomenon began when Roger Hargreaves' son Adam, then aged seven, asked what a tickle looked like. Mr Tickle was followed by a further 41 Mr Men. The books were followed by a television series narrated by Arthur Lowe which ran from 1974 to 1985. However, Roger Hargeaves (who died in 1988), perhaps by virtue of his background in advertising, realised that there might be more to the Mr Men than children's books and a television series. He endeavoured to protect his intellectual property by registering the Mr Men as trademarks. This enabled him to negotiate a series of licensing agreements with manufacturers. Thus, for those with fond memories of the books it is possible to buy a wide range of Mr Men merchandise including Mr Bump plasters, Mr Perfect boxer shorts and Little Miss Naughty underwear. Trademark registration enabled Roger Hargreaves and the executors of his estate to capitalise on the intellectual property that his creative talent was able to realise. The licensing agreements are estimated to be worth £130 million.

Source: BBC News, *29 October 2001.*

Intellectual property rights that are inherent

Copyright

Copyright is an intangible right that comes into effect through creative effort, giving rise to a wide range of creative works including literary, artistic and musical works. Other types of work are also included, such as films, sound-recordings broadcasts and typographical layouts, though with these, unlike the others, there is no requirement for originality. Copyright is automatic and comes into existence upon creation of the work. The Berne Convention requires signatories to recognise the copyright of authors of other signatory countries (currently 164), in the same way that they recognise the copyright of their own nationals.

Copyright confers an exclusive right to certain actions in relation to the work upon the owner. The actions concern the exploitation of the work and include selling copies, giving others permission to copy and the like. The significance of the exclusive right is that if someone who is not the copyright holder and does not have permission to copy makes copies and sells them, then the copyright owner can sue for infringement and seek redress, such as an injunction to forbid the sale of copies, together with damages.

The range of works covered by copyright is extensive. Literary works covers a great deal more than books. In the commercial field it extends to authorship of many things of a technical or commercial nature that perhaps would not at first seem to be literary works such as technical reports, equipment manuals, databases and customer lists as well as engineering and architectural drawings and plans. Of particular significance these days is that copyright extends to computer software. Given the growth of computer applications this is a rapidly expanding field. Thus, for a wide range of new products and services, such as videogames for instance, intellectual property rights may be less a matter of patent protection and more a matter of copyright.

The copyright owner is normally the author who created the work, and, as with many other forms of intellectual property right, he or she can assign it or sell it to another. However, there are circumstances where copyright may be conferred not on the author but on others. For instance, if authorship occurs during the ordinary course of employment then copyright belongs to the employer. Similarly, a contractor who creates a work will retain copyright unless the terms of the contract specify that he or she will not retain copyright.

The exclusive right conferred by copyright extends to a wide range of activities that includes:

- copying or reproducing
- adapting
- distributing
- issuing and renting
- public performance
- broadcasting

However, copyright legislation does provide for certain activities of an educational or academic rather than commercial nature to be undertaken without infringement. For example, it is permitted to copy at least part of a work for the purpose of private study or research. Similarly reviews and other works of criticism can copy part of a work.

The duration of copyright varies according to the nature of the work, and from country to country. As Figure 7.3 shows, in the UK the longest period of copyright protection relates to literary, musical, artistic and dramatic works where the protection lasts for 70 years beyond the lifetime of the author.

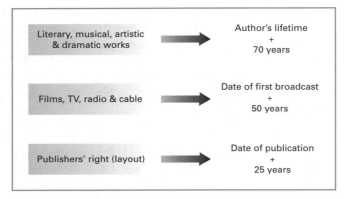

FIGURE 7.3 Copyright timescales

Mini Case

Peter Pan

27 December 2004 was the hundredth anniversary of the first public performance at the Duke of York's theatre in London of J.M. Barrie's children's classic, *Peter Pan*. The anniversary was marked by a number of special performances of *Peter Pan* as well as a number of radio documentaries about the author. Many of these detailed some of the famous performances of *Peter Pan*, not just in Britain, but in other countries such as the US. For the Great Ormond Street Hospital for Sick Children in London, the renewed interest in and performances of *Peter Pan* were of particular interest. Barrie donated the copyright of *Peter Pan* to the hospital, a move that was to benefit thousands of children over the years. However, for the hospital the anniversary itself was perhaps a mixed blessing since it was a reminder that the period covered by copyright is limited. J.M. Barrie died in 1937, so the year 2007 would be the year in which *Peter Pan* went out of copyright, thereby depriving the hospital of this source of income.

Source: Strachan (2004: pp20–21).

Design right

Registered design is not the only form of protection available for designs. In addition there is an automatic form of protection called "design right". Design right operates rather like copyright. It is a form of protection that arises automatically when a design is created. Though arising automatically, some form of tangible evidence of its creation is required.

To be eligible for design right a design must be "original": that is to say, it must not be commonplace within its field. Similarly design right only covers the shape and configuration of an article, it does not extend to two-dimensional designs.

As an intellectual property right, design right does not provide the exclusivity that comes with a registered design. Instead it provides a right to prevent copying. Design right lasts for 10 years from the date the product was first marketed, subject to a limit of 15 years from the date the design was created.

Trade secrets

Trade secrets are not registered since by their very nature they are the secret materials of an individual or an organisation (Mostert, 2007). They are covered by the law of breach of confidence, which protects confidential information by preventing its use by individuals to whom the information has been divulged in confidence (Bainbridge, 2007). Confidentiality therefore lies at the heart of trade-secret protection.

What are trade secrets? Trade secrets are confidential information that comprises the specialist "know-how" that enables a business to manufacture products or services successfully. They can range from ingredients for recipes and chemical formulae to customer lists, discount rates, credit ratings, technological know-how and manufacturing techniques. Famous examples of trade secrets include Merchandise 7X, the formula for Coca-Cola, which has remained a trade secret since it was invented in 1886, the formula for McDonald's secret sauce and Kentucky Fried Chicken's secret blend of 11 herbs and spices. For information to be a trade secret, it must not have been published or disclosed to a significant number of people. If information is in the public domain then it is clearly not confidential and no protection is available.

Trade secrets do not share the preconditions of patents or copyright in that there is no requirement for them to be "novel" or expressed in a tangible form (i.e. written down). They are likely to be valuable so that their misappropriation to others outside the business would be a matter of major concern for a commercial organisation. While there is no registration process for trade secrets, one has to be able to show that at a given time the information was actually an individual's, or individual company's, property and was being kept confidential.

To demonstrate confidentiality, firms have to take steps to ensure that the information is kept secret. This might include clearly marking information as confidential, locating information in a secure environment such as a safe or safety deposit box, restricting access to the information to a small number of individuals, and restricting access to facilities where the information is being used or might be used (e.g. through signing in requirements or the use of visitor badges, etc.)

Sometimes firms seek to maintain secrecy by requiring their employees to sign non-disclosure agreements that expressly forbid them from releasing confidential information to third parties. Nor are such security arrangements purely a matter of commercial security, they are also important legally in order to demonstrate that the information is confidential and is treated as such.

Passing off

Passing off is effectively a common-law version of trademark registration. It has no requirement for registration. Instead, passing off is based on the principle that a trader must not sell goods under the pretence that they are the goods of another. To do so is to commit passing off. Essentially passing off is a form of misrepresentation. For an action for passing off to succeed, the trader whose goods have been passed off has to show not only that misrepresentation has occurred, carried out by another trader in the course of his/her trade, but that goodwill or reputation is attached to his or her goods in the first place and that his or her trade has been damaged normally through loss of sales, though it could equally be through damage to or dilution of reputation.

Mini Case

The JIF® lemon case

An example of a passing off action was the JIF® lemon case (*Reckitt and Coleman Products Ltd v. Borden Inc.* [1990]). One of Reckitt and Coleman's best-known consumer products is JIF® lemon juice, a household bakery product used in cakes and pastries. Sold in yellow, plastic, lemon-shaped containers, JIF® lemon has been a familiar sight on supermarket shelves for many years. However, in 1990 Reckitt and Coleman, the manufacturers, took action against a competitor who was also selling lemon juice in a similar, though larger, lemon-shaped container. This was prior to the Trade Marks Act 1994 which permitted the registration of colours and shapes as trademarks. Consequently, Reckitt and Coleman took out an action for "passing off" claiming that the competitor was misrepresenting their product. To prove their case Reckitt and Coleman produced evidence from hundreds of consumers all of whom stated that they had been confused by the appearance of a very similar product. The court found in favour of Reckitt and Coleman on the grounds that members of the public had been confused, indicating that the competitor had tried to pass off its product as genuine JIF® lemon juice. The view of the court was that the shape and colour of the product ingeniously alluded to its contents and was generally recognised by the public as JIF® lemon juice.

Licensing

One of the key features of intellectual property rights (IPR) is that they provide scope for licensing, that is to say where the IPR associated with an invention has been legally established through a patent, the holder can then permit someone else to produce the invention in return for a fee. Such an arrangement is usually known as a 'licensing agreement'.

One of the attractions of licensing agreements is that the inventor does not have to complete the final stages of the innovation process, such as manufacturing and distribution. Where the inventor is an individual or a small company this can be a very important consideration. Licensing provides a means whereby small start-up businesses, lacking financial resources and complementary assets (e.g. reputation and brand name, marketing expertise, merchandising capability, product support facilities, etc.), can commercialise their technological innovation. Licensing not only means that the innovator does not have to find the capital expenditure required to build or buy the assets required, it also reduces the risk (Teece, 1986).

Both James Dyson, with his dual cyclone vacuum cleaner, and Ron Hickman, with his Workmate® portable workbench, were individual inventors. They did not work for a company or have the backing of a company behind them. Consequently, neither planned to produce their invention themselves. Both tried to interest large, well-established consumer-product companies in their invention and persuade them to take out a licence. Unfortunately both Dyson and Hickman, despite a great deal of effort, found it extremely difficult to persuade a company to adopt their invention and agree to purchase a licence, possibly because in both cases the invention was unlike anything then on the market. What is significant is that both men felt that licensing was the most sensible course of action. They recognised that they did not have the expertise or the resources to undertake the final commercialisation phase of the innovation process. Equally both men recognised the importance of asserting and protecting their intellectual property (i.e. their inventions) through patents. As it turned out both men did eventually find a company willing to take out a licence. James Dyson persuaded a Japanese company, Apex, to take out a licence for his dual cyclone technology, while Ron Hickman had to start manufacturing and selling his portable workbench on a small scale before Black & Decker agreed to take out a licence.

Mini Case

Inventive employees could be awarded royalties

Employees who dream up lucrative inventions could share in their employers' profits under government plans to radically change patent law.

The move would be the biggest shake-up for a quarter of a century. The Department of Trade and Industry is considering ways for inventors to share the fruits of their own research, such as awarding them a percentage of royalties.

Employees currently have little entitlement to the benefits brought by inventions where their employer owns the patent.

The proposal comes in a consultation launched by the DTI and the Patent Office as part of moves to bring the UK into line with changes to the European Patents Convention. Patent laws in Britain have not been significantly updated since 1977.

The DTI said it had an "open mind" on how such a scheme could work and would listen to industry's views on the subject – due by 19 February – before forming an opinion.

But drug groups said the moves would be almost impossible to implement. "Hundreds of people contribute to a product's development. It would be extremely difficult to identify specific individuals who should be rewarded", said one GlaxoSmithKline manager.

In theory, employees can claim compensation if they can prove the patent resulting from their invention has brought "substantial benefit" to the company.

But Jeremy Philpott at the Patent Office said: "That has proved to be an impossibly high barrier. I think there have been only two cases in 25 years and both failed".

Source: Sherwood (2002).

CASE STUDY: TRAMPLED UNDERFOOT – HOW BIG BUSINESS HIJACKED THE UGG BOOT

Tony Mortel's hair is standing on end, an effect created by equal doses of gel and outrage. "Who do they think they are?" he fumes. "Telling us what we can and can't call our product, trying to stop us from making a living. Well, they can stick their demands where the sun doesn't shine".

Tony comes from seven generations of boot-makers and for the last 45 years his family has been making Uggs, the once dowdy sheepskin boots now worn by the likes of Gwyneth Paltrow and Kate Moss. Their factory in Australia's Hunter Valley turns out 16,000 pairs a year. At least it used to, before a large US company across the Pacific Ocean began taking an unwelcome interest in their affairs.

Staff at Mortels Sheepskin Factory had just returned from their Christmas break when a letter arrived from the Melbourne solicitors of Deckers Outdoor Corporation, a California-based conglomerate. The letter, which was sent to 19 other Australian firms, informed them that Deckers owned all rights to the name Ugg and instructed them to stop using it or face litigation.

"I just laughed," says Tony. "I thought they were crazy. I threw it in the bin". But it was no laughing matter. Soon afterwards, at the instigation of Deckers, Mortels was ejected from eBay, the Internet auction site where it had been selling Uggs to American consumers. Last Wednesday, it was ordered by Icann, the Internet regulatory body, to stop using "Ugg" in its domain name.

The two dozen traders affected by such legal moves are reeling from shock and disbelief. For decades, they have been part of a thriving cottage industry founded on an Australian product that – according to folklore – dates back to the 1920s, when shearers used to wrap sheepskins around their feet to keep warm in the sheds.

Uggs, they argue, have always been called Uggs, originally an abbreviation of Ugly. No one bothered with trademarks, because Ugg was a generic term. Everyone knew it meant a comfortable, flat-heeled sheepskin boot, although – until the current fashion craze – few people admitted to owning a pair. Brian Iverson, owner of Blue Mountains Ugg Boots, says of Deckers' demands: "It's like saying you can't call a car a car".

The problem is: someone did bother with trademarks. In 1971 a local surf champion, Shane Steadman, decided to capitalise on the growing popularity of Uggs among Australian – and visiting US – surfers, who were starting to recognise the appeal of a snug boot when they emerged shivering from the ocean. He began selling Uggs and registered the name.

Steadman was not the only Australian wave-rider with a sharp eye for a business opportunity. In 1979, so the story goes, Brian Smith arrived in New York with a few pairs of Uggs in his backpack. He set up a company, Ugg Holdings Inc, registered the Ugg trademark in 25 countries and in 1995 sold out to Deckers.

For a long time not a peep was heard from the new American owners of the iconic Australian boot. The company sent out a flurry of warning letters five years ago, but did not follow them up. According to Middletons, its Melbourne lawyers, it was only when Australian manufacturers began selling Uggs on the Internet to meet soaring demand overseas that Deckers felt obliged to crack down.

Not surprisingly the Australian firms – most of them small family outfits with a handful of employees – are unimpressed with the Santa Barbara-based company's arguments. They say

Brian Smith was awarded the trademarks in error and are planning to have them rescinded, at least in Australia.

Their only other choice is to give up and go under – for without the name Ugg, they say, they cannot sell their boots. "People around the world know them as Ugg boots," says Tony Mortel. "My family has been marketing them as Uggs for 45 years. For Deckers to say we should give it all up, without compensation, is borderline monopolisation".

The Australian traders have united under the banner of the Ugg Boot Footwear Association and set up a fighting fund to finance the forthcoming legal battle. Those waiting in limbo include Westhaven Industries, a disabled charity that employs 65 people at its factory in Dubbo, a small town in New South Wales. Ugg boots are the charity's most profitable product and, without them, the business would not survive.

Employees include Dougie Stewart, who has been making Ugg boots at Westhaven for 30 years and travels more than 60 miles each day to work. "He's a brilliant worker and he loves what he does," says Gordon Tindall, the charity's general manager. "If we had to close as a consequence of this, it would be devastating for our workers. This is all they know, and they won't get a similar job elsewhere".

Gordon insists that Ugg is "as generic as meat pie or tomato sauce," and says he has every right to use it. "If it waddles like a duck and quacks like a duck, then it is a duck and not a chook (chicken) in my book," he says, adapting an oft-used Australian phrase. "It's like the Ford Motor Company claiming that they own the word 'sedan'".

When Westhaven received the letter from Middletons in New York, he says, "my first thought was 'Bugger, we'll have to comply'. Then I thought 'Why should I?' Our industry has agreed that we won't be bullied by these guys. We'll carry on doing what we've always done and let Deckers take some of us on".

At Mortels, situated on a light industrial estate outside Maitland, about 100 miles north of Sydney, the latest Uggs – in this season's colours of pale blue, pale pink, lavender and denim – are arrayed in a shop emblazoned with "Ugg Boots And Slippers" in huge lettering. Tony Mortel has been told to remove the word "Ugg" from the window. He has not complied.

Inside the small factory, machinists are discussing conspiracy theories about Princess Diana's death and periodically checking the temperature; if it rises above 40 degrees centigrade, they can go home early. It hovers, irritatingly, at 39.9 degrees. Beneath the laughter and good-natured banter, there is an edge of anxiety. "If we can't make Uggs anymore, I'll have to find another line of work," says Marewa Lamb, stitching a pair of tan boots.

She and the others operate a mini-production line. Tony (the "clicker") cuts out the pieces of tanned and dyed skin and passes then to Marewa, known as Ma, who sews on the heel support. Next in line is Wanda Herickwitz, who attaches the inner sole, and Andrew Cook stitches the whole thing together. Angela Daley binds the boot and adds the finishing details. Damien Lambert glues on the sole.

Cheerful, down-to-earth people, they have one word to describe the notion that they should stop calling an Ugg an Ugg. "Stupid," says Angela. "Everyone knows them as Ugg boots. If you changed the name people wouldn't know what you were talking about".

Their views are shared by Tony's father Frank – now 71 and retired, but furious about the turn of events. Frank emigrated from Holland in 1958, bringing a few sewing machines, and set up a tiny sheepskin factory. Descended from a long line of orthopaedic boot-makers, he made his first pair of fur-lined slippers for his wife, Rita, who wanted something to keep her feet warm. He then started making the slippers and boots commercially.

"We called them Uggs from the start," he says. "Although I recall other names such as 'woolly hoppers'. I'm sure this American company is just trying to frighten people off".

If that is true, the tactics have had the desired effect. Some manufacturers have excised the offending word from their trading names or websites. Westhaven no longer uses the word Ugg in its catalogues and price lists. Others, such as Uggs-N-Rugs in Western Australia, are standing firm, but with trepidation. Brian Iverson, whose family has made Uggs for three generations, is resisting. "Uggs are as Australian as the Harbour Bridge," he says.

Tony Watson, a partner with Middletons, says the portrayal of Deckers as "some big bad aggressive American company that likes squashing small businesses" is unfounded. "We don't want litigation, but people have to understand the bigger picture," he says. "It was Deckers, he says, that transformed Uggs into a high-fashion item, spending $7 million on marketing over the past decade and sending the boots to personalities such as Oprah Winfrey. Now others are reaping the benefits. My client has developed a marketplace and is now trying to protect it," he says. "They are certainly not going to throw their hands up and say, 'We've invested all this money, we've built up the brand and registered the trademark, now we're just going to walk away".

Among Deckers' competitors, those who sell over the Internet are the most vulnerable. Without "Ugg" in their domain, or trading names, they will not be located by consumers searching the web. All searches will lead to Ugg Australia, the brand name under which Deckers sells the boots around the world.

The company appears determined to protect its dominant position in the US as well as among European consumers. Yet Australian traders say they have been exporting to the US and elsewhere for decades. "Between us, we must have spent far more than Deckers on marketing," says Tony Mortel.

The irony is that, while Deckers is trying to prevent Australian traders from calling an Australian product a name by which it has always been known in Australia, it brazenly exploits Ugg's Australian origins through its choice of brand name. Claims that it uses American (rather than Australian) sheepskins are flatly denied by Tony Watson, although he admits that, as of a few months ago, "some" Uggs are manufactured in China, with the rest produced in Australia and New Zealand. He compares "Ugg" with "Biro" and "Hoover" which, although commonly used generically, are protected by trademark.

A false comparison, says Tony Mortel. In those cases, a product was developed and marketed and a name invented and trademarked. In the case of Ugg, all the hard work was put in by others, then Deckers came along and bought the name. "We've put our heart and soul into this product," he says. "It's our livelihood, our heritage".

Tony Watson does not have an answer to this point. "We'll no doubt get to the bottom of it if the case comes to court," he says. He adds that Australian traders should accept reality and develop another brand. "How about 'Surfer' Sheepskin Boots?" he suggests.

Tony Mortel refuses to acknowledge the possibility of defeat. "We're going to carry on fighting," he says. "We know we're in the right, and we know we're going to win. It's just a matter of time".

Source: The Independent *(2004)*.

Questions

1 Why was Tony Mortel told to remove the word Ugg from his shop window?

2 What is the intellectual property in this case?

3 Why have problems with the use of the word "Ugg" only recently come to a head?

4 How can Deckers instruct Australian manufacturers to stop using the name Ugg?

5 In what ways has the Internet affected trademarks?

6 Why is it important for Australian firms to be able to use the name "Ugg," especially in terms of their trade names?

7 What was Brian Smith's contribution to the present problem?

8 What are Deckers cracking down on and why?

? Questions for discussion

1 Which of the following items would not meet the criteria required for a registered design?
- a portable CD player
- a rubber sealing ring for the door of a washing machine
- a toilet disinfectant container
- a corkscrew

2 Why is computer software not normally patentable? What other forms of protection are available?

3 Why are trademarks an increasingly important piece of intellectual property?

4 Why do companies accused of infringing a patent often mount a defence based on a counter-petition claiming that the patent is not valid?

5 What is meant by diffusion? What impact does the patent system have on the rate at which new technological advances are diffused?

6 What is meant by "novelty" where patents are concerned and why is it important?

7 What is the Windsurfer test?

8 Why do inventors need to take particular care before publicising their inventions?

9 Which of the following can be registered as a trademark?
- a brand name
- the shape of a container
- a smell
- a colour
- a domain name

10 What is meant by the term "passing off"?

11 Why has the Internet been a very significant development as far as copyright is concerned?

Exercises

1 Why have trademarks become an increasingly important form of intellectual property?

2 What is intellectual property and how can a firm or individual protect it?

3 What remedies are available to holders of patents who find that their patents have been infringed?

4 Why do some patent-holders choose not to license their invention/innovation to others?

5 Carly Fiorina, the former head of Hewlett-Packard, when asked whether the company was living up to its creative traditions under her leadership, would point out the company filed 11 patents per day under her leadership compared with only three per day when she arrived. Comment critically on this statement.

Further reading

1 Bainbridge, D. (2006) *Intellectual Property,* 6th edn, Pearson Longman, London. A definitive legal textbook that provides a highly detailed technical explanation of the various forms of intellectual property. However, it is a legal text and as such is not recommended for use other than as a reference book.

2 Mostert, F. (2007) *From Edison to iPod: Protect Your Ideas and Make Money,* Dorling Kindersley. London. And now for something completely different. This is not a textbook, rather a popular introduction to the subject of intellectual property. Despite this it covers most aspects of intellectual property and in considerable detail. A big plus is the illustrations which provide highly informative examples of the various intellectual property rights. Strongly recommended as an introduction to the subject.

3 Van Dulken, S. (2000) *Inventing the 20th Century: 100 Inventions that Shaped the World,* British Library, London. This is not a book about intellectual property rights, but despite this it gives a valuable insight into the subject. Using patent records from the Patent Office, including many diagrams and illustrations, it provides an account of 100 UK patents of the twentieth century.

PART 03
How Do You Manage Innovation?

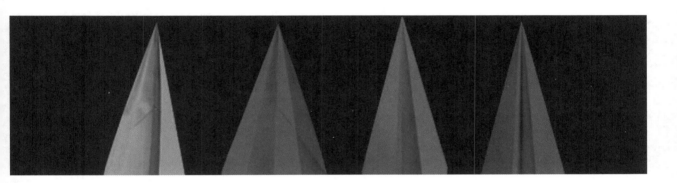

Part Contents

CHAPTER 08

Innovation strategy

❖ OBJECTIVES

When you have completed this chapter you will be able to:

❖ understand the nature of strategic management

❖ appreciate the need to take a strategic perspective on innovation

❖ explain the nature of innovation strategy

❖ recognise the various innovation strategies that are available as a means of exploiting innovations

❖ evaluate innovation strategies and determine the appropriate circumstances in which to use them

Introduction

You can have fantastic ideas, you can be very clever at inventing, you can invest a fortune in research and development (R&D) and you can be a recognised technological leader, but you may still fail when it comes to innovating. How come?

Ideas, inventions and R&D are all concerned with value creation. They are part of the creative process that leads to the development of a new product, service, or process, but as we saw in Chapter 1, there is more to innovation than value creation. The other crucial ingredient in innovation is value capture and if you don't get that right, then no matter how good you are at all the other things, the innovation may well fail, or at least you will fail to benefit from the innovation.

Value capture is about innovators appropriating (i.e. receiving) benefits from their innovation, and this is dependent on what happens in the marketplace. It is in the marketplace where innovations succeed or fail. It is often assumed that with innovation what matters is winning the race to be first-to-market. This is after all why innovation is often portrayed as a heroic endeavour, where the innovator struggles against seemingly overwhelming obstacles to get the product on to the market before anyone else. However, innovators who rush their innovations to market frequently discover that winning is not enough.

As we saw in Chapter 4, in the state of flux and discontinuity that the theories of punctuated equilibrium and dominant design predict will follow the introduction of a major new innovation, a number of competing designs may well appear. The innovator may then find that while being first-to-market is an advantage, it is not enough of an advantage. Under these circumstances seemingly attractive and useful new products can be upstaged by offerings from competitors. Sometimes these competing designs are copies which are less sophisticated and less proficient technically, but despite this they offer the consumer better value perhaps because they come with better technical support, or better availability. As a result the innovator fails to capture value, which instead goes to a competitor or competitors.

Hence, having got something to work, having developed a prototype, perhaps even having got as far as patenting it, the innovator, whether as an individual or an organisation, is then faced with some major choices in terms of how best to exploit the innovation. These choices are about how best to attack the market and they form the focus of this chapter. Because the choices have long-term consequences in terms of the life cycle of the innovation, they represent strategic decisions: that is to say, decisions that affect the long-term future of the innovation. They may even affect the long-term future of the organisation. Consequently, this chapter is all about strategic management and strategic decisions connected with innovation: in short it is about innovation strategy.

Why does strategy matter when it comes to innovation? Partly it is because market dynamics, particularly where new products and services are concerned, involve a degree of uncertainty. It can be very difficult to predict competitor reaction. It is precisely to deal with this sort of uncertainty that it is necessary to consider the bigger picture which includes not just consumers and their reaction to an innovation, but a host of other parties, including competitors. Another factor is that sometimes the resources required to bring an innovation to market are on such a scale that they require the organisation concerned to "bet the company". This means that the investment associated with the innovation, in terms of time, effort and money, is such that if the innovation fails, the future of the organisation may be at risk. Finally decisions about innovation tend to involve a relatively long timescale. It takes time to get an innovation to market and it can take time for an innovation to catch on and make money. Under these circumstances tactical decision-making involving timescales of weeks and perhaps months is not sufficient.

Mini Case

PJB-100 digital music player

"The MP3 that changes everything". That was how the American magazine *Popular Mechanics* described a pioneering new MP3 digital music player which included an integrated hard drive that allowed you to store up to a hundred CDs' worth of music. You might think that the magazine was talking about Apple's iPod, but you'd be wrong. This pioneering product was an innovation developed by a big computer company in Silicon Valley, but it wasn't Apple. It was the computer manufacturer DEC (since taken over by Compaq which in turn was acquired by Hewlett-Packard) and the digital music player was the PJB-100.

Today when almost every one has heard of the iPod, few have heard of the PJB-100. It was developed by a small team at DEC led by Cambridge-educated computer scientist, Andrew Birrell, the man who first came up with the idea of fitting the smallest available hard drive, a 2.5-in drive from a notebook computer, into an MP3 player to create what was effectively a personal jukebox. Over the course of a year Birrell's team solved the problems of energy management, navigation, file transfer and integration with a PC, and the PJB-100 went on the market almost two years before the iPod in November 1999.

Sadly although the PJB-100 was the first product of this type to reach the marketplace, it was not a commercial success. It proved to be just a little too big, a little too expensive and a little too awkward to use. So it was that while DEC pursued a first mover strategy to be first-to-market with this new type of product, it was actually Apple, with its follower/imitator strategy that struck gold, and DEC's engineers will "dwell forever in a destination they never booked – the limbo populated by creators doomed to see their great ideas realized, and hugely improved upon, by companies with more visionary bosses" (Levy, 2006: p51). They are in good company.

Source: Levy (2006).

The nature of strategy

Strategic decisions have long-term consequences and very often impact upon a lot of people. Hence strategic decisions are big ones. There is often a lot of money involved and many people are affected. Because their consequences can be so significant, strategic decisions are normally left to the most senior managers within an organisation, although particular individuals and groups lower down the organisation may be highly influential.

Strategic decisions and their associated strategies can typically be ordered in most organisations into a hierarchy (see Figure 8.1) that has business strategy at the apex, functional strategy in the middle and product/service strategy at the base.

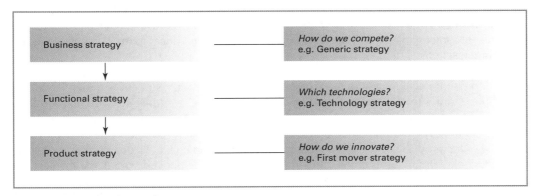

FIGURE 8.1 Hierarchy of strategies

Business strategy as its name implies is concerned with the strategy of the whole business, in particular how it achieves its long-term objectives or goals, such as growth or internationalisation. In meeting these objectives, business strategy is mainly concerned with answering the question: how does the business compete? Only by competing successfully and beating its competitors is a business likely to grow.

Within any particular business strategy there will be associated functional strategies (see Figure 8.1). These cover functional areas such as marketing, human resources and operations. They operate at a level below business strategy and they determine how each of the functional areas supports the business strategy. Hence a marketing strategy is an example of a functional strategy. Typically a marketing strategy would specify a range of goals, policies and actions designed to engage with customers and competitors in pursuit of an overall business strategy. It would aim to integrate a range of marketing activities covering advertising, merchandising, promotion, market research, market planning, marketing communications and the like, to be used in achieving the marketing goals. Strategies for other functional areas would similarly aim to take a strategic approach to the management of the function.

Among the functional areas covered in this way is technology and the relevant functional strategy is a technology strategy. Dodgson (2000: p134) describes a technology strategy as comprising, "the definition, development and use of technological competencies". Thus technology strategy is concerned with decisions about the technology that an organisation uses in order to deliver products and services to customers. These decisions are likely to include: which technologies should an organisation employ? How much money should the organisation invest in technology? How should the technology be developed?

Burgelman *et al.* (2001) argue that technology strategy is to do with the set of technological capabilities that the firm chooses to develop. Virtually all organisations employ one or more technologies. However, only certain of these technologies will be crucial to an organisation and capable of materially influencing its competitive advantage. It is these core technologies that form the focus of technology strategy. Technology strategy is concerned with the long-term development of the core technologies that make up the technology base of the organisation. In this context development has to address two issues, the breadth of the technologies that are core technologies and their depth. Breadth refers to the range of technologies, which may be set narrowly where the technology base is highly specialised, or broadly if it encompasses a number of different technologies. Similarly depth refers to the level of expertise associated with technology. This can range from a comparatively superficial level with only modest expertise where depth is limited, to extensive expertise where greater depth is present. Where technology is a crucial feature of a product or service, as in high technology industries such as computing, aerospace or biotechnology, technology strategy is likely to be critical to the competitiveness of that organisation.

Below functional strategy comes a third level, namely product strategy. This essentially sets out the long-term development of the product or service. A product strategy is rather like a roadmap in that it shows where the product or service is going over the long term. In so doing a product strategy sets out a vision for the product in terms of its long-term development and how this fits with the overall direction of the organisation. This is likely to include the anticipated life cycle of the product, details of how the product will compete (i.e. its competitive strategy), the product platform in terms of the other products that may be derived from it, the market segments in which it will compete, and the technologies to be employed. A product strategy is also likely to say something about innovation and may well include details of the relevant innovation strategy for the product. An innovation strategy is therefore likely to be an integral part of a bigger and broader product strategy.

Innovation strategy

What is an innovation strategy? At this point it is perhaps appropriate to draw a military analogy, specifically the distinction between strategy and tactics. Taking the example of the Battle of Waterloo in 1815, where an Anglo-Dutch army under Wellington and a Prussian army under Blucher defeated Napoloen, Wellington's decision to form his infantry into squares to face the French cavalry, was tactical. In contrast Wellington's decision to fight Napoleon at Waterloo, rather than retreat and fight somewhere else was a matter of strategy. Thus strategy in military terms is about big decisions such as whether, where and when to fight. Similarly with innovation, innovation strategy is about the big decisions surrounding innovation. Decisions about the level of research and development (R&D), the type of innovation, or the most appropriate intellectual property rights to employ, are tactical decisions. Important though these decisions are, they are not matters for innovation strategy. Innovation strategy is concerned with bigger, broader and longer-term issues. If the innovation equivalent of the battlefield is the market, then innovation strategy is concerned with questions of whether, where and when to fight, which when translated from the battlefield to the market comes down to:

- whether to enter a market?
- when to enter the market?
- where to enter the market?

The first of these questions may seem rather drastic, but it is a question that should be asked. It may be more appropriate to let another organisation, which by virtue of financial resources, brand name or expertise is better equipped, carry out the implementation of the innovation. With innovation being conducted by another organisation, this is innovation via an external route, a form of open innovation (as outlined in Chapter 1). The distinction between external routes to innovation and innovation strategies is highlighted in Figure 8.2. The second question is one of the most crucial and yet the timing of innovation is all too often not questioned, as it is assumed that being first to market is the best strategy. As we shall find out shortly, there is considerable evidence to suggest that this is by no means always the case. Finally, where to innovate is not so much a matter of geography as whereabouts, in terms of the market, should one innovate. In particular is there an alternative to a full-scale assault on the market? Are there particular market niches which it might be better to target?

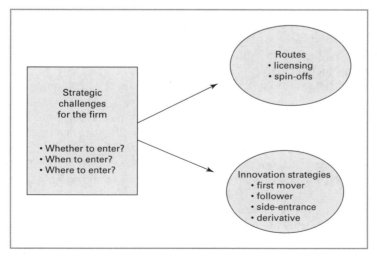

FIGURE 8.2 External routes and innovation strategies

These may seem innocuous questions but they are crucial. The market is no mere receiver of innovations. Markets, particularly for innovations, are surrounded by uncertainty and it is this aspect which makes these questions strategic. One has only to contemplate what happens if the questions aren't asked or if the wrong answers are given. Not only is history littered with failed innovations which the market rejected, but the consequences of failure can be catastrophic, precisely because in some instances innovation strategy is about "betting the company," with the result that failure brings down the whole organisation. An example of betting the company and an inappropriate choice of innovation strategy is provided by the example of the De Havilland Comet, the world's first commercial jet airliner. The British aircraft manufacturer De Havilland was the first to develop and market a commercial jet airliner, the Comet. The De Havilland Comet entered service almost six years before its nearest rival from the American planemaker, Boeing. When the Comet first entered service with the airlines, it transformed air travel by virtue of being much faster and more comfortable than the piston-engined airliners then in service. However, a series of crashes led to the Comet fleet being grounded. Investigations showed that the aircraft suffered from a design flaw. Unfamiliar with the demands of high-speed flight, the designers had underestimated the stresses imposed on the airframe, resulting in the onset of metal fatigue. Although a modified design was introduced, it was too late. Boeing's engineers were able to learn from these mistakes and produce a more robust and reliable aircraft with the result that the Boeing 707 outsold the De Havilland Comet more than tenfold and became the airline industry standard for commercial jet airliners.

Mini Case

Betting the company: EMI and the CAT scanner

EMI, or Electrical and Musical Industries to give the company its full title, is probably most familiar as the owner of several well-known record labels, including one that in the 1960s signed a then little-known band called the Beatles. However, in reality the electrical industries that also formed part of EMI were in their time as important as the musical ones. EMI had a strong record for innovation, having pioneered airborne radar during the Second World War and taken an active role in the development of early computers. Nottingham-born Godfrey Houndsfield, one of the company's senior research engineers on the computing side, was one of the first to develop software for pattern recognition – one of the early precursors of artificial intelligence. This work led him to explore the scope for linking pattern recognition to the processing of images including images generated by X-rays.

What Houndsfield did was to link together X-ray equipment and a computer. Conventional X-ray equipment was used to generate a succession of images, taken by moving in a 160° arc around a patient's head, which were then stored on a computer. He and his team then used the pattern-recognition software they had developed to process the data and display an integrated picture of the cross-section of the human brain. The resulting three-dimensional image of the brain was a big advance on the conventional two-dimensional X-ray image. EMI recognised that it had a significant "invention" on its hands and steps were taken to obtain appropriate patent protection.

However, in exploiting its CAT scanner technology, EMI faced some big challenges. It had no experience of the medical equipment market. While it had manufacturing facilities, these produced defence products not medical equipment. It was also clear that developing a commercially viable CAT scanner was going to be expensive. In the event EMI decided to exploit the technology itself by investing directly in manufacturing and marketing. EMI enjoyed early success. Within four years of launching its first CAT scanner, the sales of its electronics division had quadrupled to £207 million. But EMI soon faced stiff competition from established manufacturers like General Electric and Toshiba and soon found itself losing ground, even though it had a technically superior product. It was not long before EMI had been overtaken in terms of market share. Although Godfrey Houndsfield was awarded a Nobel Prize, the electronics division of EMI began making losses. With problems in its other divisions as well at this time, a financially weakened EMI was acquired by the Thorn group and within a year EMI withdrew from the medical equipment market and sold its scanner interests to General Electric of the US. For EMI exploiting a major technical advance in the form of the CAT scanner proved to be a case of betting the company on an innovation – and losing.

Source: Martin (1994).

External routes to innovation

In terms of strategic decisions about innovation the most crucial question is clearly: should the company enter the market with its innovation?

Drastic though a negative answer to this question may seem, it could be appropriate for a number of reasons, (Ford and Ryan, 1981):

■ Lack of resources

The company that developed the technology (i.e. the patent-holder) may lack not just the necessary finance to exploit the technology, but also the facilities or the staff. This may well occur with SMEs. Where finance is concerned it is not necessarily a case of having the necessary finance; access to finance may be just as important.

■ Lack of knowledge

The company that developed the technology may not have sufficient knowledge of manufacturing, marketing, or distribution channels. This can often occur where scientists and technologists have developed a new technology, but lack the commercial background to exploit it. Given that innovation is often initiated by outsiders, it is perhaps not surprising that lack of knowledge can be a problem.

■ A poor fit with the company's strategy

The technology may be one that has applications in markets that are too small, too remote, or too specialised to be of value for the company that has developed the technology. Under these circumstances exploitation of the technology will not fit comfortably within the strategy of the company.

■ Lack of reach

If the technology has applications that span markets across the world, then it may be that the company does not have the global reach to market technology applications in all these markets. Under such circumstances it may prefer to sell the technology, but on terms that confine it to very specific markets.

If a firm decides that these factors mean it is not wise for it to exploit the innovation itself and should instead aim to transfer the technology to a third party in order that they may complete the innovation process by bringing the innovation to market, then it has a number of routes that it can utilise. Two of the commonest routes for transferring a new technology to a third party are:

- licensing
- spin-offs

Licensing

As we saw in the previous chapter, licensing is open to organisations that can exercise control over their intellectual property rights. With patent protection in place one firm can grant another a licence to manufacture products using its technology. Under the terms of a licence the patent-holder normally retains intellectual property rights over the technology but allows the licensee to use the technology in the products or services it develops, in return for a royalty fee. However, it is normal for the licensing agreement to provide for a royalty payment that will be a percentage of the purchase price of the product. Typically this ranges between 3 per cent and 10 per cent. Licensing agreements will usually include a minimum level of royalty that is not a function of sales, so that the inventor is at least guaranteed a minimum return. But the exact financial arrangements will vary according to circumstances. If the firm selling the technology thinks there is a high level of uncertainty surrounding the products or services the licensee is planning, it may seek a significant initial payment for the licence and a smaller royalty fee.

Licensees will typically be organisations that possess assets the owner of the technology does not have, such as:

- Knowledge

    This might be market knowledge, resulting from a substantial market presence, or the result of experience working in a particular market. Alternatively it might be production knowledge derived from years of working in the trade. Whatever the field, it is likely to be "tacit" knowledge based on experience rather formal knowledge resulting from qualifications. It is precisely because tacit knowledge can take a long time to acquire and is not easily codified or assimilated through conventional learning, that it may be better to grant a licence to someone who does have this kind of knowledge.

- Access to finance

    This might be cash, but is probably likely to mean loan capital or equity capital. Certainly it needs to be some form of long-term capital since this is what the innovation is likely to require. Sometimes conventional sources of finance will not be appropriate especially if there is a high degree of risk. In these circumstances it may particularly be "patient capital" that is required: that is to say, the investor providing it needs to be willing to wait a long time for a return on their investment as innovations frequently take a long time to generate a return. Of course, it is not so much a case of having such capital as having access to individuals or organisations who themselves have access to it.

- Motivation

    Finally those seeking to exploit a technology have to have motivation. They particularly have to have the motivation to carry out innovation themselves. Innovation is a long and difficult process and requires the necessary motivation to see it all the way through. This is particularly important when one considers that innovation requires considerable commercial acumen. Inventors for their part frequently like inventing and may not be much interested in what are often commercial decisions. Under circumstances such as these the exploitation of technology through innovation is probably best left to someone else, i.e. a licensee.

According to Cesaroni (2003) the case for licensing, as opposed to in-house development, as a means of exploiting a proprietary technology, rests on three factors:

- complementary assets in production and marketing
- transactions costs associated with acquiring complementary assets
- competition in the final product market

Complementary assets are the assets required to support the production and sale of products incorporating the technology and might include manufacturing expertise, marketing expertise, product support or training. If a company does not have these complementary assets, as was initially the case with James Dyson and his dual cyclone technology (Dyson, 1997), licensing is more appropriate than in-house development. Transaction costs are the costs of transactions/ exchanges associated with in-house development (i.e. the purchase of complementary assets) or licensing the technology. If the transactions costs of licensing a technology are lower than the cost involved in purchasing the required complementary assets, then licensing is the more logical strategy. Finally, licensing the technology may be appropriate depending on the extent of competition in the final product market.

Pilkingtons, the glass manufacturers who developed the revolutionary "float glass" process for manufacturing plate glass, for instance, relied heavily on licensing. Their thinking was that licensing the technology would both provide the company with an income and prevent other companies from developing an alternative process. The strategy proved highly effective. The first foreign licence was issued to the Pittsburgh Plate Glass Company in 1962 and by the 1990s the float glass process had been licensed to 35 companies in 29 countries. This was in addition to the 14 plants operated by the company itself (Henry and Walker, 1991).

In recent years there has been renewed interest in licensing as a strategy for the exploitation of technology. One study (Kollmer and Dowling, 2004) noted that licensing was no longer confined to small companies lacking the resources to exploit a technology fully, with many large well-established concerns using it to exploit their more peripheral technology assets while focusing their internal resources on core activities.

Mini Case

ARM Holdings

Acorn Computer was a British computer firm that was among the first to develop a commercial Reduced Instruction Set Computer (RISC) processor or chip. The RISC chip is a central processing unit (CPU) that exchanges versatility for processor speed. Essentially the CPU executes a reduced number (i.e. set) of commonly used instructions very fast, thereby enhancing the overall speed of the processor. Hitherto CPUs employed a Complete Instruction Set Computer (CISC) chip that got the hardware of the CPU to do as much as possible per instruction. RISC technology operates on a quite different basis with simple instructions that get the CPU to do less per instruction.

To develop its RISC technology Acorn decided to create a spin-off company by forming a joint venture, ARM Holdings, with Apple Computer of the US, which was keen to use the new technology in its Newton notepad. Unlike other chip manufacturers such as Intel and Motorola, ARM Holdings chose to exploit the new technology in a very particular way. It became in the words of its managing director Robin Saxby, "a chipless chip company" (Garnsey *et al.*, 2008: p217). By licensing, rather than manufacturing and selling RISC chip technology, the company established a new business model that redefined the way in which microprocessors were designed, built and sold. Licensing meant that ARM Holdings could focus on design work as a core activity, leaving others to undertake manufacturing. It also enabled ARM Holdings to quickly establish a market presence that in turn enabled the company to exercise a very powerful influence over the sorts of microprocessor used in a variety of consumer products including: automotive, entertainment, imaging, security and wireless applications. Among the everyday items using ARM Holdings' RISC technology are mobile phones, digital cameras, DVD players, smart cards, set-top boxes, SIM cards, scanners and desktop printers. Some 80 per cent of the mobile phones shipped worldwide utilise ARM technology. All this from a company that makes nothing, preferring instead to license its technology.

Among the companies who are licensees of ARM technology are such household names as Motorola, Philips, Sharp, Sony and Texas Instruments, as well as a large number of specialist manufacturers of computer peripherals and similar devices. ARM Holdings now has a turnover of £250 million and employs more than 1,650 people in design centres in the UK, France and the US.

Sources: Afuah (2003); Garnsey et al. (2008); Khazam and Mowery (1994).

Spin-offs

A spin-off is where one firm quite literally creates another in order to exploit the innovation. It is likely to be an attractive option where the technology of the innovation is not closely related to the core technology of the firm, because it avoids unnecessary distractions.

In order to spin off the innovation through the sale of a subsidiary company, it is necessary to "package" the technology alongside the staff who have developed it and the associated corporate resources (e.g. equipment, facilities, etc.) and sell it off. The normal way of doing this is to locate the technology and the relevant human and other resources in a separate company and then sell off the company. This is what is meant by a "spin-off" where the parent company divests itself of the technology by selling off the subsidiary company where it is based. There are a variety of ways in which it can be sold off including:

- a company flotation via an initial public offering (IPO)
- a management buy-out (MBO) where the company is sold to its managers
- sale to a venture capital (VC) organisation who will invest in the company with a view to selling it off at some time in the future
- sale to another company

Spin-offs have the attraction that they can generate a substantial lump sum, rather than the future income stream associated with licensing. If the parent company is anxious to re-invest the proceeds in other ventures (e.g. core business, new ventures, etc.) then clearly a spin-off has attractions.

Internal routes to innovation: innovation strategies

If the answer to the question about entering the market is affirmative then there are a number of potential innovation strategies that can be employed to determine when and where market entry occurs. Some of these innovation strategies, such as first-mover/pioneer and follower/latecomer strategies are relatively well known. Others are, however, rather more obscure. Four such strategies are presented here:

- first-mover/pioneer strategy
- follower/latecomer strategy
- side-entrance strategy
- derivative strategy

The four selected innovation strategies provide an interesting contrast. There are those such as the first-mover/pioneer and follower/latecomer strategies that relate primarily to the timing of an innovation. They answer the question: when should market entry occur? In contrast the side-entrance and derivative strategies, while they also involve a strategic element because they are concerned with major decisions about innovation that have long-term consequences, are concerned not with when an innovation should enter the market, but rather with where (i.e. which part of the market).

First-mover strategy

The first-mover strategy, as its name implies, is about being first to market with a new product or service. It is the most obvious strategy and probably the most appealing for innovation. Its intuitive appeal (Suarez and Lanzolla, 2005) lies in the fact that most people probably picture innovation as being rather like a race, and a first-mover, by being first to get an innovation to market, is the race winner. This has been given renewed emphasis in recent years by the "dot-com" era (Mellahi and Johnson, 2000), where many new start-ups stressed the need to be first to market, often at the expense of profitability.

There is no shortage of examples of organisations that have successfully employed a first-mover strategy for innovation. Sony's Walkman and the Polaroid instant camera are two good examples. Sony revolutionised the audio equipment market when it brought out the Walkman music player. Though it has been copied by many other manufacturers, being the first to market such a product not only helped confirm Sony's reputation for innovation but also established the company as a major player in the audio equipment field. It also helped Sony to sell 20 million units in a little over five years (Martin, 1994).

In fact there are a number of factors put forward as potential benefits of a first-mover strategy. Firstly the first-mover, by being first, has an opportunity to establish a technological lead, thereby becoming more familiar, more practised and more competent as far as the technology is concerned. A headstart may enable a firm to get further along the "learning curve"

(Lieberman and Montgomery, 1988), thereby securing a cost advantage over rivals. In fields where technology is important this may indeed be plausible, though it is perhaps worth noting that the ability to learn and acquire knowledge isn't only a function of volume (i.e. units produced over time). In addition the learning curve varies from industry to industry and in some it is not significant. Some organisations simply have a greater capacity to learn, and this may be more important than having a headstart. A second factor is linked more directly to technological leadership. Where technological advance is a function of in-house R&D, first-movers who can protect and contain the technology, perhaps through patents or trade secrets, can deter rivals for whom intellectual property rights form a barrier to entry (Lieberman and Montgomery, 1988). A third factor, is the ability to acquire scarce resources, thereby pre-empting later arrivals in the market (Lieberman and Montgomery, 1988). The scarce resources might include locations, suppliers or distribution facilities. While the acquisition of such resources may be important in some fields (e.g. retailing, where locations can be critical), nonetheless it is by no means certain that there will be resources whose acquisition is crucial for competitiveness. Fourthly, being first-to-market provides an opportunity to build a customer base ahead of competitors. Building market share in this way provides an opportunity to "lock-in" customers, who may find it inconvenient or expensive to switch to other firms (Lieberman and Montgomery, 1988). Each of these factors represents a barrier to entry, so that one can see a first-mover strategy as being clearly linked to creating barriers that deter would-be competitors.

Other possible benefits to be derived from a first-mover strategy include: the scope for building brand recognition, shaping consumer preferences and expectations in order to define standards that effectively frame consumer preferences by positioning a product in the minds of consumers, and the acquisition of patents and other intellectual property rights that may deter potential competitors.

Though the case for a first-mover strategy appears strong with a firm rationale supported by significant potential benefits, in reality there are limits to its effectiveness. Given that there are plenty of examples of first-movers who have won the race to market, only for the innovation to ultimately fail in the marketplace, this perhaps shouldn't be a huge surprise. It has already been noted that there can be big differences between industries, in some learning effects are crucial (e.g. aerospace), while in others they are not, and the same goes for scarce resources and standards. Suarez and Lanzolla (2005) suggest that two important factors affecting the suitability of a first-mover strategy are the pace of technological change and the rate at which the market is expanding. If rapid technological change is taking place, they suggest that a first-mover advantage is unlikely because the rapid pace of change will draw in new competitors. This is closely linked to the theory of punctuated equilibrium which predicts that periods of relative stability will be broken by technological breakthroughs that lead to disequilibrium with many competing designs. The Osborne 1 portable computer provides a good example. Osborne was the first company to produce and market a portable computer. However, it weighed 24lbs and this highly innovative computer was quickly superseded by much lighter models as laptop technology rapidly evolved. The same logic is likely to apply with rapid market changes which provide potential competitors with an opportunity to enter the market.

Thus while a first-mover strategy has a number of potential benefits, whether or not they are realised is far from certain and is contingent upon a range of contextual factors. Hence, would-be innovators have to be well aware of the context within which they are innovating if a first-mover strategy is to be successful.

Mini Case

KodaVision

The first camcorders (combining a video camera and video recorder) introduced in the early 1980s were huge, weighing about 14lbs and with overall dimensions the size of a shoebox. They were so big that to operate them they had to be rested on the operator's shoulder. In part this was due to the electronics they used but it was also because for recording they used conventional VHS or Betamax video cassette tapes. Their size was not a problem for professional and semi-professional users, but they weren't really suitable for the home video equipment market. The breakthrough in developing a truly portable handheld camcorder suitable for home users came from the photography giant, Kodak. On 4 January 1984, Kodak launched the KodaVision Series 2000 video system, the first camcorder to use a narrow 8 mm video format that permitted the use of much smaller video cassette tapes. Kodak, was first to market, getting its 8 mm video format camcorder onto the market more than a year ahead of its chief rival, Sony. The tapes used by Kodak's new 8 mm video format were scaled much like audio cassettes, compared to VHS tapes which were typically the size of a book, and this, combined with new solid state electronics, resulted in a camcorder that was much smaller than any then in use, weighing a mere 5lbs. Not only did the new camcorder offer smallness and lightness, it did so without any loss of picture quality.

Kodak expected customers to come flocking to KodaVision. Although the new camcorder at $1,600–$2,600, depending on the accessories required, was a bit more expensive than conventional camcorders, the design's compact size was designed to provide a truly portable camcorder tailored to the needs of the home video equipment market. Comparable in size to a Super 8 movie camera, the KodaVision camcorder was designed to appeal directly to amateur users wanting to record events in and around the home. It was an alternative to Super 8 movie film, but because it was much easier to use it was expected to appeal to a much wider market than just amateur film-makers producing home movies. But consumers, unsure of the value the new technology could provide, failed to recognise the need for KodaVision. Sales were disappointing and Kodak was unable to capitalise on its position as the world's largest supplier of film. Convinced that consumers had rejected the innovation it had pioneered, Kodak withdrew from the market after just three years. It was left to the Japanese electronics manufacturer Sony to introduce the "Handycam," using the same 8 mm format now called Video 8, some two years later. By now consumers were much more comfortable with the idea of 8 mm video camera technology. In the late 1980s and early 1990s it caught on rapidly.

Source: Dodson (2008).

Follower/latecomer strategy

Variously described as a follower or latecomer or sometimes even an imitator strategy, this involves taking a "wait-and-see" approach, rather than perceiving innovation as a race in which being first to market is critical. The idea is to deliberately hold back when a discontinuity occurs and technological advances mean that an innovation is imminent, in order to see how both the market and the technology adapt to the innovation. When it becomes clear that there is a high level of consumer acceptance in the market or the number of competing designs begins to show signs of diminishing, then and only then does the latecomer enter the market. Clearly it is not without risk as there is always the possibility of being completely left behind and as a result shut out of the market. However, the risks may not be as great as some imagine and may well be counter-balanced by advantages derived from learning from the mistakes others have made.

Latecomer advantages can be derived in a variety of ways. The *free rider* effect (Cho *et al.*, 1998) is where a latecomer is able to utilise the benefit of investments made by pioneer firms as they entered the market earlier. These investments might include educating consumers to promote market acceptance, providing some form of infrastructure perhaps to promote ease of use or access to the innovation or gaining regulatory approval, in each case with the intention of supporting innovation. If the benefit from these investments cannot be contained or limited, then there is the very real prospect that firms other than the pioneer will use or easily copy these facilities. Hence latecomers may actually gain advantage from the work of pioneers. *Information spill-over* effects are very similar. They arise where the diffusion of technologies over time results in reduced research and development (R&D) costs for latecomers. Over time pioneer firms may find it difficult to contain in-house the knowledge and expertise that develops from working with a new technology. As it spills out into the public domain, so latecomers can access it, without having to undertake the underpinning R&D expenditure (Teece, 1986). In terms of Porter's (1980) generic strategies this (and the free rider effect) will place latecomers/followers at a cost advantage relative to pioneers.

Closely related are so-called *learning* effects, where latecomers, as in the Comet example earlier, are able to learn from the mistakes and failures of others (Schnaars, 1994). Clearly, however, the level of uncertainty is likely to be a key factor here. When the discontinuity is great, so will be the level of uncertainty. However, as the problems associated with the technology become more widely known and uncertainty reduces, so the scope for learning becomes much greater.

Other potential benefits that can accrue to follower/latecomers include a better understanding of customer requirements (Shankar *et al.*, 1998), avoiding unnecessary R&D and the provision of complementary assets. The first of these arises where consumer requirements are initially unclear. Over time these requirements are likely to be established, something that a follower can capitalise on. Where R&D is concerned, then the advantage that a follower has is being able to avoid committing research to technological paths that will not lead to successful innovations. Quite literally followers can avoid "duds," something that pioneers facing a higher degree of uncertainty find harder to do. Finally there is the matter of complementary assets. Where innovation takes place in a market where services such as marketing, manufacturing capability or after-sales service are important to consumers, latecomers may have an advantage over pioneers by virtue of having had more time to develop such complementary assets (Teece, 1986). This puts a pioneer at a disadvantage in relation to a follower.

If these sorts of factors are in evidence, then the follower/latecomer strategy may well prove the most appropriate. Despite the apparent attractions of being first, when it comes to innovation, pioneering may well have its limitations. What matters is being able to judge when these conditions are likely to apply.

Side-entrance strategy

One of the difficulties that innovations, particularly those based on a new technology, often face is that initially they are uncompetitive compared to existing products, in terms of cost and sometimes even overall performance. The first steamships provide a classic example. In terms of overall performance, wind-powered clipper ships were for many years faster than steamships. The technology S-curve outlined in Chapter 4 shows how in the early years of a new technology this can occur. Under these circumstances there is no particular reason for consumers to purchase an innovation, other than perhaps the novelty factor.

The central idea behind the side-entrance strategy is achieving market entry via a small niche in the market rather than a full-scale assault on the main market itself. The rationale behind this is that in market niches there may be groups of consumers with particular needs which are not being met, or not being met very well, in the main market. Since innovations, particularly radical innovations involving new technologies, often have new attributes such as mobility/portability, reduced size, lower power consumption or greater efficiency, innovators can use these attributes to differentiate the product and appeal to groups of consumers in market niches. With the prospect of their needs now being rather better catered for, the innovation may create value for them and they may be willing to purchase the new product. Targeting groups of consumers in this way provides an opportunity for the innovator to establish a bridgehead in specific market niches. In this way the innovator gains market presence. Then as the technology matures and costs come down and overall performance improves the innovation can be extended to the main market.

The innovation of the hydraulic excavator provides a very good example of the side-entrance strategy at work. When the first hydraulic excavators appeared, the market was dominated by cable-operated mechanical excavators. With relative simple cable technology, they met the performance requirements of their customers, large construction and mining companies, as far as the amount of earth they could shift. The new hydraulic excavators were simply not powerful enough to match mechanical excavators when it came to their primary function of shifting earth. However, though they performed relatively poorly in terms of their capacity to move earth, the new hydraulic excavators were smaller and much more manoeuvrable. Faced with this situation, firms like the British excavator manufacturer, JCB, who developed the first hydraulic excavators, targeted new market niches (Christensen, 1997) such as housebuilders, local authorities and utility companies. They had previously not used excavators. Because most of their excavation work was on a small scale, it had in the past been completed by manual labour. JCB successfully gained a foothold in this niche of the market. Thus the early users of hydraulic excavators were very different from the mainstream customers of the mechanical excavator manufacturers (Christensen, 1997). Then having demonstrated the effectiveness of the new hydraulic technology and as the technology itself improved they were able to enter the mainstream market. Eventually hydraulic excavators came to dominate the mainstream market.

This type of innovation strategy offers a number of benefits, particularly for new entrant firms. Firstly it avoids head-to-head competition with well established players in the market. This can be significant for new entrants that don't possess resources on the scale of their more established counterparts. Secondly targeting a market niche offers an opportunity to prove a new technology or a new application for a technology. There is the prospect of important and powerful "demonstration" effects, where customers and particularly potential customers can see the new technology in action and then judge its value. Hopefully having seen the new technology in action, potential customers will be convinced of its value. Thirdly, there is scope for learning the technology and thereby enhancing it. Most new technologies are gradually refined once they have been launched into the market. Thus via successive incremental innovations the technology is improved and firms start to move up the S-curve. The market niche provides a chance to learn the new technology, in what one might describe as a protected environment, certainly one that is perhaps sheltered from the full blast of competition and where the risk of problems should there be something wrong with the technology are less. Only when the technology has fully proved itself and become fully competitive will it then be launched on the mainstream market.

Sony and the transistor radio

Sony was founded in May 1946 as Tokyo Telecommunications Engineering Co. Ltd. (abbreviated to Totsuko). The founders, Masaru Ibuka and Akio Morita, had previously worked together during the War when they were assigned to a task force working on the development of heat seeking missiles, and with the coming of peace they set up in business together. Located in a single room of a former department store in central Tokyo, the company repaired radios and manufactured voltmeters. In the years after World War Two, radios were much in demand as a source of music and world news, but many had been damaged or destroyed and with spare parts in short supply, repairing them called for skill and ingenuity. The supply of parts, particularly vacuum tubes, was also problematic in the production of voltmeters. A valuable source of supply for the new company proved to be GIs selling contraband from American military bases. Both Ibuka and Morita shared a passion for technology and innovation, and their reliance on this source led to them developing an admiration for American technology and a desire to see Japan catch up.

During the first three years the company's manufacturing activity focused on the production of voltmeters. These proved popular and output planned initially to be 10 units per month soon climbed to 30 or 40. The company grew rapidly, moving to new premises at Gotenyama Heights in the southern part of Tokyo in 1947. By 1949 there were 45 employees on the payroll. In the same year Ibuka saw and heard for the first time what was to be the mainstay of the company's activities in the early 1950s, namely the tape recorder. Tape recorders had been developed in Germany in the 1930s by Grundig and Telefunken and had been used to record and disseminate Nazi propaganda. After the War tape recording, like much German technology, found its way to the US. The leading manufacturers were Ampex in tape recorders and 3M in magnetic tape. Ibuka appears to have decided on the spot that this was the product on which the new company would build its reputation.

The company's first tape recorder was the model G which weighed 100lbs and cost 160,000 yen. Intended for use by universities and government departments initial sales were extremely disappointing and only saved by an order from the Supreme Court for 20 machines to enable them to cope with a shortage of stenographers. Undaunted by this poor start Ibuka had the idea of producing a much smaller machine, the model H. This weighed only a third of its predecessor and achieved modest sales mainly to schools and educational institutions. It was followed by the model P. This was smaller still at a mere 20lbs. Light enough to be suspended from the shoulder, it proved popular with journalists who used it for "man in the street" interviews. It proved to be the company's first cash cow, selling 3,000 units in 7 months.

It may well have been the company's success in miniaturising the tape recorder that led Ibuka to turn his attention to the transistor. In 1952 while on a visit to the US, he learned that Western Electric was offering a technical licence for transistor manufacture. Invented at

Bell Labs in 1948, one of the big attractions of the transistor was that it provided a small compact and lightweight alternative to the bulky vacuum tube then widely used in electronic applications such as radios. The radio market was then dominated by giant American corporations like RCA who produced radio sets for use in the home. These were large and non-portable, very similar in size and weight to old style CRT-based television sets. Ibuka appears to have been among the first to appreciate that the transistor offered the opportunity for Sony to produce a different kind of radio. Utilising the new transistor technology it was possible to produce a radio that was a fraction of the size of a conventional radio. In fact the transistor provided scope for producing the first truly portable radio.

However, Ibuka faced an uphill struggle. He had first to gain a licence and then had to modify the transistor so that it was capable of producing the necessary high frequency signals required for radio applications. To get a licence he needed to get the support of MITI because the licence would require foreign currency which was then tightly regulated. For its part MITI was reluctant to support an upstart new company, preferring instead to support large established Japanese electronics firms like Matsushita, Hitachi and Toshiba. Despite these potential obstacles, Ibuka gained a licence and in August 1955 the company announced its model TR-55 transistor radio, the world's first commercially successful transistor radio. It was followed in March 1957 by the release of an even smaller model which represented the first "pocketable" radio which sold 1.5 million units and established Sony as the market leader.

Source: Nathan (1999).

Derivative strategy

A derivative strategy essentially involves applying a new technology to an existing product to create a new product. The original product will already have a presence in the market and the derivative strategy aims to capitalise on this existing market position, in order to gain market entry for the "new" product. Hence a derivative strategy is something of a hybrid strategy. Clearly it is not a strategy that can be used by new firms, as there has to be an existing product and it has to already be positioned in the market. However, for established products with a reputation it can be an attractive strategy. Keeble (1997) notes that the exploitation of new technologies is not confined to new-product development. It can also occur through what Rothwell and Gardiner (1989a) describe as "re-innovation". Rothwell and Gardiner note that in many industry sectors there are relatively few completely new products entering the market. Instead, one often finds a large number of what they (Rothwell and Gardiner, 1989a) describe as "post-launch improvements".

In some cases these improvements extend to a complete redesign of the product. Rothwell and Gardiner (1989b) give the example of the development of a heat gun for paint-stripping by the consumer products manufacturer Black & Decker. In this instance the product was new and Black & Decker were uncertain of whether it would be accepted by consumers. Given the uncertainty, they utilised the outer casing, motor, fan and switch from an existing product – an electric drill, thereby substantially lowering the development cost and the scale of the investment in innovation. This was an example of a derivative strategy being used, though in this case the technology was not particularly new.

Smith and Rogers (2004) show how in the aerospace industry manufacturers often use derivative strategies by adding a new technology to an existing product. Airframe manufacturers such as Boeing for instance will fit a new engine to an airliner in order to improve its performance. Smith and Rogers (2004) cite the case of Rolls-Royce's Tay engine. This was a derivative of the company's well-established Spey engine which had been in service for some 20 years. By adding a new fan utilising the advanced, wide-chord fan technology of the company's much larger RB211-535 engine, Rolls-Royce was able to develop an engine that was substantially more fuel efficient, quieter, lighter and more reliable. The use of derivative strategy in this way greatly reduced the development cost and the time taken to get the new engine into service. In particular, the certification of the engine was simpler and quicker because major systems from the old engine were used on the new one and these had already been certificated years earlier. Not only that, the Spey engine already had an established customer base, and airframe manufacturers such as the American business jet manufacturer, Gulfstream, were keen to use what they saw as a product with which they had some familiarity, though now with much improved performance characteristics.

CASE STUDY: VIDEOGAMES

Termed "recreational software," videogames originated in the US in the early 1970s. According to Lange (2002) one of the reasons why videogames developed first in the US was that US citizens had far fewer reservations about unadulterated entertainment. Among the first videogames was, Pong, an electronic table tennis game produced by Atari, that briefly mesmerised America. At this time games were often written by hobbyists working in their bedrooms and played on simple home computers. There was no one driving the development of the videogame industry.

Atari, founded in 1972 by Norman Bushnell, originally produced arcade machines, indeed Pong was played on such machines and its success led to videogame arcade machines largely replacing conventional pinball machines. But, in the late 1970s Atari branched out with a new innovation, the videogame console for the home. Campbell-Kelly (2003) credits Atari with being one of the pioneer firms that shaped the videogame console industry in the early phases of its development.

In October 1977 Atari launched its highly successful Atari 2600 videogame console. The console sold for $200 with profits coming from the sale of game cartridges that retailed for $30 but cost only one third of this to produce. A major factor in the success of the Atari 2600 was the availability of third party software which made a wide range of games available including ones produced by established media firms such as CBS, Disney and Lucas Films. When the videogame market peaked in 1982, annual sales of videogame cartridges in the US stood at $1.5 billion.

The mid-1980s saw the appearance of two new Japanese rivals to Atari, in the form of Nintendo and Sega. Nintendo was an arcade machine manufacturer that launched its first videogame console in 1983. Its Nintendo Entertainment System (NES) console represented a major advance in that it offered much improved picture quality through the use of custom rather than off-the-shelf chips. It also came with the highly successful arcade game "Mario Bros". A feature of Nintendo's console was that it could only be used with Nintendo-manufactured game cartridges. A special chip in each cartridge prevented other firms from producing compatible products. The Nintendo console was a huge success. Encouraged by Nintendo's success another Japanese arcade manufacturer, Sega, entered the market with its Sega Master System. Sega was not able to rival Nintendo, enjoying a similar market share to that of Atari. By the end of the 1980s when it launched its hand-held videogame console, the Game Boy, Nintendo was reckoned to have 85–90 per cent of the videogame market worldwide.

The start of the 1990s saw further innovation in the industry as Sega launched the Genesis, the first 16-bit console offering significantly better speed and graphics. Although it was quickly followed by a similar offering from Nintendo, this time it was Sega that had the edge helped in part by what rapidly became the videogame sensation, "Sonic the Hedgehog". Nintendo lost its market leadership as Sega became the dominant platform with an 80 per cent share of new sales.

The advent of further innovation in the form of 32-bit consoles in the mid-1990s led to major changes in the videogame industry. The industry pioneers faced a new threat, this time from new entrants from outside the industry. In 1995 the consumer electronics giant Sony, launched the PlayStation, the first 32-bit games console. The 32-bit technology of the

▶ PlayStation was a step-change from the 16-bit consoles that then dominated the market. Not only that, Sony's decision to use CDs, a technology it had pioneered, rather than the conventional games cartridges used by Nintendo and Sega, gave it a major advantage over its competitors. CDs were not only much cheaper to manufacture, they permitted much shorter lead times, allowing Sony to respond very rapidly to changes in demand. Despite having hitherto had nothing to do with videogames, Sony's PlayStation was an unparalleled success. By 1998 more than 50 million PlayStations had been sold, making it the world's best selling videogames console. One third of American households owned one. In the same year the company's game division accounted for almost half of Sony Corporation's consolidated operating profits. Three factors were critical in Sony's success: the fostering of third party software development; reducing the cost of manufacturing videogames: and the changing demographics of those playing videogames. Sony catered for the first two of these aspects by the use of CDs, while the third was catered for by the new 32-bit technology which permitted much more sophisticated games that appealed not just to teenagers, the traditional market for videogames, but young adults as well.

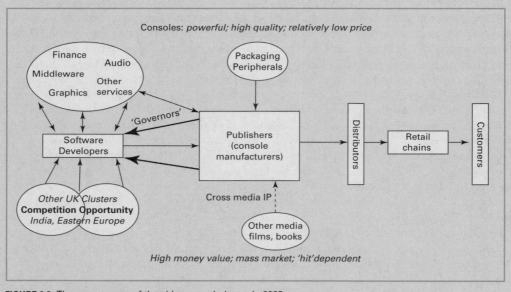

FIGURE 8.3 The governance of the videogame industry in 2005

The other new entrant was the software giant Microsoft which launched its 32-bit games console early in 2002. Microsoft's entry into this market reflected a growing concern that the growth of the videogame market threatened the PC market and a desire to diversify away from software. In any event it paid off as the Xbox quickly took market share from Nintendo's GameCube and to a lesser extent Sony's PlayStation. Indeed Microsoft's entry marked a point where, according to Grantham and Kaplinsky (2005: p189) the console manufacturers led by the two "new kids on the block" have now come to dominate a global value chain comprising software developers, distributors and retail chains to the point where in governance terms they, "define who produces what, under what terms and for what returns" (see Figure 8.3).

Success in the videogame market now requires deep pockets, extensive distribution and supply channels, and in Chaplin and Ruby's (2006: p226) words, "a willingness to take huge losses on console sales in order to establish a base of customers".

Sources: Campbell-Kelly (2003); Chaplin and Ruby (2005); Grantham and Kaplinsky (2005: p189); Lange (2002); Nathan (1999).

Questions

1 Which innovation strategy did Atari follow in the 1970s?
2 What was Atari's business model? How influential has this model been?
3 Who were the new entrants to the videogame console market in the late 1990s and early 2000s?
4 What were the attractions of the videogame console market for these new entrants?
5 What assets did the new entrants possess that facilitated their entry into the videogames console market?
6 Which innovation strategy did Sony follow?
7 Why do you think Sony chose this innovation strategy?
8 What was strategic about Sony's decision to enter the videogames market in the late 1990s?
9 What was innovative about Sony's PlayStation?
10 Draw a diagram to show the application of the theory of punctuated equilibrium to the development of videogame consoles.

? Questions for discussion

1 What are strategic decisions?
2 Give examples of strategic decisions to do with innovation.
3 What is an innovation strategy?
4 Differentiate between first-mover and follower strategies.
5 Why do first movers quite often fail?
6 What advantages, if any, do followers gain over first movers?
7 What is a side-entrance strategy and what advantages does it offer the would-be innovator?
8 Why might a firm want to take an external route in order to develop a technology or idea it has pioneered?
9 Why did many "dot-com" businesses adopt a first-mover strategy?
10 What risks does a firm expose itself to when adopting a follower/latecomer strategy?

Exercises

1 Prepare a presentation outlining the case for an innovation strategy of your choice. Assume that the presentation is being made either to the board of directors of the company that has developed a new technology or members of the financial community who are planning to invest in the company.

2 Prepare a report that compares and contrasts the relative merits of first-mover/pioneer and follower/latecomer innovation strategies.

3 Why do innovations fail? Choose an example of an unsuccessful innovation, and write a report showing how the innovation strategy contributed to the failure of the innovation.

4 As an employee of a company that has developed and patented a new technology, prepare a report for the company's senior management explaining why external routes can be an effective way of exploiting new technologies. Pay particular attention to the circumstances where external routes may be appropriate and the benefits and pitfalls associated with them.

Further reading

1 **Grant, R.M.** (2008) *Contemporary Strategic Analysis*, 6th edn, Blackwell, Oxford.
The field of strategy is extremely well catered for when it comes to texts but most such texts place comparatively little emphasis on innovation. One of the exceptions is Grant (2008). This text not only provides excellent coverage of strategy in all its forms, it also provides detailed coverage of innovation strategy. There is a whole chapter devoted to the management of innovation and this incorporates a section on strategies to exploit innovation where both external routes to innovation are outlined and specific innovation strategies. It also includes plenty of examples.

2 **Chesbrough, H.W.** (2003a) *Open Innovation: The New Imperatives for Creating and Profiting from Technology,* Harvard Business School Press, Boston, MA.
Although this isn't a book about strategy it does provide a very useful perspective on external routes to innovation. A key element of Chesbrough's thesis is that recent changes have led to much more open forms of innovation. External routes are a key element within this and are covered in considerable detail.

3 **Lieberman, M.B. and D.B. Montgmery** (1988) "First Mover Advantages", *Strategic Management Journal,* 9, pp41–58.
Although now some 20 years old, this remains one of the defining papers on innovation strategy. It focuses on first movers, explaining in detail the potential benefits to be gained from this type of strategy. At the same time, because it outlines the potential disadvantages attached to being a first mover, it also provides a clear rationale for the follower/latecomer strategy.

4 **Teece, D.** (1986) "Profiting from Technological Innovation: Implications for Integration, Collaboration, Licensing and Public Policy", *Research Policy*, 15, pp285–305.
Another "golden oldie" but it gives a clear summary of the relative merits of different innovation strategies as well as providing some very useful examples.

Technical entrepreneurs

❖ OBJECTIVES

When you have completed this chapter you will be able to:

- ❖ explain the nature of entrepreneurship
- ❖ distinguish different categories of entrepreneur
- ❖ identify the key characteristics of technical entrepreneurs
- ❖ categorise technical entrepreneurs
- ❖ analyse the factors that lead to the growth and development of technical entrepreneurs

Introduction

Silicon Valley on the southern end of San Francisco Bay in California is recognised throughout the world as a centre of innovation. However, it is not only innovations that have been created in Silicon Valley. Some of the best known names in high technology not only have their headquarters in Silicon Valley, they began life there. Silicon Valley is a veritable breeding ground of new, high technology businesses. Firms like Apple in personal computers, Intel in integrated circuits, Cisco in network computing, Oracle in database systems, eBay in on-line auctions and Google in search engines and Adobe in electronic publishing all began life in Silicon Valley. Among the first was a company which today is one of the largest, Hewlett-Packard. Founded on 1 January 1939 by two classmates from Stanford University in a garage in Palo Alto near the northern end of the valley which was then covered with fruit orchards, Hewlett-Packard has grown to the point where today it is a $100 billion business.

What marks out both the large and the small firms of Silicon Valley is not just their technological prowess and expertise and their success in launching major innovations, but the similarities in terms of their origins. They are all relatively young businesses founded in all but one case in the last 30 years by young entrepreneurs. However, they are not just entrepreneurs, that is to say individuals with visions of new products/services, the abilities to spot commercial opportunities and the determination and skill to bring together all the necessary resources required to make a new business function effectively. All the entrepreneurs listed in Table 9.1 are individuals with a strong technology background.

Founder/Entrepreneur	Company	Business
Steve Jobs/Steve Wozniak	Apple Computer	Personal computer
Gordon Moore/Robert Noyce	Intel	Integrated circuits
Larry Ellison	Oracle	Database systems
Bill Hewlett/David Packard	Hewlett-Packard	Computers/printers
Jerry Yang/David Filo	Yahoo	Search engine
John Warnock/Charles Geschke	Adobe	Electronic publishing
Larry Page/Sergey Brin	Google	Search engine

TABLE 9.1 Silicon Valley entrepreneurs

Many of them, like Larry Page and Sergey Brin of Google (Vise, 2005), have PhDs; even those that don't generally have a first degree in a technology-based subject such as computer science or electrical engineering. One exception is Steve Jobs of Apple Computer who not only does not have a technology-based degree, he actually dropped out of university after the first year, but he, like all the others, has worked for a technology-based company (the computer game maker Atari) and was a self-taught computer scientist.

Thus all the companies shown in Table 9.1, like so many high-tech businesses in Silicon Valley, were founded by entrepreneurs with a technology background. All are excellent examples of what are commonly termed "technical entrepreneurs".

Mini Case

A garage and an idea

Silicon Valley started in a garage. To be precise the garage of 367 Addison Avenue, Palo Alto, California. It was here in 1939 that William Hewlett and David Packard began making the prototype of the audio oscillator that formed the first product line of their new company Hewlett-Packard. At a time before there were science parks, starter units or incubators, many technology entrepreneurs, including Walt Disney (Disney Corporation) and Jim Casey and Claude Ryan (United Parcel Service), started their businesses in this way. Nor is it an American phenomenon. In the UK Colin Chapman, the founder of the sports-car maker Lotus, and James Dyson, the founder of Dyson Appliances, the manufacturer of the world's first bag-less vacuum cleaner, both set up initially in garages.

Both Hewlett and Packard had earlier studied electrical engineering at nearby Stanford University and become close friends. While at Stanford they had come under the guidance of Frederick Terman whose course in radio-engineering they took in their final year. On graduating both Hewlett and Packard headed to the east coast and took jobs in electrical engineering. David Packard went to work for General Electric in New York. It was at General Electric that he came into contact with the company's research department, working on the testing of vacuum tubes. This experience not only gave Packard a valuable insight into managing in a manufacturing company, it also enabled him to build up a valuable network of contacts in the electrical engineering industry.

However, he didn't stay in New York. After a couple of years at General Electric he moved back to Palo Alto to take up a one-year fellowship at Stanford. This brought him into close contact not only with Frederick Terman but also Bill Hewlett who had meanwhile moved to San Francisco. He and Hewlett were soon discussing plans for setting up their own company. So it was that Hewlett-Packard came into being, helped by much encouragement and an investment of $500 in seed capital from Frederick Terman who acted as an "angel" investor for the new firm.

Fortunately for the nascent firm, they were able to call upon more resources and facilities than those available in Packard's garage. They used Stanford University's laboratory facilities in developing and testing the first version of their audio oscillator. An early version of this device was presented at an Institute of Radio Engineers conference in Portland, Oregon. Among those who saw Bill Hewlett's presentation was Bud Hawkins, chief sound engineer at the Walt Disney company. As a result Disney ordered 8 Model 200B oscillators from Hewlett Packard. Additional orders followed and within a year the new company had out-grown the garage. Not only had what was to eventually become a giant technology-based corporation been successfully launched, the Silicon Valley model of technical entrepreneurship had emerged.

Sources: Packard (1995); Audia and Rider (2005); Gibbons (2000).

Entrepreneurship

In order to understand the role and function of the technical entrepreneur it is necessary first to look at entrepreneurship as a whole. Entrepreneurs are not managers nor are they inventors. True entrepreneurs need to know about management and they very often have to manage, but the terms "entrepreneur" and "manager" are not synonymous. There is much more to being an entrepreneur than simply managing an enterprise. To try and understand just what it is that makes the entrepreneur different, it can be helpful to look at some of the different perspectives on entrepreneurship. These have emerged over many years and taken together they provide valuable insights into the role of the entrepreneur and the nature of entrepreneurship. The perspectives can be broadly categorised into:

- economic
- psychological
- behavioural/processual

Economics

Cantillon was one of the first scholars in the emerging discipline of economics to consider entrepreneurship in his "Essay on the Nature of Commerce" published in 1755 (Glaister, 1988). Cantillon portrayed the entrepreneur as a pivotal figure within markets who acted as an organiser of production (Deakins and Freel, 2003): that is, someone who brings together factors of production such as land, labour and capital so that goods and services can be brought to market. In the twentieth century Knight (1921) took the analysis further, arguing that the entrepreneur's function was essentially one of risk taking. Since factor inputs are purchased at known prices and sold at prices that are as yet unknown, the entrepreneur has to bear risk.

A marked change of emphasis comes in the work of Schumpeter, who stressed the link between entrepreneurship and innovation. According to Schumpeter the entrepreneur is one of the prime movers in economic development and his/her function is to innovate. Schumpeter (1936) pointed out that the knowledge underlying innovation may not be newly discovered. It may perfectly well be existing knowledge that has not previously been used in products or services. For Schumpeter what matters is that the entrepreneur gives rise to some form of new combination. In a world that is generally resistant to change, the entrepreneur is a disruptive influence. By initiating new products and new processes (which may or may not include new knowledge/discoveries) the entrepreneur initiates change. In this way the entrepreneur creates opportunities. This new combination results in technological advance and it is this that makes Schumpeter's entrepreneur a key figure in economic transformation.

Finally, in the 1970s Kirzner (1973) portrayed the entrepreneur as someone who identifies and exploits opportunities for profit, resulting from an imperfect distribution of knowledge. Rather like a middleman Kirzner's entrepreneur finds opportunities that arise because knowledge is incomplete.

Psychological

In the 1960s a rather different perspective on entrepreneurship emerged. This switched the agenda away from the function of the entrepreneur within an economic system to look instead at the individual. This body of work suggested that certain individuals had a particular aptitude for entrepreneurship by virtue of certain distinctive personality "traits". These traits include:

- a need for achievement (McClelland, 1961)
- a high internal locus of control
- a willingness to take risks
- a need for autonomy and independence

While many successful entrepreneurs, especially those who come across as "heroic" figures, do possess many of these characteristics, the place of personality within entrepreneurship has been the subject of extensive critical comment. Specific traits have not proved particularly good at predicting behaviour. Other criticisms levelled at this type of approach include: personality factors can and do change over time; the search for a single factor provides a very limited perspective on the nature of entrepreneurship; it ignores learning and it takes no account of the fact that personality factors can and do change over time. Perhaps the most serious flaw is that it ignores the influence of the environment or context in which the entrepreneur operates. Consequently, work on personality traits has to an extent been overtaken by research focusing on entrepreneurial behaviour, which places considerable emphasis on context.

Behavioural/processual

These criticisms have led some researchers to look at the broader context within which entrepreneurship takes place. In particular efforts have been directed at exploring business behaviour and business context. These have looked at factors such as: ethnicity, gender, occupational background, culture and family structure related to entrepreneurial activity. This has led some to look at the different stages in the process of business development as instances of different contexts. Chell *et al.* (1997: p5) for instance point out that the "stages of development" associated with the process of business growth provide a way of "conceptualising the context in which owner-managers carry out their business affairs and enables a deeper understanding of what is driving their behaviour". People develop "repertoires" of behaviour in response to the situations and circumstances in which they find themselves. This has led to the identification of a number of typologies designed to reflect differing contexts of entrepreneurship. These typologies have included: entrepreneur, quasi-entrepreneur, administrator and caretaker (Chell *et al.*, 1991); craft-owner, promoter and professional manager (Beaver, 2002) and artisan, entrepreneur and manager (Blundel and Smith, 2001). One category of entrepreneur that has not figured prominently in these typologies and yet which resonates strongly with the notion that there are different types of entrepreneur each of which inhabits a different context is: the technical entrepreneur.

Mini Case

Mark Shuttleworth

Born in the dusty gold-mining town of Welkom in South Africa, and raised in Cape Town, Mark Shuttleworth's passion for technology started as a child when he got into computer games. His enthusiasm for computers led him to study for a BSc in Finance and Information Systems at the University of Cape Town (UCT), and it was as a student that he encountered the Internet for the first time.

In 1995, while he was still an undergraduate at the University of Cape Town, Mark took the plunge and set up his own Internet consulting business, founding a company called Thawte™. The company's focus quickly shifted to the new and emerging field of Internet security. At the time electronic commerce was in its infancy, but developing rapidly. Thawte™ became the first company outside the US to produce a full-security encrypted e-commerce web server. This brought Thawte™ into the world of "public key infrastructure," which is the basis for all encrypted and authenticated Internet transactions (required so that users can ensure the websites they are transacting with are authentic). As e-commerce began to take off, and in particular as credit and debit cards were increasingly used for making payments, the company expanded very rapidly and was one of the first to be recognised by both Netscape and Microsoft as a trusted third party for website certification. Recognition by these leading US computing companies helped the company quickly to establish a leading position in Internet security. Then in December 1999, at the height of the so – called "dot-com" bubble, Mark, then aged 26, sold Thawte™ to the American Internet security company VeriSign for a staggering $575 million. By this time Thawte™ was the fastest-growing Internet certification authority worldwide, and the leading certification authority outside of the US.

Believing that entrepreneurs in South Africa have the potential to start businesses with global impact, Mark used some of his new-found wealth to form a new venture capital team called HBD, which seeks to invest in innovative companies based in South Africa but with the potential to serve a global marketplace. Among the sectors HBD has invested in are software, pharmaceutical services, electronics and mobile phone services.

The nature of technical entrepreneurship

The term "technical entrepreneur" is synonymous with small, high-technology firms or, as they are sometimes known, new technology-based firms (NTBFs). These are small businesses that are dependent on a high level of technological knowledge and expertise. The term is often used to describe a technology-based "spin-off" business, formed by scientists and engineers leaving their current employment in a university, research-based institution or an industrial company and going it alone by setting up their own independent company. This sort of enterprise is typically to be found in industries such as electronics, computer services or biotechnology. A study by Jones-Evans and Westhead (1996) for instance found that in the UK there were large numbers of small, high-technology businesses in the computer services sector comprising specialist software companies and others providing a range of other similar services. Other sectors where there were significant numbers of this type of enterprise included medical equipment, electrical equipment, precision instruments, and pharmaceuticals (i.e. biotechnology). In these sectors there is scope for individuals who have acquired technological knowledge and expertise through their work in a large organisation to set up on their own. As an independent firm they can then specialise in the supply of specialist components or specialist services. As a number of researchers have indicated, this has been facilitated in recent years by the growth of networks as a way of linking together both large and small organisations and groups of small organisations. Clearly, becoming an independent firm involves a considerable degree of uncertainty, which is why these ventures are described as "entrepreneurial". Nevertheless, they involve a particular form of entrepreneurship, one that relies heavily on technology and the creation of new products and services. As a result this is the form of entrepreneurship that is probably most closely connected to innovation.

Definitions of technical entrepreneurs tend to emphasise the technical at the expense of the entrepreneurial. Thus Cooper (1971) quoted in Jones-Evans (1995: p29) describes this type of business as:

> a company which emphasises research and development or which places major emphasis on exploiting new technical knowledge. It is often founded by scientists and engineers, and usually includes a substantial percentage of professional technically trained personnel.

While this definition rightly highlights the importance of technology for this sort of enterprise and the connection to innovation, it tends to ignore entrepreneurship. Hence perhaps a better definition comes from Jones-Evans (1997) when he describes technical entrepreneurs as,

> … small technology-based firms (that) display a distinct form of entrepreneurship, mainly because of the dependence of the venture on the owner-manager's high degree of a technological expertise, translated into new technologies, products and processes.

This definition does rather better at including some of the key elements of the technical entrepreneur. As studies of locations populated by large numbers of technical entrepreneurs have shown, these businesses are not merely technical. Henry and Pinch's (2000a) study of Motor Sport Valley in Oxfordshire, for instance, highlighted the high rates of entry and exit into the industry as well as the dynamism of these businesses in terms of their ability to respond rapidly to change. Similarly, this type of business is likely to be closely involved in the application of technology to innovations, be they new products, new processes or new services. This was something highlighted in a major study by Pavitt *et al.* (1987) which noted that small firms had significantly increased their share of recorded innovations in the post-war period.

Consequently perhaps the most effective definition of the technical entrepreneur comes from Autio (1995) who suggested that technical entrepreneurs possess four features:

1 the founders of the company have been affiliated with the source of the technology before establishing the company.

2 the business idea of the company is essentially based on exploiting advanced technological knowledge developed or acquired in a source of technology.

3 the company is independent.

4 the company is entrepreneurial, that is, it is controlled and managed by an entrepreneur or a group of entrepreneurs.

While this definition incorporates the essential attributes of a technical entrepreneur, there are other features that are sometimes associated with this kind of business. For example, technical entrepreneurs typically make extensive use of networks comprising contact with universities, large companies and research institutes, as a source of both knowledge inputs and market opportunities. The mechanisms that help to maintain these contacts can take a variety of different forms. Autio (1995) notes that strategic alliances and R&D partnerships are often used as well as other forms of collaborative agreement. Devices such as these help to provide an interface that can be used to convey information and knowledge through the network. Similarly, the knowledge, particularly the technical knowledge, that plays such an important part in these businesses tends to be tacit rather than explicit. It is very often knowledge associated with skills and capabilities which resides in individuals. One of the great strengths of technical entrepreneurs is that they are very effective both in accessing this kind of knowledge and in applying it to practical problem-solving situations where it can contribute to the development of new products, processes and services.

Mini Case

Berghaus

Berghaus is a very recognisable brand name when it comes to outdoor wear. One does not have to be an active mountaineer to encounter Berghaus products – these days a visit to the local supermarket on a wet day will probably be quite sufficient. Yet Berghaus is much more than a well-known brand name. It is widely recognised as supplier of high-performance clothing. This reputation comes from its pioneering work developing outdoor wear made from Gore-Tex – an innovation that has helped to transform the outdoor clothing market in the last thirty years by making breathable waterproof clothing a reality for the first time. Set up in the late 1960s to run a shop specialising in outdoor wear, Berghaus began as a partnership between Peter Lockley who had worked in marketing and sales for the chocolate manufacturer Rowntrees, and Gordon Davidson who worked as a lecturer in mechanical engineering at

Newcastle Polytechnic (now Northumbria University). After an initial start in retailing, Berghaus moved into manufacturing in the early 1970s making first rucksacks and then outdoor clothing. In 1976 Berghaus was instrumental in the development of outdoor clothing made from Gore-Tex. Although W.L. Gore and Associates developed Gore-Tex fabric, it was Lockley and Davidson at Berghaus that developed the manufacturing techniques that enabled high-performance clothing to be produced using Gore-Tex, giving the consumer for the first time garments that were both waterproof and breathable.

Source: Parsons and Rose (2003).

Occupational background

Early work on technical entrepreneurs tended to portray the technical entrepreneur as an academic in a university or a researcher in a non-profit-making laboratory who had set up on his/her own, giving rise to what some have described as the "scientist entrepreneur". This model implied an entrepreneur as someone with little or no business experience and business knowledge. Later work (Cooper, 1971) extended the analysis to include entrepreneurs who had worked for large industrial concerns and therefore did have a business background. This has generally been the view of technical entrepreneurs that has prevailed. Only recently has the analysis been extended further. Work by Jones-Evans suggests that in fact technical entrepreneurs come from a more diverse range of backgrounds than hitherto noted.

Jones-Evans' (1995) typology (Figure 9.1) identifies four categories of technical entrepreneur.

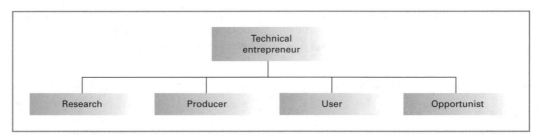

FIGURE 9.1 Typology of technical entrepreneurs

Research technical entrepreneur

The research category of technical entrepreneur includes individuals whose previous employment experience was in universities or public-research laboratories. In Jones-Evans (1995) about one-third of the technical entrepreneurs interviewed had this background. All had a scientific background that included engineers and scientists. Many continued to retain links with their former employer. While this category was clearly the equivalent of the scientist entrepreneur or academic entrepreneur of earlier studies, there were differences. Jones-Evans noted that not all had spent the whole of their previous career in an academic environment.

Some had a small amount of commercial experience, and this meant that they did have knowledge of business. Even some of those who had worked exclusively in research environments had some knowledge of business, typically extending to a modest knowledge of marketing, finance and interpersonal skills.

Producer technical entrepreneur

This category is the equivalent of the industrial technical entrepreneur identified by earlier researchers. In essence it includes entrepreneurs whose background is industrial. Typically these are people who have been involved in the development or production of commercial products, services or processes, usually in large industrial organisations. In Jones-Evans' (1995) study these were typically individuals with an engineering background and included: works managers, development managers, and technical managers, virtually all of whom were trained engineers, as well as draughtsmen, designers and project managers. A very small number had a purely scientific background and had worked as research scientists. All had a strong technical background even if their most recent position was a managerial one. As a result most combined a strong mix of both technical and managerial experience.

What is striking about this type of technical entrepreneur is how technical and managerial aspects are brought together in a single individual. Significantly this group constituted more than half the sample in Jones-Evans' survey, suggesting that although the notion of an academic entrepreneur is one that is most readily identified with technical entrepreneurs perhaps this is a misperception, certainly as far as the UK is concerned.

User technical entrepreneur

Where Jones-Evans breaks new ground is in identifying two further categories of technical entrepreneur. The first of these he calls the user technical entrepreneur. In this context the term "user" is used to denote the fact that the entrepreneur had a background in marketing/sales or product support. Such a role would therefore be likely to bring him or her into direct contact with consumers. In fact, half of the user entrepreneurs in Jones-Evans' (1995) sample had a background in marketing/sales.

The strong connection to marketing/sales helps to give credence to the notion of innovation as a demand-pull process in which consumer needs provide the stimulus to innovation. Individuals who work in marketing/sales are likely to be very familiar with consumer needs and consumer requirements. This knowledge can act as both a spur to innovation and a trigger to the decision to set up an independent business.

Obviously the user technical entrepreneur stands in sharp contrast to the two previous categories of technical entrepreneur. Whereas they have what might be described as a "supply side" perspective, the user technical entrepreneur in contrast has clear "demand side" perspective. This perspective can be particularly valuable when one is dealing with the diffusion of a generic technology. Under these circumstances, new applications are likely to take the form of specialist applications developed for very specific market niches. In the development of such market niches, detailed knowledge of the consumer is likely to be at a premium. Such knowledge is likely to be informal and tacit and the sort of knowledge that those in marketing/sales will possess. Furthermore, if the product in question has a significant technology input then marketing staff may well have a good knowledge of the generic technology.

Opportunist technical entrepreneur

The fourth and final category of entrepreneur in Jones-Evans' (1995) typology is what he describes as the "opportunist" technical entrepreneur. These are individuals who identify technology-based opportunities but who have little or no technical education and whose previous occupational experience is with non-technical organisations. Just how far removed some of these individuals can be from a technical background is illustrated by Jones-Evans' (1995) study which included a teacher, a naval officer, an insurance clerk, a civil servant, a personal assistant and an office manager.

Given that one is dealing with high-technology businesses, the lack of any technical background in these cases is surprising and is in sharp contrast with most of the previous work on technical entrepreneurs. However, it does serve to highlight the "opportunity" filling nature of the entrepreneur's role. A significant amount of research into entrepreneurship has focused on the opportunity or gap-filling nature of the entrepreneur's role. Jones-Evans' work lends support to this, while at the same time suggesting that where generic technologies are concerned and where there is scope for incremental innovations then opportunity recognition may actually be more important than technical knowledge, which may be purchased in the market either directly or through people who hold such knowledge.

Towards a synthesis

Recent work on technical entrepreneurs by Tidd *et al.* (2001) integrates earlier "trait" theories of entrepreneurship espoused by researchers such as McClelland (1961) and Roberts (1991), with work on occupational backgrounds along the lines of Jones-Evans (1995), to provide a synthesis that includes a variety of different factors that influence new venture creation by a technical entrepreneur. The resulting model (Figure 9.2) provides a composite picture of new venture creation factors. These factors are grouped into three sets of factors labelled as:

- antecedent factors
- parental experience
- environmental factors

Antecedent factors are features of the entrepreneur's personal life and cover aspects such as personality (i.e. personality "traits" highlighted by psychological theories of entrepreneurship), home context and general background. Parental experience refers to the entrepreneur's experience derived from the "host" organisation(s) where they were employed prior to setting up on their own, specifically the nature of the host organisation and the level of institutional support that it provides. Environmental factors refer to the commercial and technological environments in which the new venture is located, especially the degree of novelty associated with the market and the technology.

Figure 9.2 provides a more detailed breakdown of the factors that influence technical entrepreneurs. The value of this type of model is the degree of flexibility that it offers. Much of the early work on entrepreneurship was criticised because the pursuit of a rather narrowly defined set of personality traits did not fit easily with the diversity of entrepreneurs. There clearly is nothing like a standard case, and this model caters for a high degree of diversity.

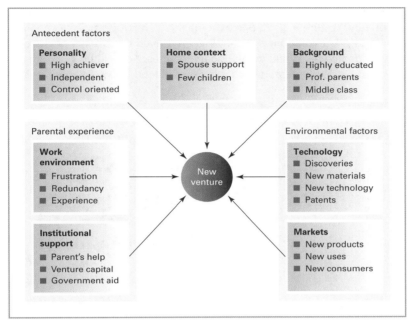

FIGURE 9.2 Factors affecting new venture formation by a technical entrepreneur
Source: Adapted from Tidd *et al.* (2001)

The model shown in Figure 9.2 also serves to highlight some additional features of technical entrepreneurs.

Technical entrepreneurs tend to be very industry specific, being found in large numbers in some industries and sectors but being almost completely absent in others. This may well be a function of low barriers to entry, which facilitate both ease of entry and exit. Thus, in sectors such as biotechnology and computing, technical entrepreneurs are to be found in abundance because entry is relatively easy.

Types of technical entrepreneur

There are some discernible patterns in the fields in which technical entrepreneurs are typically found. In general, technical entrepreneurs tend to focus on highly specialised, niche products and services which utilise the specialised, in-depth knowledge of technology possessed by the technical entrepreneur himself or herself. Quite literally these are businesses built around the technical expertise of the founder. He or she is an expert in a particular technical field and the business aims to make effective use of this expertise. Businesses like this are typically to be found in highly technology-intensive fields.

However, Autio (1995) notes that the degree of technological intensity can vary a great deal. Just as the level of technological intensity can vary so too, according to Autio can the nature of the market that the technology seeks to penetrate. In some instances technical entrepreneurs seek to create and develop new markets while in other instances the market may be relatively well established.

Recognising variations in technology and markets led Autio to differentiate four types of technical entrepreneur (Figure 9.3). At one extreme the technology may be very new, making it, in Autio's terminology, a revolutionary technology. At the other extreme, however, there are complementary technologies. While revolutionary technologies will be very different from those currently in use, complementary technologies will tend to complement existing products and services.

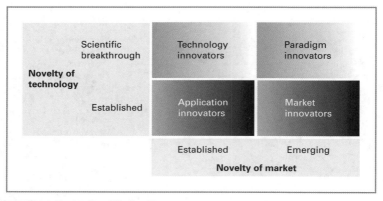

FIGURE 9.3 Technology/Market Taxonomy
Source: Autio (1995) *Entrepreneurship and Regional Development*, Taylor & Francis Ltd, http://www.tandf.co.uk/journals

Application innovator

This type of technical entrepreneur aims to utilise established technology in established markets to produce what are essentially complementary products. This will typically involve the diffusion of an existing generic technology into new, probably much more specialised, market niches. Autio (1995) gives the example of software houses that tend to provide specialist solutions using established software principles with established software languages.

Market innovator

Market innovators aim to develop new markets with existing technologies. The technology is likely to be generic and does not have to possess any radical features. The innovation comes typically from combining or configuring the technologies in a different way. Autio (1995) gives the example of the first Apple computer. This was the Apple II which used proprietary computer components that could be sourced "off the shelf" but configured in a new way to create the first effective personal computer. MessageGate, the anti-spam software firm (see mini case), spun off from aircraft Seattle-based manufacturer Boeing, would be another example.

Technology innovators

Technology innovators rely on new technologies. These technologies may well be associated with scientific breakthroughs. These technologies go into new products that are sold in established markets. They are, to use the terminology mentioned earlier, complementary products, as they enter the market alongside existing products. As Christensen (1997) has noted, however, they often threaten incumbent firms because they deliver sharply improved performance or meet customer requirements more effectively. Autio gives the example of biotechnology companies offering biodegradable materials, though the case of SSTL (see mini case) would be just as applicable since this was an instance of a new technology – micro satellites – being applied in an existing market, namely the market for space communications and earth monitoring.

Paradigm innovators

This is the most extreme form of technical entrepreneur. In this instance the entrepreneur delivers a new product concept based on a new technology into a new and as yet undeveloped market. This may well prove to be very disruptive. Autio gives the example of Intel, a new company set up as a spin-off from Fairchild Semiconductor, that developed and manufactured the first microprocessor which in time turned the computer industry upside down as personal computers displaced much larger mainframe machines. Mark Shuttleworth's Internet security start-up, *Thawte*™ (see mini case), would be another example, because in the mid-1990s when it was founded, security software was a new technology and e-commerce was a new and rapidly developing market.

Mini Case

SSTL

In April 2008, Surrey University announced that it was selling the bulk of its 80 per cent stake in its spin-off company Surrey Satellite Technologies Limited (SSTL) to Astrium, a subsidiary of the European aerospace group EADS. The sale, which was estimated to be netting Surrey University around £40 million, valued SSTL at £50 million, a significant increase in the company's initial capital of just £100.

SSTL was formed in 1986 by Surrey University at the instigation of postgraduate student Martin Sweeting. The aim was to enable the spin-off company to specialise in applying the University's expertise in satellite technology to the development of a new generation of small and micro satellites. At the time the idea that small satellites would have an important role in space seemed, in Martin, now Professor Sir Martin, Sweeting's words, "an awfully long way off". However, over the years technical advances, combined with cost pressures, have made the concept a reality and small and micro satellites are now used extensively for communications and earth monitoring. SSTL currently employs 270 staff and has launched 27 small and micro satellites, which are significantly cheaper than larger satellites and can be linked together to form powerful networks.

The rationale behind the University's sale of the bulk of its stake in SSTL after 22 years is that if SSTL is to continue to develop it must maintain and expand its R&D investment. This requires additional capital, while as Surrey's Vice Chancellor, Professor Christopher Snowdon, points out, "We are a University not a venture capital organisation".

Hence the time now appears right for the University to harvest its initial investment and to let a large aerospace group provide the additional financial resources that SSTL now needs.

Source: Milner (2008).

New venture creation

How do technical entrepreneurs start up in business? There are typically two routes that technical entrepreneurs follow in creating new business ventures. The first route is shared with conventional entrepreneurs. This is the start-up route, while the second route, the spin-off, is really unique to technical entrepreneurs.

Start-ups

A start-up is a new venture established to commercialise an entrepreneur's idea (Hague and Holmes, 2006: p7). In this context the term "venture" normally means the creation of a new company. In this instance the entrepreneur will be acting independently, without the explicit help or assistance of a parent organisation. In this case the idea is the property of the entrepreneur and he or she normally owns it.

The idea does not necessarily come from the activities of some external organisation (i.e. an employing organisation – firm or university), nor does an external organisation normally exert direct influence on the establishment of the venture. Indeed a key feature of a start-up is that the entrepreneur is acting independently. It may well be that an entrepreneur's employment or his or her employing organisation may have helped in the acquisition of experience and expertise, but the idea around which the venture is created comes from the entrepreneur. It is very much his or her idea.

Mini Case

Baby Boeings

Seattle, on the west coast of the US, is home to two household names: Microsoft and Boeing. Microsoft is a byword for software, though in fact plane maker Boeing, founded in Seattle almost 90 years ago, is not short of expertise in this field either. Boeing recently spun-off a new company, MessageGate, that sells software for filtering out junk email.

The spin-off forms part of the new initiative by Boeing designed to promote entrepreneurship on the part of its employees. The scheme, which is run by the company's Boeing Ventures Division, educates, trains and supports employees with ideas for possible new business opportunities. MessageGate itself is the product of attempts by Boeing's software engineers to control the junk email or "spam" that floods into the company's computing networks. The software is capable of evaluating email messages in terms not only of sender, but also content and context, in order to determine suitability. Furthermore, the software can be used not only on conventional email systems but on instant messaging and text messaging systems as well.

Having developed a software package to handle the 10 million spam messages flooding into the company's computer network every month, Boeing decided to market the software commercially. Given that messaging software fell outside the plane maker's core business, it was felt that the best route to market was by creating a spin-off company and Boeing sought outside venture capital through Polaris Venture Partners and Northwest Venture Associates.

The venture capital firms provided $5 million in start-up capital with Boeing retaining a minority stake. Boeing recruited local man, David Weld, a former Microsoft executive with experience of previous start-ups, to lead the new venture.

Given its parentage, MessageGate is not perhaps a typical start-up as David Weld acknowledged when he said "It's not five smart guys in a garage". However, with 20 employees and a lot of specialised technical expertise, it is a fairly typical spin-off.

MessageGate is only the third spin-off from Boeing Ventures, the others being AVChem, a chemical management company in Missouri, and an underwater survey services venture in Houston, Texas.

Source: Jung (2003).

Spin-offs

Spin-offs are also new ventures but normally ones that arise from a parent organisation which is typically a university, government R&D laboratory or established firm. They are created with the explicit goal of commercialising a technology developed by the parent organisation. Spin-offs are created by an employee, (who will typically be a scientist or technologist), leaving the parent organisation which in turn grants him or her access to a technology on which he or she has been working (Carayannis *et al.*, 1998). Often those who opt to "go it alone" in this way, have accumulated a substantial amount of knowledge and experience while working for the parent organisation. Rather than explicit knowledge that is structured and codified, the knowledge involved will be tacit, residing in the individual and often difficult to articulate. Sometimes referred to as know-how (Newell, *et al.*, 2002), this is the sort of knowledge that is gradually accumulated from working in a specialised field.

If the parent is a university and the new venture aims to commercialise some aspect of the university's research, then the venture would typically license the research. In a spin-off the parent will typically play an active role in facilitating the new venture creation process. It may well provide physical resources, e.g. equipment or premises, and certainly provide intangible resources such as knowledge, contacts, etc. Normally the parent will also take an equity stake in the spin-off both to preserve the connection and in the hope of harvesting the stake at a later date (Carayannis *et al.*, 1998).

Spin-offs are typically created because the parent does not want to or cannot commercialise the technology. Why is this? Several factors account for it. For instance, the parent may not have the resources (cash or knowledge) to fund commercialisation. By creating a spin-off an opportunity arises to attract outside capital from large corporations taking a stake or business angels or venture capitalists. On the other hand, technology may be applicable to products or markets that the parent does not wish to enter, i.e. the technology in question is not compatible with the core business. Finally, the parent may not have the flexibility or the environment in which to facilitate commercialisation. It may prefer instead to let a spin-off commercialise the technology while taking a stake in the venture with a view to harvesting it later.

Spin-offs aren't only confined to technical entrepreneurs. In the corporate sector large businesses spin off whole divisions. Good examples include Vodafone which was spun off from Racal Electronics and Experian which was spun off from Great Universal Stores.

The drivers of technical entrepreneurship

There is a long history of technically minded individuals acting as entrepreneurs and founding new ventures to produce innovations in products and services based on the application of new technology. However, they haven't always been described as technical entrepreneurs.

Early examples of technical entrepreneurs would include Alexander Graham Bell, who used his technical knowledge to found AT&T which became one of the world's largest telephone companies. Similarly with the new technology of electricity, Thomas Edison set up what eventually became General Electric, one of the world's largest producers of electrical products. In the post-war period in the UK, Joseph Bamford founded JCB to apply the new technology of hydraulics to mechanical excavators and construction equipment (Christensen, 1997), while Martin Wood founded Oxford Instruments to apply the new technology of superconductivity to the manufacture of electromagnets (Wood, 2001). More recently in the computing field newcomers like Steve Jobs and Bill Gates were the ones who established new companies to produce the first personal computers and the software they required.

However, it is really only in the last 30 years that we have started to describe entrepreneurs who found technology-based businesses, such as those mentioned above, as technical entrepreneurs. In large part this is because the scale of technical entrepreneurship has expanded so dramatically. A variety of factors or drivers have accounted for this growth in technical entrepreneurship. Among the factors that stand out are: the diffusion of knowledge; the mobility of staff (staff churn); improved institutional support; the availability of venture capital; the increased use of open innovation; the nature of new technologies; and the existence of more role models.

Diffusion of the knowledge

We now live in an age where knowledge is now much more plentiful, especially scientific and technical knowledge, and more diffused than it was in the past (Chesbrough, 2006: p44). This increased supply of knowledge is a function of the increase in the number of universities and the increase in the amount of science and technology being taught. There are now many more people studying in universities. Whereas at one time attending university was confined to a small elite group of the population comprising about 10 per cent (in the UK), it is now much more widespread with 40 per cent of the population attending university in many developed countries. Not only that, knowledge is these days very much more accessible. There is the obvious case of the Internet, but that is by no means the only factor that has helped to make knowledge more accessible. There are now many more conferences and similar activities in the field of science and technology as well as a great many more papers being published that all help to make knowledge more accessible. The net result of the increased supply of knowledge is that knowledge, particularly technical knowledge, is no longer confined to the R&D laboratories of large companies. It is quite literally all over the place and much more accessible.

Size (employees)	1981	1989	1991
< 1000	4.4	9.2	22.5
1000–4999	6.1	7.6	13.6
5000–9999	5.8	5.5	9.0
10000–24999	13.1	10.0	13.6
25000+	70.7	67.7	41.3

TABLE 9.2 Percentage of US industrial R&D by firm size
Source: Chesbrough (2006)

Staff churn

In general most employees are more mobile than they once were. It is now much rarer for employees to stay with the same company for life and many of the services and benefits provided by companies, including things like pensions and education qualifications, are much more transferable than they once were. Henry and Pinch (2000a) in their study of Motor Sport Valley in the UK, found that in small high-tech companies there was a high rate of movement of staff between companies (termed "staff churn"), with the average time spent at any single company before moving on being a little under five years. While the competitive nature of motor sport probably leads to higher rates of "staff churn," nonetheless these were well-qualified technical staff. Certainly staff mobility is much greater than it once was and this means individuals are probably more willing to leave an established company and "go it alone" by setting up their own technology-based start-up business than they once were.

Improved institutional support

It is now considerably easier to become a technical entrepreneur than it once was. In the educational field there have been institutional changes, particularly changes surrounding universities who now provide a variety of facilities that facilitate entrepreneurship both for students and academic staff. These include courses on business and management, the provision of incubators and science parks, and a much greater willingness to allow staff to engage in commercial activities and spin-offs (Hague and Holmes, 2006; Shane, 2004). Financial institutions such as banks now provide more support tailored to the needs of technical entrepreneurs, including the provision of specialist technology sections that fund high-technology start-ups and spin-offs. Nor have governments generally been idle. In the UK a variety of government institutions increasingly support technical entrepreneurship. For instance, the patent system is now more user-friendly. The government also provides financial help in the form of SMART awards (see Chapter 10) which are grants for small businesses to fund research and development on technical projects. Outside the field of central government there are also regional and local government agencies that provide support, including the provision of financial support in the form of grants for innovation, and the provision of physical facilities such as starter units and incubators.

Availability of and access to venture capital

Venture capitalists are specialist financiers who invest in companies with a view to their further growth and eventual capital gain (see Chapter 10). The first venture capitalists emerged in the

US in the post-war years, located in high-tech regions such as California and New England, as successful technical entrepreneurs sought to use some of their wealth to fund other would-be technical entrepreneurs. Over the last 30 years a similar pattern, but on a much smaller scale, has emerged in the UK and Europe.

The existence of venture capitalists provides would-be entrepreneurs with a specialist source of finance that can fund growth and expansion. Not only that, venture capitalists, by virtue of their experience are well versed in the particular needs of technical entrepreneurs. In addition, business angels – high-wealth individuals who invest in companies – who represent a form of "informal" venture capital, are often not only willing to provide loan finance, they will also provide management expertise, based on their own experiences. This all means that it is now easier to be a technical entrepreneur because appropriate funding to finance new technical start-up ventures is available.

The rise of open innovation

Another factor that has facilitated technical entrepreneurship is the increased use of open innovation by large companies. Open innovation (Chesbrough, 2003a), by placing external technologies/ideas and external paths on the same level of importance as that reserved for internal technologies/ideas and internal paths under conventional closed innovation, provides a clear role for technical entrepreneurs.

Under open innovation technical entrepreneurs can develop new technologies and new technological applications which can then be used as part of the innovation process in large firms. Quite literally large firms can access appropriate technologies for innovation through technical entrepreneurs. The value of such arrangements is that they allow technical entrepreneurs to specialise in particular technological applications while allowing the large firms to specialise in the provision of complementary assets such as marketing, distribution and product support capabilities.

The nature of new technologies

Technical entrepreneurship has also been bolstered by the nature of many of the newer technologies that have emerged in the last 50 years. Many of the technologies of the mid-twentieth century such chemicals, pharmaceuticals, aerospace, and nuclear engineering required huge amounts of capital and large and expensive facilities. The scale of these requirements acted as a barrier to entry for new start-ups. In contrast many of the new technologies to have emerged in the last 30 years are much more mobile and more flexible. This all forms part of the move towards knowledge-based economies. The result has been a significant reduction in one of the barriers to technical entrepreneurship. Nowhere is this more evident than in the case of the Internet, where new technology-based start-ups require knowledge rather than expensive facilities. Consequently we have seen a flood of new technical entrepreneurs such as Mark Shuttleworth of *Thawte*™, Jeff Bezos of Amazon, and Sergey Brin and Larry Page of Google.

Role models

Finally there are now a great many more role models of technical entrepreneurs around and they tend to have much higher public profiles. Many like Mark Shuttleworth, who grew the value of his start-up company, *Thawte*™, from nothing to more than $0.5 billion in four years, have become extremely wealthy in a very short space of time. Thirty years ago in contrast, technical entrepreneurs were comparatively rare, and little was heard of them. Shuttleworth's example and that of others has provided a very powerful "demonstration effect", showing how it is possible to become a very successful technical entrepreneur, without a need for massive financial resources. Nor are these isolated examples. Hague and Holmes' (2006) study of technical entrepreneurs in Oxford, shows that while they don't all enjoy quite the meteoric rise of those technical entrepreneurs who were able to capitalise on innovations linked to the early years of the Internet, nonetheless technical entrepreneurship is actually remarkably widely distributed.

Mini Case

Oxford Molecular

Professor Graham Richards, a chemistry academic at Oxford University, was one of the pioneers in developing computing software to analyse the molecular structure of drugs. As well as writing one of the first books on the subject, he gave talks to drug companies about his work. When they asked about the software he had developed, he gave it to them free. However, he had long harboured the idea that the software was marketable and in 1989 he teamed up with one of his former doctoral students, Tony Marchington. Marchington had worked closely with Richards on a DPhil sponsored by ICI Plant Protection under the CASE scheme for collaborative research funded by the Science and Engineering Research Council. Upon graduation he had gone on to a permanent position at ICI. Richards and Marchington decided the time was now right to create a start-up company to market the software.

Founded in 1989, Oxford Molecular started out in a prefabricated hut next to Richard's Oxford laboratory. It had three employees, including Marchington as CEO, to handle everything commercial, another former graduate student to handle the technology and a secretary. Graham Richards was non-executive chairman. They raised £350,000 from venture capitalists and split the equity three ways between the University (as owner of the intellectual property), the venture capitalists and the founders.

With a DPhil in Chemistry from Oxford, Tony Marchington had the technical knowledge which formed the basis of the company's activities. However, he was also an entrepreneur, having honed his trading skills on the family's farm in Derbyshire. At the new fledgling company he was able to put these skills to good use. He struck a number of deals with big companies, and with Marchington working full-time for the company it grew quickly. After 18 months it had 15 employees and was bursting at the seams. Having convinced its backers that it was a successful business, the company gained a second round of funding from the venture capitalists, and with the proceeds moved to Oxford University's science park and also established a small office in the US. Further expansion followed and the company took over a rival French company, Bio Structure.

By the summer of 1993, further expansion had brought the numbers employed to 30 and growth continued apace. The following year the company was floated on the London Stock Exchange. Under the terms of the flotation, one-third of the company was sold for £10 million valuing the whole enterprise at £30 million. With the new influx of capital came further changes, including the appointment of a managing director and finance director. At this time many large companies were divesting themselves of "non-core" business, and Oxford Molecular was able to make a number of acquisitions of software businesses.

By 1998 Oxford Molecular was a much bigger enterprise and had now evolved a more complex and sophisticated business model. Now one company developed and sold the software, while a second company used the software to design and synthesise molecules and a third company tested and screened them. The three companies could work in concert, or individually, or any two of the three together. By this time Oxford Molecular had 400 employees and was no longer a small business. Unfortunately, Oxford Molecular fared less well in the years after 2000 and was eventually taken over and split between two American companies, Millenium and Pharmacopeia. Though the price of the shares at the time of the takeover was less than the peak year of 1998, nonetheless it still netted Oxford University £10 million.

Source: Hague and Holmes (2006).

CASE STUDY: ONECLICK TECHNOLOGIES LTD

There is something reassuring about the little standby light on a TV or a personal computer. It is so small and so faint that the energy being used by the device must surely be minimal. Unfortunately that is not necessarily the case. Electrical devices left on standby mode may only consume a few watts of energy themselves, but when you add the associated peripheral devices like printers and speakers for PCs or the tuners, turntables, cassette decks and speakers that form part of a hi-fi system, the watts add up and when the system is left on standby 24 hours a day, the energy involved is considerable.

It was knowledge of this that inspired Peter Robertson to develop the "OneClick Intelligent Mains Panel," a six-socket extension block that can be used to power a hi-fi or PC and up to five peripheral devices which, when it senses that the main device is on standby, switches off all the peripherals, thereby ensuring that energy consumption drops to less than 5 watts an hour. The beauty of this device, which looks pretty much like an ordinary six-socket extension block, is that it is automatic. Quite literally one click is all that is required to put the principal device on standby and shut down all the peripherals.

Peter Robertson had the idea for an extension block of this type, when he worked for Yamaha selling hi-fi products. With the advent in the late 1980s of sophisticated audiovisual products incorporating Dolby "surround sound", domestic consumers were adding CD players and widescreen TVs to their hi-fi systems. As Peter himself says, "I was tired of switching off various things". He felt there was a need for an extension block into which all these devices could be plugged, and with which, with the inclusion of some sort of switching mechanism, it would be possible to switch off the peripherals along with the hi-fi. Quite literally "one click" would do the whole thing.

Peter had no formal training in electronics. Born and brought up in Nottingham where his father worked as a bus driver, he left school at 16 and had a variety of jobs. He worked first in shops and then catering, eventually becoming the catering manager of a motorway service area. In time he decided to move back to Nottingham where he got a job as an administrator, which he himself admits he "found immensely boring". As a result he soon switched to working as a coach driver for a couple of years. Peter then went into sales. To begin with he sold advertising space, then office equipment, and then hi-fi equipment. The last of these jobs was in retailing, where Peter worked as an area manager for the hi-fi manufacturer, Yamaha.

It was while working for Yamaha in the late 1980s that Peter became convinced that the proliferation of peripheral devices for hi-fi systems meant there was scope for some form of switchable extension block. Having had the idea he decided to try building a prototype. He bought a standard six-socket extension block and a heavy industrial relay. Then, using the kitchen table as his workshop, he set about building a prototype. By connecting the relay to the switched outlet fitted at the rear of virtually all hi-fi amplifiers, he was able to get the extension block to sense when the device was on standby and cause the relay to shut down the remaining five sockets. When the amplifier was switched on, it took the sensing from the back of the amplifier and fired the relay, which then duly switched on the current going to the peripheral devices. As Peter acknowledged, "I knew there was an application there". He had proved the concept. However, the relay made the extension block heavy and unwieldy and far too expensive to mass produce. With a well-paid job in retailing Peter decided that this was not the time to become a fully fledged innovator.

▶   He stayed with Yamaha for six years. As Peter said of his time at Yamaha, "I learnt a lot about how multiples work, buying and selling and that sort of stuff and I learnt a bit about electronics". But when Yamaha decided to re-structure their activities Peter opted for redundancy. There then followed a stint at EchoStar, a US-based manufacturer of satellite equipment. From there Peter spent a couple of years working as a consultant for the Franchise Centre in Manchester where he wrote franchising manuals and advised would-be franchisers and franchisees before going back into sales and marketing, working for a Danish company. When the company decided to relocate to South Wales, Peter again opted for redundancy. At this point he decided to take a career break, opting for a year out in which he studied for an MBA at Nottingham Trent University. It was while he was at university that Peter revisited his prototype intelligent mains panel. For part of his course he had to put together a business plan for the introduction of a new product and his idea for an intelligent mains panel, in the form of a switchable extension block, seemed an ideal new product. For the business plan he had to investigate costings, product viability and the market for the product. By now relay technology had moved on apace. Developments in electronics had caused relays to shrink dramatically in size, to the point where it was feasible for one to be fitted inside the extension block. The technology also meant that an electronic version was feasible which would suit any application and not just hi-fi, but Peter felt that at this stage it was important to test the market first. He opted to develop a passive version using proprietory technology, and found an extension block that could be easily adapted so that a proprietory relay could be fitted inside the space taken by one of the sockets. The intelligent mains panel had become a commercial proposition.

All the main components were proprietary products. The extension block was bought in while the relays were supplied by an electrical distributor. With a fly lead to the back of an amplifier and a similar lead to the USB socket of a computer, the intelligent mains panel could be used for either hi-fi or PC applications. By the time he came to finish the course, Peter was manufacturing 20 extension blocks a week. However, he quickly found he could not cope with making them this way, and began trying to find someone who could manufacture them for him. It did not take long but came about quite by accident. Unhappy that he was paying full price, Peter asked the distributor from whom he was buying relays for a trade discount. They refused, saying the quantities he wanted did not warrant a trade discount. However, they did suggest a firm in Hinckley that might be more interested in the sort of quantities he needed. Not only that, they mentioned that the firm might be able to do some manufacturing. And so it turned out. The firm in Hinckley could not only supply relays, but were willing to manufacture the whole extension block, and Peter placed an order for 3,000 sets.

With proper manufacturing facilities in place, he now turned his attention to marketing. With help from friends, he soon had a small website in place. Using his extensive knowledge of retailing, Peter began to target hi-fi shops. Yamaha, his former employer, agreed to place an order for 300 sets. To increase his exposure in the marketplace he decided to exhibit at a national electronics exhibition in Birmingham. However, he baulked at trying to find the £5,000 cost of hiring an exhibition stand and the additional cost of then fitting it out and staffing it. Aware that exhibition organisers often end up with unfilled stands, he approached the organisers about negotiating a discounted rate, stressing that he was a student. They agreed to rent him a stand in one of the less attractive locations for £1,000 all-in. To staff the stand he roped in some of his fellow students and to provide some publicity he purchased a supply of

T-shirts and knickers with his "Oneclick" logo printed on them. The knickers proved particularly successful. With his stand in a somewhat remote location, he needed something to get potential customers talking and they certainly provided a talking point. Orders came flooding in. They covered the cost of attending the exhibition in the first day. Several of the large electrical retailers ordered 1,000 or more.

Having successfully developed and launched his innovation, Peter began to think about expanding the market. Initially, sales were confined to the specialist hi-fi market for which it had been developed and where it had obvious applications. In the hi-fi market the attraction of the intelligent mains panel was that it helped the hi-fi enthusiast control a wide range of peripherals. There were other potential markets, however, and one was the environmental-friendly, energy-conscious market. So he approached the Energy Saving Trust, hoping that an endorsement from them would give his product an opening in this market.

They pointed out that in its present form the intelligent mains panel had some weaknesses: some consumers would not know where the USB port was; similarly the use of the switched outlet on amplifiers limited its application in the consumer electronics market. Quite literally the intelligent mains panel was not intelligent enough! This prompted Peter to commit to the development of the more advanced electronic version. Whereas the current product was a passive version that responded to external signals, he now set his sights on developing an active "current sensing version" actively able to manage the power supply.

For active power management some form of auto-calibration was needed with the capability to read a device's power consumption. Peter undertook a detailed examination of computer power-supply systems. He found that the power being used could vary enormously. Meanwhile, a patent search revealed that a similar device had been patented in Germany but had not proved successful as it was relatively primitive, working with fixed values for the power being used. Peter's solution to the problem was to use some form of programmable integrated chip linked to a software program that monitored the amount of power being used and then used a formula to decide whether to switch the slave sockets on or off. Having produced a solution was one thing; getting it to work was quite another. Development was not without its difficulties. On one occasion the only prototype blew up the night before a vital demonstration to the Energy Saving Trust. Over the course of several months more than 30 electronic prototypes of different designs either blew up or melted before Peter was finally able to come up with one that was stable and functioned effectively. At this point, having taken appropriate legal advice, Peter filed a patent for his intelligent switching device.

Since the development of an active version of his intelligent mains panel meant a major redesign of the product, Peter took the opportunity to explore alternative manufacturing facilities. He negotiated for production to be subcontracted to a British firm which arranged for manufacturing to be undertaken in China, thereby reducing the manufacturing cost by about one-third, together with a commensurate improvement in product quality. At the same time Peter set about marketing the new active version of his intelligent mains panel. An order from Powergen for 20,000 items quickly showed the potential of the improved product. The original passive version had only achieved sales of 5,000 during the period of slightly less than a year that it was on the market. Significant orders from major electrical retailers such as Maplin, Lakelands, PC World and even B&Q soon followed. When the active version went on the market in October 2003 it was soon selling at an average rate of 3,000 items a month, evidence, if such were needed, that the intelligent mains panel was a successful innovation.

Not that Peter Robertson felt innovation had to stop there. He was soon planning an improved version that would combine his patented intelligent switching system with additional features such as surge protection, full range calibration and split phone and modem outputs. He was even beginning to explore a version for the US market that would work with power supplies ranging from 100 to 250 volts, making the intelligent mains panel a product capable of taking on global markets.

Source: Personal interview with Peter Robertson, 2 June 2005

Questions

1 To what extent was Peter Robertson helped by developments in technology?
2 What kind of technical entrepreneur would you classify Peter Robertson as and why?
3 Outline the aspects of his prior working experience that you feel helped Peter Robertson with his innovation.
4 Which aspects do you think were most helpful?
5 Using the technology/market taxonomy derived in this chapter classify this innovation.
6 Give examples of institutional support that contributed to the success of the venture.
7 Outline the market developments that you consider contributed the most to success.
8 What forms of intellectual property were associated with this case?
9 Why do you think Peter Robertson registered the patent in his own name using a separate company to manufacture and market the intelligent mains panel?
10 What does the case tell us about the value of personal networks for innovation?

? Questions for discussion

1 What is the link between "garages" and innovation?
2 What is the difference between a manager and an entrepreneur?
3 What do entrepreneurs do?
4 What is the link between entrepreneurship and Silicon Valley?
5 What is a technical entrepreneur? Give examples to illustrate your answer.
6 Using an example of your choice, identify what you consider to be the main characteristics of a technical entrepreneur.
7 Using appropriate examples, distinguish the different types of technical entrepreneur.
8 What is the link between venture capital and the rise of technical entrepreneurship?
9 What is meant by the term "staff churn" and what does it have to do with technical entrepreneurship?
10 What do you consider to be the two most important drivers behind the increase in technical entrepreneurship?

Exercises

1 Select an example of a business founded by a technical entrepreneur. Develop a profile of the founder (or founders if there is a team involved) and indicate which factors you think were most influential in the creation of the business.

2 In what ways do technical entrepreneurs differ from entrepreneurs in general?

3 Select a technical entrepreneur of your choice and analyse the part played by institutional support (i.e. from government, parent organisation, public agency, etc.) in the creation of a successful new business venture.

4 How are small high-technology firms able to compete with multinationals?

5 Explain what is meant by the term "spin-off" company. Why and how do such companies arise?

Further reading

1 **Hague, D. and C. Holmes** (2006) *Oxford Entrepreneurs*, Council for Industry and Higher Education, London.
This short book comprises a collection of cases studies of Oxford University academics who have created "spin-offs" from their work at the University. Each one provides a detailed picture of how the spin-off came about. All of the case studies are technical entrepreneurs. The result is a fascinating insight into the work of the technical entrepreneur, particularly why and how they create new ventures.

2 **Packard, D.** (1995) *The HP Way*, HarperCollins, New York.
This is really an account of the origins of Silicon Valley. Hewlett and Packard in many respects form the prototype for the technical entrepreneur. The key events may have taken place in the first half of the twentieth century but all the key elements are there nonetheless.

3 **Vise, D.A.** (2005) *The Google Story*, Pan Books, London.
And now for something completely different! Oddly that is not the case at all. Despite the fact that it is describing events in the first half of the twenty-first century, the Google story has many parallels with the Hewlett Packard one.

4 **Linzmayer, O.W.** (2004) *Apple Confidential 2.0: The Definitive History of the World's Most Colorful Company*, No Starch Press, San Francisco, CA.
Many aspects of the story may already be familiar but this account is well worth reading nonetheless. Lots of detail about how Jobs and Wozniak created Apple Computer, it also provides insights into the creation of many of Apple's best known innovations.

CHAPTER 10

Funding innovation

❖ OBJECTIVES

When you have completed this chapter you will be able to:

- ❖ appreciate and understand the funding problems associated with innovation
- ❖ analyse the means employed by innovators to reduce and minimise capital requirements
- ❖ distinguish the different sources of capital available for innovation

- ❖ differentiate the various forms of capital available for innovation
- ❖ evaluate the circumstances when particular forms of capital are most likely to be appropriate
- ❖ identify some of the agencies available to assist in handling the funding innovation

Introduction

"Innovation is an expensive process" (O'Sullivan, 2005: p240) according to the *Oxford Handbook of Innovation*, surely a clear justification if one were needed for a chapter dealing with financial aspects of innovation. Why is the process of innovation expensive? Christofidis and Debande (2001: p1) offer an explanation:

> the combination of research and development, intangible assets, negative earnings, uncertain prospects and the absence of a proven track record which are character-istic of start-up and pre-commercialisation initiatives, leads to an unacceptably high perception of risk.

Though directed at the risks faced by conventional financial institutions in this instance, their comments nonetheless convey the range of factors that contribute to the high cost of innovation.

O'Sullivan puts this more succinctly, suggesting there are three particular factors that make innovation expensive:

- resources
- timing
- uncertainty

In terms of resources, it is a matter of the scale of resources required in terms of both people and technology. As Chapter 6 indicated the innovation process is complex, goes through multiple stages and requires the attention of staff from a range of functional specialisms. This all takes resources.

In terms of timing, the problem is the length of time taken to achieve a marketable product/service. In particular it is the fact that financial support has to be sustained until the innovation process is complete. Innovations, even small ones, require an outlay of funds for development which is necessary prior to innovation being achieved. Only when the innovation process is complete is there the prospect of a corresponding inflow of funds. Hence the timing problem is the gap between the outflow and inflow of funds.

Finally there is uncertainty. Uncertainty makes it difficult to predict either the outcome or the course of events. Hence the path of innovation is rarely smooth. By its nature the innovation process tends to be iterative and recursive, involving setbacks, false starts, blind alleys and recycling. As a result the level of funding required may be difficult to predict accurately. Not only that, there is also the chance that, even when the innovation process has been negotiated successfully, the innovation itself will fail in the marketplace and the anticipated future inflow of funds not occur.

Despite this, studies of innovation have generally tended to neglect consideration of the financial dimension. One exception is Joseph Schumpeter, the man who pioneered the study of innovation. Schumpeter in his early work (Schumpeter, 1996) noted that if innovation was mainly undertaken by small firms then it was external sources funding that were crucial. However, in his later work, which was heavily influenced by his experiences in America, he went on to stress the contribution of large firms to innovation, and he noted that in these circumstances it was likely that such innovation would be funded from internal sources of finance. Given that the pendulum now seems to be swinging back to small firms, with the role of spin-off and start-up companies now seen as an increasingly important source of innovation, it seems appropriate to focus in this chapter on external finance.

However, the chapter begins by first looking at the problem of timing, particularly the investment cashflow gap that arises because of the need to spend money on research and development before there is an inflow of funds from product sales (see the section on the cashflow gap below). This is then followed by an examination of the various different types of funding that are available and the sources from which they are derived. Although the focus tends to be on the case of the new venture and how it can raise the necessary funding, the overview of the capital markets that is provided is relevant to innovations developed by established ventures.

Innovation cashflow

The cashflow gap

We have clearly seen that invention and innovation are not the same thing. While individuals may be able to fund the process of innovation from their own resources, this will almost certainly not be the case with innovation. Few innovators are likely to have the resources to fund the whole of the innovation process. It is no coincidence that highly successful innovators (who also happen to be technical entrepreneurs) such as James Dyson and Ron Hickman initially tried to license their technology to large companies with substantial financial resources, rather than fund manufacturing and distribution themselves. Since innovation is about exploiting ideas and inventions to turn them into commercial products, the exploitation part of the process has to be funded and as O'Sullivan (2005) points out, it is expensive.

Figure 10.1 shows how the various phases of the innovation process (e.g. construction of a working model, prototype, etc.) generate a negative cashflow. Unlike a business deciding to start production of a well-established product, the various phases of R&D have to be undertaken prior to the start of sales. This results in a substantial negative outflow of cash without a corresponding inflow from sales. If the innovation is radical and involves an entirely new technology, the duration of this period of negative cashflow may last months or even years until the product reaches the market and sales begin to generate an inflow of cash. Even then, as Figure 10.1 shows, it may take time before break-even is achieved and the actual cashflow turns positive.

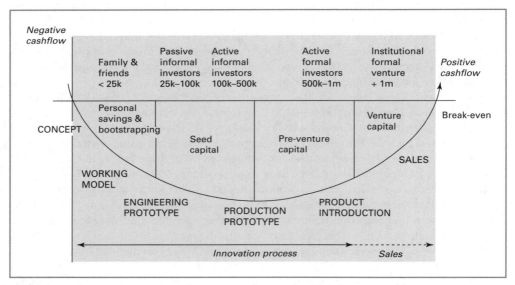

FIGURE 10.1 Innovation cashflow
Source: Adapted from Rorke *et al.* (1991: p19)

When Pilkingtons, the Lancashire-based glassmaker, developed the float glass process for the manufacture of plate glass in the 1950s, it took seven years of research and development and cost millions of pounds. The company not only built several small-scale pilot plants, it even built a full-scale plant based on the new process and ran it for a year before it produced glass of commercial quality. Only then could sales commence and the company begin to see a cash inflow. Similarly James Dyson took three years (Dyson, 1997) and built more than 5,000 prototypes before he had perfected the dual-cyclone technology for his bagless vacuum cleaner. During this time he not only had to bear the cost of his own time (i.e. he had no income) but he had to pay for materials, power, lighting, legal fees and the cost of patenting his invention. Even when he had got his technology to work successfully and secured a patent he still had no inflow of cash as he was unable to persuade any of the existing vacuum manufacturers to take out a licence to manufacture a bagless vacuum cleaner. It was to be a further three years before a Japanese company finally agreed to take out a licence and Dyson at last had a modest inflow of cash in the form of royalty payments.

Given that there may be a substantial period when the innovator has only cash going out and nothing coming in, it is perhaps not surprising that as Figure 10.1 shows there are a variety of different types of capital that can be employed according to how near the innovation is to market.

Most innovators initially at least will make use of personal savings, usually supplemented by financial inputs from family and friends. As Figure 10.1 shows these funds are likely to be supplanted by financial bootstrapping – quite literally finding ways of acquiring resources either without having to pay for them or paying a lot less for them. But this is only a small part of the story. Again, as Figure 10.1 shows, activities such as the development of production prototypes, setting up manufacturing facilities and launching a product all have to be undertaken, and the scale of these activities is likely to be much greater. Consequently, innovators require so-called "seed capital" to fund further development (see Figure 10.2). At this point they may well turn to "informal investors" willing to contribute either loan or equity capital. Informal investors, or business angels as they are known, are high net-worth individuals willing to put some of their financial resources into new ventures. They do this not to obtain an income from dividends, but in the hope of capital gain at some later stage. Eventually, however, even this source may not be sufficient and, with the innovation nearing the point where it is ready for the market, venture capitalists may be approached. They provide larger sums than informal investors but operate on the same basis – that is to say, they invest in the expectation of capital gain. Finally, depending on the size of the venture, the innovator may turn to the equity market and seek additional capital through an initial public offering (IPO) perhaps on a junior market such as the Alternative Investment Market (AIM).

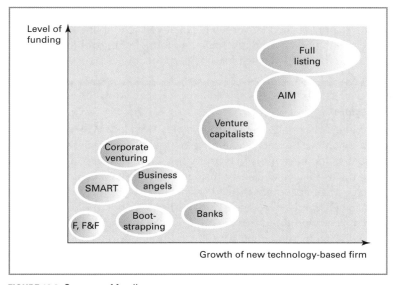

FIGURE 10.2 Sources of funding

All of these sources of capital contribute in different ways to helping the innovator bridge the "cashflow gap" that occurs while an innovation is under development prior to its being launched on the market and generating sales. This chapter explores the different ways in which organisations and individuals fund this period of negative cashflow.

Founder, family and friends

As with any small firm, the initial funding is likely to come from a combination of:

- founder
- family
- friends

Inevitably there is some overlap between this source of funding and the next one ("bootstrapping"). The founder will typically use his or her savings, or a redundancy package, or mortgage the family home. Some may be fortunate and have a legacy they can use, the less fortunate may sell a prized but valuable possession. Some may continue in employment. If friends and family are the source it is again likely to be past savings that are drawn on. The funding at this stage is likely to be used to fund the start-up stages particularly, as Figure 10.1 shows, initial development work such as building the first models or prototypes as part of proof-of-concept work. It is perhaps not unsurprising that innovators should draw on their families for funding. They are after all a logical source of funding. This was certainly the case with Martin Wood, the founder of Oxford Instruments and the first person in Europe to build a superconducting magnet, who gained financial support from his family in the early stages of his venture. Similarly, when his own savings ran out, Jeff Bezos, the creator of the world's first and biggest online bookshop, Amazon.com, persuaded his parents to invest $250,000 (Cassidy, 2002) in the venture. The ability to use friends is likely to be a function of an innovator's "social capital": that is to say, his or her personal network of friends and acquaintances, derived from recreational interests, previous work experience and even school or college. James Dyson for instance was able to get funding from his friend and former employer Jeremy Fry when he set up his first company to develop his idea for a bagless vacuum cleaner (Dyson, 1997).

Mini Case

Cybersense Biosystems

Cybersense Biosystems was established in 2001 by Dr Tim Hart. With a PhD in soil botany and microbiology and a number of years' experience of research in a university research laboratory, Hart's idea was to develop biosensors that could be used to measure land contamination. Specifically the aim was to develop sensors using bioluminescent bacteria that would permit speedy and effective identification of toxicity in contaminated land. The idea of using bioluminescent bacteria was derived from Tim's earlier research. Bioluminescence is the same principle by which glow-worms glow in the dark. The technology would potentially allow landowners, developers, environmental consultants and industrial concerns to quickly assess the toxicity of contaminated land and link the toxicity to potential pollutant triggers, thereby facilitating action to prevent further pollution.

The company's formation was linked to the award of a DTI Smart award that enabled Tim to design and build a first prototype of his toxicity measuring instrument. This was completed the following year when the company not only won a DTI Bio-wise grant but raised a substantial amount of additional capital through a syndicate of private investors. The first fully working ROTAS instrument was completed the following year and went on the market early in 2004.

Source: Talk by Tim Hart, 14 October 2004.

Financial bootstrapping

It has already been noted that business biographies provide a valuable insight into the innovation process. Such biographies usually note how difficult the process is and the obstacles and hurdles with which the innovator has to cope. At the same time business biographies also provide an invaluable insight into the ways in which innovators fund the innovation process. What is particularly revealing is the extent to which many innovators fund at least the early stages of the process, by not paying for it. Strapped for cash they look to other ways of acquiring the necessary resources: in short, they rely on bootstrapping.

Harrison *et al*. (2004: p308) define bootstrapping as involving, "imaginative and parsimonious strategies for marshalling and gaining control of resources". They go on to suggest that such strategies typically take two forms:

1 using creative ways of acquiring finance without recourse to banks or raising equity from traditional sources

2 minimising or eliminating the need for finance by securing resources at little or no cost

The first of these overlaps with funding from founder, family and friends, and is accessed through the founder's social capital network. Nonetheless, it is worth recounting some examples of this form of bootstrapping. Many innovators have relied on modest personal savings. James Dyson (Dyson, 1997) utilised this form of bootstrapping in the early stages of his work on the dual-cyclone vacuum cleaner, as did Jeff Bezos when developing his online bookshop Amazon.com.

The other category in Harrison *et al*.'s typology is probably the one that comes closest to the essence of bootstrapping, namely acquiring resources at little or no cost: in short, managing to acquire resources for free or at least for much less than one would normally expect to pay. This can take a variety of forms. One of the commonest is using domestic facilities such as a bedroom or garage (Audia and Rider, 2005). Examples proliferate. It is well known that Apple Computers manufactured its first personal computers in the garage of Steve Jobs' parents' home at 11161 Crist Drive, Los Altos in California (Linzmayer, 2004), but there is an abundance of other examples of successful businesses that started from a garage. Hewlett-Packard began in a garage (Packard, 1995) and so did Amazon.com. Founded by Jeff Bezos, the latter started life in the garage of a house he was renting in Bellevue, Seattle (Cassidy, 2002). Other domestic facilities used by innovators have included: the garden shed which gave birth to Oxford Instruments; the home workshop which Trevor Baylis used to develop his clockwork radio; and the bedroom which was used by Dan Bricklin for his early work developing VisiCalc, the world's first spreadsheet. Whatever the location, the point is that the use of domestic premises is convenient, very flexible and above all saves on rent.

The use of facilities borrowed from or provided by the parent organisation is another means by which resources can often be obtained for nothing. When Martin Wood and his embryonic company, Oxford Instruments, were developing his first magnets back in the 1960s, he was able to borrow a winding machine from the Clarendon Laboratory at Oxford University where he worked (Wood, 2001). Again when he produced Europe's first superconducting magnet he was able to use the services of Oxford University's computer in order to carry out a series of complex calculations.

The use of second-hand equipment is another way in which innovators endeavour to keep their costs down, thereby reducing the need for finance. Notable examples of innovators who have followed this route have included Joseph Bamford of JCB fame and Martin Wood of Oxford Instruments. In Bamford's case the first piece of equipment he acquired was a second-hand welder. This proved crucial in his early experiments with hydraulic loaders. In Martin Wood's case it was second-hand machine tools bought at an auction of government-surplus equipment that enabled him to embark on the manufacture of superconducting magnets.

Another popular way of acquiring resources is to get people to work for you in their spare time, preferably while paying them little or in some cases nothing. The mini case in this chapter shows that this was what Colin Chapman, the innovative designer and engineer, did when he was developing the first of his Lotus cars (Crombac, 2001).

Mini Case

Lotus

Colin Chapman was one of the most innovative car designers of the post-war era. Among a string of innovations he produced were a series of lightweight sports cars in the 1950s and the first monocoque construction Formula One racing car, the Lotus 25.

Chapman founded Lotus in 1952 with £25 borrowed from his fiancé Hazel Williams. At this time he was employed by the British Aluminium Company, working for Lotus in the evenings and at weekends. The company's first premises were former stables leased at a very modest rent from Chapman's father who owned the pub next door. Chapman was helped in his new venture by a group of volunteers. Most, like Mike Costin who later founded the engine manufacturer Cosworth, worked for nothing but the promise that they would occasionally get to drive the cars built by the company. Lacking much in the way of equipment, Chapman subcontracted the manufacture of the aluminium body of his first sports cars to Williams and Pritchard, a small engineering firm based in North London. It was apparently not unusual for Williams and Pritchard to have to chase Chapman to get their invoices paid, sometimes taking back work they had completed until the money appeared.

During the early years, the fledgling Lotus company benefited from relationships with a variety of institutions. The 750 Motor Club was particularly important. Chapman was a member and regularly participated in races organised by it. Many of the acquaintances that Chapman made through the club were customers for early Lotus sports cars. However, not all Chapman's 750 Motor Club customers paid cash, for Lotus was prepared to barter its products in exchange for services, as when Patrick Stephens, who handled Lotus's advertising, took components for his car in payment. Another important institution in the early years was the aircraft manufacturer De Havilland based near to Lotus in Hatfield. Several De Havilland employees, such as Mike Costin worked for Lotus in the evenings and at weekends, and it was through them that Lotus gained unofficial access to the plane-maker's wind tunnel for prototype testing.

By 1955, with expanded premises and a healthy order book, Lotus was sufficiently well established for Colin Chapman to give up his job with British Aluminium. By 1959 continued expansion meant a move to new premises as the company began production of the Lotus Elite sports car, an innovative design that made extensive use of glass fibre. By this time Lotus was a recognised car manufacturer, albeit on a small scale and two years later Chapman began work on his most significant innovation, the Lotus 25 Formula One car.

Sources: Crombac (2001); Lawrence (2002); Smith (2009).

Government funding

SMART awards

The Small Firms Merit Award for Research and Technology (SMART) was introduced by the Department of Trade and Industry (DTI) in 1986 as a competitive scheme designed to provide support for innovation by small firms. The rationale behind the scheme is that small firms face particular problems in raising finance for R&D associated with innovation. As Caird (1994: p58) notes, the SMART scheme:

 … recognises the failure of market forces to support high technology innovation as a result of the potential failure risks associated with innovation. It aims to encourage the formation of science and technology firms and help them to grow to a point where they are likely to attract financial support.

The objectives of the SMART scheme as specified by the DTI (1989) are:

- to bring forward highly innovative but commercially viable projects, now dormant because existing sources of finance do not wish to support them
- to encourage the formation of small firms which will develop and market new ideas in selected areas of new technology
- to help these small firms to mature sufficiently for private sources of funds to take a practical interest

Previously there had been other government-funded schemes designed to provide finance for innovation, but the SMART scheme was the first to be specifically designed to meet the needs of small firms. According to Moore (1993) the scheme was in fact inspired by the success of an earlier scheme in the US, the Small Business Innovation Research programme. Given that it was established by a government anxious not to engage in interventionism, the scheme was deliberately structured as a competition with relatively limited funding available. Similarly, it was a temporary programme designed to run for three years in the first instance. A measure of its success is that it is still in operation, albeit in a slightly different form (the SMART scheme was re-branded as *Grants for Research and Development* in 2004).

The SMART scheme is open to individuals and small firms with up to 50 employees. It aims to develop innovative but marketable technology. According to Lawrence (1997), almost any technology with the potential to be transformed into a commercial product has a chance of winning an award. Its purpose is to provide funds for a technical and commercial feasibility study as well as taking the project on to development. Under the terms of the scheme SMART awards are available to both start-up and existing companies and come in two stages. The first stage is competitive and is designed to assist small firms and individuals with technological and commercial feasibility. Applicants for an award are required to submit a detailed proposal and in 1995 over 1,100 proposals were received. Proposals are subject to detailed scrutiny by technical experts, financial advisers and commercial assessors, using a points system based on well-established criteria. The degree of innovation is an important element in the selection process, as is its technical merit, the calibre of the team putting forward the proposal, and the scope for commercial success (Lawrence, 1997). Winners receive a Stage 1 SMART award which provides 75 per cent of the first £60,000 of eligible costs in the first year up to a maximum of £45,000. This is a cash grant of which the first instalment of £15,000 is paid in advance. The Stage 2 award provides further support "to take the idea closer to the marketplace" (Jones-Evans and Westhead, 1996: p30) such as assisting with the development of pre-production prototypes. The support amounts to up to 50 per cent of eligible costs up to a maximum of £150,000 (covering both stages).

Successful projects are carefully monitored to ensure that milestones and targets are met and the money is spent as planned. Lawrence (1997) notes that one of the attractions of the scheme is that the first tranche of funds amounting to £15,000 is presented as a cheque at a formal award ceremony to mark the start of the project. The attendant publicity, as Moore (1993) observes, can have powerful indirect benefits for recipients, bringing the firm to the attention of external investors and thereby increasing its chances of obtaining external funding on appropriate terms.

That the scheme has continued (albeit with some changes along the way – see below) for almost 20 years is testimony both to the fact that market failure does exist and to the success of the scheme. Not only has the scheme resulted in innovations coming to market that would otherwise not have done so, but independent evaluation of the scheme (Moore and Garnsey, 1993) has shown SMART recipients receiving injections of finance to allow further growth and unsolicited approaches from venture capitalists.

Following the success of the SMART scheme the government introduced a new programme of support for R&D called Support for Programmes Under Research (SPUR). SPUR is open to all firms employing less than 500 employees but is targeted at larger firms since projects must have eligible costs with a minimum value of £50,000. SPUR provides a fixed grant that covers 30 per cent of eligible costs (up to a maximum of £150,000) of the development of new products and processes which involve a significant technological advance for the industry.

(The SMART scheme (branded as the Grants for Research and Development scheme) is very similar, though there are now four forms of funding available: Micro Project Grant of £2,500–£20,000 (up to 50 per cent of project costs) over 12 months; Research Project Grant of £20,000–£75,000 (up to 60 per cent of project costs) over 6–18 months; Development Project Grant of £20,000–£200,000 (up to 35 per cent of project costs) over 6–36 months; Exceptional Development Project Grant of up to £500,000 (up to 35 per cent of project costs).)

Banks

> I went to the bank first and met a very nice chap, very friendly. It turned out he was normally doing things like lending money to people to set up newspaper shops. He did not feel really qualified to comment on my adaptive non-linear pattern recognition technology. But he did give me a good piece of advice, which I carry with me even now, which is that people will always buy confectionery.
>
> *Doward (1999)*

This quote from Mike Lynch of the software company Autonomy, reflects the findings of a number of studies (Bank of England, 2001) which have noted the reluctance of banks to provide finance for innovation-related, high-technology business start-ups. A study by Moore (1994) found that only 7 per cent of high-technology companies raised start-up finance from banks compared to 40 per cent of SMEs in general. This does not mean that banks do not provide finance for innovation, it simply reflects the fact that banks generally provide working capital through the provision of overdraft facilities.

However, a recent report by the Bank of England (2001) highlights the fact that the UK banking sector has made efforts in recent years to improve its servicing of the innovation and high-technology market. The NatWest Innovation and Growth Unit for instance currently has some 225 Technology Business Managers operating in the field. They are assisted by a Technology Business Appraisal Service which offers a low-cost technology evaluation service via a network of independent technology marketing specialists who assess the technical feasibility, commercial viability and future potential of technology-based proposals. Similarly, HSBC has launched its own Innovation and Growth Unit, and Barclays has set up 15 Technology Centres across the UK. The creation of these specialist units indicates UK banks are taking a more significant role in funding innovation than in the past.

Mini Case

Dragons' Den

A popular TV series in the UK is the BBC's *Dragons' Den*. The programme hosted by presenter Evan Davies, has inventors and entrepreneurs keen to launch their new product or service, pitching for investment funding from the Dragons, five individual venture capitalists, each willing to invest his or her own money in return for a share of the equity. As individual venture capitalists, the Dragons are business angels. They are highly successful entrepreneurs, each of whom is seeking to invest some of their wealth in new ventures, using their hard-earned business acumen to identify ideas and inventions that have real potential.

The format of the programme is that one-by-one each contestant makes his or her "pitch," a short presentation, in which they briefly outline their idea/invention and the product/service they are hoping to offer together with the size of investment they are seeking and the share of the business they are willing to surrender in return. The programme is of course all about the ideas and inventions, which makes it far more personal to both the audience and the contestants. However, having had the contestants make their pitch then it is the turn of the Dragons. They probe the proposal by questioning contestants about expenditure to date, patent protection, prospective sales and the like. The probing typically comprises withering one-liners from the glowering millionaires. It is after all from the probing and questioning, not to mention the negotiating that surrounds many of the deals, that the Dragons get their name. The probing by the Dragons quickly reveals that the ideas and inventions are occasionally brilliant, but more often are not, with contestants all too often wildly deluded and in fact clutching what is all too often a rather weak idea.

A lucky few, however, get the investment they are seeking, with one or more Dragons backing the project with hard cash. Nor is that all. Like all good business angels, the Dragons don't only have cash, they also have a wealth of knowledge and expertise that they put at the disposal of the projects they back. One such project was "Rapstrap" a new patented design of cable tie for use with plants, bags and sacks, hi-fi and TV and even cycles, put forward by

Andy Harsley from Grantham in the East Midlands. Anxious to scale up production of his invention, he managed to secure an investment of £150,000 from Dragons James Caan and Duncan Bannatyne in exchange for a 50 per cent stake in his company. But it wasn't only money that the Dragons brought with them. They also brought connections with the result that within months Rapstrap had secured a £36 million three-year contract for its innovative new product.

Venture capital

Business angels

There are two principal forms of venture capital, informal venture capital provided by individuals termed business angels or angel investors and formal venture capital provided by venture capital firms which are sometimes referred to as private equity funds.

Business angels are high net-worth individuals seeking capital gains over the life of their investment in a company. Because there is no clearly visible market in which they operate or directories that list them (Mason and Harrison, 1996, 1997), business angels are often described as "informal" investors. For the same reason business angels typically have a regional focus. Good examples of business angels are the members of the panel of investors on the BBC TV programme *Dragons' Den* (see mini case above).

Recent estimates (Bank of England, 2001) suggest that there are approximately 18,000 business angels in the UK, who between them invest £500 million annually in some 3,500 companies. Although this is small compared to the £6.2 billion invested by venture capitalists, the Bank of England estimates that a high proportion of business-angel investments are in seed, start-up and early stage capital, making the "informal" venture capital market (i.e. business angels) of equivalent importance in terms of funding innovation to the formal market, even though the latter is many times bigger (Bank of England, 2001).

A study of business angels by Coveney and Moore (1997) found that business angels are by no means a homogeneous group. Business angels vary greatly on any one of a number of different aspects of their activities including:

- number of investments made per year
- the level of funds they have available to invest
- the size of individual investments, which varied from £10,000–£1 million+
- net-worth of individual investors, which ranged from about a quarter with less than £200,000 to a similar proportion with more than £1 million
- the extent of their experience of business start-ups, which ranged from about a third with no experience to some who had been involved in several
- the reasons for investing, with only half investing primarily for financial gain

In the light of such variation, Coveney and Moore (1997) divided business angels into two broad categories – active and passive informal investors – which they then further subdivided to create a total of six categories:

1 active business angels
- entrepreneurs
- wealth-maximising
- income-seeking
- corporate

2 passive business angels
- latent
- virgin

The entrepreneur business angels are generally self-made, very wealthy and interested in a broad range of business opportunities. The members of the *Dragons' Den* would all fit into this category (see mini case above). Typically they invest in start-up situations and are motivated as much by fun and a desire to contribute to a successful venture as a desire for financial gain. For these individuals the most important criterion tends to be the personality of the innovator/founder. Surprisingly, they are often less active in the management of the venture than other types of business angel.

Income-seeking business angels are generally interested in smaller investments and are looking for high rates of return. Their background is generally the least entrepreneurial and they have less net-worth. Investing mainly locally and in sectors with which they are familiar, their motivation is clearly income, and for them it is a serious business rather than a matter of enjoyment and satisfaction.

Wealth-maximising business angels are, to quote Coveney and Moore (1997: p73), "a contradictory bunch". They invest mainly for financial gain and, though they normally only take minority stakes, they often get involved in company management. Richer than income-seeking business angels, they are less focused in terms of what they invest in. Their backgrounds are generally not entrepreneurial, most having acquired their wealth through inheritance.

Corporate business angels are, as their name implies, companies making investments in unquoted companies, and they are dealt with in more detail in the next section under the heading of corporate venturing.

Latent business angels are ones who have invested in the past but do not currently have any investments. Coveney and Moore (1997) found they are generally very wealthy, highly educated and older than other business angels. Their main reason for not investing is a lack of suitable investment opportunities.

Virgin business angels are those who want to invest but have not yet done so. In general their backgrounds are very varied with few having been involved in a business start-up before.

The Bank of England (2001) suggests that the presence of latent and virgin business angels is a sign of market inefficiency, reflecting information gaps and unnecessarily high search costs. These factors reflect the informal nature of this capital market. However, recent moves to create networks of business angels together with greater awareness of this source of finance (Dodgson, 2000) may have gone some way to alleviate the problem.

A key feature of the business-angel market is the extent to which it complements the formal venture capital market. Recent research by the British Venture Capital Association suggests that this is the case, with more than half of business-angel investments being for less than £50,000

(Bank of England, 2001), and less than a quarter over £100,000, compared with 86 per cent by venture capitalists. The extent to which venture capitalists concentrate on bigger deals confirms that the business-angel market is the main source of private-sector finance, after the founder's initial resources have dried up (Mason and Harrison, 2000a, 2000b). As such, business angels normally provide capital after the immediate start-up phase and before the company has reached a size where it is likely to be of interest to venture capitalists. Business-angel investment may even contribute to the due diligence required by venture capitalists. More significantly, they perform an invaluable networking function by bringing together the innovator, capital and managerial expertise.

One final word of caution regarding business angels is that in the UK they are a much rarer species than in the US. In addition, only a small proportion appear to be active in innovation through investing in high-technology companies. However, the Bank of England's (2001) report does note that the evidence on this appears contradictory with some studies suggesting that around a third of business-angel investments are in high-technology companies, while other studies put the proportion as low as 5 per cent.

Mini Case

Amazon.com

Having studied engineering and computer science at university, Jeff Bezos worked briefly for a small software house before moving to Bankers' Trust, a big Wall Street bank. Two years later he switched to another financial institution, the hedge fund D.E. Shaw. It was here, a couple of years later in 1994 that he was asked to investigate the possibility of making money from the Internet. When he came to look at the Internet he was immediately struck by the dramatic growth of traffic in the World Wide Web. Yet there were few businesses on the web, and Bezos figured that it was only a matter of time before this changed. His analysis led him to the conclusion that of all the items that could be sold over the web, books offered the best prospect.

Bezos recommended that D.E. Shaw set up an online bookstore. When Shaw rejected his idea, he left and set up on his own. At the time it was a big gamble. Bezos chose Seattle as the home for his new company. Why Seattle? It was the home of Microsoft, it was close to Roseburg, Oregon, the home of the biggest book distributor in the US and he had friends there. Bezos called his new company Amazon.com, the first use of the ".com" suffix. Bezos employed two computer scientists to develop a website and paid them out of his own pocket. When he ran out of money his parents invested $250,000. With such a risky venture raising money from outsiders was not really an option. Amazon.com began business from the garage of his rented house in Bellevue, a suburb of Seattle, in mid-1995. Amazon.com was not the first Internet bookstore, but it was the first to allow customers to search through a catalogue of a million books. At first the business grew slowly. Needing more money Bezos began to look for outside capital. With great difficulty he raised $1 million. Then Bezos got a lucky break. In May 1996, a short article on the front page of the Wall Street Journal reported how Bezos had quit his Wall Street job to set up an online bookshop. The day the story was published Amazon.com's business doubled and then went on doubling over a very short space of time. In no time at all he was inundated with venture capitalists offering to invest in his company.

Source: Cassidy (2002).

Venture capital firms

The Macmillan Report (1931) first identified the existence of an "equity gap," describing the inability of small firms to access long-term risk capital. At the time the gap was said to lie between founder, friends and family and the stock market. To bridge this gap the Bank of England and the UK clearing banks established 3i, the first venture capital organisation in the UK. Despite this early start, venture capital firms, or private equity funds as they are sometimes known, are a relatively recent phenomenon (Deakins and Freel, 2003), since it was only in the 1980s that venture capital emerged as a significant source of funding both in the UK and the US.

In the US the growth of venture capital was linked closely to the success of Silicon Valley in California (Howells, 2005). Among the first venture capital firms established in this region were well known names like Kleiner Perkins, Caufield & Byers and Sequoia Capital, all of which were established in the early 1970s. Set-up by successful entrepreneurs keen to put their new found wealth to good use, their rapid growth was linked to the growth of technology-based industries in Silicon Valley, based initially on semiconductors and later computers. Their numbers grew from a handful at the start of the 1980s to 650 by the end of the 1980s. Recession at the start of the 1990s brought a halt to growth only for another boom to occur in the second half of the decade fuelled by the "Internet Bubble".

Country	Venture capital investment as percentage GDP	
	1989	1999
Austria	0.01	0.03
Belgium	0.05	0.26
Denmark	0.01	0.05
Finland	0.01	0.11
France	0.05	0.12
Germany	0.01	0.13
Greece	n.a.	0.06
Ireland	0.05	0.09
Italy	0.02	0.05
The Netherlands	0.05	0.02
Portugal	0.02	0.25
Spain	0.02	0.09
Sweden	0.02	0.19
United Kingdom	0.13	0.20
EU	0.04	0.12
US	0.11	0.56

TABLE 10.1 Venture capital investment as a percentage of GDP
Source: Christofidis and Debande (2001: p20)

Europe remains some way behind the US in terms of the development of venture capital, and within Europe there are marked variations with the Netherlands, Belgium, Sweden and the

UK well ahead of countries like France and Germany in terms of the scale of venture capital activity (see Table 10.1).

The UK venture capital industry is the largest in Europe (Bank of England, 2001). It is second only to the US and in per capita terms it is the largest in the world. Between 1984 and 1998 British Venture Capital Association members invested some £35.5 billion in more than 19,000 companies.

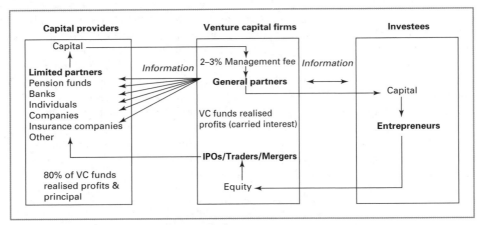

FIGURE 10.3 Venture capital funds structure
Source: Christofidis and Debande (2001: p10)

Predominantly structured as limited partnerships, venture capitalist firms manage "pools of capital" (Christofidis and Debande, 2001: p1) by borrowing from institutional investors such as pension funds, life assurance companies and banks as well as companies and individuals and investing in private companies requiring funding for seed, start-up and second/third stage development (see Figure 10.3). Their aim is to make a capital gain by the time they harvest their investment via a "trade sale" or initial public offering (IPO) some years later. As intermediaries, venture capital firms' expertise lies in evaluating the risks and growth potential of companies which they back with equity investments.

However, venture capital firms provide only a very small proportion of the external finance used by SMEs in the UK. Similarly, only a small proportion of investment by venture capital firms goes into financing start-ups and early growth. This reflects what appears to be a growing preference within the venture capital industry for large deals. In fact, the average size of deal has risen from less than £1 million in 1988 to over £3 million in 1998. This rise reflects a shift away from start-up and early-stage funding in favour of later-stage deals that require larger sums (Bank of England, 2001).

A variety of factors have been put forward to explain this, including increasing reliance on pension funds as a source of finance and the greater cost of managing small-technology investments. Whatever the reasons, venture capital firms are of declining importance as a source of funding innovation undertaken by small companies.

Corporate venturing

Corporate venturing is yet another type of venture capital operation. A report by the CBI (1999) describes corporate venturing as,

> " a formal, direct relationship, usually between a larger and an independent smaller company, in which both contribute financial, management or technical resources, sharing rewards equally for mutual growth. "

Such arrangements involve the larger company taking a financial stake in the smaller one in return for a share in its development. The rationale behind a corporate undertaking investing in this way is that it is seeking to invest in technologies perceived to help it fulfil its strategic objectives (Christofidis and Debande, 2001). In particular it wishes to keep in touch with and potentially influence the development of specific technologies. Typically this would be connected to the development of an innovation in the form of a new product or process. This sort of arrangement most often occurs in high-technology sectors such as pharmaceuticals and software, and reflects developments in the US where the trend towards larger companies investing in smaller ones is increasingly a feature of high-technology clusters like Silicon Valley.

For the small company corporate venturing affords another means of funding innovation, although it often brings with it other benefits including access to managerial expertise and sometimes to the larger company's manufacturing and marketing resources.

The benefits, however, are by no means all one way. For the larger company, corporate venturing offers benefits too. It facilitates access to new ideas and skills, allows an assessment of new markets and provides the means to exploit potentially attractive returns on new technologies.

Initial public offering (IPO): the Alternative Investment Market (AIM)

Launched in 1995, the Alternative Investment Market (AIM) is a London-based equity market aimed at meeting the needs of smaller companies, especially ones that are technology based. As such it is designed to meet the needs of smaller companies by offering a streamlined admission process and a flexible approach to regulation (i.e. financial reporting). Specifically this means:

Accessibility

Unlike the main equity market of the London Stock Exchange, AIM does not stipulate minimum criteria for:

- company size
- track record
- number of shares in public hands

Instead a nominated adviser ensures that the applicant company is suitable for entry to AIM. This type of approach is much more flexible than that taken by the main market and is therefore much more in line with the needs of small high-technology companies.

Admission process

Again the process is a much simplified version of that required for the main market. As a result it is relatively quick, normally taking 24 weeks from the start of the process to a successful listing. The nominated adviser carries out due diligence and ensures that all the requirements are met and all appropriate information is included in the admission document.

Regulatory regime

All AIM-listed companies are required to disclose their financial performance through the publication of interim and full-year results, as well as making appropriate disclosures regarding any issues relevant to future performance. But they are not required to publish details regarding acquisitions and disposals.

At launch there were just ten companies on AIM. By the end of 2000 this had risen to 524 with a market capitalisation of £14.5 billion. Of these, around a fifth are technology-based companies with a market capitalisation of £3.26 billion. In fact, 2000 was a record year for the admission of technology-based companies (Figure 10.4) with 62 joining the market that year.

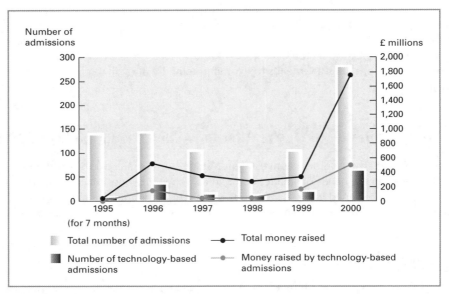

FIGURE 10.4 Technology-based AIM admissions
Source: Bank of England (2001: p47)

As with any public equity market AIM offers a number of benefits beyond raising equity capital. These include:

- an exit route for existing shareholders
- enhanced visibility for the enterprise
- a broader shareholder base
- an objective market valuation of the enterprise

The market is aimed specifically at the unique community of innovative and entrepreneurial companies.

Formation of the company

Oxford Instruments was started by Martin Wood and his wife Audrey. Martin Wood came from a solid, middle-class professional family. Required to do three years' national service before going to university, Martin Wood opted to do his national service working in the coal mines of South Wales instead of going into the army. He then gained a BSc from Imperial College, London and an MA in Engineering from Cambridge. Having finished his studies, he decided to pursue a career in industry working initially as a management trainee for the National Coal Board. However, he became frustrated with working for such a large organisation, decided to look around for something else and got a job as Senior Research Officer at the Clarendon Laboratory, part of Oxford University's physics department.

It was while he was working at the Clarendon Laboratory that he founded Oxford Instruments. In fact, the company began very much as a part-time venture, with Martin Wood continuing his work at the University, for a further ten years. To begin with the work of the new venture was all concerned with design and consultancy. This was a time when the university system in the UK was expanding and Martin Wood initially assisted and advised new departments on the equipping of laboratories. Since it did not actually make anything, Oxford Instruments did not need any premises. Most of the work came through Martin Wood's contacts at the Clarendon Laboratory.

In time Martin Wood and his wife Audrey came to realise that some of his customers, especially those in public research laboratories, such as the Royal Radar Establishment (RRE) in Malvern and the Harwell Laboratory of the UK Atomic Energy Authority (UKAEA) had a requirement for magnets that they were finding difficult to fulfil. As a result Oxford Instruments moved into the manufacture of magnets. The move into manufacturing required rather more in the way of assets than the design and consultancy business. The need for premises was met by the Woods installing a large garden shed which had once been half a post-war "prefab" house at the bottom of their garden. For equipment the company bought an old lathe at auction and arranged to borrow Clarendon Laboratory's special machine for winding magnetic coils. Material supplies were less of a problem, because Martin Wood was dealing with the same suppliers that he dealt with regularly at the University. The company employed a retired Clarendon Laboratory technician on a part time basis and most of the rest of the jobs were undertaken by Audrey Wood.

The company delivered its first magnet, a specialist laboratory magnet, manufactured in the shed at the bottom of the garden of the Woods' North Oxford home to the Royal Radar Establishment, and other orders soon followed.

Superconductivity and magnets

Now initiated into the intricacies of manufacturing, Martin Wood continued his academic work. He and his wife attended an academic conference at Boston in the US. This was a routine event for university staff such as Wood, but the conference was to have a far from

▶ routine impact on the new company. At the conference several research groups reported research into new developments in the field of superconductivity. Superconductivity is essentially a property of certain metals which means that at very low temperatures they suddenly lose all electrical resistance. Superconductivity had been first identified in 1911, but from then until the second half of the twentieth century it remained an interesting curiosity with no practical applications. The conference raised the prospect that this might be about to change, with the development of new materials that were sufficiently versatile to be used in practical products. Since electrical resistance dramatically reduces the efficiency of materials for transmitting electricity, any material that has a low resistance (in superconducting materials resistance falls to zero) is likely to have a dramatic impact on the efficiency of transmitting electricity. This was especially important for research laboratories working with high magnetic fields. Hitherto the scope for research had been limited by the need to employ large magnets that required enormous amounts of electrical power and special water-cooling facilities. An indication of the problems posed by the use of conventional magnets can be gauged by the fact that at the time the Clarendon Laboratory at Oxford University had one magnet which alone used 10 per cent of the city of Oxford's electricity. Such was this magnet's requirement for electricity that permission had to be sought from the electricity board every time it was switched on. In essence, developments in superconductivity meant there was the prospect of a completely new generation of magnets (and a whole host of products using magnets) that would no longer be dependent on large quantities of electrical power.

While these developments offered the prospect of a new type of magnet, to develop a commercial superconducting magnet still required many obstacles to be overcome. The new superconducting materials, such as niobium zirconium (NbZr), tended to be inconsistent and unreliable. Not only that, to achieve the very low temperatures required for the material to become superconducting required a supply of liquid helium, a liquified gas that was costly and hard to obtain.

Undeterred by these problems, Oxford Instruments purchased a pound of niobium zirconium wire from the US and Martin Wood set out to make Europe's first commercial superconducting magnet. Knowledge was extremely sparse. There were no books or manuals on how to manufacture a superconducting magnet. From university sources Martin Wood had access to reports and papers from academic conferences, but even though these told him a lot about the properties of the materials with which he was working, they did not focus on issues directly relevant to manufacturing. He was fortunate in being able to use Oxford University's computer to calculate the quantities of material required and to predict the new magnet's performance characteristics.

With the design completed, the first magnet did not take long to build. Using liquid helium and liquid nitrogen borrowed from the Clarendon Laboratory, the new magnet was carefully tested. Much to everyone's surprise it worked perfectly, producing a magnetic field far more powerful than had previously been possible in a laboratory without major engineering, power and cooling installations. This prototype worked well and was shown and demonstrated at a variety of exhibitions and conferences. Oxford Instruments was soon talking to prospective customers and by the end of the year had had many enquiries and ten orders for the new type of magnet. Though busy manufacturing conventional magnets, Oxford Instruments developed and manufactured its first superconducting magnet, which was delivered to Birkbeck College, at the University of London.

It was at this time that the company moved out of the Woods' garden shed and into a disused stable in North Oxford, rented from a local butcher. To provide additional manufacturing capacity, the company acquired and installed some redundant machine tools bought at auction, and took on its first full-time employee. Within a year the workforce had risen to four. Further equipment such as cryostats for storing liquid helium was manufactured by Clarendon Laboratory technicians working in their spare time.

The need for at least some administration, covering aspects such as payroll and invoicing, personnel and selection, and the purchasing and storing of materials, was now beginning to emerge. Nor was it only a matter of routine administration, since there was also a need to plan production and schedule the delivery of materials so that deliveries were met on time. These were aspects that neither Martin Wood nor his fellow workers with their scientific backgrounds and interest in technical issues knew much about. As a study of the company noted, "we were rather arrogant, imagining that it would not be difficult for people with a scientific training to grow a company successfully". Oxford Instruments was fortunate that Martin Wood's wife, Audrey, was able to handle most aspects of the administrative side of the business at this time, using a second-hand caravan that served as an office.

Funding development of the company

Although growing fast the company did not yet need outside finance. Overheads were still low and the operation sufficiently small for costs not to get out of hand. The limited finance that was needed, could be provided by the Woods themselves, supplemented by loans from family members and an overdraft from the bank.

One problem that the company did face at this point in its development was obtaining reliable supplies of raw materials. Liquid helium was a particular problem. Their supplier, British Oxygen Company (BOC), would not deliver supplies of the gas – so that the vacuum flasks containing the gas had to go by train – resulting in delays and losses of gas due to heat and vibration. Not only was this making manufacturing difficult, it was deterring potential users of superconducting magnets because they could not ensure a reliable supply of liquid helium to enable them to operate the magnets. So it was that Oxford Instruments undertook a major new investment, purchasing a helium liquefier from the US. It cost £35,000, a great deal more than the total investment in the company to date. The company was able to finance the purchase by extending its overdraft with the bank, supported by suitable guarantees from members of Martin Wood's family. A separate company was formed, Oxford Cryogenics, and additional premises were acquired to house the new equipment, in the form of a disused laundry rented from Oxfordshire County Council on a temporary basis pending planning decisions in the area. Oxford Cryogenics was soon supplying laboratories across the country and the new service gave a major boost to low-temperature research in the UK.

Meanwhile Oxford Instruments was growing fast. Production of both types of magnet was expanding and the following year the company moved to new larger premises by the river Thames in Oxford. Three years after it had been formerly registered, the company's annual turnover was £41,000 on which the company made a net profit of £2,460, representing a return of some 6 per cent. By this point Oxford Instruments had 25 employees almost all of whom were engineers, scientists and technicians.

Within a couple of years, however, finance was beginning to become a problem. The company relied heavily for profits on systems produced to individual requirements. This stretched the technology to its limits and made profits unpredictable. By this point the existing sources of capital – family loans and guarantees and the bank overdraft – were simply proving inadequate. The company looked at several potential sources of venture capital including:

- large companies investing in technology
- merchant banks
- insurance companies
- rich private individuals

Although they came very close to agreeing a deal on several occasions throughout this period, the terms were never quite right. Eventually the venture capital firm 3i put in substantial loans and equity finance. This involved 3i purchasing 20 per cent of the equity of Oxford Instruments for £45,000, while at the same time providing a similar sum in debentures (loan finance). With adequate capital Oxford Instruments continued to grow rapidly. Martin Wood finally quit his job at Oxford University. By this time the company had 105 staff on the payroll and the following year turnover reached £350,000. It was a small company no longer.

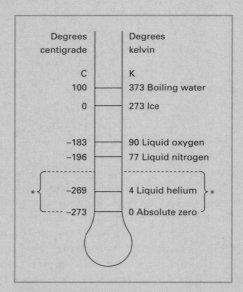

FIGURE 10.5 The range of superconductivity
Range of superconductivity

Source: A. Wood (2001) from *Magnetic Venture: The Story of Oxford Instruments,* by permission of Oxford University Press

Questions

1 What sources of venture capital did Oxford Instruments consider and which source did it ultimately opt for?

2 What is the name usually given to high net-worth individuals who invest in new ventures, especially ones that take the form of technology-based companies?

3 What innovation did Oxford Instruments develop?

4 What kind of entrepreneur would you classify Martin Wood as?

5 What aspects of Martin Wood's previous work experience proved helpful in founding Oxford Instruments and why?

6 What institutional support did Oxford Instruments get in the early years and from whom?

7 What instances of "financial bootstrapping" can you identify in this case?

8 What sources of venture capital did Oxford Instruments consider and which source did it ultimately opt for?

9 How important do you consider Martin Wood's personal network to have been in the success of this venture?

10 Which organisation was Oxford Instruments "parent" and to what extent did the company continue to maintain links with it?

11 What other problems besides funding did Oxford Instruments face as it grew and why are these sorts of problems likely to be particularly significant for technical entrepreneurs?

? Questions for discussion

1 Why is cashflow an important issue for technological innovation?

2 What is the cashflow gap that innovators typically face?

3 What is venture capital?

4 What is bootstrapping and why do innovators often resort to it as a way of funding innovation?

5 Why are personal networks often important when it comes to funding innovation?

6 What are business angels?

7 What motivates business angels to risk their capital?

8 What is the rationale behind the government making funds available to support innovation?

9 What is the SMART scheme?

10 Why are banks often reluctant to lend to small high-technology businesses?

11 What is AIM? Why is it likely to be of particular interest to smaller high technology companies?

12 What is an IPO and why are IPOs attractive to technical entrepreneurs?

13 What is the difference between a "passive" and an "active" informal investor?

14 What is the difference between formal and informal investors?

Exercises

1 Explain what is meant by the term "business angel" and explain how such individuals can contribute to the process of innovation.

2 Select a technical entrepreneur who has been active in innovation and outline the problems he/she faced regarding funding and indicate how they overcame these problems.

3 Explain what is meant by the term "bootstrapping" and then using an account of an innovation show how one innovator (either an individual or an organisation) used it to fund innovation.

4 Analyse the reasons for a cashflow gap when it comes to the provision of "seedbed capital" for technical entrepreneurs and/or technology-based small firms.

5 "The best place for an innovator to get finance is a bank". Discuss.

Further reading

1 **O'Sullivan, M.** (2005) "Finance and Innovation", in Fagerberg, J., D.C. Mowery and R.R. Nelson (eds.) *The Oxford Handbook of Innovation,* Oxford University Press, Oxford. There is actually very little on financial aspects of innovation. This article gives a broad overview of the topic. It doesn't go into detail but does outline some of the key issues.

2 **Mason, C. and R. Harrison** (1994) "Informal venture capital: a study of the investment process, the post-investment experience and investment performance", *Entrepreneurship and Regional Development,* 8, pp105–125.
Mason and Harrison are the pioneers of this subject. Having been ignored by academics for years, they were among the first to open the subject to serious academic scrutiny. The result has been a torrent of research on the subject which has produced a stream of articles stretching back over a decade and a half. Their particular interest is informal venture capital, but this and other papers give a good account of the other forms of start-up capital as well.

3 **Smith, D.J.** (2009) "Financial Bootstrapping and Social Capital: How technology-based start-ups fund innovation", *International Journal of Entrepreneurship and Innovation* (forthcoming).
Perhaps not the best article on the subject, but it does explain this particular form of finance and at the same time give an insight into the problems facing innovators who choose to innovate via a technology-based start-up. If nothing else it does contain some useful references for those doing research on this topic.

4 **Wood, A.** (2001) *Magnetic Venture: The Story of Oxford Instruments*, Oxford University Press, Oxford.
Actually any business history or business biography would do. However, this one is better than most because it provides a detailed picture of the problems facing technology-based start-ups and what they do about finance. Of particular value is the fact that this company used several different forms of finance at the start-up stage. And a very readable and interesting account of the start-up process as well.

11

Managing innovation

❖ *OBJECTIVES*

When you have completed this chapter you will be able to:

- ❖ evaluate the scope of management activities relating to innovation

- ❖ appreciate and understand the contribution that planning makes to effective innovation

- ❖ appreciate and understand the contribution of organisation to effective management

- ❖ appreciate and understand the contribution that monitoring and control makes to effective management

- ❖ appreciate and understand the contribution leadership makes to effective management

Introduction

For every successful innovation there are probably ten times as many unsuccessful ones. Among many well-known examples of unsuccessful innovations are the CAT scanner, the world's first body-scanner developed by EMI in the 1970s (Teece, 1986), the C5 electric car developed by Sinclair Research in the 1980s and British Rail's Advanced Passenger Train (see case study at the end of this chapter). It is tempting to see innovation failures as the result of unreliable or ineffective technology, but while innovations sometimes either do not work or fail to work reliably because of weaknesses in the technology, often there are other factors in play. Sometimes the fault lies with the market, or rather the failure of the innovation to deliver what the market wants. However, innovation does not occur in a vacuum. Most forms of innovation are organised and directed by individuals working either on their own or within an organisation. Consequently sometimes the reason for the failure of an innovation is managerial failure, that is, the particular way in which the various parts of the innovation process were managed.

Mindful of this, this chapter explores some of the issues surrounding the management of innovation. It explores what is involved in managing an innovation and then proceeds to examine a range of tools and techniques available to assist those responsible for management. Rather than present little more than a list of tools and techniques, the chapter begins by considering the nature of management itself, particularly the range of activities that managers engage in when they manage something, whether it be a manufacturing process, a service facility, a construction project or the development of an innovation. These activities are then used as categories in order to present a range of appropriate techniques under each heading.

The functions of management

Management is one of those activities where it is pretty clear when it is being done well and also when it is failing. Actually determining what is involved in managing is more complex and open to debate. It was one of the early pioneers of managerial thought, the Frenchman Henri Fayol (Fayol, 1916), who categorised management as essentially comprising four (Figure 11.1) principal elements:

- planning
- organising
- leading
- controlling

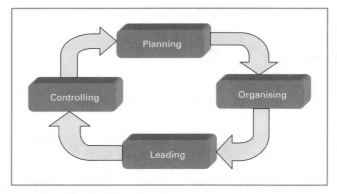

FIGURE 11.1 The functions of management

Planning is very clearly a decision-making activity. It involves looking into the future and making decisions that will enable a particular outcome to be achieved. Appropriate goals need to be set in order to achieve the desired outcome. It is then necessary to identify and select courses of action or activities to achieve these goals with appropriate resources then being allocated to enable the activities to be carried out. Organising, in contrast, tends to be a more people-centred activity. It involves specifying and structuring working relationships between individuals. This is required to enable the planned activities to be carried out by ensuring that an appropriate mix of skills is available, that coordination can takes place and that the necessary human input is available. Leadership involves conveying a sense of purpose to the whole organisation and individuals (i.e. at a variety of different levels within the organisation).

At one time seen primarily as a matter of directing individuals, leadership involves providing a vision of where the organisation is going, and motivating individuals to make the necessary effort to see that the vision is achieved. Finally control involves monitoring and evaluating the progress of activities to ensure that they are going according to plan.

Why does innovation have to be managed? What is it about the context of innovation that makes management an important activity? Although innovation may appear to be something of a spontaneous activity that cannot be managed, in fact there are many features of the context within which innovation takes place, that make effective management essential. These contextual factors are:

- uncertainty
- complexity
- messy/untidy
- disruptive
- creative

Innovation by its very nature involves much uncertainty. For some innovations there will be uncertainty about how a new technology will perform. For others there will be uncertainty about how consumers will react to a new product. Similarly there will often be uncertainty about the level of resources or the time required to get an innovation ready for the market.

Complexity is associated with innovation because the development of something new almost invariably draws on a variety of different types of expertise. Innovation not only requires technical expertise to get the technology right, it also requires commercial expertise (e.g. marketing, finance, etc.) to get the product or service ready for market. The involvement of staff from a range of disciplines inevitably leads to complexity, whether it is communication channels, the transfer of information or just different ways of working. Not only that, these days innovation very often requires expertise from outside the organisation which makes things more complex still.

Given that one is dealing with something new, innovation does also tend to be messy and untidy. Rarely is innovation smooth and straightforward. Rather as studies of innovation frequently show (Nayak and Ketteringham, 1993; Brown, 2002; Seabrook, 2008) innovation all too often comprises false starts when avenues of exploration prove to be blind alleys, shocks and triggers when external events cause the course of innovation to take new directions, and serendipity as chance events give rise to new insights.

The fact that one is dealing with the novel and the new also tends to mean that innovation is disruptive. When the innovation is radical, it can be very disruptive, requiring entirely new ways of doing things. Even when the innovation is merely incremental it can still be disruptive, leading to significant changes for the organisation.

Finally innovation almost invariably requires a degree of creativity. While management cannot make people creative, it can through appropriate leadership and organisation, help to provide the conditions in which creativity can flourish.

Faced with the uncertain, complex, messy, disruptive and creative nature of innovation, this chapter presents a range of tools and techniques that managers can employ to help and assist them with the difficult task of managing innovation. They will not guarantee success for an innovation. Quite apart from anything else there is nearly always far too much uncertainty attached to every innovation to ensure that. However, applied in the correct way the techniques can help to make the process of innovation management more effective, and this in turn should help to increase the likelihood that an innovation will succeed. But the chapter not only imparts knowledge of managerial techniques, it also hopefully provides some powerful insights into what managing innovation involves, and why it is needed.

Planning

Two planning techniques that are commonly associated with innovation are project management and the development funnel.

Project management

Project management (henceforth abbreviated to PM) is a general purpose planning technique that is widely used to help with the management of projects, particularly ensuring that they are completed on time and within budget. A project is any one-off, even unique, activity which is time constrained and has a specific goal. Since the development of a new product or service is typically a one-off experience, it is not surprising to find that PM can be extremely useful when applied to managing innovation projects.

As a management technique, PM comprises five main steps:

- determine the goal (s)
- identify the activities or tasks to be undertaken
- estimate the duration of the activities/tasks
- determine the sequence in which the activities/tasks have to be completed and link them into a model of the overall project
- develop a project plan that provides an overall schedule for the project

With innovation the project will involve the development of a new product or service and the goal will be to launch it on the market at an appropriate time, normally before competitors can launch rival products/services. The activities/tasks to be completed will generally be those identified in the previous chapter as part of the innovation process and include activities such as design, testing, commissioning and so forth. Identifying the tasks to be undertaken is likely to be a useful discipline because it forces those involved in the project to think, not just about the immediate tasks on which they are working, but also about future tasks. Similarly, while estimating the duration of these activities/tasks may be difficult, having to provide an estimate means that those involved have again to think carefully about the future course of the project. So too does working out the sequence or order in which they will have to be completed. Once the sequence has been established then the activities/tasks can be linked together in a plan or model of the project.

Constructing a project plan is where the planning actually produces plans. There are two types of plan commonly used in PM. The first is a simple Gantt or bar chart where the activities are listed on the vertical axis and the duration of them is recorded on the horizontal axis. With activities/tasks shown as strips the chart will show the cumulative time taken to complete the project. The other type of chart is a network diagram (Figure 11.2). In this the activities/tasks are typically denoted as nodes and arrows showing how they are linked together. In this way the project is built up as a series of arrows and nodes beginning with the start of the project on the left-hand side and ending with completion of the project on the right-hand side.

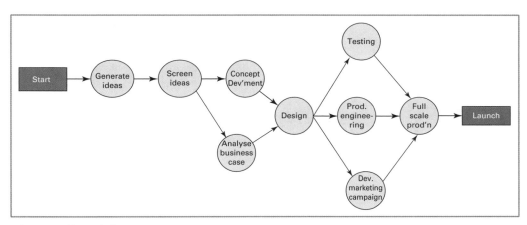

FIGURE 11.2 Network diagram

Whichever type of chart is used the net result is a map of the whole project, forming a plan indicating what has to be undertaken and when. With innovation projects the level of uncertainty can make it difficult to keep to the original plan. It may well prove necessary to divert from the plan or to modify it extensively. Under these circumstances one might well ask the question why bother with PM? The answer lies not in the plan that results, but rather in the process that those involved in PM go through. Not only does the PM process force managers and those working on the innovation to think about the future, it also requires them to talk about and discuss the future. This is a future that involves not only a technical dimension but also a commercial one. Hence it is necessary to think about the innovation in much broader terms. This is what planning is really all about. Out of the discussion should come a better understanding of the tasks to be completed and the uncertainties faced.

Development funnel

The development funnel, or cyclone as it is sometimes termed, represents a "structured" approach to getting from an idea or ideas to the successful launch of a new product or service. The principle is simple. One begins with many ideas and then provides a systematic method of filtering them so that only a relatively small number are actually developed and launched as commercial products or services (Wheelwright and Clarke, 1992). Ideally there should be lots of ideas going in, with the mouth of the funnel deliberately kept wide to encourage a wide range of potential new products and services. The narrowing of the funnel represents the filtering processes as the large number of ideas is reduced to a much smaller number. As Figure 11.3 shows, the funnel may comprise multiple filtering points. In this instance filtering consists of a screening process where ideas are screened, initially to demonstrate that the technical principles work effectively, then for marketability and then for manufacturability. Those ideas which are not technically feasible, too expensive to manufacture or lacking commercial potential are successively screened out.

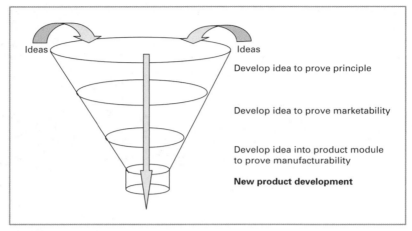

Ideas

Ideas

Develop idea to prove principle

Develop idea to prove marketability

Develop idea into product module
to prove manufacturability

New product development

FIGURE 11.3 The development funnel/cyclone

The result is a much smaller number of ideas going forward as acceptable concepts which can then be pushed forward into a rapid new product development process. The aim of this type of process is not simply to back only those concepts which offer the highest pay-off, but rather, by employing the planning dimension, to use the funnel to build a portfolio of development projects that meet the needs of the business. This will typically mean ensuring a steady stream of new products coming on to the market, and this is something that clearly results from careful planning.

Organising

In managerial terms organising concerns the arrangement or structure of the internal shape of an organisation. Typically this means locating people in groupings (i.e. departments or teams) that facilitate effective working. Where innovation is concerned it is about the choice of internal structure or architecture/configuration conducive to innovation (i.e. that caters for the creativity and flexibility required for innovation). Structures that facilitate conventional work activities such as manufacturing are not necessarily conducive to innovation.

Why is the internal shape or structure of an organisation so important and how does it facilitate innovation? The answer is that the internal structure affects a great many aspects of work activities including:

- communication channels (between individuals and groups of individuals)
- flows of information
- working relationships
- working practices
- work environment
- corporate culture

Innovation has particular requirements where the above are concerned. In particular, communication and information flows have to be effective in order to facilitate the knowledge transfer which the theory of absorptive capacity (Chapter 4) suggests is such a vital ingredient of innovation. Similarly working relationships and working practices have to be flexible and able to cope with uncertainty and unpredictability.

Innovation specific structures: corporate venturing

Much has been written about the problems that large firms encounter in delivering innovations. These include technological and resource lock-ins and routine and cultural rigidities. A number of organisational or structural solutions are available to tackle these sorts of problems. They represent ways of "shaping" an organisation internally in order to circumvent some of the problems caused by large size.

We have already encountered the term "corporate venturing" in the context of funding innovation, where it was used to describe large organisations taking a stake in small ones. In the current context, corporate venturing refers to attempts by large organisations to establish conditions conducive to innovation through a range of initiatives that take the form of internal structural devices that provide a focus for innovation. These usually involve the creation of an internal unit that allows mainstream commercial activity to coexist side-by-side with more speculative activities associated with innovation.

Tidd and Taurins (1999) suggest that such arrangements are designed to permit a trade-off between learning and leverage. Their typology of internal corporate venturing arrangements is presented in Figure 11.4.

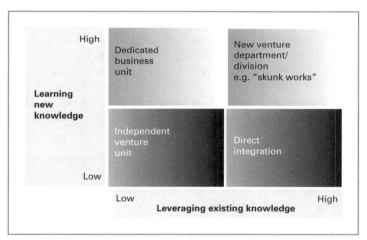

FIGURE 11.4 A typology of corporate venturing
Source: Tidd and Taurins (1999) *Creativity and Innovation Management,* Blackwell Publishing

Direct integration

With this arrangement there is no separate entity created to conduct innovation. Rather, individuals drawn from across the organisation are brought together in a team which has responsibility for the development of a new product or service. The individuals may be secondees, attached to the team for a given period, or they may simply belong to the team and join in its activities alongside their normal work. This type of arrangement has the advantage that it is easy and quick to set up, but it is very dependent on the existing corporate culture being "innovation tolerant," because integration means it is still very closely bound up with the parent organisation.

Dedicated business unit

Although it remains within the existing organisation structure, a dedicated business unit is a separate entity. Such units sit alongside existing business units and may be difficult to distinguish from others. This kind of arrangement is only suitable for innovations with a very short development phase, or ones that are close to being launched, because as a business unit it will be expected to stand on its own feet in terms of profitability. It is also likely to be the case that the innovation will be incremental simply because the organisation will need to be sure that it is likely to break into profit fairly rapidly.

New-venture department

In its more extreme form this is the 'skunk works' solution (see mini case below), where a separate, somewhat secret department is created within the organisation with the very specific brief of coming up with innovations – particularly radical innovations which are a significant departure from the existing product/service portfolio. The aim is to create an "organisation within an organization," but where the newly created inside organisation differs markedly from its parent being much more dynamic and entrepreneurial. Consequently, differentiation is encouraged, often leading to different sorts of behaviour, such as greater informality, teamwork, creativity and dynamism, alongside a lack of hierarchy. While it is staffed by people drawn from the organisation, some may be somewhat independently minded, with behaviour that might be regarded as problematic in mainstream departments. However, a new-venture department will always remain an organisation within the organisation and as such subject to administrative control from the centre, although if run by a strong, powerful personality, or a charismatic figure, it is possible that such control will be relatively weak.

During the 1970s and 1980s a number of large corporations established "development departments" designed to create new ventures that would foster diversification. Britain's BP was typical. In 1974 it established BP New Ventures, a department designed to take over responsibility for developing activities other than oil and coal.

Mini Case

Skunk Works

The term "Skunk Works" is the name given to the Lockheed Aircraft Company's Advanced Development Projects Office. It was formed in 1943 to build secretly the company's first jet fighter, the P-80 Shooting Star. Given 180 days to design and build the aircraft, Lockheed's chief designer Kelly Johnson established a small team within Lockheed's main plant at Burbank, California. The small team was located close to a plastics plant whose noxious smell not only kept the curious at bay but helped give the team its nickname (Rich and Janos, 1994). The team met their target, building the P-80 in a mere 143 days.

The initial Skunk Works operation set the standard for what followed. Lockheed's senior management agreed that the chief engineer could maintain his small research and development operation as long as it was kept on a shoestring budget and did not distract the chief engineer from his principal duties. The team moved into permanent accommodation in Building 82 within the Burbank plant but their activities were kept highly secret. However, it was not so much that the work was kept secret that distinguished the Skunk Works, it was the way it worked. Staff, many of whom were "mavericks," were handpicked by Johnson. Dress was informal. Designers, analysts and engineers were all located close to the shop floor. The emphasis was on building prototypes in the shortest possible time. Often this meant "quick and dirty" solutions to problems such as using stock parts rather than designing new ones.

Among the outputs of the Skunk Works over the years have been the U-2 spy plane of the 1960s, the world's first corporate jet, the Jetstar, and the F-117 Stealth fighter – all new developments, that in their own way, pushed forward the frontiers of aviation.

Source: Rich and Janos (1994).

Independent-venture unit

As their name implies independent venture units are separate entities that typically take the form of a company set up for the express purpose of developing innovative new products. The company may be wholly owned by the parent company or it may be a joint venture. It was this type of arrangement that was described in Chapter 10.

Independence gives rise to a number of important features. Most important is that it gives the unit a high degree of autonomy. This stems from the fact that it is a separate legal entity. This should mean that the unit will be free of internal politics and the corporate mindset. Ideally it should have or at least begin to develop its own sub-culture. Autonomy should mean less interference, greater freedom to experiment and try new approaches and less "baggage" in the sense that there is less need to comply with the requirements of an existing technology or meet the needs of an existing set of consumers; yet, should the unit need further expertise or resources, perhaps for marketing or distribution, these can be tapped into within the parent organisation. As well as greater autonomy, an independent-venture unit should also benefit from greater focus. Without the distraction of corporate policies or internal politics, the team within such a unit should be more cohesive and able to focus specifically on innovation. They ought not to be distracted by the need to update, improve and revise existing products. In short, they should be able to focus on radical innovation free of the need to engage in incremental innovations. Tidd *et al.* (2001) also note that within a separate, independent-venture unit managers may be more highly motivated because they feel in control of their own destiny. If the unit is a joint venture then there will also be advantages in terms of additional resources and the sharing of risk.

Leading

Leadership is about setting a direction or vision for others to follow. Clearly where innovation is concerned the vision needs to be one in which innovation is seen as important and highly valued by the organisation. Leadership can be exercised in a variety of ways. One way is to create roles, within an organisation, that individuals can assume and which they can then use in order to provide leadership to others. Another way is for those in leadership roles to create the kind of culture or climate within an organisation where innovation can flourish. Addressing motivation more specifically, there are a number of practices or schemes that some companies have introduced, which are designed to provide employees (and others) with an opportunity to exercise their creativity by developing new products and services and process innovations.

While such practices tend to be very specific, leadership is about creating the kind of climate within an organisation where employees feel motivated to exercise their creativity and engage in activities that can lead to innovation.

Leadership roles

In managerial terms there are a number of well known and much used leadership roles. The role of chief executive for instance is a widely recognised leadership role, taken by a person who has overall responsibility for managing an organisation. As well as having day-to-day control over the organisation, the chief executive would also be expected to guide its long-term direction by providing a vision of what the organisation will be like in the future.

Just as there are a number of generic leadership roles in management, so there are a number of more specific leadership roles that are, or at least can be, associated with the management of innovation. Some of these roles are formal in that they are designated posts where an individual is assigned to a role, while others are informal in that they don't involve a formal title, nor are they designated roles; instead they are roles that individuals choose to assume at their own behest.

These leadership roles, both formal and informal, include:

- project leader
- product champion
- godfather
- gatekeeper

What are the roles? What do they involve? How do they facilitate innovation?

Project leader

The role of project leader is a formal one that would normally involve an individual being formally designated. He or she is likely to be a figurehead, the person probably most closely associated with the project. In leadership terms, their job is to take responsibility for the project and provide it with an appropriate sense of direction. Obviously project leaders need to have a strong technical knowledge but they also need a breadth of knowledge and experience to enable them to co-ordinate and draw together the various functions required to bring an innovation to market successfully. A project leader should be someone who doesn't get completely bogged down in detail, but instead is able to maintain a sense of perspective, so that they don't lose sight of the overall goal – successful innovation.

Thus, a project leader is likely to possess a mix of talents, combining the communicating and motivating skills required to provide a sense of direction to a team that is multidisciplinary, alongside the analytical skills required to ensure effective organisation and management.

Product champion

The idea of a product champion was first put forward by Schon (1963) in the early 1960s. He noted how new developments, especially innovations within large corporations, frequently run into trouble. Why? Schon (1963: p83) argued that the novelty of an innovation often challenges "accepted ways of doing things and long-established skills". Both managers and staff may feel threatened by their lack of knowledge of the new technology, and possible potential structural changes. Hence innovations can easily come up against powerful vested interests.

Nor, according to Schon, are vested interests the end of the story, as often within large corporations the systems and procedures designed to screen new ideas can also provide a series of formidable obstacles for innovations.

In order to assist new developments in battling their way through the corporate minefield, Schon proposed the idea of someone who would act as a champion, doing all in their power to promote the innovation in order to ensure its success. Essentially the role of product champion implies someone who will act as an *advocate* for the innovation, prepared to support and defend it even in the most difficult circumstances. In Schon's (1963: p84) words:

 … the champion must be a man willing to put himself on the line for an idea of doubtful success. He is willing to fail. But he is capable of using any and every means of informal sales and pressure in order to succeed.

To carry out the role, product champions clearly need political support within the organisation. More importantly the product champion has to identify with the innovation. He or she has to regard it as their "child" to be defended and protected at all times. They also need to be individuals who are familiar with the organisation, who know their way around and in particular know where the power lies. Finally, the product champion has to be a leader who can communicate, in order to win over others to the cause.

Godfather

The godfather role is probably the least formal of these four roles. At first glance it might not seem like a leadership role because it is something of a "behind-the-scenes" role, involving the provision of political support to those involved in innovation, through a capacity to "pull strings" (Tidd *et al.*, 2001). To be effective, a godfather has to be able to exercise power and influence within the organisation, hence the role is likely to be taken by a senior manager preferably working at board level. The role typically involves providing support for the innovation (including the staff associated with it) and affording it protection (Smith, 2007), particularly from reactionary forces within the organisation. Such forces might include those who are risk averse, those possessed of a "not-invented-here" perspective, those who find it difficult to see future potential, or those who just see their powerbase threatened. As well as acting in a defensive capacity, the godfather can take a more proactive stance. Typically this might mean removing potential obstacles, be they people or potential hurdles. It might mean providing access to resources. These could be financial, but are probably more likely to be people or equipment or facilities. Finally, a godfather may simply exercise moral support for the innovation team. As the mini case of the Sony Walkman (below) shows, the involvement of a senior company figure, in this particular instance Sony chairman, Akio Morita, in a godfather role, can be vitally important in maintaining the motivation and commitment of an innovation team.

Gatekeeper

There is an increasing awareness that knowledge is critical to innovation. Studies have shown that in particular it is an organisation's ability to transfer knowledge that leads to innovation. Cohen and Levinthal's (1990) theory of absorptive capacity, for instance, highlights the importance of external sources of knowledge to the process of innovation. In this context the phrase "it is not what you know but who" has a ring of truth about it. Certainly individuals can play a key part in the networking that forms part of the knowledge-transfer process. In the process they are acting as gatekeepers. Individuals taking on this gatekeeper role effectively hold the key to accessing knowledge. Quite how they operate is likely to vary but it might include:

- acting as a repository of knowledge
- knowing who possesses knowledge
- exercising skill in making connections
- acting as a "go-between" for parts of the organisation or between organisations

At the simplest level, gatekeepers may be repositories of knowledge. This is rarely a matter of formal codified knowledge; it is much more likely to be tacit knowledge, the sort that is informal, unstructured and difficult to capture in a structured way. Often gatekeepers' actual knowledge is limited and instead their value lies in what they know about others, especially the knowledge that these others hold. Gatekeepers also tend to be skilled in making connections to others. Such skills are likely to be social ones that enable individuals to make very effective use of the informal structure of an organisation. Finally, it is worth observing that gatekeepers often act as a bridge between different parts of an organisation. This may have nothing to do with knowledge or skill. Instead, it may be more a matter of culture or background or perhaps social ties. Whatever the reason, gatekeepers of this type can be very valuable as they can act as a conduit to facilitate knowledge transfer. Allen (1977), in a study of the Apollo space programme noted the importance of informal communication flows, linked not to formal positions or posts, but instead to individuals' places within the informal structure of the organisation.

Mini Case

The Sony Walkman

The Sony Walkman was the world's first portable stereo tape player. Introduced in July 1979, it proved to be a highly successful innovation. With cumulative sales of 250 million units by 1998, it transformed the way we listen to music.

By the end of the 1970s, truly portable tape recorders were rare and confined to monaural sound. With Sony racking up losses on its Betamax video recording technology and its compact disc (CD) technology not yet ready for the market, the company's tape recorder division was under pressure to come up with something new. The division's engineers tried modifying one of the company's best-selling portable monaural tape recorders, the Pressman, to create a stereo machine. They discarded the speakers and the recording mechanism so that the machine consumed less power and ran on smaller batteries. This resulted in a smaller, lighter and more portable machine, but it required headphones to play pre-recorded music cassettes. The need for headphones was problematic because headphones were associated with deafness, a taboo subject in Japan. Consequently the machine remained confined to the laboratory.

No more would have been heard of this machine had not Masaru Ibuka, Sony's co-founder and honorary chairman, dropped in on the tape recorder division. Ibuka was impressed by the quality of the sound. He had recently seen the prototype of a new set of lightweight headphones being developed by Sony's Research Laboratory. He insisted on combining the portable stereo tape player with the new headphones. The result was a lightweight machine ideal for listening to music on the move. However, Ibuka was not in a position to request the development of this hybrid product. Instead he called on Akio Morita, Sony's chairman.

From the start Morita was enthusiastic. He borrowed the machine for the weekend and took it with him when he played golf. He was convinced there was a market for the product among young people. But his enthusiasm was not shared by others. As he himself said, "it seemed nobody liked the idea". The engineers were sceptical. Both the engineers from the tape recorder division and the engineers from the Research Laboratory were "polite but non-committal". Approval for the development to proceed was granted in February 1979. Believing that the market for the new portable stereo tape player would be primarily amongst the young, especially students, Morita was adamant that the product be launched to coincide with the summer vacation. This was six months away and new products typically took two years to develop. Given the timescale, major components like the tape transport and the stereo circuitry were taken from other Sony products.

Sony's accountants were unenthusiastic, worrying that at a price of $165, the Walkman wouldn't even recoup the costs of development. The marketing staff too showed little enthusiasm, saying the Walkman wouldn't sell. Nor were they alone, for retailers felt consumers wouldn't want a cassette recorder that couldn't record. Morita, however, was undeterred, but for the first three months after the launch it looked as if his Sony colleagues were right. Japanese teenagers failed to buy the product in anything like the numbers anticipated. But sales picked up in September, and by the end of the month the first production run of 30,000 units had sold out. As the idea took hold Sony found it had a runaway success on its hands. Production could not keep pace with demand as the first production model of the Walkman, the TPS-L2, sold 1.5 million units in the first two years.

Source: Smith (2007).

Motivational schemes

All sorts of practices and schemes have been developed to enable employees to contribute actively to innovation. In recent years as innovation has become more "democratic" (Von Hippel, 2005) and more "open" (Chesbrough, 2003a), so companies have increasingly seen their employees as a valuable resource where innovation is concerned, and have made greater use of such schemes. Their function is to tap into the creativity of employees by motivating them to participate in innovation by coming up with ideas that can form the basis of new products/services or process enhancements.

Bootlegging

According to Augsdorfer (2005), bootlegging occurs when motivated individuals secretly work on the development of new products based on their own ideas. Covert research of this type is typically associated not with radical innovations but with incremental innovations comprising improvements to existing products/services and processes (Augsdorfer, 2005). However, inevitably there are exceptions. Sometimes bootlegging can lead to the development of entirely new products that represent a significant departure from a company's existing product portfolio. Here the case of the Post-it note at 3M is a very good example. Bootlegging offers a number of advantages, in particular it offers a way of motivating individuals to make effective use of their own knowledge which may be a realtively underutilised resource (Augsdorfer, 2005).

Bootlegging by its nature is an undercover activity that individuals undertake more or less in secret and the idea behind bootlegging schemes is to provide an official sanction of such work. Among the best-known and best documented examples are the bootlegging schemes operated by 3M and Google. For 60 years 3M has operated a policy known as the "15 per cent rule" (Nayak and Ketteringham, 1993) which allows 3M staff at all levels of the organisation to spend up to 15 per cent of their time pursuing projects of their own choosing and outside their primary assignment. The policy is not operated in a mechanistic way with all staff expected to work in this way all of the time. Rather the message to 3M scientists is that there is some slack in the system such that if they have got a good idea, even if no one else appears greatly interested, they can squirrel away some time to develop it further. This bootlegging policy has been the catalyst behind some of 3M's most successful innovations, including the Post-it note, Scotchgard and Scotch Tape.

More recently the Internet company Google has introduced a bootlegging policy, known as the "20 per cent rule" (Vise, 2005), which allows the company's software engineers to spend a day a week on whatever projects interest them. Introduced by Google's founders as a way of encouraging innovation, both Sergey Brin and Larry Page see the policy as essential in establishing a culture where bright technologists will want to work and feel motivated to come up with 'breakthrough ideas' (Vise, 2005: p131). Among a number of innovations that have resulted from this policy are *Google News* and *Google Suggest* (Matthews, 2007). A key feature of the policy is that it is seen as providing time when staff can explore things that they see as important and are passionate about.

Ideas programmes

Ideas programmes are employee-based schemes designed to encourage employees to come forward with ideas. They represent a development of the staff suggestion scheme, among the first of which was a scheme introduced by Eastman Kodak in 1898. However, these days the focus is firmly on ideas linked to innovation. Ideas programmes generally encourage employees to come forward with ideas, which are then carefully evaluated by the company and if the idea is adopted the employee is duly rewarded. Programmes such as this tend to result in process innovations, as employees, by virtue of their familiarity with a firm's processes, are often well placed to come forward with process improvements and enhancements.

A programme introduced by BMW at its car plant at Cowley in Oxford manufacturing the Mini generated no less than 14,333 ideas from shopfloor staff over a two-year period. The ideas ranged from cutting unnecessary use of paper to more complex engineering solutions and nearly three-quarters were implemented, saving the company £10.5 million between 2002 and 2004 (Matthews, 2007). Another company to have recently implemented a successful ideas programme is the Nottingham-based retailer, Boots. Its "All Ideas Matter" programme encourages employees to present their thoughts through a variety of channels including emails, letters, the company intranet and the company magazine (Matthews, 2007). The scheme generates around 1,200–1,500 ideas a year, of which around one-third are taken up by the company. In its first year the scheme generated savings of around £250,000 of which around 25–30 per cent was ploughed back into running the scheme, including providing cash awards for staff (Beddows, 2001). Other well known companies that have established ideas programmes include high street optician Dollond and Aitchison with its "Every Idea is a Good Idea" scheme and parcel carrier TNT Express with its "Grand Idea" scheme, which offers £100 cash per submission accepted and £1,000 for the best ideas.

Research clubs

Research clubs are a way of facilitating innovation through collaboration rather than through individuals. They aim to bring together companies with common interests in particular research areas. An example is DRINC which is the Diet and Health Research Industry Club. This is a £10.5 million, five-year partnership between the Biotechnology and Biological Science Research Council (BBSRC) and a consortium of companies which aims to help companies in the food industry develop products that deliver enhanced health benefits for consumers.

Corporate culture

Corporate culture refers to the shared values and beliefs, both implicit and explicit, that shape the behaviours and experiences of individuals working within an organisation (Hargadon, 2003). Just as the national culture of a country affects things such as attitudes to work, attitudes to and the use of authority and styles of decision-making, so the corporate culture of an organisation influences how things are done within that organisation. This in turn can influence and affect innovation. Corporate culture can have a profound effect on innovation via the value it places on things like challenging existing ideas and practices, willingness to take risks, and the stigma attached to failure. It is notable that some of the organisations that are particularly good at innovation, like W.L. Gore and Associates (the makers of Gore-Tex), 3M (the makers of Post-it notes and a whole lot more), Dyson Appliances and the design agency IDEO have quite distinctive corporate cultures.

Mini Case

IDEO

Given that corporate culture is something that is internal to a company, most companies don't normally say much, if anything, about their culture. One notable exception is the design consultancy, IDEO. Based in Palo Alto, California, but with offices in Europe and Asia, IDEO is one of the world's leading design consultancies, having been responsible, among other things, for the first Apple mouse and the Palm V personal digital assistant and having been named one of the 20 most innovative companies in the world by *BusinessWeek* in 2005. IDEO's web site proudly outlines the company's corporate culture as a "special mix" of:

- mad scientist (curious, experimental)
- bear-tamer (gutsy, agile)
- reiki master (hands-on, empathetic)
- midnight tax accountant (optimistic, savvy)

While the roles may seem a little bizarre, the associated qualities convey very clearly the qualities that make up the company's culture. And this culture in turn promotes and stimulates innovation because, using a gardening metaphor, these qualities are "… the medium in which great ideas are borne and flourish".

Source: IDEO (2009).

In general, organisations with a strong record of innovation will have a corporate culture that values and promotes the following:

- outward-looking orientation
- facilitating communication
- openness to new ideas
- challenging established ideas
- acceptability of failure
- promotion of evaluation and reflection

By outward looking we mean that the organisation has strong links to external parties (e.g. users, competitors, professional groups, knowledge sources, etc.) and is responsive to signals and stimuli from them. This type of external orientation stands in contrast to insular inward-looking organisations where the "not-invented-here" syndrome is prevalent. A culture that facilitates communication is one where lateral links across the organisation are strong and communication is easy and frequent, thereby helping to bring people with different perspectives into contact with each other so as to facilitate the transfer of knowledge. Openness is characterised by a sense of freedom where individuals feel able to experiment and try things out. It typically involves both people being willing to put forward new and different ideas and being receptive to such ideas. Challenging established ideas is all about not taking things for granted, in particular a willingness to challenge and question the *status quo*. Assumptions are constantly questioned and staff actively seek new and better ways doing things. Because innovations don't always succeed, a culture of accepting and tolerating failure is essential if innovation is to be encouraged. In particular failure needs to be accompanied by a lack of recriminations and instead a desire to learn from what has gone wrong. Finally one would expect to find an emphasis on reflection, where individuals don't rush to hasty and unconsidered judgments but instead seek evidence and analyse it carefully.

Promoting these qualities will not guarantee innovation. As Nayak and Ketteringham (1993: p325) put it, "breakthroughs can occur in any environment". However, they do acknowledge that the internal environment (i.e. the corporate culture) within an organisation can make a difference and that some cultures are more conducive to breakthroughs and innovations than others. In organisations with a culture such as that outlined above, those engaged in innovation are likely to find that the barriers they face are likely to be fewer and lower.

Mini Case

W.L. Gore and Associates Inc

Probably best known for its high-performance waterproof fabric Gore-Tex, W.L. Gore and Associates is one of the world' s most innovative companies with a product range that extends from Gore-Tex fabrics to heart patches and synthetic blood vessels, air filters, parts for fuel cells, dental floss and even guitar strings. It is also a company with a very distinctive corporate culture.

W.L. Gore and Associates Inc was formed in 1958 when Bill Gore left the chemical giant Du Pont, having become frustrated at his employer's unwillingness to take up his ideas about techniques for fabricating materials from the newly discovered polymer Teflon (Hounshell and Smith, 1988). He and his wife decided to go it alone and with capital raised from their bridge club, they set up a company to manufacture wire insulated with Teflon, which found applications in the electronics and aerospace industries. Gore is still a private company, and the term "associates" is present in the company title for a sound reason. It refers to the whole workforce, all of whom are known as associates. There is very little hierarchy, with few ranks and titles. There are no job descriptions. Gore is organised into what are effectively autonomous teams of up to 150–200 people. These are small enough for people to know one another and work together with minimal rules, very much in the manner of a task group tackling a problems. New staff are allocated a sponsor or mentor whose job is to help the newcomer integrate.

The corporate culture is one that facilitates innovation. It is a culture where people feel free to pursue ideas on their own, communicate with one another and collaborate because they want to rather than out of a sense of duty (Deutschman, 2004) Gore encourages associates to engage in what others would probably call "bootlegging" – that is, spending 10 per cent of their time on speculative new ideas. It is also a company that is very patient with the development of innovations. The company takes the long view where innovations are concerned. As a private company it does not have the pressure of frequently reporting to the financial community and can instead take its time over the process of getting an invention ready for market. As long as there is a possibility that a new idea will lead to an innovation, staff are encouraged to keep a project going.

Source: Deutschman (2004).

In so far as corporate culture facilitates and stimulates innovation and can be determined by management, then it is something that requires leadership. As the example of W.L. Gore and Associates Inc shows, the lead given by those at the top of an organisation can exert a very powerful influence upon the development of a corporate culture conducive to innovation. It is worth reflecting on other examples of companies with a strong reputation for successful innovation, the nature of their corporate culture, and the part that culture plays in promoting and stimulating innovation activity. But it isn't an easy task, quite apart from anything else the unwritten nature of corporate culture makes it difficult to change, but some organisations have managed it very successfully, creating highly distinctive cultures that are an integral part of a policy of fostering innovation.

Controlling

Control may seem to be the very antithesis of innovation. While there is no doubt that excessive control can seriously deter innovation, nonetheless it does have a part to play in the effective management of innovation projects. The very fact that innovation is associated with a high degree of uncertainty is one of the key reasons why control is important. A lot of uncertainty, combined with the multidisciplinary nature of development teams and the unique nature of most innovations, means that some kind of control is necessary in order to provide a review of the progress of an innovation project.

There is in fact a very close link between planning and control techniques that can be used for managing innovation projects. The development funnel for instance serves both as an aid to planning and a way of controlling and structuring the flow of new ideas and discoveries.

Similarly the stage-gate process outlined below aids both planning and control. However, unlike the development funnel its primary function is to provide a means of exercising a degree of control both over the innovation process and the multidisciplinary teams working within it.

The stage-gate process of innovation

Derived originally from NASA's moon programme of the late 1960s (Cooper, 1994), the stage-gate process is a technique that provides a series of evaluation points during the course of an innovation project. Innovation projects are structured by breaking them down into well-defined phases at the end of which come evaluation points, which are integrated into a systematic process designed to move a new product innovation forward from idea to market launch. The stage-gate process is designed to filter out potentially unsuccessful innovations early on in the development process before extensive resources have been committed. The filtering out comes about as a result of the evaluations carried out at each "gate," where there are three possible decision outcomes: GO or HOLD or KILL. If the decision outcome is the last of the three, then clearly the project is terminated.

Cooper (1988) suggests that there are a minimum of three possible gates in the course of any one project, although it is common practice to have more. These three gates are:

- *initial screening* – decision to commit resources
- *business/finance analysis* – aimed at deciding whether to go to full-scale development
- *pre-commercialisation business analysis* – decide whether to move to full-scale production and market launch

Each of these gates represents a key decision point in the new product development process where, depending on the outcome of the decision made at the gate, major resources, in terms of finance, people and equipment can potentially be committed to the project.

How are these decisions arrived at? Cooper (1988) suggests that at each gate it is necessary to pose three questions:

1 does the project continue to make economic/business sense?
2 have the essential steps (necessary to pass that particular gate) been completed?
3 is the project on time and budget and have the milestones been hit?

The answers that come back from posing these questions determine what happens, in terms of the three possible decision outcomes at the gate in question. The outcomes will be arrived at on the following basis:

- *GO* – if the answers to questions 1 to 3 are positive
- *HOLD* – if the answer to question 2 is negative
- *KILL* – if the answer to question 1 is negative

As important as the decisions being made at each gate is the question: who is making the decisions? This is where one of the key features of the stage-gate process emerges. The decisions are made by representatives of *all* the functional disciplines involved. This means that a project cannot move forward unless both technical and commercial parts of the business have signed up to it. This is essential. Not only does it help to prevent costly alterations and modifications in the later phases of a project, it also ensures buy-in from all parts of the business, thereby avoiding the so-called "silo" mentality, where decisions are made in isolation rather than on an integrated basis.

Thus the control provided by the stage-gate process is not only filtering out weak projects: the structured nature of the process ensures overall control of the project so that vital activities, particularly what Cooper (1988) describes as "up-front" activities associated with the early phases of a project such as preliminary market assessments, are not omitted. Another dimension to the discipline provided by the stage-gate process is the degree of control it provides over the people involved. Although the stage-gate process does have its weaknesses, chiefly where high-risk projects are concerned in which the level of uncertainty may make decision-making very difficult, it does make a very valuable contribution to ensuring an integrated approach to new product development.

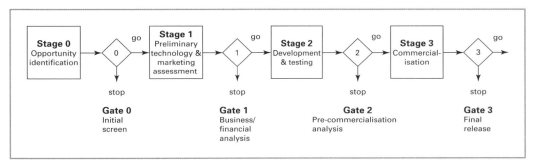

FIGURE 11.5 The stage-gate process
Source: Adapted from Ettlie (2006: p273)

Conclusion

The tools and techniques presented here enable managers to provide a degree of structure and order to the development of new products and services, in ways that will counteract the uncertainty, complexity and messiness surrounding much of the innovation process. Being able to provide a degree of structure means innovations can actually be managed rather than being handled in a purely *ad hoc* way. The result should be more effective new product development that significantly increases the prospect of successful innovation.

Some observers would doubtless point out that the tools and techniques presented here are generally better suited to the development of incremental rather than radical innovations. It is worth reflecting that as Stefick and Stefick (2004: p3) have observed, "breakthroughs take people by surprise". Nor is it only people for whom breakthroughs or radical innovations come as a surprise: they typically take organisations by surprise as well. For surprise one can also read uncertainty. The much greater uncertainty surrounding radical innovations, particularly the changes they often bring in their wake, mean they are much harder to manage. Fortunately, however, breakthroughs are comparatively rare. Hence the managerial framework presented here combined with many of the associated tools and techniques is likely to be effective in most instances of innovation.

Finally it should be noted that this chapter has focused primarily on the management of innovation as a process. Given that the cause of many innovation failures is a failure to manage the process effectively, this is justified. However, managers' responsibilities really should extend beyond the innovation process. For organisations to compete in the twenty-first century, there is also a need for them to develop a *capability* for innovation. Being able to manage the innovation process will contribute towards this, but managers need to do more. The extra is likely to cover intangible aspects of innovation such corporate culture, attitudes to learning, opportunity recognition and leadership.

CASE STUDY: THE ADVANCED PASSENGER TRAIN (APT)

In moves designed to improve the speed and quality of service offered to rail passengers, Virgin Trains has invested nearly £1 billion in new "tilting trains", designed to operate at speeds up to 155 mph. The trains, built by Alstom in Italy, will eventually reduce the journey time for the 401-mile London–Glasgow route from five hours to four by 2014. A feature of these trains is their "tilting technology" which enables them to travel at high speed even on curved tracks such as those on West Coast Main Line (London–Glasgow). However, "tilting technology" is not new. In fact it is not even new to Britain. In the 1980s British Rail developed a tilting train – the Advanced Passenger Train (APT).

Although the 1960s was marked by a contraction of the railway system in Britain, developments abroad, particularly the introduction of the Japanese Shinkansen or "bullet train" at the time of the Tokyo Olympic Games, led to much interest in the possibility of high-speed trains (Potter, 1987). Against this background, the British government gave British Rail, the state-owned railway operator, the go-ahead in the early 1970s to begin work on an experimental high-speed train. Government funding restrictions meant that any new train had to be developed within tight constraints, including a requirement that it should be able to operate on the existing rail network. On the UK's principal inter-city route, the West Coast Main Line (WCML) connecting the capital to Scotland's second city, Glasgow, via England's second and third largest cities, Birmingham and Manchester, speeds were restricted by curves in the northern section of the line beyond Preston. These were designed to ensure passenger comfort by restricting the lateral g-force which would otherwise cause objects to slide off plates, spill drinks and knock over standing passengers. Consequently the R&D programme for the new high-speed train included, in addition to a requirement that it be quiet and energy efficient with operating costs comparable to existing trains, the following objectives:

1 maximum speed 50 per cent higher than existing trains (i.e. 155 mph)

2 curving speed 40 per cent higher than existing trains

3 operate on existing tracks within the limits of existing signalling

4 maintain standards of passenger comfort at high speed

These demanding objectives led to a number of innovations for the new train:

- advanced bogie and suspension design (using new anti-hunting technology)
- low unsprung weight through the use of articulated bogies (i.e. wheel sets shared between coaches as on French TGV, to reduce weight and track maintenance)
- hydro-kinetic brakes able to stop the train within existing signalling from 155 mph
- tilting body to maintain comfort when running on curves at high speed
- lightweight aluminium construction (i.e. to reduce weight and increase safety)

Of these innovations, the one that attracted the greatest public attention was the "tilting technology". Being able to tilt at up to 9°, it was possible for the train to take curves 40 per cent faster than conventional trains by eliminating g-force. The tilt was to be achieved by an active, powered, tilt mechanism that would use sensors and hydraulics to automatically tilt the coaches when taking curves at high speed.

Known as the Advanced Passenger Train (APT), the project was to have three distinct phases, an experimental R&D phase involving the construction of a single experimental train (APT-E), a prototype design/development phase involving the construction of three prototype trains (APT-P), and a final production phase involving the construction of a squadron fleet of 80 trains (APT-S).

Research phase

The experimental proof-of-concept train was gas turbine powered and incorporated several of the new systems in a small "test-bed" train designed to test out a number of the planned innovations. Trials proved successful and the new train set a new British speed record of 152.4 mph on a run between Swindon and Reading. By now British Rail Research had proved the basic viability of the high-speed train concept running on the existing rail network. On the London–Glasgow service it was anticipated that journey times would fall from five hours to three and a half. Since this was city centre to city centre, such times were directly comparable with air travel.

Development phase

The project then moved to the "Design-Build-Test" phase. From being a relatively self-contained project housed at the Railway Technical Centre in Derby, development of the APT now became the responsibility of the Chief Mechanical and Electrical Engineer (CM&EE). The CM&EE was structured on a traditional "functional" basis (i.e. according to the broad engineering divisions in the railway organisation), which was effective for conducting routine operational tasks efficiently. However, as a study of the project (Potter 1989: p106) noted,

> the concept of a project team was totally alien to the way in which the CM&EE department was organised.

Inevitably given the strong operational focus (i.e. running a railway) at CM&EE, some managers gave the APT a low priority. Though consideration was given to setting up a separate company (i.e. an equity joint venture) owned jointly by CM&EE and British Rail's research department, such a move was not at that time acceptable to the British Rail board.

The three electric powered prototype APT-Ps were assembled by British Rail's manufacturing arm, British Rail Engineering Limited's (BREL) in Derby. Although the three prototypes were able to make a series of fast runs on curved lines, there were, as one would expect with prototypes, technical problems, particularly tilt failures, binding brakes and gearbox failures (Potter, 1989: p108). Since the government would only authorise a production run of APTs once the prototypes had proved themselves in passenger service there was intense pressure to show results, which led British Rail to launch a series of demonstration runs. The first run from Glasgow to London, undertaken in a blaze of publicity, was completed on time, but on the return trip the driver took a bend too fast, setting off a safety mechanism which shut down the tilt mechanism. On its own the problem was not a major one, but then a fault developed in the main traction motor causing the train to be late into Glasgow. This attracted much adverse publicity. In addition some members of the press complained of "motion sickness". This was caused by the tilting mechanism effectively working too well.

The eyes sensed turning for a curve, but the body, because the tilting mechanism compensated for lateral g-forces, did not feel it. Though this was easily cured by turning down the tilting a couple of degrees so that the body did get a slight turning sensation, it all added to poor publicity. Further services were then affected by the worst winter weather for 30 years. British Rail, unwilling to see the prestigious train operate unreliably, took the APT out of service.

Technical v. organisational problems

Most of the problems arose from putting prototypes, rather than production models into passenger service. Problems with the tilt mechanism jamming proved to be caused not by the tilt technology itself but by inadequate wiring which automatically shut down the tilt mechanism. Similarly problems with the hydro-kinetic brakes resulted from bearing failures. These were easily re-designed but the possible serious consequences of brake failure meant that trials had to be halted while the problem was sorted.

However, the problems with the APT were often not so much technical problems as manufacturing ones. A breakdown on the APT's third run in public service was caused by failure to fit a rubber grommet over a wire correctly, leading to the wire chaffing through and causing a short circuit which then disabled the train's entire control system because it had not been wired correctly during the manufacturing process. Similarly when one APT suffered a derailment at 125 mph, it transpired that a ring of bolts securing the axle to the hydro-kinetic brakes had simply not been tightened during assembly!

Staff at the BREL workshops in Derby, where the trains were built, were simply not used to the production standards required. In contrast to high technology industries such as aerospace, older, medium technology industries, such as the railway, were still rooted in "craft" traditions, where the craftsman was expected to exercise a high degree of skill and personnal judgment. It was normal practice for the shop floor to modify and amend design details. The "craft" tradition held that the experience of shop-floor employees, usually built up in the workplace over many years through the apprenticeship system, was a valuable and necessary final check on the designer. Sometimes described as a "workshop culture" (Potter, 1989: p110), it led to shop floor staff modifying and amending design details during the manufacturing process for the APT and, since they were used to working in this way, they didn't always tell the design team about the changes they'd made. As a study by Potter and Roy (1999: p35) found:

> in some cases people on the shop floor simply did not believe that the light-weight APT designs would work because they were so different from familiar traditional designs.

Nor were the problems confined to the workshops of BREL where the trains were assembled. Locating the development work on the APT within CM&EE meant that work had to be undertaken alongside routine railway work which led to delays and also affected the quality of work carried out. Again, Potter, Roy and Wield (1999: p36) note:

> There were significant differences in the quality of work between workshops where the manager was enthusiastic about the APT and those where the manager was not.

▶   Not only was there a divided attitude to the APT within the organisation, some senior members of the APT team, while they had a very high level of scientific and technical skills, often had little in the way of project management experience.

Aware of some of the problems, the British Rail board eventually stepped in and brought in external consultants to evaluate the project and suggest changes. The consultants reported that the technology was basically sound. However, they recommended major organisational and managerial changes. These involved the appointment of a new APT project manager, whose role was to coordinate work on the APT. There was a move to a matrix structure for the project, with staff drawn from different departments across British Rail. The new matrix structure for the project provided a settled situation that as well as improving coordination, meant it was possible to change the composition of the project team as the mix of skills required changed.

Sadly the changes came too late. Although the APT was in regular passenger service between mid-1984 and mid-1985, the success was short-lived. In 1984 the government authorised the electrification of the East Coast Main Line (ECML) between London and Edinburgh. On this route the track was much straighter and there was no need for a tilting train. With the adverse publicity of the APT's first public appearance still a recent memory and an alternative high speed route between London and Scotland, British Rail quietly terminated the APT project in 1986. However, much of what had been learnt on the APT was applied to a new train. Simpler and less advanced, the Intercity 225/Electra took only two years to develop. Although slower (maximum speed 140 mph) than the APT it nonetheless substantially reduced the journey time between London and Edinburgh. It has been in regular service on the ECML since 1989. With no need for tilting technology, British Rail sold the patents for its tilting bogie to Fiat (later taken over by Alstom) who duly utilised the technology in a new generation of Pendolino trains. It was a custom-designed version of the Pendolino train (termed the Class 390) that Richard Branson's Virgin Trains brought into use on the West Coast Main Line franchise in 2003. Currently limited by signalling limitations to 125 mph, the trains are capable of operating at 155 mph. Interestingly the fastest run between Glasgow and London by a Pendolino train to date (a one-off non-stop run for charity) is 3 hours 55 minutes, whereas an APT completed the run 25 years earlier in 1984 in 3 hours 52 minutes!

Sources: Potter (1987); Potter, 1989; Potter and Roy (1999).

Questions

1 What was the root cause of many of the APT's problems when it was first brought into service?

2 Why would it generally be regarded as bad practice to put prototypes into passenger carrying service ?

3 If the failure of the hydro-kinetic braking system described in the text was not a technical problem, what kind of a problem was it?

4 Why are organisations organised along functional lines and what are the potential benefits of this type of structure?

5 What is meant be a "workshop culture" and why is such a corporate culture likely to be inappropriate for high-tech innovation projects like the APT?

6 What type of corporate venture was the joint venture considered for this innovation and had it been implemented would it have been appropriate for a radical innovation like the APT?

7 What is a matrix structure and why would it have helped the management of this innovation project?

8 Why would project management experience have been advantageous for senior members of the APT team?

9 Why did the consultants recommend the appointment of a project manager and how would such a post help the management of this innovation project?

10 Outline what you consider to be the main failings in terms of the management of this innovation project?

Questions for discussion

1 Why is innovation not just a matter of providing a technologically superior product?

2 What is it about innovation that makes it difficult to manage?

3 What evidence is there to suggest that the perspective of those such as Schumpeter, who suggest that only large organisations can undertake innovation successfully, may be flawed?

4 How can management techniques assist in controlling innovation projects effectively?

5 What sort of corporate culture is likely to be conducive to innovation?

6 What is meant by corporate venturing and what are some of the forms that it can take?

7 Why have large organisations increasingly turned to corporate venturing as a means of fostering innovation?

8 How can managers encourage staff to be more innovative?

9 What is a strategic alliance and why have organisations increasingly turned to them as a means of facilitating innovation?

10 What can management contribute to innovation?

Exercises

1 Explain what is meant by the term "gatekeeper" and show why this role is important for effective innovation.

2 Select an organisation, analyse its corporate culture and show how it contributes to successful innovation.

3 With reference to appropriate managerial techniques, show why planning is important for effective innovation.

4 Explain why a relatively large US corporation like W.L. Gore and Associates Inc would want to team up with a specialist supplier of outdoor wear like Berghaus.

Further reading

1 **Henry, J. and D. Mayle** (2002) (eds) *Managing Innovation and Change,* 2nd edn, Sage
Publications, London.
A diverse collection of papers dealing with various aspects of innovation. The focus on
management isn't quite as strong as it might be, but the papers are interesting and useful
nonetheless. There are contributions from some of the leading researchers in the field, as
well as practitioners who know a thing or two about innovation.

2 **Katz, R.** (ed.) (2004) *The Human Side of Managing Technological Innovation: A Collection of
Readings*, 2nd edn, Oxford University Press, Oxford.
Though confined to human aspects of managing innovation, this is a very useful collection of
papers. It is the sheer diversity of the papers that is impressive. What makes it unusual is that
from an academic perspective there are some classic papers, while at the same time the
practitioner side is covered too, with papers that provide insights into some well-known
innovations.

3 **Dodgson, H., D. Gann, and A. Salter** (2008) *The Management of Technological Innovation,*
revsd edn, Oxford University Press, Oxford.
A new textbook on the subject. Not only is this a comprehensive treatment of the subject it is
supported by some superb case studies derived from both practitioners and well regarded
academic journals. The choice of material is well chosen, resulting in a range of topics
relevant to the managerial side of innovation. Worth knowing about for the references alone!

4 **Goffin, K. and R. Mitchell** (2005) *Innovation Management: Strategy and Implementation
using the Pentathlon Framework*, Palgrave Macmillan, Basingstoke.
A text that focuses not just on innovation but the management of innovation. It provides a
detailed treatment of management techniques, particularly those associated with new
product development. One of its strengths is that there is extensive treatment of services and
innovation in services. It is also strong on the strategic side.

PART 04
How Do You Foster Innovation?

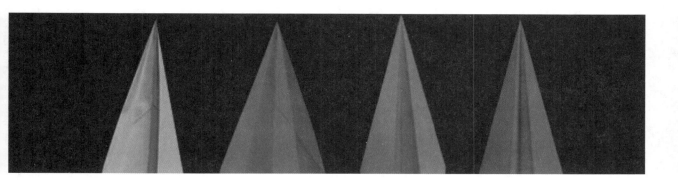

Innovation policy

Introduction

Most governments are favourably disposed towards innovation. It is viewed positively as something to be encouraged and fostered. This is because innovation is linked to economic growth through the creation of new firms and new jobs. Also, innovation is closely associated with technology which has similar positive overtones and is linked to high-skill/high-quality/high-income jobs. For politicians and policy-makers innovation forms part of a virtuous circle of more and better products and services leading to more and better jobs. Consequently, innovation is something that governments and other public agencies try to foster and encourage and they do this through the use of policies employing a variety of policy instruments. This chapter explores the policies and policy instruments employed by governments and endeavours to provide some evaluation of their effectiveness. It should be noted that this chapter does not cover broader government policies that can and do have an impact on the "environment" within which innovation takes place. These aspects are covered in Chapter 14 which deals with National Innovation Systems, leaving the emphasis in this chapter firmly on specific policy measures targeted at innovation.

Rationale for government intervention

The case for government intervention to aid and assist innovation rests upon a variety of factors:

- public nature of knowledge
- uncertainty
- complementary assets
- network externalities
- market inflexibility

Scientific knowledge especially has a number of public properties that make it difficult for firms or individuals to extract rent from it (Afuah, 2003). This is very much a problem of appropriability in the sense that it can be difficult for those with knowledge and expertise to appropriate benefit from it. The problems that can arise when the innovator tries to appropriate his or her knowledge include:

- imitation or copying
- non-rivalrous aspects
- spill-overs and leakages
- knowledge in the public domain

Imitation may simply mean that a third party has "reverse engineered" an innovation and acquired the knowledge that way. A non-rivalrous aspect of knowledge occurs where A sells the knowledge to B, but A still has it and can use it. Spill-overs or leakages occur where knowledge cannot be retained within an organisation, perhaps through staff leaving. Finally, much knowledge, particularly explicit, codified knowledge, is in the public domain anyway and can be accessed by all. Factors such as these reduce the incentive for commercial organisations to invest in knowledge creation, particularly in the form of R&D. Under these circumstances the level of innovation may be lower than it would otherwise be and there is a rationale for some form of government intervention.

Similarly, there is often a high level of uncertainty surrounding innovation. The uncertainty can be of the technical or market varieties. Technical uncertainty arises because research and development may not lead to innovation. There may be uncertainty as to whether an invention can be commercialised, whether a device that works well in the laboratory will operate effectively in the hands of the consumer, whether there is a potential safety problem as yet not identified. The market presents a similar range of uncertainties. Will consumers want the innovation? Will consumers be willing to pay for it? Will the market have changed by the time the device enters service? Hence, for a range of reasons associated with technical and market uncertainties, firms may choose not to proceed with an innovation. If this means a loss to consumers, there is again a rationale for government intervention.

Complementary assets are an important, but often neglected, aspect of innovation. They consist of things like market knowledge, access to distribution channels and facilities for product support. While no one would normally suggest that government should provide assets such as these, there are others which are more public by nature. Examples include transport facilities, power, sites and infrastructure facilities. The absence of such complementary assets may defer innovation, leading again to a case for government intervention either to provide them or assist in providing them.

Network externalities arise where the more people use a technology, the greater they value it. Afuah (2003) gives the example of an old technology which is valued because large numbers use it. There may then be a reluctance to switch to a new technology. Under these circumstances there can be a case for government intervention perhaps as a lead user.

Finally, market inflexibilities can mean that the institutions available to support and service a technology are outmoded when a new technology comes along. Market conditions should induce institutional changes, but markets can be slow and unresponsive to change and under these conditions governments may wish to induce institutional changes.

Hence there are a variety of reasons for governments engaging in interventions designed to facilitate innovation. However, the forms of intervention can vary greatly as the following section indicates.

Policy initiatives

Support for innovation can have a variety of different objectives and take a variety of different forms. The policy objectives pursued by the UK government in recent years include:

- technology forecasting
- knowledge transfer
- location
- R&D
- exploitation/licensing
- lead user

The objective of *technology forecasting* is to increase awareness of current trends in technology development and to highlight the future implications. The "Foresight" programme introduced in 1994 is an example of a policy initiative designed to achieve this objective. In terms of *knowledge transfer* the objectives are self-evident, being the transfer of knowledge between organisations, and the "Knowledge Transfer Partnership" programme run by the DTI and the UK Research Councils exemplifies policy initiatives in this field. The *location* objective is to affect the location of innovative firms with a view to them being clustered together. Science parks are an example of the sort of policy initiative designed to achieve this. R&D involves encouraging and stimulating research and development by firms. The SMART award scheme and R&D tax credits are examples of policy initiatives in this field. The penultimate objective is *exploitation/licensing* of technology and, while it is not a policy initiative as such today, the activities of BTG plc exemplify work to try and achieve this objective. Finally there is the *lead user* objective. Research by Von Hippel (1988) highlighted the crucial role that users can play in the process of innovation. However, it is the case that potential users do not always know that they need a product. This may particularly be the case if the technology is entirely new or is a radical innovation. In situations such as these the uses of an innovation or potential users may be unclear. Under such circumstances governments can have an important part to play, taking the role of lead user. In this role they can undertake activities that will help to establish an innovation. These activities can include:

- allowing time for new/potential users to develop
- acting as a "demonstrator" showing possible uses
- interacting with the innovator to facilitate further development and improvement
- stimulating demand

Afuah (2003) refers to these activites as "shepherding". He cites the case of the transistor where the US Department of Defense played a crucial role in establishing its viability. At the time the technological paradigm of electronics was dominated by the thermionic valve. However, the Department of Defense recognised that the transistor offered significant benefits in terms of: less weight; less heat; greater reliability; lower power consumption and smaller size. By awarding contracts for the application of transistor technology to military projects, the Department of Defense was able to procure new uses for the transistor, thereby enabling this innovation to become established.

Foresight

The Foresight Programme is a UK government initiative introduced following the White Paper "Realising our Potential" (DTI, 1993). It aims to identify potential opportunities for the economy and society that may be present in new science and technologies and to consider how future science and technology might address future challenges for society with a view to initiating actions to realise these opportunities. The programme brings together key people, knowledge and ideas to look beyond the normal planning horizons in order to identify potential opportunities.

The first round of Foresight was launched in 1994 and brought together experts from industry, government and academia into a series of sector-based panels:

1 Agriculture, horticulture and forestry
2 Chemicals
3 Construction
4 Defence and aerospace
5 Energy
6 Financial services
7 Food and drink
8 Health and life services
9 IT, electronics and communications
10 Leisure and learning
11 Manufacturing, production & business processes
12 Marine
13 Materials
14 Natural resources and environment
15 Retail and distribution
16 Transport

During the main analysis phase, these panels considered emerging market and technological opportunities over a 20-year timescale, emerging priorities for research, and actions needed to exploit them. Following widespread consultation the panels published their findings in 1995. The reports identified likely social, economic and market trends over the next 10–20 years and the developments in science, engineering, technology and infrastructure required to best address future needs. The reports included 300+ recommendations for action.

The Materials Panel played a key role in gaining acceptance of nanotechnology as one area, if not the key area, of technology for the future. In terms of action it encouraged support by research councils such as the Engineering and Physical Sciences Research Council (EPSRC) for the establishment of two Interdisciplinary Research Centres in nanotechnology.

Similarly, the Foresight Toolkit allowed the benefits of Foresight to be delivered to SMEs. The Toolkit is a training tool that can be used by training facilitators to encourage companies to plan towards a future vision and anticipate challenges and opportunities.

The outputs of the Foresight programme are meant to inform and influence those who make decisions about research funding including business, government departments and charities.

The criteria for selecting topics as Foresight projects include:

- significant current developments in science or technology, with potential to bring radical change, crossing the boundaries of established disciples

- important challenges for society or the economy, to which science and technology have the potential to make a substantial contribution

- scope to put together a group of people, with an interest in exploring the science and technology and ways of making it useful

Knowledge transfer partnerships

The Knowledge Transfer Partnership (KTP) programme (formally known as the Teaching Company Scheme (TCS)) is a government department/research council scheme that aims to transfer technology (in the broadest sense) between universities/colleges and small companies. This is achieved by the KTP programme providing funding for specific projects of up to three years' "duration" as part of which an "Associate," who is normally a recent graduate, is recruited to undertake the development work managing the project, applying their knowledge and ensuring that the expertise of the university/college is transferred to the business. The Associate works full time in the company and is paid a salary with most of the cost being met by the KTP funding, which also provides for academics to work on the project. The academics in the university/college remain closely involved throughout the project, working with senior managers in the business in order to contribute their knowledge and experience. One of the benefits of the programme is that, as well as improving links between universities and industry, it gives the SME access to the resources, especially in terms of knowledge, of a university. In some 70 per cent of cases the Associate goes on to work permanently for the company.

The projects undertaken by KTP Associates include:

- improving existing products
- developing new products
- streamlining manufacturing processes
- improving logistics processes
- developing a marketing strategy

As Figure 12.1 shows the aim of KTP programmes is for research staff from the university/college to work with the KTP Associate and company staff on a project that will lead to an innovation which could be a new product, new service or new process.

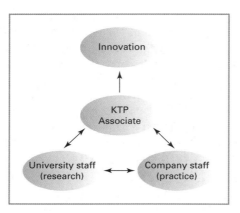

FIGURE 12.1 Knowledge transfer partnerships

An instrument manufacturer's KTP

The company made hand-held instruments for monitoring potentially harmful chemicals that could pose a threat to health safety. A chemistry graduate was employed as a KTP Associate to improve their existing products and create a completely new one. The new product was an ethanol analyser that measured alcohol levels in beer, wine and cider. The new instrument was used by breweries, trading standards departments and Customs and Excise (as it was called then). These were entirely new markets for the company. During the course of the two-year project employment at the company rose from three to eight and the company now exports to more than 30 countries.

Science parks

The concept of a science park is based on the idea of high-technology firms undertaking similar work being located close to each other and close to a knowledge base, usually in the form of a university. This model originated in the US. Frederick Terman, the dean of electrical engineering at Stanford University at Palo Alto in California, established one of the first science parks on a 600-acre site adjoining the university in the early 1950s. Terman was keen to develop what he termed a "community of interest between the University and local industry" (Saxenian, 1983: p9). The park was landscaped and leases granted only to high-technology firms. The first company to move to the park was Varian. Hewlett-Packard moved to the park in 1954. By now Terman's notion of a "community of technical scholars" had become a reality and there was the nucleus of what was to become Silicon Valley. By 1955 there were seven firms; by 1960, 32; by 1970, 70; and by the 1980s, 90; with total employment amounting to 25,000 (Castells and Hall, 1994).

Encouraged by the success of Stanford University science park, similar facilities began to spring up around the world in the 1980s and 1990s. One of the first science parks in the UK was established at Cambridge. Established in 1970 following the Mott Report of 1969 (Castells and Hall, 1994), Cambridge Science Park was in fact developed by Trinity College, Cambridge. It received its first occupants in 1976. Since then it has grown dramatically and has been joined by two more science parks set up in Cambridge. By 1999 the number of high-tech establishments had grown to 959 employing more than 31,000 people (Athreye, 2000). Many other universities have now set up their own science parks including Cranfield, Nottingham and Warwick.

Among the benefits that high-tech start-up companies can derive from a science park location are:

- access to a university knowledge base – i.e. researchers
- scope for university spin-offs and joint ventures
- access to specialist institutions – e.g. venture capitalists
- role models
- access to a pool of specialist labour

However, while the science park concept is very attractive and has been widely embraced, it should be noted that attempts in Europe and Asia to emulate the early US experience of Silicon Valley and Boston's Route 128 through the provision of university science parks, appears to have met with only mixed success in part at least because the American experience was based on high levels of expenditure on defence research in the 1960s and 1970s. Comparative studies of firms located on and off university science parks have found little difference between such locations, in terms of measures of innovation such as expenditure on R&D, patents and outputs of new products and services (Bessant and Tidd, 2007). Indeed one major study (Bessant and Tidd, 2007: p264) concluded that, "science parks provide little more than cheap, short-term leases and a prestigous address".

SMART awards

The Small Firms Merit Award for Research and Technology (SMART) scheme, which is analysed in depth in Chapter 10, was initiated by the UK government's Department of Trade and Industry (DTI) in 1986 (Dodgson and Bessant, 1996), to provide financial support to small firms for research and product development.

As Dodgson and Bessant (1996) note, the rationale of the SMART scheme is to bridge the funding gap faced by small firms seeking to undertake innovation, particularly a shortage of seedcorn capital and investment funding for firms in the early stages of growth (Moore and Garnsey, 1993). This gap arises for two reasons. First, the presence of an information gap covering technological and commercial aspects, which makes it difficult for venture capitalists to evaluate the technical strengths and development potential of a project. This is exacerbated by an asymmetry of interest between innovators who do not know want to lose control and venture capitalists who typically demand a substantial stake.

Evaluations of the SMART scheme have proved positive and highlighted a number of important benefits including impetus to small-firm formation, stimulating firm growth and making the innovation more attractive for potential investors (Moore, 1993; Moore and Garnsey, 1993).

The SMART scheme has benefited from a number of high-profile innovation successes, including Bookham Technologies which developed a range of components utilising optical communications (ASOV) technology.

Mini Case

Lasers Are Us

Husband and wife team Simon and Debbie Lau set up Laser Application Unlimited in 1999. Their partnership aimed to develop a new laser-marking technique that would be both faster and applicable to a wider range of plastics than previously. As an experienced laser physicist, it was Simon who handled technical development, while Debbie began test marketing the concept among industrial clients. "We were impatient with the performance and high cost of existing laser systems and reckoned we could develop a better system at half price" said Simon. Early development was carried out in a spare bedroom of the couple's home in Porthcawl, South Wales and it was at this stage that the partnership sought and won a £45,000 SMART award to cover technical development and market research. Lasers Are Us Ltd was formed in May 2001 and began operations from a factory unit in Bridgend in November 2001.

Source: DTI (2005).

Mini Case

Iskra Wind Turbines

Redlands Primary School in Worksop, Nottinghamshire is unusual. It is one of the first schools in the country to install its own wind turbine in order to generate power. The 12-metre-high turbine uses a 5-foot diameter rotor that generates 5kw, enough electricity to light the school. The wind turbine is produced by Iskra Wind Turbine Manufacturers Ltd based in Nottingham. In October 1999 Iskra won a DTI SMART award for innovative technology which was used to fund development of the turbine, which is a small-scale version of the wind turbines installed in so-called "wind farms" now springing up in windy spots around the UK such as the Lake District. This phase of development work culminated in the installation and testing of a prototype turbine in the Derbyshire Dales. Following encouraging results of these trials, Iskra gained a further SMART award to develop a production version. Product development aimed at reducing:

- cost
- complexitiy
- weight

while at the same time improving:

- reliability
- corrosion protection

The result was the AT5-1 wind turbine which is now in production and in 2003 achieved a "Highly Commended" in the commercial enterprises category of the Eurosolar UK awards for inspiring renewable energy projects.

Source: Iskra (2009).

R&D tax credits

The R&D tax credit is another recent policy initiative from the UK government that aims to help and assist SMEs working on innovations. The scheme applies to SMEs that are registered limited companies spending more than £25,000 per year on research and development. Three different types of tax relief are available:

- basic R&D tax relief: treats expenditure as equal to 150 per cent of actual
- pre-trading R&D tax relief: expenditure creates a tax loss
- R&D tax credit: a tax refund of 16 per cent of unused loss

R&D is defined as "creative" work undertaken on a systematic basis in order to increase the stock of knowledge and the use of this knowledge to devise new applications.

The scheme is aimed specifically at SMEs endeavouring to "break new ground" by developing new products. Unlike the SMART scheme which provides a grant, it provides tax relief instead. It is a relatively flexible scheme that aims to benefit not only companies that have already started trading but also those which are at a point where they have not yet started. Since it is a relatively new scheme, it is too early for there to have been any formal evaluation of its effectiveness.

Mini Case

BTG and Isis to develop diagnostic tests and treatments for wheat intolerance

Coeliac disease (CD) is a lifelong illness caused principally by intolerance to protein in wheat and other grains. Also known as gluten intolerance, it is a genetic disorder that has symptoms that include stomach pain, diarrhoea, vomiting and failure to thrive, and correlate with inflammation and subsequently destruction of the surface of the intestine. The current blood tests for coeliac disease are frequently non-specific, leaving an intestinal biopsy as the only specific diagnostic test. The only treatment is the complete withdrawal of the toxic protein from the diet.

The Oxford researchers, led by gastroenterologist and principal investigator Dr Robert Anderson, have carried out extensive studies into the "toxic" protein fractions in cereal crops and have identified the particular part of the wheat protein that, following modifications by gut enzymes, causes the immune reaction associated with coeliac disease.

This opens the way for a specific diagnostic test for the disease as well as new prevention and treatment strategies, and even the possibility of producing wheat that does not contain the rogue sequence.

BTG and Isis, the technology transfer arm of Oxford University, recently announced an agreement that granted BTG exclusive rights to Oxford's proprietary technology, which provides for new prevention, treatment and diagnosis strategies for coeliac disease. The new technology has the potential to be the world's only therapeutic treatment for the disease which may affect up to 1 per cent of the population of the UK.

Under the terms of the Isis agreement BTG will have exclusive access to the University's technology for use in the diagnosis, prevention and treatment of coeliac disease. The technology is based on identification of the particular epitopes that cause priming of the immune system in coeliac disease. BTG will underwrite the development and commercialisation of the technology and will share any revenue from commercialisation of the technology with Isis and the university.

Source: BTG (2002).

Agencies promoting innovation

Unlike the situation 20 years ago there are now a number of agencies in both the public and private sectors that are able to provide a variety of forms of assistance to organisations and individuals engaged in innovation. It would not be possible to detail them all, but two very different agencies – Business Link and BTG plc – indicate the range of assistance available.

Business Link

Business Links are publicly funded agencies set up as a "one-stop-shop" to provide advice and training primarily for small businesses and start-ups. Business Links operate in close collaboration with the regional development agencies in their area. While their principal function is small-business support, this does not extend to innovation. Most Business Links have a Technology and Innovation adviser (Lawrence, 1997). They can advise on any grants (e.g. SMART) that may be available, they can also advise on the availability of local sources of professional services (e.g. patent agents) as well as the services provided by national agencies (e.g. Patent Office).

BTG plc

BTG was established in 1981 through a merger of two government bodies – the National Research and Development Corporation (NRDC) and the National Enterprise Board (NEB) (Dodgson and Bessant, 1996: p147). Its role is to help exploit technology drawn from both public and private sector organisations. BTG finds, develops and commercialises emerging technologies in the life and physical sciences. These innovations are protected by a strong portfolio of intellectual property (IP) that BTG develops and enhances. BTG then captures the value of these technologies through licensing and venturing activities. BTG was privatised in 1992. From its inception back in 1949, BTG has commercialised several major innovations including magnetic resonance imaging (MRI), recombinant factor IX blood-clotting protein, Campath® (calemtuzumab) and Multi Level Cell (MLC) memory.

BTG's function is essentially to evaluate inventions, ensure appropriate IP rights protection is in place through patents and then achieve effective exploitation normally through some form of licensing agreement. Dodgson and Bessant (1996) summarise its particular strengths as a willingness to:

- take a long-term view – in some cases a 10–15-year time horizon
- provide a depth of knowledge in the protection of IP rights on a worldwide basis
- provide technical, legal, commercial and patent resources

In recent years it has focused particularly on "latent innovation" – that is, helping larger firms make effective use of underused or unused technologies.

CASE STUDY: MALAYSIA'S MULTIMEDIA SUPER CORRIDOR

In the space of a generation Malaysia has been transformed from a developing country exporting primary products into an industrially oriented economy. Throughout the 1970s government industrial policies sought to diversify the economy in order to diminish its reliance on primary commodities (e.g. rubber, palm nut oil and tin) and encourage manufacturing. In the 1980s the government became ever more interventionist, launching an industrial strategy that set priorities for specific industry sectors. Manufactured goods which made up only 19 per cent of exports in 1980 had risen to 77.4 per cent of a much larger total by 1995 (Jomo and Felker, 1999).

However, by the 1990s Malaysia had reached a critical point in its development. The growth in manufacturing had occurred largely in the field of labour-intensive manufacturing. Malaysia presented a curious picture of burgeoning high-technology exports (mainly electronics) with little local innovation activity. The country's industrial structure was somewhat shallow with poor inter-industry linkages and an underdeveloped capital-goods sector. Much of this was a function of foreign direct investment (FDI) attracted to the country on the basis of low wages and resource availability. There was an increasing awareness on the part of policy-makers that for economic development the country had to move towards an industry structure based on higher value-added, technology-intensive production. Vision 2020, the Malaysian Prime Minister's ambitious plan for the country published in 1991, highlighted the importance of technology development. It stressed the need for Malaysia to enhance the scope of its industrial activities beyond simple assembly and production through the development of indigenous technology.

The Industrial Master Plan (IMP) 1986–1995 had already identified a weak indigenous technology base as a threat to future growth. It noted that what technological competence did exist was largely foreign owned, with the country heavily dependent on external sources of technology. The IMP recommended aggressive strategic investment in key industry sectors to build up local capabilities.

Then in 1996 the Malaysian Prime Minister Dr Mahathir announced the country's most ambitious industrial technology policy initiative – the establishment of the Multimedia Super Corridor (MSC).

The MSC is a 50 × 50-km zone stretching from the capital Kuala Lumpur to the newly built Kuala Lumpur International Airport at Sepang. It comprises a number of "clusters", including Putrajaya (a newly built federal seat of government), Cyberjaya (a new high-tech city housing multimedia industries, research centres and the Multimedia University) and Technology Park Malaysia – a zone providing engineering and IT facilities for entrepreneurs and industrial organisations.

The government's role in the project has been absolutely central. In the first place it has ensured a first-class environment. For instance, Putrajaya, the new federal seat of government, has been constructed as a garden city and the hub of the government's e-government project. Cyberjaya offers not only high-class multimedia working facilities including a very high level of connectivity but also residential and civic facilities. At the Petronas Twin Towers complex which serves as the northern gateway to the MSC there are extensive commercial, recreational, entertainment and retail facilities in a park-like setting. At the southern end of the MSC is the Kuala Lumpur International Airport built at a cost of more than US$3.5 billion, which acts as regional logistics hub and has the capacity to cater for 25–50 million passengers per year.

As well as providing an appropriate infrastructure for the MSC, the Malaysian government has also provided a range of financial incentives designed to attract investment from foreign companies that meet appropriate high technology criteria. These financial incentives include:

- a five-year exemption from Malaysian income tax renewable to 10 years or a 100 per cent investment tax allowance
- duty-free importation of multimedia equipment
- eligibility for R&D grants for Malaysian-owned MSC companies
- special guidelines to regulate foreign currency transactions and loans

As well as financial incentives the Malaysian government has also revised its regulatory requirement for MSC-status companies to facilitate innovation. The measures taken include:

- unrestricted employment of foreign knowledge workers
- freedom of ownership within the MSC (i.e. avoiding the requirement for local Malay participation)
- extensive IP protection

In addition the Malaysian government has promoted a number of "flagship application" projects designed to promote new uses for new technologies. There are seven flagship applications in total:

- electronic government
- smart schools
- smart card (My Kad)
- telemedicine
- R&D clusters
- borderless marketing centres
- manufacturing co-ordination

The flagship applications are designed to transform core elements of Malaysia's technology infrastructure and social systems in areas where there is normally a high level of public-sector involvement. Driving the development of the seven flagship applications are government agencies that report directly to the MSC Implementation Council chaired by the Prime Minister. These agencies work in close collaboration with leading international and local companies on concept planning and project implementation. Pilot schemes are identified jointly by project team members through a mechanism known as the Concept Request for Proposal (CRFP). This provides guidelines for bidding for consortia interested in undertaking multimedia projects within the MSC.

The Smart card is typical of the flagship application projects. The aim is to provide a multi-purpose card that will provide the holder with a range of applications. The primary purpose of the card is to act as an identity card for all adults over the age of 12 and this is why the lead agency is the National Registration Department. Other public agencies involved include: the Road Transport Department, the Immigration Department, the Health Ministry and the Royal Malaysian Police. The other dimension to this flagship application is that the card should also act as a payment card to provide access to a wide range of financial services, e.g. as a credit card.

Source: Ramasamy et al. *(2004)*

Questions

1 Why is the Malaysian government interested in innovation?
2 Why had Malaysia's industrial development up until the 1990s done little to embrace the country's innovation capability?
3 What is foreign direct investment?
4 What is the purpose of the Multimedia Super Corridor?
5 Which well-known location famous for its capacity for innovation is the Multimedia Super Corridor trying to emulate?
6 Towards which of the innovation policy objectives of the Malaysian government is the Multimedia Super Corridor targeted?
7 To what extent is the Multimedia Super Corridor an example of the Malaysian government pursuing the lead user objective?
8 What is the Smart card contributing to innovation in Malaysia?

? Questions for discussion

1 Why should governments provide assistance to innovators?
2 Why is market failure sometimes associated with innovation?
3 What are the UK government's objectives in promoting innovation?
4 What does Afuah (2003: p312) mean when he says that governments have a role to play "shepherding" innovations by being a lead user?
5 When has the UK government acted as a lead user?
6 How do knowledge-transfer partnerships transfer knowledge?
7 How can science parks help to facilitate innovation?
8 Which university invented the science park and why?
9 What is the function of the SMART award scheme?
10 How do SMART awards help innovators?
11 How do R&D tax credits help innovators?
12 Why are regional development agencies increasingly involved in innovation?

Exercises

1 Choose one government initiative designed to foster innovation. Describe the initiative, outline its purpose and provide an evaluation of its effectiveness.

2 Why do governments try to stimulate innovation?

3 With the aid of appropriate examples, explain what is meant by the term "lead user".

4 Explain why in the early life of an innovation there is typically a lot of technological and market uncertainty.

5 Prepare a presentation explaining the nature of SMART awards and showing how they can help innovators.

6 Prepare a briefing document explaining the role that BTG plc undertakes in connection with innovation.

7 Explain the nature and purpose of the DTI's Knowledge Transfer Partnership (KTP) scheme.

8 Evaluate current UK national policies for innovation, illustrating your answer with reference to recent policy initiatives.

Further reading

1 Dodgson, M. and J. Bessant (1996) *Effective Innovation Policy: A New Approach*, International Thomson Business Press, London.
An unusual book simply because there is very little material on innovation policy. This is virtually the only book on the subject. By now somewhat dated, but worth knowing about nonetheless.

2 DIUS (2008) *Innovation Nation: Unlocking Talent*, Department for Innovation, Universities & Skills, Cm 7345, March 2008, The Stationery Office, London.
A recent White Paper on innovation, it outlines the importance of innovation, as well as recent changes in both its nature and the environment within which takes place. It provides a useful overview of developments in innovation, particularly the extent to which new ideas have infiltrated the subject. In terms of policy it highlights recent measures taken by the government to stimulate innovation.

3 DCITA (2004) *Backing Australia's Ability: Building our Future Through Science and Innovation*, Department of Communications, Information, Technology & Arts, Commonwealth of Australia, Canberra.
The same thing, only this time it's the Australian version. It provides an interesting comparison with the UK's *Innovation Nation*. But really the best thing about it is the way that it briefly outlines the various policy measures that the Australian government has taken over the last decade to stimulate innovation.

Innovation clusters

Introduction

Silicon Valley, or to give it its real name, Santa Clara County, on the southern flank of San Francisco Bay in California, is synonymous with innovation and high-technology. It comprises the densest concentration of high-technology firms in the world. Once a sparsely populated agricultural area, today more than 8,000 firms, most of them employing less than 50, provide employment for more than quarter of a million people. Since the 1970s Silicon Valley has exhibited an extraordinarily high rate of new-firm formation. Many of these firms are "spin-off" companies where new firms are formed by employees leaving their existing employer in order to go it alone, by founding their own company. This has helped Silicon Valley become associated with an entrepreneurial culture where, to quote one leading study (Castells and Hall, 1994: p12), "new ideas born in a garage can make teenagers into millionaires, while changing the way we think, we live, and we work".

Focusing originally on electronics, Silicon Valley evolved to become a centre for information industries. Some of the most important innovations of the second half of the twentieth century, including the integrated circuit and the personal computer, originated in Silicon Valley. The region also specialises in breeding highly successful and innovative high-technology companies including Hewlett-Packard, Apple, Intel, Oracle and eBay (Lee *et al.*, 2000).

The extraordinary success of Silicon Valley has attracted the interest of politicians, policy-makers and industrialists around the world, all anxious to reproduce the "Silicon Valley effect" by establishing concentrations or clusters of high-technology firms through direct government action. In each case policy-makers hoped not only to create large numbers of high-technology jobs, but also to stimulate the national rate of innovation in pursuit of a more dynamic and expansive economy. In France the government has created a high-technology cluster at Sophia Antipolis near Nice where large numbers of multinational companies have established manufacturing plants and research laboratories (Longhi, 1999). In Taiwan the government sponsored the Hsinchu Science Park which is home to large numbers of indigenous IT companies (Castells and Hall, 1994; Saxenian, 2004). In India the government has been instrumental, through a range of fiscal incentives, in establishing the southern city of Bangalore as an internationally recognised software cluster of more than 200 firms comprising both foreign MNEs and locally owned software companies (Balasubramanyan and Balasubramanyan, 2000). Malaysia in the late 1990s saw the launch one of the most ambitious attempts to replicate Silicon Valley in the form of the Multimedia Super Corridor, a 50 km by 50 km high-technology zone, stretching southwards from the federal capital Kuala Lumpur, that houses a range of information-related digital businesses (Bunnell, 2002).

A development sponsored by a provincial rather than a national government is a science park called the Innovation Hub, at Pretoria in Guateng Province in South Africa. It was developed in partnership between the Guateng provincial government and the University of Pretoria (The Innovation Hub, 2008). Established in 2001 on a site adjacent to the University of Pretoria, the Innovation Hub aims to support the creation, nurturing and growth of technology-led businesses. The first businesses arrived in 2005 and the Innovation Hub currently houses some 68 enterprises employing almost 900 people and with a combined turnover of R43 million. The businesses located in the Innovation Hub range from start-up businesses and SMEs to multinational enterprises (including such well-known names as Cisco Systems and SAP), and they are engaged in activities ranging from R&D and testing, to piloting technology commercialisation and the development of business spin-off technologies in the biotechnology, electronics and ICT sectors.

Clusters like these have been variously described as "high-technology clusters," "innovative milieux" and "innovation clusters". This reflects the fact that the growth and development of clusters is associated with innovation and the development of a strong knowledge base (Armstrong and Taylor, 2000). Using the generic term "innovation cluster" to describe clusters of high-technology firms, this chapter looks at the link between innovation and such clusters. The characteristics of these clusters are analysed and the factors reputed to contribute to innovation identified. Not only does this enable us to understand more about the geography of innovation and why it is that some locations appear to be extraordinarily successful as centres of innovation, it also serves to deepen our knowledge of innovation and the factors that can both enhance and inhibit the process of successful innovation.

The nature of clusters

Whether they are termed "innovation clusters," "high-technology clusters" or "innovative milieux," there are a number of attributes or characteristics associated with this kind of cluster. These attributes include:

- geographical concentration
- high degree of specialisation

- large number of mainly small and medium-sized firms
- ease of entry and exit
- high rate of innovation

Geographical concentration is the defining attribute behind the concept of a cluster. Porter (1998: p78) for instance describes clusters as, "geographic concentrations of interconnected companies and institutions in a particular field".

In this sense "geography matters" because a cluster consists of a number of firms belonging to the same or related industries, grouped in relatively close proximity within a particular location. The proximity of firms, and the fact that they work on related activities, differentiates the cluster from other forms of industrial location.

At the same time one normally finds that the presence of a number of firms, most of which are probably small, gives rise to a high degree of specialisation. In this context "specialisation" describes the way in which firms are narrowly focused in terms of the range of outputs they provide. This is in contrast to a situation where firms offer a broad range of products and might be described as "general purpose" concerns. The significance of specialisation is not merely that it is an attribute that serves to define the nature of the cluster. It is linked to the nature of a cluster because it is the presence of a significant number of firms that enables specialisation to occur. The presence of a number of firms justifies specialisation.

The requirement that there should be a number of firms is self-evident. Too few firms and there simply is no grouping. However, the characteristics of the firms that make up a cluster are also important. Though there can be variations, in general clusters comprise small firms. There may be large firms present within a cluster, but for a location to be recognised as a cluster one would normally expect many, if not most, of the firms to be small.

Another attribute of clusters is that there should be ease of entry and exit. In other words it should be possible for start-up and spin-off companies to spring up and join a cluster with relative ease. In economic terms, barriers to entry should be absent. At the same time it should also be possible for firms to leave an industry and therefore the location.

Finally, clusters are usually associated with a high rate of innovation. New ideas, new concepts, new designs and new processes can be commercialised quickly and easily, by setting up a new company or spinning one off from an existing one. This does not necessarily make innovation easy, but it does facilitate the process of innovation, as there are likely to be fewer hurdles to overcome, such as criteria for funding, for continuation or for the use of resources, as one might find in a large firm.

The cluster concept

The notion of a cluster was first put forward by Alfred Marshall (1890). He used the term "industrial district" to describe agglomerations of small specialised firms found in particular localities. He cited as examples the cotton industry in Lancashire and the cutlery trade in Sheffield. He explained the success of these industrial agglomerations in terms of external economies of scale, where the close proximity of large numbers of small firms generated a market for increasingly specialised services.

According to Marshall (1890), agglomeration economies centre around three sources of collective efficiency, namely:

- a local pool of specialised labour
- firms specialising in the intermediate stages of production
- knowledge spill-overs

The availability of a pool of specialised labour occurs within industrial districts because the existence of a large number of similar firms encourages the concentration of supplies of skilled labour. For firms this can mean lower costs because they can poach skilled labour from other firms rather than going to the expense of investing in training and skills development. The scope for firms specialising in the intermediate stages of production occurs because agglomeration can result in a significant demand from local firms. Knowledge spill-overs occur informally. Proximity makes it relatively easy for firms to observe better business practices and copy working methods from their neighbours. Similarly, new ideas and knowledge of new technologies can be shared through informal contact between the employees of different firms.

While the logic of industrial districts rests primarily on economies derived from the proximity of large numbers of similar firms leading to lower costs, Marshall himself recognised that agglomeration could be a spur to innovation, where the level of expertise available leads via human ingenuity to some firms exploring different ways of doing things.

For much of the twentieth century, however, large firms and internal economies resulting from size were dominant. A revival of interest in economic localisation, particularly on the part of economic geographers, occurred in the 1980s, spurred among other things by studies of small specialised firms in Northern Italy. Work by Piore and Sabel (1984) and others identified "flexible specialisation" as an alternative to the prevailing logic of mass production. Since flexible specialisation was a form of production pursued by small firms, particularly concentrations of small firms, this led to a revival of interest in industrial districts.

However, although the "new industrial districts" as they were termed by economic geographers, subsumed Marshall's ideas from a century earlier they also added new ones. These focused particularly on the importance of "institutional factors" associated with concentrations of small firms. These institutional factors included the presence of:

- supportive socio-cultural attributes associated with working practices
- a network of public and private institutions supporting firms in the locality
- an intense set of backward, forward and horizontal linkages between firms based on non-market as well as market exchanges

The socio-cultural attributes comprise a range of local conventions, rules, routines, and norms that influence behaviour particularly in a work context. These attributes are often informal and non-systematic being based on tradition and practice. They often involve a certain "way of doing things" within a locality. As such they serve to define a "local world of production" and will often involve tacit knowledge. The institutions comprise a variety of organisations including training agencies, financial institutions, development agencies, marketing board and the like. A feature of these institutions is that they are for the most part collaborative, not-for-profit bodies. The presence of such institutions is termed "institutional thickness" and its significance is that it supports and assists the firms present in the locality. They not only provide support to potential entrepreneurs contemplating the establishing of new firms, they also serve to embed existing firms in the locality. The significance of the linkages, which economic geographers term "untraded interdependencies," is that they assist knowledge transfer and dissemination.

Hence, this new strand of thinking has helped revive the concept of the industrial district. This owes much to the nature of the agglomerations to which the analysis has been applied. A feature of many modern agglomerations is that, like Silicon Valley, they comprise high-technology firms that are active in innovation. At the same time new ideas about innovation, particularly those that stress the importance of networking (e.g. Rothwell's (1992) fifth-generation innovation process) and knowledge assimilation (e.g. Cohen and Levinthal's (1990) absorptive capacity) have emphasised the importance of transfer and learning. As a result neo-Marshallian industrial districts and the institutional factors associated with them have been seen as vehicles for stimulating and enhancing innovation. Neo-Marshallian industrial districts are often associated with innovative milieux and innovation clusters which in turn have been pursued by policy-makers as a way of reproducing the Silicon Valley effect.

However, the biggest factor behind the return of industrial districts to the forefront of the policy agenda and in particular interest in and promotion of clusters has come from quite another source, namely the work of two economists, Michael Porter (1990) and Paul Krugman (1991). They did much to re-ignite interest in industrial agglomerations, now re-branded as clusters. Porter's work on clusters, coming a decade after his earlier work had drawn attention to the importance of competitiveness, proved particularly influential. Policy-makers the world over seized on Porter's notion of business clusters as a tool for promoting both national and regional competitiveness as well as growth and innovation.

However, while Porter may have done much to popularise the cluster concept in recent years, there are those who argue that the rush on the part of policy-makers to endorse and apply the concept has helped to sow the seeds of its destruction. Martin and Sunley (2003) have criticised the cluster concept, arguing that Porter has turned it into something approaching a "brand" that is applied far too frequently. They argue that the cluster concept has now become much too "elastic" (Martin and Sunley, 2003: p28), being applied so widely to all sorts of geographical concentrations that its power to explain a link between agglomeration and local economic growth has been severely diminished.

Types of cluster

Mini Case

Galway's ICT cluster

Over the last 30 years Ireland's economy has developed rapidly, principally by attracting large amounts of FDI (foreign direct investment). In Galway the process began in the 1970s when the American computer company Digital established a manufacturing operation. At this point Galway was effectively a greenfield site with virtually no previous experience of the computer industry. Digital's plant in Galway expanded rapidly and through FDI was joined by other branch plants of American multinationals including Compaq and Nortel in the computing field and Medtronics AVE and Boston Scientific in the medical instruments field. While local linkages were at first extremely limited, over time these plants have become more firmly embedded in the local economy of Galway. Digital became not only a major provider of advanced training and development for the largely locally recruited workforce, it also became a source of broader research linkages and collaboration, including a major research project on computer integrated manufacturing with Renault, Compaq and NUI Galway (Green *et al.*, 2001).

Similarly the shortage of experienced professional ICT staff in the area forced inward investors to co-operate with each other for skills, infrastructure and market opportunities, rather than just compete.

The local linkages were such that, when Digital closed its Galway plant in 1993, the repercussions reverberated throughout the local economy. However, efforts by the local business chamber and national and regional development agencies ensured that the pool of skills and professionalism within Digital's workforce was not lost. The provision of business support, training and "incubator" facilities working together with informal networks among ex-Digital staff contributed to further development of Galway's software cluster. While some ex-Digital staff moved to other ICT-based branch plants in the area, others chose to go it alone. As a result, helped by some early successes such as Toucan Technology, the number of small start-up companies within the local economy of Galway has increased substantially. While the cluster continues to be dominated by branch plants, it has become more diverse over the course of the last decade as an increasing number of small plants working in the computing sector have been established.

Source: Green et al. (2001).

Renewed interest in clusters and industrial agglomeration has led to the identification of a number of variations on the conventional Marshallian industrial district. Work by Markusen (1996) differentiates four distinct types of cluster (see Figure 13.1):

1 neo-Marshallian industrial district (ID) cluster
2 hub-and-spoke cluster
3 satellite platform cluster
4 state-anchored cluster

Neo-Marshallian industrial district cluster

The first of these four types of cluster is the conventional ID as identified by Marshall and extended in recent years to include Italian-style industrial districts. This type of cluster possesses a structure characterised by the presence of large numbers of small, locally owned firms. Firms being locally owned, investment and production decisions are typically made within the region. There will be a substantial amount of local trading, with inputs bought locally, resulting in strong inter-firm linkages within the cluster. Outputs on the other hand may well be exported from the region, reflecting the specialist nature of production in the region. The labour force too will be recruited locally with both immigration and outmigration largely absent. According to Markusen (1996: p301), the presence of a high proportion of workers engaged in design- and development-type activities ensures that such clusters are "seedbeds of innovation". Given its record for innovation and the presence of a large number of small firms with strong inter-firm linkages, specialist suppliers and local sources of capital, Silicon Valley in California represents an example of a technologically oriented, neo-Marshallian industrial district. In Britain, Motor Sport Valley in Oxfordshire provides another example of this type of cluster. It comprises a world-leading agglomeration of small and medium-sized firms clustered in a 50-mile radius around Oxford (Henry and Pinch, 2000a). Within this area are more than 600 firms engaged in

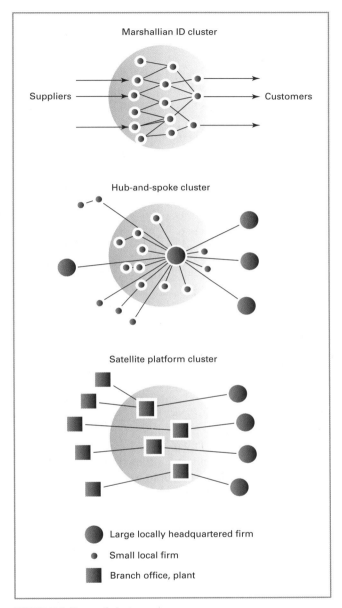

FIGURE 13.1 Types of cluster

Source: Markusen (1996) *Economic Geography,* reprinted with kind permission of Clark University

the design, development and manufacture of racing cars and their components (Aston and Williams, 1996). What makes the cluster a neo-Marshallian industrial district reminiscent of Silicon Valley (Beck-Burridge and Walton, 2000) is not merely the presence of many leading racing-car constructors, but also of large numbers of specialist component suppliers, a pool of skilled staff and a "knowledge community" (Henry and Pinch, 2000b: p127) comprising inter-firm links that facilitate knowledge generation and diffusion leading to a high rate of innovation.

Hub-and-spoke cluster

While small firms predominate in neo-Marshallian IDs, hub-and-spoke clusters are characterised by having a number of large firms or facilities that act as a hub around which are to be found many small firms that may well be tied to the hub firm by virtue either of origin or of ongoing exchange relationship. Hub firms are typically large, with an international outlook that may involve exchange relationships with branch plants, suppliers, customers and competitors outside the region as well as locally. They may be vertically integrated, incorporating several distinct stages of the production process. According to Markusen (1996) they are also likely to be oligopolistic and dominate a single industry. Linkages between the hub firms and the small firms that make up the spokes typically take the form of supply contracts. Unlike relations within a neo-Marshallian cluster, relations within a hub-and-spoke cluster are unlikely to be collaborative and co-operative in nature, but instead will tend to be confined to being contractual. The disparity in size between the hub firms and the others means that the hub firms tend to play a dominant role within the local economy, giving rise to a unique local culture. Gray *et al.* (1996) suggest that the success of hub-and-spoke clusters is dependent on the ability of a hub that emerges in one industrial era to tolerate and encourage the development of hub organisations in another era.

Gray *et al.* (1996) cite the Seattle region of the US as exemplifying the hub-and-spoke configuration. In this instance, Boeing, the world's largest aerospace company, acts as a hub. As a hub firm, Boeing's focus is firmly international as it has dominated the market for commercial airliners for many years and this international orientation has resulted in arm's length, purely contractual relationships with local suppliers (Gray *et al.*, 1996). In fact only a small proportion of Boeing's suppliers are locally based. Despite this, Boeing has been a powerful agent in shaping the regional economic infrastructure and the labour market of Seattle. Just how influential can be gauged by reaction to lay-offs at Boeing. In the early 1970s during one of the periodic downturns in the civil airliner market, Boeing cut its Seattle workforce by two-thirds, from 150,000 to 50,000. In April 1971 two Seattle residents put up a sign on a large roadside advertising hoarding that read: "Will the last person leaving SEATTLE – Turn out the lights" (Rodgers, 1996: p302).

On a more positive note, Gray *et al.* (1996: p658) comment that:

> Boeing has helped to make the region an attractive place to live and work, which translates palpably into strong affinities for the region on the part of both long-term residents and newcomers.

Significantly, Boeing's role in defining the region as a high-technology centre has been a tolerant one that has permitted the rise of other hubs, most notably in the field of computing, with Seattle becoming home to more than 500 software companies, including Microsoft.

Satellite platform cluster

The third variant of the cluster form is the satellite platform cluster characterised by a concentration of branch plants of large externally owned and headquartered organisations. The firms to be found within satellite platform clusters can range from routine assembly functions to relatively sophisticated research. However, one distinguishing characteristic is that they are likely to form what Markusen (1996) describes as "stand alone" facilities detached in spatial terms, with few linkages to other firms in the cluster. As a result commitments to local suppliers are likely to be for the most part "conspicuously absent". Linkages where they exist will be to the parent corporation or other branch plants of the same concern located in other regions. Because the plants located within satellite platform clusters tend to be owned by absent multinational corporations, their destiny, especially with regard to things like key investment decisions, will largely be determined outside the region. The main sources of finance, technical expertise and business services will tend to be external to the region. In contrast to the strong external focus associated with the provision of capital, local government and local development agencies typically play an important role in the provision of infrastructure, tax incentives and generic support services. Despite the absence of many of the cluster features that foster innovation, satellite platforms can nonetheless prove to be important centres of high-technology activity.

With an economic structure dominated by branch plants of major, high-technology companies (Longhi and Keeble, 2000), Sophia Antipolis in France provides a good example of a satellite platform cluster (Longhi, 1999). Among the companies represented are IBM, Digital, Thomson, Rockwell and Dow Corning, attracted to Sophia Antipolis as a *parc de prestige*. Attempts to encourage the growth of SMEs through incubator schemes (Castells and Hall, 1994) have generally met with only limited success, resulting in a cluster polarised into large and small organisations. However, recent research by Longhi (1999) indicates a move away from exogenous growth in favour of endogenous growth as the SME sector at last began to flourish in the late 1990s and form linkages with some of the large foreign firms.

Another example of the satellite platform type of cluster is the software cluster in Bangalore in southern India. This is another government-sponsored cluster (Balasubramanyam and Balasubramanyam, 2000) comprising more than 60 foreign MNEs including Motorola, Texas Instruments, Hewlett-Packard, Oracle and Siemens, as well as many indigenous software firms. However, in this case linkages between large foreign firms and small local ones are a feature of the cluster. According to Balasubramanyam and Balasubramanyam (2000) this is thanks to the nature of the software which consists primarily of bespoke systems tailored to specific client needs that demand a high degree of collaboration.

State-anchored cluster

The fourth type of cluster in Markusen's (1996) typology is the state-anchored cluster. This occurs where some form of public sector or not-for-profit organisation acts as an "anchor tenant" within a region. Examples of the sorts of organisation that might undertake this anchoring function include:

- a military base
- a large defence plant
- a public laboratory
- government offices

As examples Markusen (1996) cites Denver in Colorado which houses the second largest concentration of government offices in the US and Ann Arbor in Michigan, where a university acts as the anchor. The structure of the state-anchored cluster is likely to resemble a hub-and-spoke cluster in the sense that one organisation, or a small number of organisations, will tend to dominate the economic landscape, so much so that the local business structure is likely to reflect strongly the anchor organisation(s). Because the anchor organisation is not a conventional commercial organisation (i.e. it is in the public or not-for-profit sectors) it is likely to be relatively immune from the threat of a sudden exodus caused by corporate failure or a downturn in the business cycle. Indigenous firms are likely to play a smaller role than in neo-Marshallian industrial districts or hub-and-spoke clusters, although over an extended period of time supplier sectors will often grow up to meet the needs of the anchor organisation. In the case of universities and military and scientific establishments, labour markets will generally reflect national, or in the case of universities, even international market conditions.

Examples of state-anchored clusters to be found in the UK include Cambridge and the so called "M4 Corridor," an area of high-technology firms that stretches from the western side of London to Bristol following the westbound motorway and covering counties such as Berkshire, Hampshire and Wiltshire. The M4 Corridor's claim to be this type of cluster configuration rests on the presence of several large government research establishments (GREs) in the counties to the west of London (Castells and Hall, 1994; Hall *et al.*, 1987). Mainly established in the years before the Second World War, they expanded rapidly during the Cold War years when their links to high-technology industries were extended. The Royal Aircraft Establishment at Farnborough in Hampshire, the Atomic Weapons Research Establishment at Aldermaston in Berkshire and the National Physical Laboratory at Bushy Park in Middlesex are all publicly-funded laboratories located in this area. Similarly, the M4 Corridor is also home to a number of major military establishments including the British Army's home base of Aldershot and GCHQ at Cheltenham. The rapid development of the military-industrial complex in the post-war years led the GREs to "form the nodes of an intricate web defence procurement in which close and intimate contacts between research establishments and high-technology clusters became the everyday rule" (Hall *et al.*, 1987: p121).

Cambridge similarly represents a state-anchored cluster but by virtue of its university. Cambridge University dates back to medieval times and has had a profound influence on the development of the local economy. Since the 1960s the University's global reputation for research and scientific activity has spawned a substantial cluster of technology-based SMEs in the Cambridge region. Sometimes described as the "Cambridge phenomenon," the number of local high-technology firms has mushroomed from 30 in 1960 to more than 700 by the late 1990s (Keeble *et al.*, 1999). This growth has occurred as start-up firms have been spun off from the University or been attracted in because of it. The technologies represented in the cluster are diverse but include computing, electronics and biotechnology, the latter linked to the University's pioneering work in the field of genetics. A significant proportion of the high-technology firms in the cluster maintain close links with the university. In the manner of state-anchored clusters, the University's generally liberal attitude towards "research collaboration, sharing and the development of new knowledge" has, according to Keeble *et al.* (1999), spilled over and helped to shape attitudes in the local business community. Such attitudes have been particularly conducive to innovation.

The innovative milieux

In 1841, Richard Birkin, a Nottingham lace machinery manufacturer, giving evidence before a Parliamentary committee on the export of machinery, noted (Church, 1966: p78):

> 66 … it is not the machines themselves in which value exists, but the great practice we in Nottingham have had and the ideas we have from being congregated together, that enables us to apply our various improvements to the machines. 99

Nottingham, through the cluster of lace manufacturers in the lace market area of the city at this time, formed a major centre of lace production and was the source of a string of innovations that created the machine-made lace industry. Hence Richard Birkin was suggesting that the rate of innovation was a direct function of the lace-manufacturing cluster in and around Nottingham's lace market.

What is the connection between clusters and innovation? How do clusters facilitate innovation?

There are a number of features of clusters that are particularly conducive to innovation. These features include:

- networking
- specialisation
- ease of entry and exit
- resource mobility

Networking

Research in the 1990s (Rothwell, 1992) highlighted the importance of networking. Innovation is portrayed not as something that is completely internalised within the organisation, but as something which is carried on as a multi-actor process that requires a high level of inter-firm integration. This model notes how firms do not operate in isolation but tend to draw on other firms for ideas, knowledge and services. In so far as they comprise small tight-knit groups of people working in the same field but within a number of different firms located in close proximity, clusters can facilitate networking. Proximity gives rise to a "community of practice" where different occupations rub shoulders with their counterparts in rival firms enabling knowledge to circulate on the back of shared practice, thus allowing each firm to draw upon a wider knowledge base than it would otherwise have access to. Research by Henry and Pinch (2000a) into Motor Sport Valley in Oxfordshire has shown just how important such a "knowledge community" can be in enabling a cluster to maintain its position as an internationally recognised centre of innovation. Nor are the benefits of networking confined to accessing knowledge. As a community of practice, clusters ensure that firms know a lot about other firms, especially what their competitors are doing. It becomes relatively common knowledge which firms are good at particular tasks. In this way a form of collective benchmarking, where firms are constantly looking over their shoulders at what their competitors are doing, drives them to innovate.

Specialisation

A second feature of clusters that helps to stimulate and encourage innovation is the scope they provide for specialisation. The presence of a large number of firms in the same industry or at least in similar sectors, located in close proximity to each other, enables firms to specialise in those activities they are good at, and to provide specialist products or services. As a result firms located in a cluster can draw on a range of specialist suppliers. These can extend to subcontractors and fabricators who can perform production tasks vital to innovation such as those associated with the development of prototypes. In addition, specialisation is likely to lead to a range of "subsidiary trades" being present. These are likely to include firms providing specialist services that support innovation and new-venture development such as venture capitalists and patent agents. Hence, through specialisation clusters can provide the sort of infrastructure that will support and enable innovation.

Ease of entry and exit

Most high-technology clusters feature the presence of significant numbers of small and relatively young firms. This is a function of the conditions within the cluster which allow for ease of entry into the cluster. Thus it is relatively easy for enterprising individuals to break away from their existing employer and "go it alone". While it used to be argued that large firms were more likely to innovate (Galbraith, 1956), on the grounds that they had the resources to sustain the level of R&D required for new discoveries and thence innovation, an increasing body of evidence points to small firms being a more suitable environment for innovation. Why? Essentially they lack the baggage associated with old technology. Second, small firms can provide rapid decision-making in a way that large firms, with several tiers of management, find hard to match. Last, knowledge can circulate more rapidly within small firms. Thus, where clusters have a tradition of new start-ups combined with the facilities to make the process of start-up relatively easy, they will provide a climate in which innovation can flourish.

Resource mobility

Resource mobility, especially where the resource is people, is a feature of many high-technology clusters. Several studies of such clusters have noted that they are frequently characterised by a high level of labour mobility. This mobility encourages innovation in a number of ways. First, if people move then so too will ideas. Second, the high level of mobility is likely to mean that there is an active and responsive market for human skills. Under these conditions rewards will be an accurate reflection of skills and individuals, especially those with a high level of skill, can gain rewards that accurately reflect their abilities. Finally, the mobility of labour means that firms are likely to be very well aware of what others firms are doing, thus providing a powerful spur to innovation.

CASE STUDY: THE BRITISH HI-FI INDUSTRY CLUSTER

A hi-fi cluster?

The market for audio equipment in Britain as in other parts of the world is dominated by producers from the Far East, particularly well-known Japanese brands such as Sony, Pioneer, Sanyo and Panasonic (Milne, 1989). Despite this, British manufacturers continue not only to survive but even to prosper. A key feature of their relative success is that they occupy a niche within the global audio equipment market, dedicated to producing hi-fi equipment that provides the best possible sound quality. In this market segment the emphasis is on quality rather than cost, and in the quest for the best possible sound quality British manufacturers actively embraced innovation in order to maintain their position in the marketplace.

The British hi-fi manufacturers are distinctive in a number of ways. First, there are a remarkably large number of them. A recent study by May *et al.* (2001) identified no less than 65 British hi-fi manufacturers. Not only are there a lot of them, but most of them are relatively small. Typically they employing 25 people or less, which makes them a great deal smaller than their Japanese competitors. Third, they are for the most part concentrated in the South East of England, being clustered in an arc that stretches from Cambridge through London and on into Kent, Sussex and Hampshire. Unlike their Japanese counterparts who mass-produce a range of consumer electronics products, the British hi-fi manufacturers specialise in hi-fi products. These extend to the design and manufacture of:

- compact audio systems
- amplifiers
- specialist audio products
- CD players
- loudspeaker systems

Recently some manufacturers have moved into the nascent market for home cinema amplifiers and loudspeaker systems. The extent to which British manufacturers engage in the quality end of the audio equipment market can be gauged by the way their products do not tend to make use of modern display aids. Most renounce such design gimmicks as a distraction, preferring instead to rely upon the sound quality their products offer.

Though small, the British hi-fi manufacturers are very active in terms of innovation. While some of the major technological breakthroughs that have transformed the audio equipment field in recent years, such as video and CD formats, have been introduced by global consumer electronics companies like Philips and Sony, May *et al.* (2001) in their study of the industry showed that the small British hi-fi companies have nonetheless been responsible for many significant product innovations including: stereo sound, small bookshelf speakers and flat-panel loudspeakers. The highly innovative nature of the small British hi-fi companies is reflected in the large number of international awards they have gained in recent years. May *et al.* (2001) point out that between 1992/1993 and 1996/1997 the European Imaging and Sound Association placed them second to the Japanese in terms of the number of awards granted. In the awards organised by the US Consumer Electronics Show the small British companies were close behind the US and Japanese companies that dominated the event. British hi-fi companies in 1994/1995 and 1995/1996 received as many awards as all their European counterparts combined. In addition, many British firms are regularly used as consultants by large Japanese concerns such as Sony, Canon and Pioneer. The British firm NXT has been at the forefront of developing the flat-panel loudspeaker technology being used by Japanese companies, and Meridian developed the "home cinema" speaker system used by Canon. The record of small British companies in terms of innovation led May *et al.* (2001: p367) to observe that:

> Other nations also have many significant specialist hi-fi firms (such as Audio Access, Cello, Krell, Mark Levinson, Proceed and Revel to name but a few from the US) but British manufacturers certainly seem to excel in this sector.

How did the cluster arise?

In some respects it is surprising to find a hi-fi industry in Britain, since most of the early innovations were made elsewhere. The phonograph for instance was invented by an American, Thomas Edison, in 1877. Later improvements such as the disc phonograph, the forerunner of the vinyl-record player, also came from America. However, the country's interest in audio technology gained a boost when Marconi, the pioneer of radio, moved to Britain in the early part of the twentieth century. He established the Wireless and Telegraphy Company at Chelmsford near London. Despite a late start Britain has in recent years been responsible for several major innovations in the field of audio technology. A.D. Blumlein pioneered the early development of two channels on a single disc to produce stereo recording. Similarly D.T.N Williamson and Harold Leak were responsible for the development of amplifiers. Developments such as these owed much to government support, often indirect rather than direct from the interwar years onwards.

The formation of the BBC in the 1920s not only fostered interest in radio, but also provided trained engineers. Similarly, another government initiative, the setting up of the National Grid in 1926, helped to open the market for wireless sets, by extending the provision of electricity to all parts of the UK and ensuring a common standard for electrical supply. Both of these publicly funded schemes contributed to the development of a thriving amateur radio community in Britain in the interwar years and after. According to May *et al.* (2001), the amateur input to the industry, in which a strong esprit de corps results from the hobbyist and enthusiast origins of the industry, has close parallels with motor sport (Pinch and Henry, 1999), another industry in which innovation clusters are much in evidence.

While a small number of the British hi-fi manufacturers, such as Wharfdale, were founded in the 1930s, it was in the 1960s that there arose the first of a series of waves of new company formations associated with the creation of a cluster of small specialist hi-fi manufacturers in the South East of England. The Second World War had seen a big investment by the government in research into radio and associated electronic technology. Much of this work was connected with the development of radar, designed to check the threat posed by German U-boats and aerial bombing by the Luftwaffe. This produced a generation of engineers trained in the Armed Forces, who went on to develop civilian audio products in later years. Typical were John Bowers and Roy Wilkins who, having been trained in radio technology in the Armed Forces, went on to found B & W Loudspeakers in the 1960s, a company that has developed a range of innovations in the field of loudspeaker design.

This trend towards new company formation was boosted in the 1970s as major British mass market consumer electronics firms such as Thorn, EMI, GEC and Rank, all of which had extensive research laboratories in the London area, began to rationalise their activities in the face of intense competition from Japan. As these large concerns rationalised, so skilled engineers left and set up their own businesses focusing on a specialist field of audio equipment. The process of ever-more specialised companies being spun off in this way continued throughout the 1980s and 1990s as employees of existing companies spotted market niches for new products and services and decided to set up on their own. May *et al.* (2001) give the example of Myriad, a manufacturer of amplifiers and tuners, spun off from NAD Electronics (which was itself established in the 1970s) a manufacturer of similar products, but aiming for a more expensive market segment. As Curran and Blackburn (1994) have noted, those involved in spinning off new firms can be very dependent in the early stages on linkages, in the form of contacts and market knowledge, to their previous employment.

When it comes to market and industry knowledge, those setting up new firms are also able to benefit from the numerous hi-fi shows that are held in the UK each year. These provide an opportunity for those who have set up on their own to meet old friends and maintain contacts as well as making new connections. As with all trade fairs, gossip and rumour serve to disseminate information about market trends and technological innovations. However, it should be noted that for the most part technological innovation by hi-fi firms is an "internalised and self-sufficient enterprise" (May *et al.*, 2001: p372) using the resources of their own R&D departments. This is because hi-fi is a field where the pursuit of technical excellence provides scope for taking different approaches.

Source: May et al. *(2001).*

Questions

1 What is the evidence for suggesting that the British hi-fi industry constitutes a cluster?

2 How did Britain's hi-fi cluster originate?

3 What are spin-off companies and what part did they play in the development of Britain's hi-fi cluster?

4 What similarities, if any, are there between Silicon Valley and Britain's hi-fi cluster in terms of the part played by public institutions in the development of the cluster?

5 Which of Markusen's (1996) four types of cluster most appropriately applies to the British hi-fi industry in your view and why?

6 What evidence is there that innovation is a feature of this cluster?

7 What evidence is there to suggest that the success of the hi-fi cluster is based on what Marshall (1890) terms "agglomeration economies"?

8 If the British hi-fi industry cluster stretches from Cambridge to Hampshire (120 miles), is it feasible to describe this as an industrial agglomeration?

9 How valid is Martin and Sunley's (2003) critique of the cluster concept in this instance?

10 Martin and Sunley (2003) suggest that one of the weaknesses of the cluster concept is the extent to which policy-makers have uncritically endorsed the concept – how valid is that criticism in this instance?

Questions for discussion

1 Explain what is meant by the term "agglomeration economies".

2 What is "flexible specialisation" and how has it contributed to a revival of interest in clusters/industrial districts?

3 Explain the value of typologies, such as Markusen's (1996) typology of clusters.

4 What are knowledge spill-overs, how do they arise and how do they contribute to collective learning within a local economy?

5 What is the link between clusters and competitiveness?

6 Why should would-be innovators be aware of clusters?

7 What according to Martin and Sunley (2003) are some of the weaknesses of the cluster concept?

8 Indicate what you consider to be high-technology industries. Provide a rationale for your choice.

9 In an era of globalisation, how can a local economy be competitive?

Exercises

1 Using any innovation cluster of your choice, prepare a presentation that provides an overview of the cluster in terms of its location, scale, and activities and also highlights the benefits for firms of locating within the cluster.

2 Compare and contrast an innovation cluster established as a result of deliberate government policy with one that has emerged without any public policy intervention.

3 Explain what is meant by the term "agglomeration economies" and show how it can contribute to stimulating and encouraging innovation.

4 Prepare a presentation for a group of policy-makers (e.g. a regional development agency) showing how institutional factors can contribute to economic dynamism within a local economy.

5 Using a biography of any innovator, show how he or she has been assisted by being located within an innovative cluster.

6 Using Markusen's typology of clusters, analyse an innovation cluster of your choice.

Further reading

1 **Piore, M. and C. Sabel** (1984) *The Second Industrial Divide: Possibilities for Prosperity*, Basic Books, New York.
Another classic text. Not actually a book about clusters, but it provides a fascinating account of some very distinctive clusters in Northern Italy. It is a bit over the top in its enthusiasm for clusters, but well worth reading, though with a critical eye.

2 Markusen, A. (1996) "Sticky Places in Slippery Space: a Typology of Industrial Districts", *Economic Geography*, 72, pp293–313.

A short article that nonetheless provides a first-class overview of the subject. Don't be put off by the title, industrial district is the term used by Alfred Marshall, the man who came up with the concept, for a cluster. Markusen explains what a cluster is, provides a typology to make sense of the term and then provides some highly informative examples.

3 Storper, M. (1987) "Flexible Specialisation and Regional Agglomerations: the Case of the US Motion Picture Industry", *Annals of the Association of American Geographers*, 77(1) pp104–177.

A different perspective this time. Everyone is familiar with Hollywood and its outputs and the article shows how those outputs are the product of an unusual cluster.

4 Martin, R. and P. Sunley (2003) "Deconstructing Clusters: Chaotic Concept or Policy Panacea", *Journal of Economic Geography*, 3, pp5–35.

As a contrast to the very positive image of clusters presented elsewhere, this paper presents a thorough and robust critique. Martin and Sunley highlight the limitations of the cluster concept and cast doubt on its applicability. In particular they question the readiness of policy-makers to endorse and apply the concept.

CHAPTER 14

National innovation systems

❖ OBJECTIVES

When you have completed this module you will be able to:

- ❖ distinguish those nations with a stronger record of innovation

- ❖ distinguish the institutions and policies that influence the rate of innovation

- ❖ analyse the nature of the institutions that contribute to innovation

- ❖ evaluate the policies that contribute to innovation

Introduction

Some countries appear to be better at innovation than others. In the late eighteenth and early nineteenth centuries Britain was widely recognised as the leading innovator amongst nations. However, the country's success in innovation was, as Freeman (1987: p313) points out:

> ❝ not just a succession of remarkable inventions in the textile and iron industries. Rather it can be attributed to a unique combination of interacting social and economic and technical changes within the national economic space. ❞

Britain at the time was notable because of the strong links which existed between scientists and entrepreneurs; organisational structures (e.g. partnerships) that enabled inventors to raise capital; efficient capital markets at national and local levels that brought capital to where it could be used for innovation; policies of deregulation that helped to reduce restrictions on trade; and reduction in the power of medieval guilds that restricted the movement of labour. These factors all helped to contribute to innovation. They supported and facilitated innovation and they were at the time peculiarly British. Today we would identify these factors as forming part of a national system of innovation. This chapter aims to explain what national systems of innovation are and to show how such systems can encourage or constrain innovation within a particular country.

The public nature of innovation

In the popular imagination, innovation tends to be portrayed as a private activity conducted by individuals. Accounts of well-known innovations, particular in familiar fields such as household products, tend to endorse this picture. James Dyson and the bagless vacuum cleaner, Ron Hickman and the Workmate® workbench are prime examples of the innovator-entrepreneur – individuals working seemingly in isolation to bring about successful innovation. Even when one is dealing with corporate innovation, individuals tend to surface in accounts of innovation. Accounts of the development of "Post-it®" notes by the 3M company give a prominent role to Art Fry, a product designer with 3M, and his realisation that an adhesive developed by a colleague some years earlier might have commercial potential precisely because of its poor sticking qualities.

Nonetheless, whether one is dealing with corporate innovation or individual innovation, there is an important public dimension to innovation. The public dimension arises because many of the inputs and outputs of innovation are in fact public, that is to say they accrue to the public at large. The outputs become public when a successful innovation is diffused through the economy. Then it begins to generate new jobs and new firms, higher incomes and greater prosperity as well as increased tax revenues and know-how. The inputs include such things as education and training, knowledge and intellectual property rights. These assets tend to have "public" properties (Afuah, 2003). Much knowledge, for instance, is publicly available. Even if it has been developed by individuals or organisations, it enters the public domain and becomes publicly available. In a knowledge-based economy specialised knowledge tends to be held by an ever-increasing number of institutions, including many that are public by nature. This trend means that individuals and firms have increasingly to be able to access a range of sources of knowledge and apply them to their own needs if they wish to be successful.

A recent report by the OECD (1997) has extended the public dimension still further. It notes that the overall performance of an economy depends not so much on how specific institutions (firms, research institutes, universities) perform, but on how they interact with each other as elements of a "collective" system of knowledge creation and use, and their interplay with social institutions such as values, norms and legal frameworks.

The notion of a collective system recognises that, although innovation is often introduced by private individuals and private firms, it is ultimately the product of a system of institutions that are closely linked together by economic and social relationships (Simonetti, 2001). The term "system of innovation" describes the configuration of institutions and the resulting flows of knowledge. Such systems can operate at the level of the nation state, the region or the industry sector:

- *National innovation systems*

  I.e. a country-specific system such as the national innovation system of the UK or Japan

- *Regional innovation systems*

  I.e. an innovation based on a specific location or place such as Silicon Valley in California or Motor Sport Valley in Oxfordshire in the UK

- *Sector innovation system*

  I.e. an industry-specific innovation system such as those of the pharmaceutical or aerospace industries

National innovation systems

Dahleman (1994: p554) defines a national innovation system as:

> the network of agents and set of policies and institutions that affect the introduction of technology that is new to the economy … [including] policies toward foreign direct investment, arm's length technology transfer, intellectual property rights, and importation of capital goods. The innovation system also comprises the network of public and private institutions and agents supporting or undertaking scientific and technological activities, including research and development, technology diffusion, and creation of technical human capital.

The idea of a national innovation system is that it describes the arrangements pertinent to innovation that prevail within a particular nation state. "National" implies that we are dealing here with aspects influenced by the nation state. Thus, we are dealing primarily with institutions established by or specific to a particular nation state. In an age of globalisation, the nation state still exerts a high degree of influence. There are big differences in the innovative performance of nations and this is increasingly recognised as having links to the characteristics of particular national innovation systems. Innovation here describes the processes by which firms market and put into practice product designs and manufacturing processes that are new to them (Barker and Goto, 1998). In terms of knowledge, innovation in this context includes both the creation of new knowledge and existing knowledge. In either case it refers to knowledge from inside the firm and outside and, where the latter is concerned, primarily knowledge that resides within the country where the firm is based (though it could also be from outside).

The term "system" refers to the set of institutions whose actions and interactions have a bearing on the innovative performance of national firms. As the quotation from Dahleman (1994) indicates, it includes aspects of the financial system, the educational system, the attitudes and behaviours of firms and the role of government organisations.

Simonetti (2001) stresses that the notion of a system of innovation recognises that tacit knowledge has a vitally important role to play in the innovation process. If all knowledge was explicit and codified, firms could just purchase it like any other factor of production. However, the presence of tacit knowledge means that firms have to interact with other firms and a variety of different organisations in order to acquire knowledge and use it effectively.

Governance

The pressure of interactions and linkages in a system raises the issue of governance – in other words how the system itself is governed (Simonetti, 2001). National innovation systems tend to exhibit three types of governance mechanism.

- corporate governance
- political governance
- network governance

Corporate governance describes the mechanism surrounding the exercise and control of corporate ownership. Within capitalist economies it operates through the market mechanism. Two main approaches to corporate governance are generally recognised. Albert (1992) terms the first "Anglo-Saxon" and the second "Nippon Rhineland". Under the Anglo-Saxon model, which is found in the US and the UK, there is a clear separation of ownership of corporate undertakings from their control. Ownership lies in the hands of stakeholders, many of whom are institutional innovators such as pension funds, while control is left to a cadre of professional managers. The two are mediated through the stock market. Shareholders know little about the internal operation of the firms in which they invest. An efficient stock market means they can switch investments quickly and easily and investors' motivation to hold a particular stock is high due to increasing dividend payments, generally based on short-term profits. Professional managers are trained to deliver such profits through MBA courses in the US and accountancy training in the UK. This model of corporate governance tends to favour the active management of a portfolio of businesses with the harvesting of assets within a fairly short timescale. Some argue that it is not conducive to innovation since the short-term perspective means that it may not provide the "patient capital" required for innovation.

Under the Nippon-Rhineland model of governance, which as its name implies is found in countries such as Japan and Germany, there is no sharp division between ownership and control. The presence of multiple stakeholders means that banks, suppliers and even employees have a stake in the management of the firm. In Germany, for instance, banks have been important as sources of investment capital and as a consequence have often been closely involved in the day-to-day governance of the firm (Moran, 2001). As well as having a stake in the firm these stakeholder groups have usually had detailed knowledge of, and taken a detailed interest in, internal aspects of the firm including its technological competence. This has important consequences as far as innovation is concerned. The stakeholders are in a much better position to evaluate the long-term commercial potential of R&D activities. This is reflected in a tendency for firms in countries strongly influenced by the Nippon-Rhineland model to invest more strongly in R&D than those in the UK and the US (Tidd and Brocklehurst, 1999).

However as Tidd and Brocklehurst (1999) point out, during the 1990s there have been growing doubts about the supposed superiority of the Nippon-Rhineland model in terms of R&D. In particular the US appears to have reasserted its lead in information technology and biotechnology.

Political governance refers to the role of government in fostering innovation. This role centres around two functions: the policy function and regulating function.

The regulatory function covers intellectual property rights and environmental protection. Intellectual property rights (IPR) are critical for innovation. IPR regimes are generally designed to promote innovation. Without a strong IPR regime, it is difficult for innovators to appropriate the benefits of their endeavours. Instead imitation, copying and even counterfeiting tend to proliferate. Clearly, if the rewards for genuine innovation appear to be low, this will discourage innovation and a country's overall performance will be poor.

While the remit of government in providing environmental protection falls outside of the remit of national innovation systems, it can influence innovation in that a requirement to meet environmental standards can act as a useful spur to innovation.

The National Literacy Strategy

In 1998 the UK government introduced the National Literacy Strategy into primary schools in England. Using ideas and teaching methods developed in New Zealand and Australia, the strategy was the first prescribed scheme for the teaching of literacy to be used in England. The strategy introduced learning objectives for three aspects of literacy:

- text level (reading and writing)
- sentence level (grammar)
- word level (spelling and vocabulary)

These formed a part of a comprehensive scheme of objectives for each term for each primary school year group, from Reception (aged 4–5 years) to Year 6 (aged 10–11 years). Included in the strategy was the introduction of a "literacy hour," a sequence of one-hour-per-day lessons involving whole class teaching, independent work and a plenary session.

The strategy was implemented in primary schools in England the following year. As an education initiative it was the first time a nationwide comprehensive scheme for literacy had been adopted in England, where the education system had developed at local level and left the delivery of the curriculum to individual schools.

The strategy was supported by resources and support developed at a national level. These included high-quality teaching and learning resources that extended to:

- intervention programmes for children who are just below the age expected levels
- lesson plans
- materials to support areas of teaching, e.g. grammar for writing, spelling banks and progression in phonetics

The support included locally based consultants able to provide guidance and support as well as running regular training sessions.

A year later a National Numeracy Strategy followed.

Network governance recognises that increasingly innovation takes place through firms working together with other organisations. These organisations are likely to include many of the institutions that play an important role within national systems of innovation such as universities, educational establishments, research bodies and financial institutions. Within such networks relationships will not necessarily be governed by the market mechanism. While some services within the network may be bought and sold, some, in particular those associated with advice and guidance, may be provided on a non-market basis through common interest and mutual trust reinforced by some form of common cultural background.

Simonetti (2001) gives the example of links and relationships between firms and universities. These links can take a variety of different forms. Firms and universities may work together on government-sponsored research programmes. Scientists working in firms may well retain informal contact with the universities where they were trained. Scientists working in firms will attend conferences where they meet and have contact with their counterparts in universities. Links such as these all provide opportunities for knowledge transfer, especially the transfer of tacit knowledge which can play a vital role in the process of innovation. Nor need the contact be confined to the scientific, for activities such as design, marketing and production may all benefit from links with universities.

Arrangements such as these will tend to be self-organising and self-governing. In some instances where shared interests emerge between the parties in a network then mutual interest bodies such as trade associations and professional bodies may have a part to play in governing relationships. Such bodies may work to pool information, identify common interests and agree strategies designed to promote collaboration. Sometimes the collaboration can extend to the setting of standards. These can be important actions as a new technological paradigm emerges. The early phases of such a paradigm will typically see a number of competing product architectures or configurations. Competition of this sort can lead to compatibility problems for consumers and users that ultimately slow the diffusion of an innovation. By agreeing and setting standards, trade associations can help to further innovation.

Institutions

At the heart of any system of innovation lies what Freeman (1987) describes as: "The network of institutions in the public and private sectors whose activities and interactions initiate, import, modify and diffuse technologies".

Inevitably the range of institutions that this encompasses is extremely broad as it includes all those that in some way influence the creation and use of technology (Dodgson and Bessant, 1996) (see Figure 14.1).

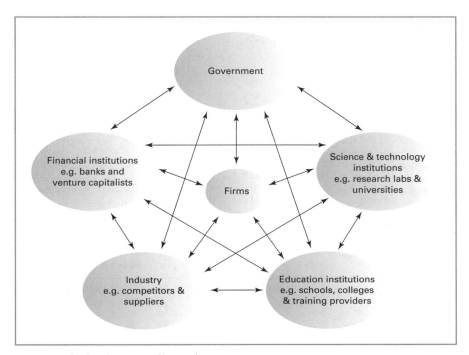

FIGURE 14.1 National systems of innovation

A broad categorisation of those institutions would include:

- industrial institutions, e.g. firms and industry sectors
- financial institutions, e.g. banks and venture capitalists
- science and technology institutions, e.g. universities and public research laboratories
- educational institutions, e.g. schools, colleges and training providers

Industrial institutions

Industrial institutions encompass both the broad industry structure that prevails within an economy and the range of industrial undertakings with which a firm competes and from which it obtains components and materials. Industry structure covers the mix of industries present within an economy, especially the proportion of high-technology industries and the size distribution of firms. Both of these dimensions can influence the level of innovation.

In terms of competition a key factor is likely to be the overall level of competitiveness within an economy. While Schumpeter argued that monopoly conditions might actually be beneficial for innovation, in that monopoly profits could provide scope for funding high levels of R&D – generally competitive conditions are associated with economic dynamism, which in turn facilitates the diffusion of innovation.

Similarly, supply conditions can be important in facilitating innovation. The availability of high-quality components at appropriate prices can be a powerful boost to innovation. The development of the personal computer industry in the US in the late 1970s would undoubtedly have been much slower had it not been for the ready availability of microprocessors, disk drives and other computer accessories.

The significance of industrial institutions comes into sharp relief when one compares national innovation systems. Table 14.1 compares the national systems of innovation of Japan and the USSR in the 1970s. Although the USSR spent more, in fact much more, on R&D than Japan, it had a relatively poor record of innovation. A key factor was the USSR's poorly developed industrial system.

Japan	USSR
High R&D/GNP Ratio (2.5%)	Very high R&D/GNP Ratio (4%)
Low proportion of Military/Space R&D (<2% of R&D)	Very high proportion of Military/Space R&D (>70% R&D)
High proportion of R&D at firm level (>60%)	Low proportion of R&D at firm level (<10%)
R&D and imported technology integrated into production	R&D, imported technology and production poorly integrated with weak linkages
Strong user–producer and subcontractor linkages	Weak or non-existent linkages between marketing, production and procurement
Strong incentives to innovate at the firm level	Largely top-down innovation following government policy objectives
Intensive experience of competition in international markets	Relatively weak exposure to international competition

TABLE 14.1 National systems of innovation: Japan and USSR (1970s)
Source: Freeman and Soete (1997) *The Economics of Industrial Innovation*, 3rd edn, Continuum International Publishing Group

Mini Case

CERN and the World Wide Web

CERN is the European particle physics laboratory. It is a public research laboratory devoted to basic research in physics. It is located close to Mont Blanc just outside Geneva in Switzerland. CERN employs scientists from all over Europe. In 1980 these scientists included a young software engineer who had recently graduated from Oxford University where he studied physics. His name was Tim Berners-Lee.

Berners-Lee soon noticed that his fellow scientists tended to bring their own computers and their own software with them when they joined CERN. Given that they came from all over Europe, this often made it difficult to track what they were doing. Berners-Lee began to think about creating a space in which every computer at CERN would be available to him and to others in the laboratory. When he returned to CERN in 1984, this time as a full-time researcher, he began to pursue this idea further.

By 1990 he had developed the necessary software. It would sit on top of the Internet using its computer networking facilities. It comprised three elements:

- a computer language for formatting hypertext files: Hypertext Markup Language (HTML)
- a protocol for switching between files: Hypertext Transfer Protocol (HTTP)
- a unique address code: Universal Resource Locator (URL)

By the end of 1990 the software was running successfully on the computers of CERN. It now needed a name. Unhappy with his first attempt "The Information Mine" which produced the acronym TIM, Berners-Lee eventually opted for World Wide Web. Because he was an employee of CERN, the laboratory owned the intellectual property rights to the World Wide Web. The bosses at CERN were unsure what to do with these intellectual property rights. Eventually they came round to Berners-Lee's view that as a public research facility they should release the rights and allow the public access to the World Wide Web without charge.

Source: Cassidy (2002).

Mini Case

Oxford Instruments

It was while working as a Senior Research Officer at the Clarendon Laboratory at Oxford University that Martin Wood, together with his wife Audrey, founded Oxford Instruments. The company began as very much a part-time venture in the early years, with Martin Wood advising on the equipping of laboratories and most of the work coming through his contacts at the Clarendon Laboratory. In time he and his wife came to realise that many of these laboratories such as the Royal Radar Establishment (RRE) in Malvern and the Harwell Laboratory of the UK Atomic Energy Authority (UKAEA) had a requirement for powerful magnets that they were finding hard to fulfil. As a result Oxford Instruments moved into the manufacture of industrial magnets. Using their garden shed as a workshop, they bought an old lathe at auction and arranged to borrow the Clarendon Laboratory's special machine for winding magnetic coils. Material supplies were less of a problem because Martin Wood was dealing with the same suppliers that he dealt with regularly at the University. The new company employed a retired Clarendon Laboratory technician on a part-time basis with the administration being undertaken by Martin's wife Audrey.

Source: Wood (2001).

Science and technology institutions

We have already seen that innovation is in many respects an example of "public goods" where the benefits accrue not just to private individuals but to society at large. This causes problems in funding R&D, because individuals or firms may be reluctant to fund it if they feel they are unlikely to appropriate the benefits. One way round this difficulty is for the government to step in and fund R&D.

Public funding of R&D in this way can provide additional benefits beyond finding a way around the problem of appropriability. Afuah (2003) identifies four such benefits:

- training the workforce in skills needed for innovation
- stimulating private firms to invest in related innovations
- gaining economies of scale in R&D
- reducing the cost of firms entering new markets

The training function occurs where large publicly funded research projects require large numbers of scientists/technicians to be trained in particular skills. Afuah (2003) gives the example of the US Defense Department's Advanced Research Projects Agency (DARPA) sponsoring research into computer networks, with the result that when the Internet began to take off it was relatively easy for firms to find employees with the necessary computing skills. Silicon Valley provides a good example of stimulating private firms to invest in related innovations. Much of the early development of Silicon Valley was based on government-funded research into electronics in the aerospace field in the 1950s and 1960s which produced a string of related innovations in the computing field in the 1970s (Castells and Hall, 1994). Space programmes provide an example of economies of scale in R&D. The European Space Agency (ESA), for example, funds research that would be prohibitively expensive if undertaken by individual European nations or single firms. Finally, governments can facilitate market entry, as in the case of the US's entry into the commercial jet airliner market where the R&D costs associated with developing the Boeing 707 airliner were largely paid for by the KC-135 tanker aircraft developed for the US Air Force.

Government sponsorship of R&D can take a variety of contexts. Afuah (2003: p311) identifies four:

- public research laboratories
- universities
- firms
- consortia

Public research bodies include organisations like the National Physical Laboratory at Bushey Park in Hertfordshire, the Atomic Energy Research Establishment at Harwell in Oxfordshire and the Royal Aircraft Establishment at Farnborough in Hampshire. They are funded by the UK government and undertake both basic and applied research. A good example of research carried out in a government research laboratory is the work undertaken in the 1960s by the Royal Aircraft Establishment at Farnborough into carbon fibre. This work not only resulted in an in-depth understanding of the process for producing carbon fibre, but led to a patent being granted in 1968 and the negotiation of licences for commercial manufacture to three firms: Courtaulds, Morgan Crucible and Rolls-Royce.

Government-sponsored research is also carried out by universities. In the UK this can take a variety of forms of which the commonest are research projects carried out directly for government departments and those undertaken by the government-funded research councils such as the Engineering and Physical Science Research Council (EPSRC) and the Medical Research Council (MRC). As with government research laboratories this can involve both basic and applied research. An outstanding example of the latter would be the discovery of the double helix structure of DNA by Watson and Crick at Cambridge University in conjunction with work by Wilkes and Franklin at King's College, London (Maddox, 2002).

The government also sponsors R&D that is carried out by firms. This sort of work tends to be applied rather than basic research with a view to the development of specific products. The "Launch Aid" provided to the UK aerospace industry to facilitate the development of new aircraft and engines is typically of this type of R&D. For instance, when Rolls-Royce developed the all new 25,000-lb thrust V2500 engine for the Airbus A320, it received £70 million in launch aid from the UK government (Kavianto, 1997).

The fourth category of government-sponsored research is the funding of consortia, which typically comprise government research laboratories, universities and industrial firms or some combination of the three.

Finally, Afuah (2003) reminds us that the range of innovations that have benefited from government funding of R&D includes a wide range of high-technology products including: the Internet, UNIX, computers, semiconductors, RISC technology and the jet engine.

Financial institutions

As we saw in Chapter 10, innovation requires finance. Within a market economy, the capital market will be the source of funding for innovation. The function of the capital market is to link savers and investors. The latter in this instance will be individuals and organisations undertaking innovation. The capital market is made up of a variety of financial institutions which act as intermediaries. These financial institutions fall within the following categories:

- commercial banks
- investment banks
- venture capitalists

Banks as we have already seen play a role in innovation. However, the support they provide tends to be in the form of banking services rather than capital. This reflects the generic nature of commercial banks in the UK, which serve the full range of industry sectors rather than providing specialist finance for innovators. The generic nature of commercial banks means they do not normally fund innovation directly. Most banks simply do not have the capability to evaluate the risks – both market and technical – involved.

Investment banks are specialist financial institutions. They specialise in corporate finance, particularly equity finance through the stock market (e.g. initial public offerings (IPOs)) and mergers and acquisitions. This sort of finance can play an important part in innovation. However, it has to be said that historically this sort of finance has tended to be used later in the innovation cycle, when an innovation has already achieved at least some market success. This is because, in order to access equity finance, it is normally necessary to have a track record in terms of sales and profitability.

In terms of institutions, this leaves venture capitalist organisations. These are specialist financial institutions which take an equity stake in firms in order to provide funding for major developments such as innovation. In the UK the leading venture capital organisation is 3i. Since it was founded in 1945 it has funded a large number of firms, though usually only when they have reached a certain size. Venture capitalist organisations like 3i typically invest substantial sums of £100,000 or more. Hence it is mainly innovation in larger firms that is funded by venture capitalists.

Educational institutions

Human capital is vital to innovation. It is a source of both knowledge and skills. The institutions that provide knowledge and skills are:

- schools
- colleges
- universities

The school system provides the generic skills required for innovation. These include skills in literacy and numeracy as well as a range of generic skills associated with learning, problem-solving and creativity.

Colleges generally provide technical and vocational training to develop a range of work-related skills. Historically such training in the UK has been highly fragmented. There have been attempts to re-organise and re-structure the system, such as the creation of a Technician Education Council (TEC) in the 1970s and the introduction of National Vocational Qualifications (NVQs) in the 1990s. Although influenced by the highly structured and very effective German model of technical education, none of these reforms had a significant impact on the relatively low skills levels that prevailed in the UK. As Howells notes (2005: p241): "In this regard, the British 'reform' had continuity with the old-style, voluntary institutions of informal British apprenticeship".

The third level within this institutional framework comprises the universities, who provide degree-level and postgraduate courses. In terms of their contribution to innovation, there are two crucial aspects of university education. First, the proportion of the population that attends such institutions and, second, the proportion of those who attend that take science, engineering and technology courses. In the UK the university system has historically been highly elitist, with only about 10 per cent of the population attending university. This has resulted in an outstanding record of achievement in terms of scientific breakthroughs; but it has equally been blamed by some for Britain's apparently poor record in terms of successful innovations.

CASE STUDY: BACKING AUSTRALIA'S ABILITY

A case by Renu Agarwal and David Smith

In recent years the Australian economy has been relatively prosperous. The country has enjoyed a high rate of economic growth with the annual rate of growth averaging 3.5 per cent for the last decade and a low level of unemployment. A factor in this has been relatively high commodity prices, which have benefited economies like Australia which have large agricultural and natural resource sectors. Productivity in these sectors has also increased markedly. Consequently rising resource exports have fostered growth and prosperity.

Despite this apparently good performance, concerns have been expressed about Australia's international performance in terms of the level of innovation. Although Australia enjoys levels of expenditure on research and development and education that are comparable to other OECD countries, and has a well-developed and well-regarded university system, from the early 1990s a range of concerns were raised over Australia's relatively poor track record on commercialisation of research. The view was expressed that, despite the country having a strong track record on scientific research, this was not feeding through into the commercialisation of research to deliver new products and services. Some suggested that academics felt reluctant to be seen to be profiting from their research. Added to this were concerns over the lack of well-developed venture capital markets in Australia and the comparatively unsophisticated nature of the venture capital provision that was available. Some even argued that these inadequacies were leading to a "brain drain" as young scientists, researchers and entrepreneurs left the country for less risk-averse environments overseas. Against this background, the need for Australia to invest in research and development was seen as critical to the nation's ability to maintain its international competitiveness.

A measure of the concern felt about the country's capability to sustain innovation can be gauged from some of the policy initiatives designed to boost innovation activity introduced by the Australian government in the late 1990s and early 2000s. In 1997 the government's "Investment for Growth" statement introduced a programme designed to boost the innovative capacity of firms. Two years later in August 1999, the government commissioned Australia's Chief Scientist, Dr Robin Batterham, to review the effectiveness of the country's science, engineering and technology base in supporting innovation. In the same year the government published a White Paper entitled "Knowledge and Innovation", outlining a new policy and funding framework to enable universities to contribute more effectively to the national system of innovation. In addition the government also injected $614 million into health and medical research in response to a report by the Health and Medical Research Strategy Review, a move designed to double the National Health & Medical Research Council's annual budget by 2005. The government also introduced a new capital gains tax (CGT) system designed to encourage risk-taking and entrepreneurial behaviour, and set up the Innovation Investment Fund (IIF) in order to stimulate overseas and domestic early-stage venture capital investment in new technology.

Then in 2000, the government, working closely with the Business Council of Australia, called a National Innovation Summit. Attended by more than 500 senior figures from across the scientific and business communities, it met to assess the strengths and weaknesses of Australia's system of innovation. The Summit's recommendations highlighted the need for government, business, education and research organisations to work together in order to enhance the country's capability for innovation.

Finally, in 2004 the government published, "Backing Australia's Ability," a five-year strategy for science, research and innovation, designed to "pursue excellence in science, research and technology, to build an even more highly skilled workforce and increase opportunities for the commercialisation of new ideas" (DCITA, 2004: p3).

The strategy had three principal aims:

1 to strengthen Australia's ability to generate ideas and undertake research

2 to accelerate the commercial application of these ideas

3 to develop and retain skills

The first of these aims was designed to bolster the flow of new ideas which underpin innovation, to create critical mass in leading research fields, and to build competitive advantage in key sectors, especially ICT and biotechnology. In support of this the strategy provided significant investment comprising both additional funding and incentives. Funding included an extra $736 million for the Australian Research Council for competitive grants, $337 million for infrastructure projects, $246 million for upgrading universities' infrastructure and $176 million to establish Centres of Excellence in ICT and Biotechnology. The incentives were designed to stimulate business investment in R&D, and included new tax concessions to encourage companies to increase their R&D (estimated to be worth $115 million over five years), a rebate to assist small companies to undertake R&D and continued direct grant assistance via the START scheme valued at $535 million over five years.

The second of these aims, accelerating the commercial application of ideas focused on improving the flow of finance into business innovation and stimulating innovative firms by improving the country's capability to commercialise research and new technologies. It included a range of initiatives focused on enhancing the country's capacity to create innovative enterprises, encouraging spin-offs, strengthening IP and increasing access to global research and technologies. Specific measures included doubling the value of the Commercialising Emerging Technologies (COMET) programme which provides assistance to firms in improving their commercialising skills, enhancing spin-off opportunities by providing an additional $227 million for the Cooperative Research Centres Program, an additional $100 million for the Innovation Access Program, and sector specific assistance to biotechnology and agriculture.

Finally the third aim of developing and retaining skills included a range of initiatives designed to enhance the nation's skill base and encourage a wider interest in science, mathematics and technology. It included measures to increase university places in critical fields such as ICT, mathematics and science, support ongoing skills development and enhance science and technology literacy, provide increased access to online learning opportunities and boost the skills base through immigration.

The total value of the initiatives that formed part of the strategy was some $2.9 billion spread over five years. This expenditure was designed to underpin the $6 billion contributed to research made by business and research organisations. However, as important as the financial resources was the theme of the "Backing Australia's Ability" strategy which emphasised "the complex nature of innovation and the importance of the people, linkages and interactions between the different system elements" (DCITA, 2004). Evidently, Australia's

National Innovation System had several excellent outcomes, yet in reality it lacked strategic effectiveness, which was compromised due to the lack of policy focus and collaborative thinking in government, public agencies, businesses and academic institutions with major gaps at both the strategic and operational levels. Not only that, a survey by ABS-DITR (2006) entitled "Patterns of Innovation in Australian Business" identified the focus being limited to technological innovations, rather than organisational or institutional innovations. Similarly a recent report by the Committee of Economic Development of Australia (CEDA 2007) entitled "Competing through Innovation – An International Perspective" identified shortcomings of the strategy that require urgent attention.

It is in this context that the Australian Labor government (appointed in November 2007) recently completed a review of the Australian National Innovation System detailed in their report "Venturous Australia – Building Strength in Innovation" (DIISR, 2008). The government is currently considering the review's recommendations and preparing a ten-year White Paper on Innovation. This will hopefully address some or all of the shortcomings of the current strategy, promoting both the generation and systematic application of knowledge within and across sectors, and building up dynamic capabilities at the firm and organisational levels to position Australia for long-term competitive success in global markets. The outcomes of this review are awaited; however, the collaborative efforts of the government working jointly with business, industry and academic institutions should help contribute to the innovation performance of the Australian economy as a whole, providing an integrated national policy and a funding framework for the development of a knowledge-based economy.

Sources: DCITA (2004); Ferris (2001); Mazzarol and Reboud (2007); ABS-DITR (2006); CEDA (2007); DIISR (2008).

Questions

1 What aspects of the Australian economy were the concerns of the 1990s directed at?
2 Which institutions within the national innovation system were seen as failing (refer to Figure 14.1)?
3 Which of the linkages between institutions within the national innovation system were seen as inadequate?
4 What is meant by commercialisation of research?
5 How can one have a strong record of scientific research and a relatively poor record of innovation?
6 Using Figure 14.1 as a template, draw a diagram that shows the institutions affected by the Australian government's strategy "Backing Australia's Ability". What does the diagram indicate about the extent to which the strategy affected Australia's national innovation system?
7 What is venture capital? What is the connection between venture capital and innovation?
8 In terms of its national innovation system, why should a country be concerned about a lack of venture capital?
9 What features of Australia's national innovation system are likely to be improved as a result of the measures taken in the late 1990s and early 2000s? (In your answer refer to Figure 14.1.)
10 What were some of the weaknesses of the "Backing Australia's Ability" strategy which required urgent attention and focus?

?   ## Questions for discussion

1 If innovation is conducted by individuals or organisations, how can there be a public domain to innovation?
2 Who are the agents involved in the introduction of new technology?
3 What are the institutions associated with intellectual property rights?
4 What is the difference between the Anglo-Saxon and Nippon-Rhineland systems of corporate governance?
5 What are the institutions typically associated with science and technology?
6 How can corporate governance affect innovation?
7 What is a regional system of innovation?
8 How do financial institutions contribute to a national system of innovation?
9 What part do schools play in a national system of innovation?
10 Using examples show how changes in higher education have affected the UK's national innovation system.
11 What part do financial institutions play within a national system of innovation?
12 What is the national science base and how does it contribute to innovation?

Exercises

1 Using an example of a public research institution of your choice, show how such institutions contribute to the UK's national system of innovation.
2 Critically review the UK's education system in terms of its contribution to the national system of innovation.
3 Take any country of your choice and identify the main features of its national system of innovation.
4 From the perspective of an innovator, how useful is the concept of a regional system of innovation?
5 What has tacit knowledge to do with a system of innovation?

Further reading

1 **Nelson, R.R.** (1993) *National Innovation Systems: A Comprehensive Analysis*, Oxford University Press, NY.
   The main text on the subject. Well worth consulting. It is authoritative and balanced, and in any event Richard Nelson virtually invented the concept of a national innovation system.
2 **OECD** (1997) *National Innovation Systems*, OECD, Paris.
   Similarly authoritative, but this time for different reasons. It provides an overview of the national innovation systems of OECD countries.

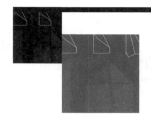

Bibliography

Abernathy, W.J. and J. Utterback (1978) "Patterns of industrial innovation", in M.L. Tushman and W.L.Moore (eds) *Readings in the Management of Innovation*, pp97–108, Harper Collins, New York.

ABS-DITR (2006) *Patterns of Innovation in Australian Business*. Department of Industry, Tourism and Resources, Commonwealth of Australia, Canberra.

Afuah, A. (2003) *Innovation Management: Strategies, Implementation and Profit*, 2nd edn, Oxford University Press, New York.

Albert, M. (1992) *Capitalism against Capitalism*, Whurr, London.

Allen, T. (1977) *Managing the Flow of Technology*, MIT Press, Cambridge, MA.

Amesse, F., C. Denranleau, H. Etermad, Y. Fortier and L. Seguin-Dulude (1991) "The Individual Inventor and the Role of Entrepreneurship: A Survey of the Canadian Experience", *Research Policy*, 20, pp13–27.

Anderson, I. and R. Kennedy (1986) *Sinclair and the Sunrise Technology*, Penguin Books, Harmondsworth.

Anderson, P. and M.L. Tushman (1990) "Technological Discontinuities and Dominant Designs: A Cyclical Model of Technological Change", *Administrative Science Quarterly*, 35, pp604–633.

Andriopoulus, C. and P. Dawson (2009) *Managing Change, Creativity and Innovation*, Sage Publications, London.

Ansoff, I. (1988) *Corporate Strategy*, revd edn, Penguin Books, Harmondsworth.

Armstrong, H. and J. Taylor (2000) *Regional Economics and Policy*, 3rd edn, Blackwell, Oxford.

Aston, B. and M. Williams (1996) *Playing to Win: The Success of UK Motorsport Engineering*, Institute for Public Policy Research, London.

Athreye, S. (2000) "Agglomeration and Growth: A Study of the Cambridge High-Tech Cluster", in T. Bresnahan and A. Gambardella (eds) *Building High-Tech Clusters: Silicon Valley and Beyond*, Cambridge University Press, Cambridge.

Audia, P.G. and C.L. Rider (2005) "A Garage and an Idea: What More Does an Entrepreneur Need?" *California Management Review*, 18(1), 4–2005, pp6–28.

Augsdorfer, P. (2005) "Bootlegging and Path Dependency", *Research Policy*, 34(1), pp1–11.

Augsdorfer, P. (2008) "Managing the Unmanageable", *Research-Technology Management*, 51(4), pp41–47.

Autio, E. (1995) "Four Types of Innovators: a Conceptual and Empirical Study of New, Technology-Based Companies as Innovators", *Entrepreneurship and Regional Development*, 7, pp233–248.

Bainbridge, D. (1999) *Intellectual Property*, 4th edn, FT/Pitman Publishing, London.

Bainbridge, D. (2007) *Intellectual Property*, 6th edn, Pearson Longman, London.

Baker, M. and S. Hart (1999) *Product Strategy and Management*, FT Prentice Hall, Harlow.

Balasubramanyam, V.N. and A. Balasubramanyam (2000) "The Software Cluster in Bangalore", in J.H. Dunning (ed) *Regions, Globalization and the Knowledge Economy*, Oxford University Press, Oxford.

Bamfield, J. (1994) "The Adoption of Electronic Data Interchange by Retailers", *International Journal of Retail and Distribution Management*, 22(2), pp3–11.

Bank of England (2001) *Financing of Technology-based Small Firms*, Bank of England, London.

Bardsley, G. (2005) *Issigonis: The Official Biography*, Icon Books, Cambridge.

Barker, B. and A. Goto (1998) "Technological Systems, Innovation and Transfers", in G. Thompson (ed) *Economic Dynamism in the Asia-Pacific*, Routledge, London.

Barnatt, C. and K. Starkey (1994) "The Emergence of Flexible Networks in the UK Television Industry", *British Journal of Management*, 5(4), pp251–260.

Basalla, G. (1988) *The Evolution of Technology*, Cambridge University Press, Cambridge.

Baxter, P. (1997) *The Inventor's Guide to How to Patent and Profit from Your Idea*, British Library, London.

Baylis, T. (1999) *Clock This: My Life as an Inventor*, Headline Publishing, London.

Beaver, G. (2002) *Small Business, Entrepreneurship and Enterprise Development*, FT Prentice Hall, Harlow.

Beck-Burridge, M. and J. Walton (2000) *Britain's Winning Formula: Achieving World Leadership in Motorsports*, Macmillan, Basingstoke.

Beddows, A. (2001) "Suggestion Scheme for the Future", *Management Services*, February 2001, 45(2), pp14–15.

Bentley, L. and B. Sherman (2001) *Intellectual Property Law*, Oxford University Press, Oxford.

Berlin, L. (2007) *The Man Behind the Microchip: Robert Noyce and the Creation of Silicon Valley*, Oxford University Press, Oxford.

Berners-Lee, T. (1999) *Weaving the Web: The Past, Present and Future of the World Wide Web by its Inventor*, Texere, Andover.

Berto, F.J. (1999) *The Birth of Dirt: Origins of Mountain Biking*, Van Der Plas Publications, San Francisco, CA.

Bessant, J. and J. Tidd (2007) *Innovation and Entrepreneurship*, John Wiley & Sons Ltd, Chichester.

Betje, P. (1998) *Technological Change in the Modern Economy: Basic Topics and Developments*, Edward Elgar, Cheltenham.

Black, T. (1989) *Intellectual Property in Industry*, Butterworths, London.

Blundel, R. and D.J. Smith (2001) *Business Networks: SMEs and Inter-firm Collaboration: A Review of the Research Literature with Implications for Policy*, Small Business Service, Sheffield.

Branscomb, L. and J. Keller (eds) (1998) *Investing in Innovation*, MIT Press, Cambridge, MA.

Bresnahan, T. and A. Gambardella (eds) (2004) *Building High-Tech Clusters: Silicon Valley and Beyond*, Cambridge University Press, Cambridge.

Brown, D.E. (2002) *Inventing Modern America: From the Microwave to the Mouse*, MIT Press, Cambridge, MA.

Bruce, M. and J. Bessant (2001) *Design in Business: Strategic Innovation through Design*, FT Prentice Hall, Harlow.

Bruce, M. and S.T. Moger (1999) "Dangerous Liaisons: An Application of Supply Chain Modelling for Studying Innovation within the UK Clothing Industry", *Technology Analysis and Strategic Management*, 11(1), pp113–125.

BTG (2002) "UK Scientists Make Breakthrough in Fight Against Coeliac Disease", BTG plc, Press Release 16 October 2002, accessed at *http://www.btgplc.com/News/218/PressReleases.html*.

Bunnell, T. (2002) "Multimedia Utopia? A Geographical Critique of High-Tech Development in Malaysia's Multimedia Super Corridor", *Antipode*, 34(2), pp265–295.

Burgelman, R.A., M.A. Maidique and S.C. Wheelwright (2001) *Strategic Management of Technology and Innovation*, 3rd edn, McGraw-Hill, New York.

Burns, T. and G. Stalker (1961) *The Management of Innovation*, Tavistock, London.

Caird, S. (1994) "Sources of Technological Innovative Ideas and their Significance for Commercial Outcomes in Small Companies", in R. Oakey (ed) *New Technology-based Firms in the 1990s*, Paul Chapman Publishing, London, pp57–67.

Campbell-Kelly, M. (2003) "The Rise and Rise of the Spreadsheet", in M. Campbell-Kelly, M. Croarken, R. Flood and M. Robson (eds) *The History of Mathematical Tables: From Sumer to Spreadsheet*, Oxford University Press, Oxford.

Campbell-Kelly, M. (2004) *From Airline Reservations to Sonic the Hedgehog: A History of the Software Industry*, MIT Press, Cambridge, MA.

Carayannis, E.G., E.H. Robert, K. Kurimara and M.M. Allbritton (1998) "High Technology Spin-Offs from Government R&D Laboratories and Universities", *Technovation*, 18(1), pp1–11.

Cassidy, J. (2002) *Dot Con: the Greatest Story Ever Sold*, Penguin Books, London.

Castells, M. and P. Hall (1994) *Technopoles of the World: The Making of 21st Century Industrial Complexes*, Routledge, London.

CBI (1999) *Connecting Companies: Using Corporate Venturing for Growth*, Confederation of British Industry, London.

CEDA (2007) *Competing through Innovation: An International Perspective*, Committee for Economic Development of Australia, Melbourne.

Cesaroni, F. (2003) "Technology Strategies in the Knowledge Economy: The Licensing Activity of Himont", *International Journal of Innovation Management*, 7(2), pp223–245.

Chaplin, H. and A. Ruby (2006) *Smartbomb: The Quest for Art, Entertainment and Big Bucks in the Videogame Revolution*, Algonquin Books, Chapel Hill, NC.

Chapman, S.D. (2002) *Hosiery and Knitwear: Four Centuries of Small-Scale Industry in Britain c1589–2000*, Pasold Research Fund/Oxford University Press, Oxford.

Chell, E., J.M. Haworth and S.A. Brearley (1991) *The Entrepreneurial Personality: Concepts, Cases and Categories*, Routledge, London.

Chell, E., N. Hedberg-Jalonen and A. Miettinen (1997) "Are Types of Business Owner-Manager Universal? A Cross Country Study of the UK, New Zealand and Finland", in R. Donckels and A. Miettinen (eds) *Entrepreneurship and SME Research: On its Way to the Next Millenium*, Ashgate, Aldershot.

Chesbrough, H. (2003a) *Open Innovation: The New Imperatives for Creating and Profiting from Technologies*, Harvard Business School Press, Boston, MA.

Chesbrough, H. (2003b) "The Era of Open Innovation," *Sloan Management Review*, 44(3), pp35–41.

Chesbrough, H. (2006) *Open Business Models : How to Thrive in the New Innovation Landscape*, Harvard Business School Press, Boston, MA.

Chesbrough, H. and R. Rosenbloom (2002) "The Role of the Business Model in Capturing Value for Innovation", *Industrial and Corporate Change*, 11(3), pp529–566.

Chibber, K. (2009) "The Man who Saved the BBC", *Wired*, 15 April 2009.

Cho, D-S., D.-J. Kim and D.-K. Rhee (1998) "Latecomer Strategies: Evidence from the Semiconductor Industry in Japan and Korea", *Organization Science*, 9(4), pp489–505.

Christensen, C.M. (1992) "Exploring the Limits of the Technology S-curve: Part 1 Component Technologies", *Production and Operations Management*, 1(4), p334.

Christensen, C.M. (1993) "The Rigid Disk Drive Industry: A History of Commercial and Technological Turbulence", *Business History Review*, 67, pp531–588.

Christensen, C.M. (1997) *The Innovator's Dilemma: When New Technologies Cause Great Firms to Fail*, Harvard Business School Press, Boston.

Christofidis, C. and O. Debande (2001) "Financing Innovative Firms Through Venture Capital, EIB Sector Papers", February 2001, European Investment Bank, Luxembourg.

Chu, B. (2008) "Wii: More than Just a Game", *The Guardian*, 30 April 2008.

Church, R.A. (1966) *Economic and Social Change in a Midland Town: Victorian Nottingham 1815–1900*, Frank Cass, London.

Cohen, W.M. and D.A. Leventhal (1990) "Absorptive Capacity: A New Perspective on Learning and Innovation", *Administrative Science Quarterly*, 35, pp128–152.

Collings, T. (2001) *The Piranha Club: Power and Influence in Formula One*, Virgin Books, London.

Conner, M. (2001) *Hans Von Ohain: Elegance in Flight*, American Institute of Aeronautics and Astronautics, Renton, VA.

Conway, S. and F. Steward (2009) *Managing and Shaping Innovation*, Oxford University Press, Oxford.

Cooke, P., M. Heidenreich and H. Braczyk (2004) *Regional Innovation Systems*, 2nd edn, Routledge, London.

Cooper, A. (1999) "The Material Advantage", *Motor Sport*, LXXV, March 1999, pp32–37.

Cooper, A.C. (1971) *The Founding of Technologically-based Firms*, Center for Venture Management, Milwaukee, WI.

Cooper, R.G. (1988) "The New Product Process: A Decision Guide for Management", *Journal of Marketing Management*, 3(3), pp238–255.

Cooper, R.G. (1994) "Third Generation New Product Development Processes", *Journal of Product Innovation Management*, 11, pp3–14.

Cooper, R.G. (2001) *Winning at New Product Development: Accelerating the Process from Idea to Launch*, 3rd edn, Basic Books, New York.

Cooper, R.J. (1990) "Stage-Gate Systems: A New Tool for Managing New Products", *Business Horizons*, May–June, pp20–29.

Coveney, P. and K. Moore (1997) "A Typology of Angels: A Better Way of Examining the Informal Investment Phenomena", in R. Donckels and A. Miettinen (eds) *Entrepreneurship and SME Research: On its Way to the Next Millennium*, Ashgate, Aldershot.

Cox, H., S. Mowatt and M. Prevezer (1999) "From Frozen Fish Fingers to Chilled Chicken Tikka: Organisational Responses to Technical Change in the Late Twentieth Century", *Research Papers in International Business*, 18–99, Centre for International Business, South Bank University, London.

Cox, H., S. Mowatt and M. Prevezer (2003) "New Product Development and Product Supply within a Network Setting: The Chilled Ready-meal Industry in the UK", *Industry and Innovation*, 10(2), pp197–217.

Crombac, G. (2001) *Colin Chapman: The Man and his Cars*, Haynes Publishing, Sparkford.

Curran, J. and R. Blackburn (1994) *Small Firms and Local Economic Networks*, Paul Chapman Publishing, London.

Cusumano, M.A., Y. Mylonadis and R.S. Rosenbloom (1992) "Strategic Maneuvering and Mass-Market Dynamics: The Triumph of VHS over Beta", *Business History Review*, 66, pp51–94.

Dahleman, C.J. (1994) "Technology Strategy in East Asian Developing Economies", *Journal of Asian Economics*, 5(4), pp541–572.

Dahlin, K. and D. Behrens (2005) "When is an Invention Really Radical? Defining and Measuring Technological Radicalness", *Research Policy*, 34(5), pp717–734.

David, P. (1985) "Clio and the Economics of QWERTY", *Economic History*, 75, pp332–357.

Davis, W. (1987) *The Innovators*, Ebury Press, London.

DCITA (2004) *Backing Australia's Ability: Building our Future Through Science and Innovation*, Department of Communications, Information, Technology & Arts, Commonwealth of Australia, Canberra.

Deakins, D. and M. Freel (2003) *Entrepreneurship and Small Firms*, 3rd edn, McGraw-Hill, Maidenhead.

Deutschman, A. (2001) *The Second Coming of Steve Jobs*, Broadway Books, NY.

Deutschman, A. (2004) "The Fabric of Creativity", *Fast Company*, December 2004.

DIISR (2008) *Venturous Australia: Building Strength in Innovation*, Department of Innovation, Industry, Science and Research, Commonwealth of Australia, Canberra.

Dodgson, M. (2000) *The Management of Technological Innovation: An International and Strategic Approach*, Oxford University Press, Oxford.

Dodgson, M. and J. Bessant (1996) *Effective Innovation Policy: A New Approach*, International Thomson Business Press, London.

Dodgson, M., D. Gann and A. Salter (2006) "The Role of Technology in the Shift Towards Open Innovation", *R&D Management*, 36(3) pp333–346.

Dodgson, M., D. Gann and A. Salter (2008) *The Management of Technological Innovation: Strategy and Practice*, revd edn, Oxford University Press, Oxford.

Dodson, S. (2008) "A Cheap Camcorder in Every Pocket", *The Guardian*, 4 September 2008.

Dogannis, R. (2001) *The Airline Business in the 21st Century*, Routledge, London.

Donaghu, M. and R. Barff (1990) "Nike Just Did It – International Subcontracting and Flexibility in Athletic Footwear Production", *Regional Studies*, 24(6), pp537–552.

Dosi, G. (1982) "Technological paradigms and technological trajectories", *Research Policy*, 11, pp147–162.

Doward, J. (1999) "@business: E is for Autonomy", *Observer*, 5 December 1999, Business Section, p9.

Dowling, T. (2001) *The Inventor of Disposable Culture: King Camp Gillette: 1855–1932*, Faber & Faber, London.

DTI (1989) *Applications and Guidance Notes for the SMART Competition*, Department of Trade and Industry, London.

DTI (1993) *Realising Our Potential: A Strategy for Science Engineering and Technology*, Department of Trade and Industry, London.

DTI (2004) *Succeeding Through Innovation, Creating Competitive Advantage through Innovation: A Guide for Small and Medium Sized Businesses*, Department of Trade and Industry, London.

DTI (2005) "R & D Case Studies", Department of Trade and Industry, London. Available online at: *www.dti.gov.uk/r-d/studies/lasers.htm*.

du Gay, P., S. Hall, L. Janes, H. Mackay and K. Negus (1997) *Doing Cultural Studies: The Story of the Sony Walkman*, Sage, London.

Dyson, J. (1997) *Against the Odds*, Orion Business, London.

Dyson, J. (2003) *Against the Odds*, updated edition, Orion Business, London.

Eaglesham, J. (2001) "Hoover Loses Dyson Appeal", *Financial Times*, 5 October 2001.

Economist, The (2007a) "Out of the Dusty Labs", 3 March 2007, 382(8518), pp79–81.

Economist, The (2007b) "Lessons from Apple", 9 June 2007, 383(8532), p11.

Edwards, F. (1972) *Catseyes: Biography of Percy Shaw*, Blackwell, Oxford.

Ellis, C.D. (2006) *Joe Wilson and the Creation of Xerox*, John Wiley and Sons, New York.

Ettlie, J.E. (2006) *Managing Innovation: New Technology, New Products, and New Services in a Global Economy*, 2nd edn, John Wiley & Sons, NY.

Ettlie, J.E., W.P. Bridges and R.D. O'Keefe (1984) "Organizational Strategy and Structural Differences for Radical vs. Incremental Innovation", *Management Science*, 30, pp682–695.

Fagerberg, J. (2005) "Innovation: A Guide to the Literature", in J. Fagerberg, D.C. Mowery and R.R. Nelson (eds) *The Oxford Handbook of Innovation*, Oxford University Press, Oxford, pp1–26.

Fayol, H. (1916) *Administration Industrielle et Générate* (General and Industrial Management), I. Gray (ed), C. Storrs (trans) (1988), rev edn, *Financial Times*, Prentice Hall, London.

Ferris, W.D. (2001) "Australia Chooses: Venture Capital and a Future for Australia", *Australian Journal of Management*, 26, pp45–64.

Fildes, N. (2007) "Game On: Console Makers in Three-way Shoot-out", *The Independent*, 27 October 2007.

Fiol, C.M. (1996) "Squeezing Harder Doesn't Always Work: Continuing the Search for Consistency in Innovation Research", *Academy of Management Review*, 24(4), p1012.

Florida, R. (2002) *The Rise of the Creative Class: And How It's Transforming Work, Leisure, Community and Everyday Life*, Basic Books, NY.

Forbes, N. and D. Wield (2002) *From Followers to Leaders: Managing Technology & Innovation*, Routledge, London.

Ford, D. and C. Ryan (1981) "Taking technology to market", *Harvard Business Review*, March–April, pp117–126.

Foster, R.J. (1986) *Innovation: The Attacker's Advantage*, Summit Books, NY.

Freeman, C. (1974) *The Economics of Industrial Innovation*, Frances Pinter, London.

Freeman, C. (1986) "The Role of Technical Change in National Economic Development", in A. Amin and J.B. Goddard (eds) *Technical Change, Industrial Restructuring and Regional Development*, Unwin & Hyman, London.

Freeman, C. (1987) *Technology Policy and Economic Performance*, Frances Pinter, London.

Freeman, C. and F. Louçã (2001) *As Time Goes By: From Industrial Revolutions to Information Revolution*, Oxford University Press, Oxford.

Freeman, C. and L. Soete (1997) *The Economics of Industrial Innovation*, 3rd edn, Continuum, London.

Fry, S. (2008) "Dork Talk", *The Guardian*, 30 August 2008.

Gabler, N. (2008) *Walt Disney: The Biography*, Aurum Press, London.

Galbraith, J.K. (1956) *American Capitalism*, Houghton Mifflin, Boston.

Galbraith, J.K. (1958) *The Affluent Society*, Penguin Books, Harmondsworth.

Gapper, J. (2005) "Europe is Right to Take a Patent Risk", *Financial Times*, 23 June 2005, p19.

Garnsey, E., G. Lorenzoni and S. Ferriani (2008) "Speciation through entrepreneurial spin-off: The Acorn-ARM story", *Research Policy*, 37(2) pp210–224.

Geroski, P.A. (2000) "Models of Technology Diffusion", *Research Policy*, 29, pp603–625.

Gibbons, J.F. (2000) "The Role of Stanford University" in C.-M. Lee, W.F. Miller, M.G. Hancock and H.S. Rowen (eds) *The Silicon Valley Edge: the Habitat for Innovation and Entrepreneurship*, Stanford University Press, Stanford, CA, pp200–217.

Glaister, K.W. (1988) "The Entrepreneur: Enigma of Economic Theory", *Economics*, Spring 1988, pp2–6.

Goffin, K. and R. Mitchell (2005) *Innovation Management: Strategy and Implementation Using the Pentathalon Framework*, Palgrave Macmillan, Basingstoke.

Golley, J. (1996) *Genesis of the Jet: Frank Whittle and the Invention of the Jet Engine*, Airlife, Marlborough.

Grant, R.M. (2008) *Contemporary Strategic Analysis*, 6th edn, Blackwell, Oxford.

Grantham, A. and R. Kaplinsky (2005) "Getting the Measure of the Electronic Games Industry: Developers and the Management of Innovation", *International Journal of Innovation Management*, 9(2), pp183–213.

Gray, M., E. Golob and A. Markusen (1996) "Big Firms, Long Arms, Wide Shoulders: The Hub-and-Spoke' Industrial District in the Seattle Region", *Regional Studies*, 30(7), pp651–666.

Green, R., J. Cunningham, I. Duggan, M. Giblin, M. Morony and L. Smyth (2001) "Boundaryless Clusters: Information and Communications Technology in Ireland", *The Future of Innovation Conference*, ECIS, Eindehoven, Netherlands, 20–23 September 2001.

Griffiths, K. (2004) "BTG Sues Amazon over Tracking Software", *The Independent*, 16 September 2004, p48.

Gundling, E. (1999) The *3M Way to Innovation: Balancing People and Profit*, Kodansha International, Japan.

Hague, D. and C. Holmes (2006) *Oxford Entrepreneurs*, Council for Industry and Higher Education, London.

Hall, K. (2006) "The Big Ideas Behind Nintendo's Wii", *Business Week*, 16 November 2006.

Hall, P. (1981) "The Geography of the Fifth Kondratieff Cycle", *New Society*, 25 March 1981, pp535–537.

Hall, P., M. Breheny, R. McQuaid and D. Hart (1987) *Western Sunrise: The Genesis and Growth of Britain's Major High Technology Corridor*, Allen and Unwin, London.

Hamilton, J. (2005) *Thomas Cook: The Holiday Maker*, Sutton Publishing, Stroud.

Hands, D., J. Ingram and R. Jerrard (2001) *Design Management Case Studies*, Routledge, Oxford.

Hargadon, A. (2003) *How Breakthroughs Happen*, Harvard Business School Press, Boston, MA.

Harrison, R.T., C.M. Mason and P. Girling (2004) "Financial Bootstrapping and Venture Development in the Software Industry", *Entrepreneurship and Regional Development*, 16, pp307–333.

Henderson, R.M. and K.B. Clark (1990) "Architectural Innovation: The Reconfiguration of Existing Product Technologies and the Failure of Established Firms", *Administrative Science Quarterly*, 35, pp9–30.

Henry, A. (1988) *Grand Prix Design and Technology in the 1980s*, Hazleton Publishing, Richmond.

Henry, J. and D. Walker (1991) *Managing Innovation*, Sage Publications, London.

Henry, N. and S. Pinch (2000a) "Spatialising Knowledge: Placing the Knowledge Community of Motor Sport Valley", *Geoforum*, 31, pp191–208.

Henry, N. and S. Pinch (2000b) "(The) Industrial Agglomeration (of Motor Sport Valley): A Knowledge, Space, Economy Approach", in J. Bryson, P. Daniels, N. Henry and J. Pollard (eds) *Knowledge, Space, Economy*, Routledge, London.

Henry, N., S. Pinch and S. Russell (1996) "In Pole Position? Untraded Interdependencies, New Industrial Spaces and the British Motor Sport Industry", *Area*, 28(1), pp25–36.

Hertel, G., S. Niedner and S. Herrmann, (2003) "Motivation of Software Developers in Open Source Projects: An Internet Based Survey of Contributors to the Linux Kernel", *Research Policy*, 32(7), pp1159–1177.

Herz, J.C. (1997) *Joystick Nation: How Videogames Gobbled Our Money, Won Our Hearts, and Rewired Our Minds*, Abacus Books, London.

Hickman, L. (2006) "Is It OK…to Use an MP3 player?" *The Guardian*, 17 October 2006.

Hitzik, M. (2000) *Dealers of Lightning: Xerox PARC and the Dawn of the Computer Age*, Harper Business, New York.

Hodges, M. (2007) *AK47: The Story of the People's Gun,* Sceptre, London.

Hounshell, D.A. and J.K. Smith (1988) *Science and Corporate Strategy: Du Pont R&D, 1902–1980*, Cambridge University Press, Cambridge.

Howells, J. (2005) *The Management of Innovation and Technology*, Sage Publications, London.

Hughes, T.P. (1989) *American Genesis: A Century of Innovation and Technological Enthusiasm* 1870–1970, Viking, NY.

Huston, L. and N. Sakkab (2006) "Connect and Develop: Inside Proctor and Gamble's New Model for Innovation", *Harvard Business Review*, March, pp58–68.

IDEO (2009) *Culture*, IDEO: Palo Alto, CA. Available online at *URL:http://www.ideo.com/ culture* (accessed 14 April 2009).

Innovation Hub, The (2008) *Annual Report 2007–08,* The Innovation Hub, Pretoria, South Africa. Available online at *http://www.theinnovationhub.com*.

Iskra (2009) *Case Studies*. Available at *http://iskrawind.com*.

Jewkes, J.D., D. Sawers and R. Stillerman (1969) *The Sources of Innovation*, Macmillan, London.

Jomo, K.S. and G. Felker (eds) (1999) *Technology, Competitiveness and the State: Malaysia's Industrial Technology Policies*, Routledge, London.

Jones, D. (2005) *iPod Therefore I am: A Personal Journey*, Weidenfield and Nicholson, London.

Jones, G. (2005) *Reinventing Unilever: Transformation and Tradition*, Oxford University Press, Oxford.

Jones, G. and A. Kraft (2004) "Corporate Venturing: The Origins of Unilever's Pregnancy Test", *Business History*, 46(1), pp100–122.

Jones, L. (2007) *easyJet: The Story of Britain's Biggest Low Cost Airline*, Aurum Press, London.

Jones-Evans, D. (1995) "A Typology of Technology-based Entrepreneurs: A Model Based on Previous Occupational Background", *International Journal of Entrepreneurial Research and Behaviour*, 1(1), pp26–47.

Jones-Evans, D. (1997) "Technical Entrepreneurship, Experience and the Management of Small Technology-based Firms – Exploratory Evidence from the UK", *Entrepreneurship and Regional Development*, 9, pp65–90.

Jones-Evans, D. and P. Westhead (1996) "The High-Technology Small Firm Sector in the UK", *International Journal of Entrepreneurial Research and Behaviour,* 2(1), pp15–35.

Kamm, A. and M. Baird (2002) *John Logie Baird: A Life*, National Museum of Scotland Publishing, Edinburgh.

Kavianto, K. (1997) *UK Launch Aid Experience*, Research Paper No. 260, Warwick Business School, Warwick.

Keeble, D. (1997) "Small Firms, Innovation and Regional Development", *Regional Studies*, 31, pp281–293.

Keeble, D., C. Lawson, B. Moore and F. Wilkinson (1999) "Collective Learning Processes, Networking and 'Institutional Thickness' in the Cambridge Region", *Regional Studies*, 33(4), pp319–332.

Kerin, R.A., P.R. Varadarajan and R.A. Peterson (1992) "First Mover Advantage: A Synthesis, Conceptual Framework and Research Propositions", *Journal of Marketing*, 56, pp33–52.

Khazam, J. and Mowery, D. (1994) "The Commercialization of RISC: Strategies for the Creation of a Dominant Design", *Research Policy*, 23(1), pp89–102.

Kingston, W. (2000) "Antibiotics, Invention and Innovation," *Research Policy*, 29, pp679–710.

Kirzner, I. (1973) *Perception, Opportunity and Profit: Studies in the Theory of Entrepreneurship*, University of Chicago Press, Chicago.

Knight, F.H. (1921) *Risk, Uncertainty and Profit*, University of Chicago Press, Chicago.

Kollmer, H. and M. Davling (2004) "Licensing as a Commercialisation Strategy for New Technology-based firms", *Research Policy*, 33, pp1141–1151.

Krugman, P. (1991) *Geography and Trade*, MIT Press, Cambridge, MA.

Kuhn, T.S. (1970) *The Structure of Scientific Revolutions*, University of Chicago Press, Chicago.

Landis, S. (1987) *The Workbench Book: A Craftsman's Guide to Workbenches*, The Taunton Press, Newtown, CT.

Lange, A. (2002) "Report from the PAL Zone", in L. King (ed) *Game On: The History and Culture of Videogames*, Laurence King Publishing, London.

Lawrence, M. (2002) *Colin Chapman: Wayward Genius*, Breedon Publishing, Derby.

Lawrence, P. (1997) *The Business of Innovation: How to Turn a Patentable Idea into a Profitable Product*, Management Books 2000, Chalford.

Lawson, B. (2005) *How Designers Think: The Design Process Demystified*, 4th edn, Architectural Press, Oxford.

Leadbeater, C. (2006) *The User Innovation Revolution: How Business can Unlock the Value of Customers' Ideas*, National Consumer Council, London.

Lee, C.M., W.F. Miller, M.G. Hancock and H.S. Rowan (2000) *The Silicon Valley Edge: The Habitat for Innovation and Entrepreneurship*, Stanford University Press, Stanford, CA.

Leonard-Barton, D. (1991) "Inanimate Integrators: A Block of Wood Speaks", *Design Management Journal*, Summer 1991, pp61–67.

Levy, S. (1994) *Insanely Great: The Life and Times of Macintosh, The Computer that Changed Everything*, Penguin, London.

Levy, S. (2006) *The Perfect Thing : How the iPod Became the Defining Object of the 21st Century*, Ebury Press, NY.

Lieberman, M.B. and D.B. Montgomery (1988) "First-Mover Advantages", *Strategic Management Journal*, 9, pp41–58.

Linzmayer, O.W. (2004) *Apple Confidential 2.0: The Definitive History of the World's Most Colorful Company*, No Starch Press, San Francisco, CA.

Littler, D. (1988) *Technological Development*, Philip Alan, Oxford.

Loch, C.H. and B.A. Huberman (1999) "A Punctuated Equilibrium Model of Technology Diffusion", *Management Science*, 45(2), p160.

Longhi, C. (1999) "Networks, Collective Learning and Technology Development in Innovative High Technology Regions: The Case of Sophia Antipolis", *Regional Studies*, 33(4), pp333–342.

Longhi, C. and D. Keeble (2000) "High Technology Clusters and Evolutionary Trends in the 1990s", in D. Keeble and F. Wilkinson (eds) *High Technology Clusters, Networking and Collective Learning in Europe*, Ashgate Publishing, Aldershot.

Lüthje, C., C. Herstatt and E. Von Hippel (2005) "User-innovators and 'Local' Information: The Case of Mountain Biking", *Research Policy*, 34, pp951–965.

McClelland, S. (1961) *The Achieving Society*, Van Nostrand, Princeton, NJ.

McElenhy, V.K. (1998) *Insisting on the Impossible: the Life of Edwin Land*, Perseus Books, Reading, MA.

McGinn, R.E. (1991) *Science, Technology and Society*, Prentice Hall, Englewood Cliffs, NJ.

Macmillan Report (1931). See Report of the Committee on Finance and Industry, chaired by Hugh Pattison Macmillan, HMSO, London.

McRae, H. (2000) "However the Internet Develops, it is the Consumer who will Benefit", *The Independent*, 25 February 2000, p23.

Maddox, B. (2002) *Rosalind Franklin: The Dark Lady of DNA*, HarperCollins, London.

Marks, K. (2004) "Trampled Underfoot: How Big Business Trampled the Uggboot", The *Independent*, Review Section, 17 February 2004, pp1–3.

Markusen, A. (1996) "Sticky Places in Slippery Space: a Typology of Industrial Districts", *Economic Geography*, 72, pp293–313.

Marshall, A. (1890) *Principles of Economics*, Macmillan, London.

Martin, M.J.C. (1994) *Managing Innovation and Entrepreneurship in Technology-Based Firms*, John Wiley and Sons, New York.

Martin, R. and P. Sunley (2003) "Deconstructing Clusters: Chaotic Concept or Policy Panacea?", *Journal of Economic Geography*, 3, pp5–35.

Mason, C. and R. Harrison (1996) "Informal Venture Capital: A Study of the Investment Process, the Post-investment Experience and Investment Performance", *Entrepreneurship and Regional Development*", 8, pp105–125.

Mason, C. and R. Harrison (1997) "Business Angels are the Answer to an Entrepreneur's Prayer", in S. Birley and D. Muzyka (eds) *Mastering Entrepreneurship*, FT/Prentice Hall, London, pp110–114.

Mason, C. and R. Harrison (2000a) "The Size of the Informal Venture Capital Market in the UK", *Small Business Economics*, 15, pp137–148.

Mason, C. and R. Harrison (2000b) "Informal Venture Capital and the Financing of Emergent Growth Businesses", in D.L. Sexton and H. Langstrom (eds), *The Blackwell Handbook of Entrepreneurship*, Blackwell, Oxford, pp221–239.

Mason, C. and R. Harrison (2004) "Improving Access to Early Stage Venture Capital in Regional Economies: A New Approach to Investment Readiness", *Local Economy*, 19, pp159–173.

Matthews, C. (1998) *Case Studies in Engineering Design*, Arnold, London.

Matthews, V. (2007) "Giving Staff Time Off to Think Creatively Can Pay Dividends", *Personnel Today*, 16 January 2007.

May, W., C. Mason and S. Pinch (2001) "Explaining Industrial Agglomeration: the Case of the British High-Fidelity Industry", *Geoforum*, 32, pp363–376.

Mayle, D. (2006) *Managing Innovation and Change*, 3rd edn, Sage Publications, London.

Mazzarol, T. and S. Reboud, (2007) "Innovation Management in Small Firms: A Comparison of French and Australian Companies", *37th Entrepreneurship, Innovation and Small Business Conference*, 13–14 September 2007, University of Ljubljana, Slovenia.

Mellahi, K. and M. Johnson (2000) "Does it Pay to be a First Mover in E-commerce? The Case of Amazon.com", *Management Decision*, 38(7), pp445–457.

Mensch, G. (1979) *Stalemate in Technology: Innovations Overcome the Depression*, Ballenger, NY.

Metrick, A. (2006) *Venture Capital and the Finance of Innovation*, John Wiley & Sons, New York.

Meyers, M.A. (2007) *Happy Accidents: Serendipity in Modern Medical Breakthroughs*, Arcade Publishing, New York.

Milne, S. (1989) "Small Firms, Industrial Reorganisation and Space: the Case of the High Fidelity Audio Sector", *Environment and Planning* A, 21, pp833–852.

Milner, M. (2008) "UK Satellite Firm Set Up With £100 Sells for £40m", *The Guardian*, 8 April 2008, p26.

Moody, G. (2002) *Rebel Code: Linux and the Open Source Revolution*, Penguin Books, London.

Moore, B. (1994) "Financial Constraints to the Growth and Development of Small High-technology Firms", in A. Hughes and D.J. Storey (eds) *Finance and the Small Firm*, Routledge, London.

Moore, G. and K. Davies (2004) "Learning the Silicon Valley Way", in T. Bresnahan and A. Gambardella (eds) *Building High Tech Clusters: Silicon Valley and Beyond*, Cambridge University Press, Cambridge.

Moore, I. (1993) "Government Finance for Innovation in Small Firms: the Impact of SMART", *International Journal of Technology Management*, Special Issue, pp104–118.

Moore, I. and E. Garnsey (1993) "Funding for Innovation in Small Firms: The Role of Government", *Research Policy*, 22, pp507–519.

Moran, M. (2001) "Governing European Corporate Life" in G. Thompson (ed) *Governing the European Economy*, Sage Publications, London.

Morrison, P.D., J.H. Roberts and E. Von Hippel (2000) "Determinants of User Innovation and Innovation Sharing in a Local Market", *Management Science*, 46(12), pp1513–1527.

Mostert, F. (2007) *From Edison to iPod: Protect Your Ideas and Make Money*, Dorling Kindersley, London.

Mowery, D. and N. Rosenberg (1989) *Technology and the Pursuit of Economic Growth*, Cambridge University Press, Cambridge.

Nahum, A. (2004) *Issigonis and the Mini*, Icon Books, Cambridge.

Nathan, J. (1999) *Sony: The Private Life*, HarperCollins, London.

Naughton, J. (1999) *A Brief History of the Future: The Origins of the Internet*, Phoenix, London.

Naughton, J. (2002) "Never ask permission to innovate", *The Observer*, 3 November 2002, p17.

Naughton, J. (2008a) "Thanks, Gutenberg – But We're Too Pressed For Time to Read", *The Observer*, Business Section, 27 January 2008, p12.

Naughton, J. (2008b) "Google's Android Could Smash iPhone's Locked Gateway", *The Observer,* Business Section, 28 September 2008, p14.

Nayak, P.R. and J.M. Ketteringham (1993) *Breakthroughs!* Mercury Business Books, Didcot.

Nelson, R.R. (1993) *National Innovation Systems: A Comprehensive Analysis*, Oxford University Press, NY.

Nelson, R. and S. Winter (1977) "In Search of a Useful Theory of Innovation", *Research Policy*, 6, pp36–76.

Nelson, R. and S. Winter (1982) An *Evolutionary Theory of Economic Change*, Cambridge University Press, Cambridge.

Newell, S., J. Robertson, H. Scarborough and J. Swan (2002) *Managing Knowledge Work*, Palgrave, Basingstoke.

Newton, D. (2008) *Trademarked: A History of Well-known Brands from Aertex to Wright's Coal Tar Soap*, The History Press, Stroud.

Nordström, K. and M. Biström (2002) "Emergence of a Dominant Design in Probiotic Functional Food Development", *British Food Journal*, 104(9), pp713–723.

Norton, R.D. (2001) *Creating the New Economy: The Entrepreneur and the US Resurgence*, Edward Elgar, Cheltenham.

OECD (1997) *National Innovation Systems*, OECD, Paris.

O'Sullivan, D. and R. Dooley, (2009) *Applying Innovation*, Sage Publications, London.

O'Sullivan, M. (2005) "Finance and Innovation", in J. Fagerberg, D.C. Mowery and R.R. Nelson (eds) *The Oxford Handbook of Innovation*, Oxford University Press, Oxford.

Owen, D. (2004) *Copies in Seconds: How a Lone Inventor and an Unknown Company Created the Biggest Communications Breakthrough since Gutenberg – Chester Carlson and the Birth of the Xerox Machine*, Simon Schuster, New York.

Packard, D. (1995) *The HP Way: How Bill Hewlett and I Built Our Company*, HarperCollins, New York.

Parsons, M.C. and M.B. Rose (2003) *Invisible on Everest: Innovation and the Gear Makers*, Northern Liberties Press, Philadelphia, PA.

Parsons, M.C. and M.B. Rose (2004) "Communities of Knowledge: Entrepreneurship, Innovation and Networks in the British Outdoor Trade, 1960–1990", *Business History*, 46(4), pp609–639.

Pavitt, K. (2005) "Innovation Process", in J. Fagerberg, D.C. Mowery and R.R. Nelson (eds) *The Oxford Handbook of Innovation,* Oxford University Press, Oxford.

Pavitt, K., M. Robson and J. Townsend (1987) "The Size Distribution of Innovating Firms in the UK: 1945–1983", *Journal of Industrial Economics*, March 1983, pp43–54.

Perez, C. (1983) "Structural Change and the Assimilation of New Technologies in the Economic and Social System", *Futures*, 15, pp357–375.

Petroski, H. (1992) *The Evolution of Useful Things*, Alfred A. Knopf, NY.

Pinch, S. and N. Henry (1999) "Paul Krugman's Geographical Economics, Industrial Clustering and the British Motor Sport Industry", *Regional Studies*, 33(9), pp815–827.

Pinch, T. and W. Bijker (1987) "The Social Construction of 'artefacts'" in W. Bijker, T. Hughes and T. Pinch (eds) *The Social Construction of Technological Systems: New Directions in the Sociology and History of Technology*, MIT Press, Cambridge, MA.

Piore, M. and C. Sabel (1984) *The Second Industrial Divide: Possibilities for Prosperity*, Basic Books, New York.

Porter, M.E. (1980) *Competitive Strategy: Technologies for Analysing Industries and Competitors*, Free Press, New York.

Porter, M.E. (1990) *The Competitive Advantage of Nations*, Macmillan, London.

Porter, M.E. (1998) "Clusters and the New Economics of Competition", *Harvard Business Review*, November–December, pp77–90.

Potter, S. (1987) *On The Right Lines? The Limits of Technological Innovation*, Frances Pinter, London, p48.

Potter, S. (1989) "High-speed Rail Technology in the UK, France and Japan: Managing Innovation – the Neglected Factor", *Technology Analysis and Strategic Management*, 1(1), pp99–121.

Procter, J. (1994) "Everyone versus South West", *Airways*, November–December 1994, pp22–29.

Quinn, J.B. (1991) *The Strategy Process: Concepts, Contexts, Cases*, Prentice Hall, Englewood Cliffs, NJ.

Ramasamy, B., A. Chakrabarty and M. Cheah (2004) "Malaysia's Leap into the Future: an Evaluation of the Multimedia Super Corridor", *Technovation*, 24, pp871–883.

Rich, B.R. and L. Janos (1994) *Skunk Works: A Personal Memoir of My Years at Lockheed*, Warner Books, London.

Roberts, E.B. (1991) *Entrepreneurs in High Technology: Lessons from MIT and Beyond*, Oxford University Press, Oxford.

Rodgers, E. (1996) *Flying High: The Story of Boeing and the Rise of the Jetliner Industry*, The Atlantic Monthly Press, New York.

Rogers, E.M. (1995) *Diffusion of Innovation*, 4th edn, The Free Press, NY.

Rorke, M.L., H.L. Livesey and D.S. Lux (1991) *From Invention to Innovation: Commercialisation of New Technology by Independent and Small Businesses*, Mohawk Research Corporation, Rockville, MD; cited in Norton (2001).

Rosen, P. (2002) *Framing Production: Technology, Culture, and Change in the British Bicycle Industry*, MIT Press, Cambridge, MA.

Rosenbloom, R.S. and M. Cusumano (1987) "Technological Pioneering and Competitive Advantage", *California Management Review*, 29(4), pp51–76.

Rothwell, R. (1986) "The Role of Small Firms in the Emergence of New Technologies", in C. Freeman (ed) *Design, Innovation and Long Cycles in Economic Development*, Frances Pinter, London, pp231–248.

Rothwell, R. (1992) "Successful Industrial Innovation: Critical Success Factors for the 1990s", *R&D Management*, 22(3) pp221–239.

Rothwell, R. (1994) "Towards the Fifth-generation Innovation Process", *International Marketing Review*, 11(1), pp7–31.

Rothwell, R. and D. Gardner (1989a) "The Strategic Management of Re-innovation", *R&D Management*, 19(2), pp147–160.

Rothwell, R. and P. Gardiner (1989b) "Design Management Strategies", in M. Dodgson (ed) *Technology Strategy and the Firm: Management and Public Policy*, Longman, Harlow.

Roy, R., S. Potter and D. Wield (1999) *Innovation, Design, Environment And Strategy*, T302 Technology, Block 4 Case Studies, Open University, Milton Keynes.

Rutherford, P. (2007) *A World Made Sexy: Freud to Madonna*, University of Toronto Press, Toronto.

Sabbagh, K. (1996) *21st Century Jet: The Making of the Boeing 777*, Pan Books, London.

Sahal, D. (1981) *Patterns of Technological Innovation*, Addison-Wesley, Reading, MA.

Sanderson, S. and M. Uzumeri (1995) "Managing Product Families: The Case of the Sony Walkman", *Research Policy*, 24, pp761–782.

Saunders, R. (1999) *Business the Amazon Dot Com Way*, Capstone Milford CT.

Saxenian, A.L. (1983) "The Genesis of Silicon Valley", *Built Environment*, 9(1), pp7–17.

Saxenian, A.L. (2004) "Taiwan's Hsinchu Region: Imitator and Partner of Silicon Valley", in T. Bresnahan and A. Gambardella (eds) *Building High-Tech Clusters: Silicon Valley and Beyond*, Cambridge University Press, Cambridge.

Schnaars, S. (1994) *Managing Imitation Strategies: How Later Entrants Seize Markets from Pioneers*, Free Press: New York.

Schon, D.A. (1963) "Champions for Radical New Inventions", *Harvard Business Review*, 41, March–April, pp77–86.

Schumpeter, J. (1936) *Capitalism, Socialism and Democracy*, Harvard University Press, Boston, MA.

Schumpeter, J. (1939) *Business Cycles*, McGraw-Hill, New York.

Schumpeter, J. (1950) *Capitalism, Socialism and Democracy*, 3rd edn, Harper Row, New York.

Schumpeter, J. (1996) *The Theory of Economic Development*, Transaction Publishers, New Brunswick.

Seabrook, J. (2008) *Flash of Genius: And Other True Stories of Invention*, St. Martin's Griffin, New York.

Segal, Quince and Wicksteed (2000) *The Cambridge Phenomenon Revisited*, Segal, Quince and Wicksteed Ltd, Market Street, Cambridge.

Shah, S. (2000) *Sources and Patterns of Innovation in a Consumer Products Field: Innovations in Sports Equipment*, Sloan Working Paper 4105, March 2000.

Shane, S.A. (2004) *Academic Entrepreneurship: University Spin-offs and Wealth Creation*, Edward Elgar, Cheltenham.

Shankar, V., G.S. Carpenter and L. Krishnamurthi (1998) "Late Mover Advantage: How Innovative Late Entrants Outsell Pioneers", *Journal of Marketing Research*, 35, February 1998, pp54–70.

Shelton, J. (2008) *Schneider Trophy to Spitfire: The Design Career of R J Mitchell*, J.H. Haynes & Co Ltd, Sparkford.

Sherman, E. (2002) "Inside the Apple iPod Design Triumph", *Electronics Design Chain*, Summer 2002, accessed at *http://designchain.com*.

Sherman, J. (2001) *Jeff Bezos: King of Amazon*, 21st Century Books, New York.

Sherwood, B. (2002) "Inventive Employees could be Awarded Royalties", *Financial Times*, 4 December 2002.

Shurkin, J.N. (2006) *Broken Genius: The Rise and Fall of William Shockley, Creator of the Electronic Age*, Macmillan, Basinstoke.

Sigafoss, R.A. (1988) *Absolutely Positively Overnight: The Unofficial Corporate History of Federal Express*, Peachtree Publishers, Atlanta, GA.

Simon, H.A. (1972) "Technology and Environment", *Management Science*, 19(10), pp1110–1121.

Simonetti, R. (2001) "Governing European Technology and Innovation", in G. Thompson (ed) *Governing the European Economy*, Sage Publications, London.

Smil, V. (2005) *Creating the 20th Century: Technical Innovations of 1867–1914 and Their Lasting Impact*, Oxford University Press, Oxford.

Smil, V. (2006) *Transforming the 20th Century: Technical Innovations and Their Consequences*, Oxford University Press, Oxford.

Smiles, S. (1862) *The Lives of George and Robert Stephenson*, John Murray, London.

Smith, A. (1776) *An Inquiry into the Nature and Causes of the Wealth of Nations*, Strahan and Cadell, London.

Smith, D.J. (2007) "The Politics of Innovation: Why Innovations Need a Godfather", *Technovation*, 27(3), pp95–104.

Smith, D.J. (2009) "Financial Bootstrapping and Social Capital: How Technology-based Start-ups Fund Innovation", *International Journal of Entrepreneurship and Innovation Management,* 10(2), pp199–209.

Smith, D.J. and M.F. Rogers (2004) "Technology Strategy and Innovation: The Use of Derivative Strategies in the Aerospace Industry", *Technology Analysis and Strategic Management*, 16(4), pp509–527.

Spinardi, G. (2002) "Industrial Exploitation of Carbon Fibre in the UK, USA and Japan", *Technology Analysis and Strategic Management*, 14(4), pp381–398.

Stefick, M. and B. Stefick (2004) *Breakthroughs: Stories and Strategies of Radical Innovation*, MIT Press, Cambridge, MA.

Strachan, A. (2004) "The Lost Boy", *The Independent*, 27 December 2004, pp20–21.

Suarez, F. and G. Lanzolla (2005) "The Half-Truth of First-Mover Advantage", *Harvard Business Review*, April 2005, pp121–127.

Taylor, E. (1996) "Craig's Boot", *Innovation: Design, Environment and Strategy, T302*, Open University, Milton Keynes.

Teece, D.J. (1986) "Profiting from Technological Innovation: Implications for Integration, Collaboration, Licensing and Public Policy", *Research Policy*, 15, pp285–306.

Tidd, J., J. Bessant and K. Pavitt (2001) *Managing Innovation: Integrating Technological, Market and Organizational Change*, 2nd edn, J. Wiley and Sons, Chichester.

Tidd, J. and M. Brocklehurst (1999) "Routes to Technological Learning and Development: An Assessment of Malaysia's Innovation Policy and Performance", *Technological Forecasting and Social Change*, 62, pp239–257.

Tidd, J. and Hull, F.M. (2002) *Service Innovation*, Imperial College Press, London.

Tidd, J. and S. Taurins (1999) "Learn or Leverage? Strategic Diversification and Organizational Learning through Corporate Ventures", *Creativity and Innovation Management*, 8(2), pp122–129.

Toumi, I., (2006) *Networks of Innovation: Change and Meaning in the Age of the Internet*, Oxford University Press, Oxford.

Trott, P. (2002) *Innovation Management and New Product Development*, 2nd edn, FT Prentice Hall, Harlow.

Tushman, M.L. and P. Anderson (1986) "Technological Discontinuities and Organisational Environments", *Administrative Science Quarterly*, 31, pp439–465.

Tushman, M.L. and P. Anderson (2004) *Managing Strategic Innovation and Change*, 2nd edn, Oxford University Press, New York.

Tylecote, A. (1992) *The Long Wave in the World Economy: The Present Crisis in Historical Perspective*, Routledge and Kegan Paul, London.

Ulrich, K.T. and S.D. Eppinger (2003) *Product Design and Development*, 3rd edn, McGraw-Hill, New York.

Usher, A.P. (1954) *A History of Mechanical Inventions*, revd edn, Harvard College, Boston, MA.

Uttal, B. (1983) "The Lab that Ran Away from Xerox", *Fortune*, 5 September 1983.

Utterback, J.H. (1993) *Mastering the Dynamics of Innovation*, Harvard University Press, Boston, MA.

Vaitheeswaran, V. (2007) "Something New under the Sun", *The Economist*, 13 October 2007, pp3–24.

Van Dulken, S. (2000) *Inventing the 20th Century: 100 Inventions that Shaped the World*, British Library, London.

Van Dulken, S. (2001) *Inventing the 19th Century: The Great Age of Victorian Inventions*, British Library, London.

Van Dulken, S. (2003) *Inventing the American Dream: A History of Curious, Extraordinary and Just Plain Useful Patents*, British Library, London.

Vise, D.A. (2005) *The Google Story*, Pan Books, London.

Von Hippel, E. (1976) "The Dominant Role of users in the Scientific Instrument Innovation Process", *Research Policy*, 5(3), pp212–219.

Von Hippel, E. (1988) *The Sources of Innovation*, Oxford University Press, New York.

Von Hippel, E. (2005) *Democratizing Innovation*, MIT Press, Cambridge, MA.

Von Tunzelmann, N. (1995) *Technology and Industrial Progress: The Foundations of Economic Growth*, Edward Elgar, Cheltenham.

Walker, R. (2003) "The Guts of the New Machine", *The New York Times*, 30 November 2003, p68.

Wetzel, W.E. (1983) "Angels and Informal Risk Capital", *Sloan Management Review*, 24, pp23–34.

Wheelwright, S.C. and K.B. Clark (1992) *Revolutionizing Product Development: Quantum Leaps in Speed, Efficiency and Quality*, The Free Press, New York.

Winborg, J. and H. Landstrom (2001) "Financial Bootstrapping in Small Businesses: Examining Small Business Managers' Resource Acquisition Behaviours", *Journal of Business Venturing*, 16, pp235–254.

Womack, J.P., D.T. Jones and D. Roos (1990) *The Machine that Changed the World*, Rawson Associates, NY.

Wood, A. (2001) *Magnetic Venture: The Story of Oxford Instruments*, Oxford University Press, Oxford.

Wood, J. (2005) *Alec Issigonis: The Man Who Made the Mini*, Breedon Books Publishing, Derby.

Wozniak, S. and G. Wood (2006) *iWoz: Computer Geek to Cult Icon – Getting to the Core of Apple's Inventor*, Headline Review, London.

Wray, R. and J. McCurry (2008) "Clearer Picture Emerges in Battle over High Definition Viewing", *The Guardian*, 19 February 2008, p27.

Young, J.S. and W.L. Simon (2005) *iCon Steve Jobs: The Greatest Second Act in the History of Business,* John Wiley & Sons Ltd, Chichester.

Resources

There are a wide range of resources to support the study of innovation and they are available in a range of media. Printed media dominate and, though innovation is a comparatively young discipline, the range of printed materials has grown dramatically over the last couple of decades. Among printed resources, books are clearly important along with articles in academic journals. However, there are other sources. Newspapers can be a valuable source as occasionally can magazines. More recently have been added video resources available as videocassettes (if you can find a video recorder to play them on!), DVDs or online. To these has been added over the last decade or so a range of web-based resources available online.

This section on resources is divided up on the basis of printed materials, online (websites) materials and video/DVD materials. However, there is clearly a degree of overlap with some items being available in more than one format. This applies particularly to video materials which are increasingly becoming available online.

Printed materials

Books

Biographies

For an introduction to some of the practicalities of participating in innovation, autobiographies and biographies are a very valuable resource. They often provide detailed accounts of how an innovation was undertaken. In particular, they often provide a mass of detail about the process of innovation, including the various steps or stages that form part of the process. However, a word of caution is necessary. One has to be careful because they are prone to being subjective, not unsurprisingly, and they do tend to emphasise the "heroic" nature of innovations brought about by individuals. Hence one needs to disentangle extraneous detail or the writer's personal views regarding obstacles and hurdles, from the detail of what actually happened. But they have the great advantage that they usually provide an insider's view and one usually gets quite a lot of detail.

In terms of autobiographies, good examples of the genre are James Dyson's (1997) *Against the Odds: An Autobiography*, Tim Berners-Lee's (2000) *Weaving the Web: The Original Design and Ultimate Destiny of the World Wide Web By Its Inventor*, Dave Packard's (1995) *The HP Way: How Bill Hewlett and I Built Our Company*, Trevor Baylis's (1999) *Clock This: My Life as an Inventor* and Steve Wozniak's (2006) *iWoz – Computer Geek to Cult Icon: Getting to the Core of Apple's Inventor*. James Dyson's autobiography includes a detailed account of the innovation process that led to the introduction of the dual cyclone vacuum cleaner. Covering the 15-year period from Dyson having the idea for a vacuum cleaner using cyclone dust extraction, to his finally getting it into production and onto the market, it explains in detail the steps involved including: how the idea arose, the building of prototypes, testing them, design of the product, the acquisition of manufacturing facilities and the problems he faced in getting his new cleaner into the shops. The chapters on development, i.e. building and testing 5,127 prototypes, are particularly informative for those without a strong technical background.

Good examples of biographies are Bardsley (2005) *Issigonis: The Official Biography*, Berlin (2007) *The Man Behind the Microchip: Robert Noyce and the Creation of Silicon Valley*, Deutschman (2001) *The Second Coming of Steve Jobs*, Dowling (2001) *Inventor of the Disposable Culture: King Camp Gillette 1855–1932*, Edwards (1972) *Catseyes: Biography of Percy Shaw*, Nathan (2000) *Sony: The Private Life*, Owen (2004) *Copies in Seconds: How a Lone Inventor and an Unknown Company Created the Biggest Communications Breakthrough since Gutenberg – Chester Carlson and the Birth of the Xerox Machine,* Shelton (2008) *Schneider Trophy to Spitfire: The Design Career of R J Mitchell,* Shurkin, (2006) *Broken Genius: The Rise and Fall of William Shockley, Creator of the Electronic Age*, Wood (2005) *Alec Issigonis: The Man Who Made the Mini* and Young and Simon (2005) *iCon Steve Jobs: The Greatest Second Act in the History of Business*. Interestingly service innovations are also well served by biographers, some notable examples being Gabler (2008) *Walt Disney: The Biography* and Hamilton (2005) *Thomas Cook: The Holiday Maker* and Sherman (2001) *Jeff Bezos: King of Amazon*.

Owen's biography of Chester Carlson, the inventor of the plain-paper copier, is typical, providing a fascinating and detailed picture of the difficulties faced by Carlson and the Haloid company in bringing about an innovation that was to have a significant impact not merely on administrative work but education, libraries and a host of other aspects of modern life. It is particularly useful given the problems Haloid encountered in marketing its first copier, the Xerox 914, and the business model it employed.

Company histories

There are also company histories that, as well as detailing how a particular company developed and changed over time, can also provide valuable insights into innovations that the company in question developed. As with biographies a critical perspective is essential. Good examples are: Jones (2005) *Renewing Unilever: Transformation and Tradition*, which provides valuable insights into a number of Unilever innovations including the Clearblue pregnancy testing kit, Ellis (2006) *Joe Wilson and the Creation Of Xerox*, Gundling (1999) *The 3M Way to Innovation: Balancing People and Profit*, Hitzik (2000) *Dealers of Lightning: Xerox PARC and the Dawn of the Computer Age*, Hounshell and Smith (1988) *Science and Corporate Strategy: Dupont and Research and Development*, Jones (2007) *easyJet: The Story of Britain's Biggest Low-cost Airline*, Linzmayer (2003) *Apple Confidential,* Sigafoss (1988) *Absolutely Positively Overnight*: *The Unofficial Corporate History of Federal Express*, Vise (2005) *The Google Story* and Wood (2001) *Magnetic Venture: The Oxford Instrument's Story*.

The last-named of these studies is the story of Oxford Instruments, a firm at the forefront of innovations in magnets and magnetism. The section dealing with the introduction of superconducting magnets in the 1960s shows how small start-up companies innovate, particularly the ways in which they tackle the various stages of the innovation process. Given that Oxford Instruments is a high-technology business it provides a fascinating account of the interaction between academic and industrial communities and how small firms acquire the resources to enable them to engage in R&D. Another very informative study is Levy (1994) *Insanely Great: The Life and Times of Macintosh, the Computer that Changed Everything* which tells the story of the personal computer maker, Apple. The section on the Mackintosh, the first PC to employ a graphical user interface and a mouse, is particularly detailed.

Another book that provides a history of high-technology companies is Hague and Holmes (2006) *Oxford Entrepreneurs*. This isn't a single-company history but rather a collection of short histories. It briefly details the origins and innovations of several high-technology businesses spun-off from Oxford University and in the process provides a valuable insight into the nature of spin-off companies and the spin-off process and the work of technical entrepreneurs.

Innovation studies

Another possible avenue is books about specific innovations. There are several accounts of innovations in the field of computing, most notably Levy (1994) *Insanely Great: The Life and Times of Macintosh, the Computer that Changed Everything*, Campbell-Kelly (2004) *From Airline Reservations to Sonic the Hedgehog: The History of the Software Industry*, and Moody (2001) *Rebel Code: Linux and the Open Source Revolution*. And there are plenty of books dealing with innovations other than those in the field of computing. Good examples are Levy (2006) *The Perfect Thing: How the iPod Became the Defining Object of the 21st Century*, Jones (2005) *iPod, Therefore I am: A Personal Journey Through Music,* du Gay et al. (1997) *Doing Cultural Studies: The Story of the Sony Walkman* and in a very different context Hodges (2007) *AK47: The Story of the People's Gun*.

Campbell-Kelly (2004) is particularly useful. A study of the development of the software industry, it describes how a host of important innovations in computing came about. Not only that, for those who want to take the study of a particular innovation further, there are a large number of references.

Innovation case studies

Another potential seam of material about innovations comes from books that provide a collection of innovation case studies. Rarely written as case studies, they often provide useful, if brief, accounts of well-known innovations. Again, one needs to be slightly careful because they often focus on the "heroic" aspects of invention rather than the less dramatic but often more significant "nuts and bolts" of innovation. Good examples include, Van Dulken (2000) *Inventing the 20th Century: 100 Inventions that Shaped the World*, Van Dulken (2001) *Inventing the 19th Century: The Great Age of Victorian Inventions,* Nayak and Ketteringham's (1993) *Breakthroughs!,* Stefik and Stefik (2004) *Breakthrough: Stories and Strategies of Radical Innovation,* Smil (2005) *Creating the 20th Century: Technical Innovations of 1867–1914 and Their Lasting Impact*, Smil (2006) *Transforming the 20th Century: Technical Innovations and Their Consequences* and, though now rather old, Jewkes et al. (1969) *The Sources of Invention*.

Two collections of case studies with a distinctively American focus are Brown (2003) *Inventing Modern America: From the Microwave to the Mouse,* and Van Dulken (2004) *Inventing the American Dream: A History of Curious, Extraordinary and Just Plain Useful Patents*.

The value of all of these books lies not so much in them providing highly detailed accounts of innovation (most of them don't have the space to do that), rather they give an overview of the innovation process which can be a useful starting point for further research.

A book which does contain detailed in-depth case studies is Christensen (1997) *The Innovator's Dilemma: When New Technologies Cause Great Firms to Fail* which includes case studies of innovations in hard disk drives and hydraulic excavators. Another recent addition to provide considerable detail about the innovation process of a number of innovations is Seabrook (2008) *Flash of Genius: And Other True Stories of Invention*. It is one of these innovations, the development of the intermittent windscreen wiper by Bob Kearns, that forms the basis of Marc Abraham's film of the same name.

Books on specific aspects of innovation

Books that deal with specific aspects of innovation have been highlighted in the "Further Reading" section at the end of each chapter. There remain some additional texts which are likely to be useful for very specific aspects of innovation. The literature on service innovation as opposed to product innovation is limited and a useful collection of readings on this subject is provided by Tidd and Hull (2002) *Service Innovation*. Similarly in the field of intellectual property rights, because much of the literature has a very strong legal focus, more general works can be difficult to locate. Baxter (1997) *The Inventor's Guide to How to Patent and Profit from Your Idea* provides a valuable non-legal practitioner perspective on patents and the patent system. Similarly a useful study of trademarks is Newton (2008) *Trademarked: A History of Well-known Brands from Aertex to Wright's Coal Tar Soap*. The same applies to financial aspects of innovation which form part of a very large financial literature. A couple of particularly useful resources here are the Bank of England's (2001) *Financing of Technology-based Small Firms*, a survey that provides a detailed picture of the sources of finance used by small technology-based firms in the UK, and Metrick (2006) *Venture Capital and the Finance of Innovation*, one of very few texts to address specifically financial aspects of innovation.

In terms of the innovation process there are a number of texts, such as Baker and Hart (1999) *Product Strategy and Management*, that deal with the management of new product development. However, there are also some more specialised texts that focus on particular aspects of new product development. For example, Lawson (2005) *How Designers Think: The Design Process Demystified* explores the role of the designer in new product development. There are also a small number of texts that provide detailed case studies of specific aspects of new product development. Two examples are Hands, Ingram and Jerrard (2001) *Design Management Case Studies,* which provides case studies of design management in a range of industries and Matthews (1998) *Case Studies in Engineering Design,* which provides case studies illustrating some of the key design issues that arise in new product development. Both of these texts are based on case studies and they therefore provide plenty of illustrations and examples of the nature of new product development.

Journal articles

Articles in academic journals are clearly an important source for the study of innovation. Not only do they cover the latest theoretical developments in the subject as well as reporting the results of major pieces of research, they also provide in-depth case studies of particular innovations. Many of the journals in the field of innovation are cited in the "Further Reading" section of each chapter, but it is worth providing a more comprehensive list here:

- *Research Policy*
- *R&D Management*
- *Industry and Innovation*
- *Technovation*
- *International Journal of Innovation Management*
- *Technology Analysis and Strategic Management*
- *Journal of Product Innovation Management*
- *Creativity and Innovation Management*
- *European Journal of Innovation Management*
- *International Journal of Innovation and Learning*
- *Technological Forecasting and Social Change*

As well as innovation journals there are journals in other academic disciplines, including business history, economics, general management and marketing, that can be useful. Many of the journals dealing with business history for instance, such as *Business History; Industrial and Corporate Change; Business History Review*; and *Enterprise and Society,* from time to time include articles on the development of particular innovations, and when they do they typically provide very detailed accounts of the innovation process.

Newspapers and magazines

Finally newspapers and magazines represent an important and valuable source of material on innovation and they have the advantage that back issues can often be accessed via their respective websites. *The Guardian* has a weekly technology section which often features more technologically oriented innovations, *The Independent* and *The Financial Times* too have special features from time to time that focus on new technologies and innovations.

The Economist has a special quarterly technology issue that reviews recent developments in technology. Similarly the *New York Times,* regularly features articles about specific new technologies and innovations, and its magazine section has an annual "Year in Ideas" edition which provides details of all sorts recent inventions – some of which become innovations.

With magazines it is very difficult to make specific recommendations. However, there are several magazines that focus on science and technology and they can be a very useful source. Among those that focus on science are titles like *New Scientist* and *Scientific American*. They cover developments in science, particularly breakthroughs and discoveries, but the latter does include a technology section which reports on both new technologies and new applications of technology. Among magazines that focus on technology, the outstanding example is *Wired,* which, as well as reporting on new developments in technology especially in relation to computing, also includes highly detailed, in-depth articles on particular innovations.

Finally a valuable source of case study material illustrating design aspects of the new product development process is the *Design Council Magazine.*

Websites

There are lots of websites on particular innovations, but be warned, many provide only very superficial details. Rarely do they provide the level of detail or the level of analysis that is a part of academic study.

There are a number of websites that provide background information on innovation. Among the most useful is: *http://www.dius.gov.uk/policy/innovation.html*. This is the website of the UK government's Department for Business, Innovation and Skills and it provides an excellent overview of innovation in the UK. It includes links to the White Paper *Innovation Nation*, the R&D Scorecard, a wide range of statistics about the scale and scope of innovation in the UK (including data on patents and venture capital), and the *DIUS Annual Report* which contains a number of case studies of recent innovations.

Websites covering more specific aspects of innovation include several dealing with intellectual property. Prominent among these are:

- *http://www.ipo.gov.uk*, the website of the Intellectual Property Office. This provides authoritative and wide ranging guidance on all forms of intellectual property

- *http://www.invent.org.uk,* the website of the Institute of Patentees and Inventors which provides valuable background information and practical information on various forms of intellectual property
- *http://www.cipa.org.uk*, the website of the Chartered Institute of Patent Agents

There are also a number of websites of organisations in the field of design and innovation that provide some valuable case studies of innovations. Some of the case studies are a little short and don't always say much about the development process leading to innovation, but they nonetheless provide useful insights and illustrations. Such websites include:

- *http://design-council.org.uk*, the website of the UK's Design Council which includes a number of short case studies of well-known innovations ("10 lessons for Successful Invention") about The Workmate, Dyson DC01, Sony Walkman, Pilkington Float Glass and the Lotus bicycle as well as some slightly longer case studies taken from the *Design Council Magazine,* including the Toyota Prius, Stannah stairlift, Umpqua Bank and Owlstone Nanotechnology
- *http://designmuseum.org*, the Design Museum's website. This site includes profiles of several well-known innovators including: Craig Johnson (Adidas Predator boot), R.J. Mitchell (Spitfire), Alec Issigonis (Mini), George Cowardine (Anglepoise lamp), Percy Shaw (Cats-eyes), Jonathan Ive (iPod), Tim Berners-Lee and Sam Hauser and Terry Doran (Grand Theft Auto). The profiles provide details of the innovations themselves, and often include fascinating illustrations covering things like design sketches, pictures of mock-ups and prototypes and advertisements
- *http://www.americanhistory.si.edu*, the website of the Smithsonian Institution in the US. As the principal museum of technology in the US, the Smithsonian Institution is a valuable source on all things technological
- *http://www.stanford.edu/group/wellspring,* which features profiles of Stanford alumni and the companies and innovations they have created
- *http://www.sussex.ac.uk/spru/* the website for Sussex University's Science Policy Research Unit (SPRU), which amongst other things provides a series of working papers covering a range of different aspects of innovation

Some corporate websites also form an important source of data about innovation. They tend to be few in number, being generally confined to companies with a particularly strong record for innovation. Some notable examples are:

- *http://www.dyson.co.uk,* this is the website of James Dyson's company Dyson Appliances and it provides some superb materials covering a wide range of different aspects of innovation. These include: details of James Dyson's early career, the innovation process surrounding the development of the first bagless vacuum cleaner the DC01, and details of a number of design 'icons'. The website also contains several video clips including some in which James Dyson describes how he developed 'the world's first vacuum cleaner that doesn't loose suction' and others in which he explains various aspects of the innovation process including sources of ideas, design, prototypes, product development and testing. Not only is there a wealth of information about what innovation involves, there are loads of fascinating illustrations too.

- *http://www.3m.com/US/office/postit/pastpresent/history.html,* the history of the Post-it® note by the people that made it. Another excellent website, though one that doesn't have quite the same level of detail, but nonetheless provides a useful account of the development of the ubiquitous Post-it® note
- *http://ibm.com/innovation/guide,* this is the website of computer maker IBM. It presents a rather glossy and technology-driven perspective on innovation that lacks specifics. However, despite this it does provide a perspective on innovation in the twenty-first century, particularly the fields that are currently being most affected by innovations

There are also the websites of specific individuals that provide insights into innovations. They include the websites of those directly involved in innovations and those with a particular interest in innovation, particularly technology and innovation.

- *http://www.bricklin.com,* this is the personal website of Dan Bricklin the inventor of the spreadsheet. It provides a first-hand account of the innovation process surrounding the development of the first spreadsheet, including examples of early designs and advertisements, as well as a copy of the first commercial spreadsheet, *VisiCalc,* that you can download and use
- *http://www.stevenlevy.com,* the website of the technology journalist and writer, Steven Levy. Levy, who for many years wrote a technology column for *Newsweek,* currently contributes a similar column to *Wired,* and is the author of two excellent texts on innovation, *Insanely Great,* about the development of Apple's innovative Mackintosh PC in the 1980s and *The Perfect Thing* which provides the background story on the development of the iPod. The website not only includes a number of useful articles, it also includes links to others
- *http://www.molly.ac.uk,* the website of academic and *Observer* columnist, John Naughton. The website provides links to many of Naughton's articles for *The Observer,* as well as a number of thought provoking essays on a variety of aspects of innovation
- *http://britishlibrary.typepad.co.uk/patentsblog,* this is the blog of Steve Van Dulken at the British Library. Steve is an expert on patents and other forms of IPR and has written a number of books on innovation. His blog provides a lively commentary on issues associated with IPR

Video/DVD

There has been a great deal of excellent material about innovation broadcast over many years. Unfortunately, however, locating videos of these programmes isn't easy, though university libraries often have recorded copies of the programmes. Examples include well-known documentary series such as the BBC's *Horizon* and Channel 4's *Equinox.* The latter has covered innovations in video games, aircraft fly-by-wire systems and the lean burn engine. During the 1990s the BBC broadcast a series called *Design Classics* and this featured several well-known innovations including; the Sony Walkman, the VW Beetle, the Aga cooker and the Harley-Davidson Electraglide.

There are also some specialist documentary films available on DVD. A most notable example is *Klunkerz* a documentary by Billy Savage that traces the origins and evolution of the mountain bike. Not only does it include some cine film footage of early mountain bikers, their machines and the tracks they raced them on, it also includes interviews with some of the leading innovators themselves such as Charlie Kelly, Tom Richey and Gary Fisher. Another useful documentary now available on DVD is *Giant of the Skies: The Making of the Airbus A380*. This provides a perspective on the development of high-tech products such as modern aircraft and aero engines, as well as a detailed picture of many of the activities that form part of the new product development process, such as the construction of mock-ups and prototypes and testing programmes.

The popular BBC series *Dragon's Den* also provides a useful insight into innovation, but it is important to remember that it only focuses on individual innovation. How do individual inventors commercialise their inventions, in particular how do they get access to finance, marketing and organisational expertise? The answer is that the successful ones very often team up with a "dragon" or, as they are more commonly termed, a "business angel". The essence of the programmes lies in would-be innovators and their inventions being evaluated by a group of business angels (i.e. the dragons). The evaluations make good television as the would-be innovators are often shown to be ill-prepared and unrealistic in their understanding of what successful commercialisation demands. But this is also the value of the series: each programme highlights, usually in considerable detail, just what commercialisation requires.

The Massachusetts Institute of Technology (MIT) provides s number of video documentaries covering a variety of aspects of innovation. These are available from MIT's website at *http:// mitworld.mit.edu*. Among the most relevant is one on corporate culture and innovation entitled *Nurturing a Vibrant Culture to Drive Innovation*. This is a talk by Terri Kelly (the CEO of W.L. Gore and Associates) that outlines and discusses Gore's corporate culture and its contribution to innovation. Others in this series include:

- James Dyson *The Art of Engineering*
- Steve Wozniak *iWoz: From Computer Geek to Cult Icon*
- Eric Von Hippel *Democratizing Innovation*
- Tim Berners-Lee *The Semantic Web*
- Jeff Bezos *An Interview with Jeff Bezos*
- Clayton Christensen *How Technology is Transforming Existing Industries and Creating New Ones*

Perhaps surprisingly there have been a number of films about innovators and many are now available on DVD. The most recent is Marc Abrahams' film, *Flash of Genius*, released in 2008 in the US and in 2009 in the UK. This tells the story of Bob Kearns the inventor of the intermittent windscreen wiper and his legal battles with the US car companies whom he claimed had infringed his patent. Kearns is a classic example of the lone inventor, but the film does provide a fascinating insight into many of the issues surrounding innovation, most notably intellectual property rights. Details are available at the film's website at *http://www. flashofgenius.net*. Other films on innovators include: *Tucker, the Man and his Dream* (1988) about Preston Tucker and the Tucker car, *The Aviator* (2004) about aviation pioneer Howard Hughes, *The First of the Few* (1942) about R.J. Mitchell, the designer of the Spitfire fighter aircraft, and *Edison, the Man* (1940) which as its title implies is a film about Thomas Edison, starring Spencer Tracy.

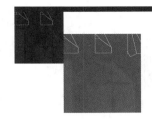

Index